Praise for *Everything You Need to Know about Homeschooling*

Lea Ann has hit a home run with her new book about homeschooling. How timely this book is in the midst of at least twenty million families now doing some form of schooling at home because of the pandemic. We know that many will try homeschooling as a result of getting their appetites whetted. What Lea Ann has provided is a one-stop shop for all you need to know about homeschooling, as well as all you need to know to be able to effectively homeschool. Not that homeschooling is easy—it's not—but this book makes it as easy as possible to do it. The book covers everything you will encounter in homeschooling and more in a very readable, easy-to-understand manner. *Everything You Need to Know about Homeschooling* is not hype. As moms and dads consider homeschooling, there will be many avenues presented. This book will direct you down the right road. It's a must buy for anyone contemplating homeschooling.

MIKE SMITH
President, Home School Legal Defense Association

A grab bag of homeschool help and how-to! Lea Ann covers every concern a new homeschool parent could have, from socialization to spelling to spiritual guidance. This book will equip parents to persevere past common pitfalls with confidence from preschool to graduation. No denim jumper required!

JENNIFER CABRERA
HifalutinHomeschooler.com

COMPELLING. If I only had one word to describe this book, THAT would be it! If you've ever mused about the possibility of homeschooling your brood, Lea Ann Garfias's book is the one to read. It provides a plethora of extremely valuable information and resources about the whole process—from A to Z. *Everything You Need to Know about Homeschooling* covers all the nuts and bolts with compelling anecdotes and a Q&A style that imparts valued information and stirs your imagination. By providing concise and accurate answers without wading into the weeds, this book will move you to feel "I CAN DO THIS!" Even if you already homeschool, you will appreciate the thoroughness of this book as it will offer new insights, firm up your foundation, and strengthen your resolve. I'm thankful this book was written and highly recommend it!

RAY BALLMANN
Homeschool Author and Conference Speaker

Everything You Need to Know about Homeschooling is exactly the book I needed when I began homeschooling my boys almost a decade ago. Lea Ann offers practical and real-life ideas, support, and encouragement for the parent just getting started with homeschooling. I think this is a must read for new homeschoolers—like having another mom come alongside and help you along the way. Even veteran homeschoolers will find inspiration and encouragement as Lea Ann expertly provides solutions for every grade level. What a wonderful gift to the homeschooling community!

SHAWNA WINGERT
CEO of Different By Design Learning and Homeschool Mom of Two

EVERYTHING YOU NEED TO KNOW

ABOUT HOMESCHOOLING

EVERYTHING YOU NEED TO KNOW ABOUT HOMESCHOOLING

A Comprehensive, Easy-to-Use Guide for the Journey
from Early Learning through Graduation

LEA ANN GARFIAS

TYNDALE
MOMENTUM®

The Tyndale nonfiction imprint

Visit Tyndale online at www.tyndale.com.

Visit Tyndale Momentum online at www.tyndalemomentum.com.

Visit the author's website at lagarfias.com.

TYNDALE, Tyndale's quill logo, *Tyndale Momentum*, and the Tyndale Momentum logo are registered trademarks of Tyndale House Ministries. Tyndale Momentum is the nonfiction imprint of Tyndale House Publishers, Carol Stream, Illinois.

Everything You Need to Know about Homeschooling: A Comprehensive Easy-to-Use Guide for the Journey from Early Learning to Graduation

Designed by Lindsey Bergsma

Edited by Deborah King

Published in association with the literary agency of Kirkland Media Management, LLC.

For information about special discounts for bulk purchases, please contact Tyndale House Publishers at csresponse@tyndale.com, or call 1-800-323-9400.

ISBN 978-1-4964-3904-8

Printed in the United States of America

27	26	25	24	23	22	21
7	6	5	4	3	2	1

*To my husband, David: this is all your fault for making
me homeschool and then making me write about it.*

CONTENTS

Foreword *xi*

Preface *xiii*

Introduction *1*

PART ONE MAKING AND DEFENDING THE DECISION *7*

CHAPTER 1 Finding Your Homeschool Why *11*

CHAPTER 2 Get Ready for the Questions *23*

PART TWO GETTING STARTED *37*

CHAPTER 3 Ready, Set, Go! *39*

CHAPTER 4 We Aren't in School Anymore *51*

CHAPTER 5 How to Be a Great Teacher *57*

CHAPTER 6 The Way You Teach Best *77*

CHAPTER 7 How Children Learn *119*

CHAPTER 8 Books and Stuff *147*

PART THREE GROWING AND LEARNING *159*

CHAPTER 9 What Grade Are We In? *161*

CHAPTER 10 Early Learning: The Preschool and Kindergarten Years *179*

CHAPTER 11 Elementary School: The First- through Fifth-Grade Years *233*

CHAPTER 12 Middle School: The Sixth- through Eighth-Grade Years *291*

CHAPTER 13 High School: The Ninth- through Twelfth-Grade Years *341*

PART FOUR **OVERCOMING OBSTACLES** *395*

CHAPTER 14 The Dangers of Homeschooling *397*

CHAPTER 15 Making Homeschool Life Easier *449*

CHAPTER 16 Special Children, Special Needs *479*

Conclusion *501*

APPENDIX A Finding Your Teaching Style *503*

APPENDIX B Sample Routines *509*

APPENDIX C Student Essay Editing Checklists *513*

APPENDIX D Sample Essay Grading Rubric *519*

APPENDIX E High School Transcripts and Course Descriptions *523*

APPENDIX F Homeschool Resources *529*

Bibliography *547*

Notes for Callout Quotes *553*

Notes *555*

Index *561*

Acknowledgments *571*

About the Author *573*

FOREWORD

MANY PARENTS have had to unexpectedly facilitate their kids' education at home because of the COVID-19 pandemic. Not surprisingly, many of them have been very surprised that homeschooling is not what they expected it to be, even if this type of virtual schooling isn't necessarily true homeschooling. While some of these parents and kids like doing their schooling at home, others can't get past what seem like never-ending distractions, especially the lure of the TV, phone, computer, or video games. Others like the flexibility they have at home and find that they have fewer distractions, as they don't have to be concerned about other kids in the classroom.

So what is true homeschooling? Who homeschools their kids? Are these students able to play sports, have friends, or actually learn anything? There is a lot of mystery around these things, isn't there?

Even as a pediatrician, I was once misled into believing some of the stereotypes about homeschoolers. Luckily, I have also met some wonderful families who have helped teach me that homeschoolers are much like everyone else.

Lea Ann Garfias is a mom of one of those families.

She was homeschooled and has done a great job homeschooling her own children—all six of them!

Is homeschooling for everyone? Of course not. Unfortunately, I see some families jump into homeschooling thinking it will be easy or looking to correct a problem that can't be easily fixed just by leaving school.

Is homeschooling for you and your child? This book will help you figure that out. It is a great resource, both for parents who have just started thinking about homeschooling and for those who need some help along the way.

Unlike some books, *Everything You Need to Know about Homeschooling* doesn't sugarcoat things. It helps you to understand that whether your child is in public school, private school, or a homeschool, none of these things is guaranteed. It is your responsibility.

Vincent Iannelli, MD
Fellow of the American Academy of Pediatrics
and Author of The Everything Father's First Year Book

PREFACE

To the families who are
distance learning

SO I WROTE THIS BOOK, sent it to my publisher, and a few months later, *BOOM*: 2020 came and everything changed. Even homeschooling.

By the fall of that year, the percentage of American homeschoolers doubled from 5% to 10% of school children, for the first time exceeding the number of those enrolled in private schools.[1] Parents suddenly had to navigate distance learning and hybrid learning. Millions of children were studying outside the classroom, and parents became involved in their child's education like never before.

In uncertain times, homeschoolers proved themselves uniquely prepared. In the face of quarantine, these parents were able to provide continuity of education and a stable home environment. Many families struggling with distance learning craved that stability and looked at the benefits of homeschooling wistfully.

Indeed, the events of 2020 caused all parents to examine their child's education more closely and to intentionally choose what was best for their family. Regardless of whether their changes were temporary or permanent, parents became even more deliberate in educating their child. This is a very good thing for everyone.

You yourself may have chosen distance learning, or a hybrid of distance and classroom instruction, rather than full-on homeschooling. No matter what your at-home learning choice, there are many things you can learn

[1] Megan Brenan, "K-12 Parents' Satisfaction With Child's Education Slips," *Gallup*, August 25, 2020, https://news.gallup.com/poll/317852/parents-satisfaction-child-education-slips.aspx.

from the homeschool community. With time and experience, homeschool parents have developed unique tools and strategies to manage home education. We face many of the same challenges you do:

We struggle having our child home all day.
We wonder if our child is on track.
We worry we aren't prepared to teach our child or to help with his homework.
We are intimidated by hard subjects.
We are concerned if our child has a learning issue.
We are tired, discouraged, and frustrated.

We aren't struggling with all of these things all of the time. But we do face these issues at one time or another, maybe even much of the time. We have developed coping methods to overcome them. And I wrote this book to put these tools and information all in one place to support parents through each challenge.

So this book is for you, too.

Rather than read this book from beginning to end, you may want to jump right into some specific sections that will help with your unique distance-learning life:

If you want some tips for just getting started, turn to chapter 3.
There you'll find encouragement for starting off right from the very first day. Besides giving suggestions for your first day's schedule, I talk about working through the emotions of that beginning, even if you feel like you or your child are having a rough start.

If you feel uncertain about your ability to teach, turn to chapter 5.
You are doubtless already helping your child understand lessons and complete difficult homework assignments. This chapter will give you perspective on your own teaching abilities and encourage you that you definitely do have what it takes.

If you want to make learning easier for your child, turn to chapter 7.
This chapter provides several perspectives on how children process information. As you identify your child's learning style, you'll

understand how to help her learn and retain new information with fewer tears. This may be my favorite chapter.

If you want to know for sure your child is in the right grade, turn to chapter 9. There I discuss what grade levels mean and what determines if a child is on track. I'll also give you an overview of what to expect in the early learning, elementary school, middle school, and high school years.

If your child is in preschool or kindergarten, turn to chapter 10. In this chapter, you'll find benchmarks for physical, mental, social, and emotional development during this period, as well as thoughts on character development. I give you examples of what your child might learn in various subjects and suggestions for curriculum and supplies you might use. I'll even teach you how to teach reading.

If your child is in elementary school, turn to chapter 11. This chapter also provides benchmarks for physical, mental, social, and emotional development—and thoughts on how your child's personal character may develop during these years. For every school subject, I'll give you ideas of what he might be learning, and I'll answer your most common questions.

If your child is in middle school, turn to chapter 12. As with the previous two chapters, you will find benchmarks for physical, mental, social, and emotional development and an explanation of how your child is developing personal character during these years. For each subject, I give you ideas for what your child should be learning and how you can help. Then I answer common questions about middle schoolers: for example, questions addressing behavior and attitudes about schoolwork.

If your child is in high school, turn to chapter 13. I again begin with physical, mental, social, emotional, and character development you may see during these years. For each academic subject, I suggest which classes may fulfill the necessary graduation requirements. We look at some of the academic hurdles during these years and discuss how to meet each challenge. I answer a lot of graduation questions, including questions about honors credits, CLEP classes, and college entrance exams. I even tell you my secret to teaching subjects that are too hard for me.

If you feel tired, frustrated, or burned out, turn to chapter 15. Of course I and the rest of homeschooling moms everywhere completely identify with these feelings. So in this chapter, I answer some of the biggest concerns we have about living with our children at home all day and how to manage the learn-at-home lifestyle with grace.

If you suspect your child has a learning difficulty or special needs, turn to chapter 16. There I explain some basics of special needs and give examples of what many special needs look like so you can decide if your child needs evaluation. I also explain where to first look for help and give ideas for how you can help your unique child learn.

If you have ever wondered if homeschooling might be right for you, go back to chapters 1 and 2. Chapter 1 gives information about homeschooling and how parents can decide if it is the right choice for their family. Chapter 2 answers many objections and concerns you might have about homeschooling.

If you want help right where you are, reach out to a homeschool mom. Tell her you aren't ready to convert fully to homeschooling, but you do want to learn some strategies to help your child learn at home. Ask her questions about how she manages the homework, how she juggles life and learning, and how she gets away from it all. Most homeschool moms would love to support you.

No matter how you choose to educate your child, she's *your* child. You are stepping up to take responsibility for her education, and you are putting your all into it. You have what it takes, and now you have the information you need. And most of all, you have an entire community just waiting to help you.

Enjoy the learn-at-home life.

INTRODUCTION

I NEVER WANTED TO HOMESCHOOL. I had the very best reason to avoid such a fate: I'm a homeschool graduate.

I was homeschooled in the late eighties and early nineties. This is the period known to our children now as the Late Stone Age, back when phones were attached to walls and computers took up entire floors of large office buildings and people wrote letters on paper with stamps to mail them and the news was also a paper that was thrown on your lawn every morning. Most children went to school on yellow buses or the wayback seat of station wagons, and few had ever heard of homeschooling and even if they had, they'd never met an actual homeschooler in real life.

Back in those days of yore, there were basically two kinds of homeschoolers. The country kind lived in the boonies and ran barefoot through the tall grass reciting Latin and Shakespeare to the goats and reading classic literature to the cattle and making cheese and denim jumpers. That wasn't me.

I was the city kind of homeschooler, the ones that had desks in the basement loaded with school textbooks and posters of maps on the walls and a used microscope on the shelf and an American flag hanging prominently from the ceiling. Mornings began with pledges, chores, and worksheets. We basically were a school at home, with a mom teacher and a dad principal and regular field trips and tests and projects and the whole nine yards. Only we had to be very secretive about the whole setup because homeschoolers were being regularly removed from their parents or detained for questioning since no one really believed parents could properly educate their own children in a basement.[1]

And yet I survived being taught at home seventh through twelfth grade. I graduated one year early with a congratulatory proclamation from my state senator and a letter from then-president Bill Clinton and high enough test scores to warrant multiple college scholarship offers. I chose a private Christian college instead, however, dropping out two years later to marry a hot Latino, birth four children, adopt two more, and live happily ever after.[2]

So when my husband suggested that I homeschool our firstborn, I said, "No way!" And for a very good reason: I knew how hard it is to homeschool. And I knew how much pressure it is to homeschool. I knew homeschooling takes everything from the mother, every moment of every day. And sadly, I have met homeschoolers who have grown up to become very smart, highly trained adults who want nothing to do with their family.[3]

I didn't want any of that. Not the denim jumpers, the fifteen-passenger vans, the spelling bees, or the basement desks. None of it.

My ever-optimistic husband, David, issued me a challenge, then, of a short-term experiment. What if we homeschooled our first son for just one year that didn't even hardly count—preschool? What if we tried it out to see if we could do it differently, if we could break the mold and forge a new path? What if we could homeschool in a unique, specialized way that built our family rather than strained it? What if we could find the faith that God could use homeschooling for good in our lives and in the lives of our children?

If you give me a challenge, I have to accept. Homeschoolers are no losers. And seriously, what did I have to lose in just one preschool year? Alas, those are the famous last words for homeschooling; everyone starts for "just one year." During those brief months, I found amazing joy and satisfaction and excitement and fulfillment in the everyday learning moments, those simple pleasures of reading and learning and talking and playing and growing together. And when my son sounded out his first word, when he taped words to his train cars to make sentences, when he sorted his shapes into a matrix across the floor, I found myself hopelessly addicted. No one was going to see all those "firsts" before I did! I wanted to be there with him every magical step of the way.

So "just one" preschool year became a new lifestyle. First at the kitchen table, then in an attic schoolroom with desks, and finally scattered across floors and tables and beds around the house, we created a homeschool that was uniquely us. A homeschool that was about building people, training young adults, molding minds. A homeschool that was about strengthening relationships and growing love. A homeschool that was filled with hard subjects and moral dilemmas and opposing worldviews and tricky calculations. A homeschool that was messy and frustrating and boring and terrifying and funny and relaxing and bold and beautiful. A homeschool of sinners seeking a Savior. A homeschool that changed us all.

Today, we have six homeschooled students: two elementary, one middle school, and one high school, plus that first preschooler and his younger sister, who are now working full time and in college, respectively. Most of our children have never sat in a schoolroom,[4] and the ACT was our teens' first standardized test. We've been through hard days, we've questioned ourselves many times, and we've cried ourselves to sleep. We've changed curricula, changed course, and changed our minds. But we made the right decision. We found the faith that God could grow all of us, and we've seen him work every day.

Can homeschooling be different from the norm? I'm here to tell you that *homeschooling must be different.* Your homeschool must be different from mine, from your friend's, from the expert at the convention's. Your homeschool must be different from that of the previous generation, from that of the boxed set, from that of the how-to guide. Your homeschool must be as different as the family you lead. Because each child is unique, each family culture is unique, and each day has its own unique challenges.

But that's a terrifying statement, isn't it? If we throw out all the rules and guidelines and manuals, what does that leave us with? How do we know how to begin, what to do on the first day, or how to level up to the next stage of learning? How can a homeschool parent know what to expect? That's a paralyzing fear—that we won't know what to do next or that we might mess up our children or that we'll fail homeschooling.

I fear failure every day of the week. It's a very real problem I struggle with constantly. And there's nothing more serious than taking on the full-time training of a child. But what my husband realized all those years ago, and I learned slowly over time, was that we will fail. We'll get exhausted and overworked, we'll make mistakes and hurt our children, and they'll make mistakes and hurt us. But God is gracious in it all. He will forgive us, and our families will find grace and forgiveness with each other as we humble ourselves to grow together.

So can we avoid burnout, failure, and conflict? I don't think so. I think, instead, we have to expect it. We have to expect that if we are fallen, sinful parents raising our own crop of sinners, it will be tough going. We have to expect that we'll mess up and need to apologize regularly. We'll have to expect that our children will mess up and say hurtful things and act disrespectfully and get bad grades and scare us to death. If we plan for all of that, if we realize that all of that comes with parenting and teaching, then we'll know that these difficulties don't mean the end of our relationship with our children. Instead, these challenges are the beginning of the most important lessons.

We need to understand that our most frustrating, difficult, scary homeschool moments are actually our most powerful teaching opportunities. How we handle these trials, how we love and forgive and seek forgiveness and persevere—these actions set powerful examples our children will follow throughout their lives. Those survival moments are sacred lessons. The F in science is the most important test paper our child receives. The year we slow down and complete only one chapter of a math book—over and over, ad nauseam—is the year we learn the most. The months we struggle with homework, character issues, and hormones are the months our family grows the most. Our most lasting lessons come not from those books but from these lives.

The answer, then, to the dilemma about how to shape a bold, new, different homeschool is in relationships—between mother and father, parent and child, and child and sibling. Those relationships impact each of us for eternity. Homeschooling gives each of us an exciting opportunity to grow alongside our child, to teach him while we ourselves learn from the Savior, to humble ourselves each day yet more and more as we marvel at how greatly God works.

I want to be your companion through that journey. This book is a resource to get you started on day one of your own unique homeschool journey, and it's a steaming cup of coffee with a smile on the tough days when you feel like giving up. In each section, I'll answer your questions on a variety of topics to help you get going and keep going.

First, in part one, we'll look at how to make the decision to homeschool and how to solidify your commitment. We'll also look at how you can answer those hard-to-answer objections to homeschooling from those around you.

Next, in part two, I'll help you get started on that very first year—first day, even—of homeschooling. We'll explore how your homeschool is vastly different from a traditional school, and I'll give you some basic tips on excelling as a teacher. Then we'll look at different homeschool teaching styles so you can consider how you most enjoy teaching and which style might be the best fit for your family. We'll also discuss the various learning styles and how they describe the ways your student may approach new subject matter. Then we can look at how you want to choose the books and materials right for you.

In part three, we'll dive into the meat of homeschooling: determining your child's grade and knowing what your child should be learning each step of the way from early learning and elementary school to middle school and high school. The chapters in this section discuss the physical, mental, emotional, and spiritual developments typical of each age, which I hope will help you find assurance that your child is not behind—or know which areas to address to strengthen his skills. In each chapter I'll also answer your questions on how to teach academic subjects at each stage.

Finally, in part four, I'll talk about some obstacles you may face in homeschooling. We'll look first at some of the dangers inherent to homeschooling and how to avoid them. We'll look at the ins and outs of homeschool life and how we can make things easier. Finally, I discuss special needs issues and how to help your child if you suspect he is struggling.

The appendices contain goodies to help you out. There's a survey to help you find your teaching style and some sample homeschool routines to peruse. There are helps to edit and grade your students' essays. I share a sample homeschool transcript so you can easily create one of your own. Then I list a gazillion homeschool resources to meet your needs.

Since the majority of homeschool teaching typically falls to Mom, I'm primarily speaking to her in this book. However, a growing number of fathers are taking over teaching the family's homeschool. I address them personally in section 15.4. I applaud these men and encourage them to apply this book's suggestions to their own endeavors.

I'm still learning, but what I share with you here comes from homeschooling for two decades with my marriage and my family and my sanity (mostly) intact. I know how exciting it is to start homeschooling, the thrill of watching a child read his first words, the anxiety of standardized tests, and the satisfaction of graduation. And I know my friends have overcome trials and difficulties to emerge quite successfully on the other side. So I have every faith in you. I know that God will keep giving you wisdom when you seek him, and I know he plans for your family to have an extraordinary impact on each other and the world around you through your homeschooling experience.

So let's get started!

PART ONE

MAKING AND DEFENDING THE DECISION

LIKE YOU, my parents did not make the decision to homeschool my sister and me lightly. It is a big decision to take your child out of school. Besides the scary reality of taking on the oversight of an entire education, homeschooling can feel like a lonely, countercultural path. In other words, most of your friends probably don't homeschool. Who wants to be the weirdo friend?

Not me.

My mom had long wanted to homeschool. She spent hours teaching my younger sister to read, gathering her own large children's library, taking us on field trips, and doing crafts. Teaching—especially early education—was in her bones.

So her outlet was school volunteering. She was always the class mom, the field trip chaperone, even one of the lunch ladies. You'd better believe her bake sale contributions were on point. She regularly tutored students during school hours in her favorite subject of reading.

My dad was also very involved in our education. He was a driven man, intent on providing the very best of everything for his family. And that included education. He took pride in sending us to a good private school and taking an acute interest in our progress. I learned to spell (okay, not great, but at least a little) and to memorize my multiplication facts only because of his patient drilling.

My mom brought up homeschooling once in a while, but my dad was not interested.

Then my sixth-grade year was less than stellar. My class had two different teachers and made very little progress. Most of the class fell behind. I spent most of each day doing my homework during the lesson time then trying to hide the book I was reading. My parents found themselves tutoring many of my fellow students in language arts and math. They ended the year dissatisfied with the quality of the education we received and wondering if they could do better. But they did go ahead and register both my sister and me for the following school year.

So they were surprised when *two* families they knew well decided to begin homeschooling that coming school year. That was weird. One family would be strange, two was mind-boggling. How could they do that?

Then one family invited my mom and dad to travel from Michigan down to Ohio to a homeschool convention. There they listened to seminars and perused curricula from new and established publishers. They became convinced that, though people might think *they* had become the weirdos, they could try this out for themselves.

Thus began my parents' one-year experiment that turned into a complete homeschool education. I graduated homeschooled after completing seventh through twelfth grade in five years. My sister was homeschooled from third grade on. It wasn't always easy, but we did it. And I'm glad we did.

Yes, people thought we were strange, even prideful to have left a great school to do things ourselves. My parents became so uncomfortable with the reaction from their friends that they changed churches. But it seemed like the more questions they got, the more committed they became to the decision they had made.

And as I homeschool my own children, I find that to be the case for me as well. The more I need to explain or even defend homeschooling, the more I reaffirm my own commitment. Explaining my own *why* and how we live this life helps me recognize God's plan and provision in our lives. I know God wants me to homeschool, and now I'm bold to tell you so.

You may not be at that place, though. Maybe you are still casting about, trying to figure out if this is right for you. Maybe you bought this book "just in case I want to later." Perhaps you are starting out for the first time. Or maybe you've been homeschooling for a long time, but your purpose has become muddied a little. That's okay. Because now we are looking at all of that together.

In this section, we'll consider some reasons people choose to home-school and how to make a decision that is right for your family based on your fundamental *why*. Then we'll discuss quick but substantive answers to others' questions about our decision—and maybe to some questions of our own.

I'm cheering you on. You can do this if God leads. Look around you, dig deep in your soul, seek God in prayer, and find your homeschool *why* right now.

FINDING YOUR HOMESCHOOL *WHY*

"WHY WOULD YOU WANT TO DO THAT?"

My fork froze midair, Southwest chicken salad dangling from the tines, as my mouth choked on a response. The restaurant owner gazed at me steadily, waiting for my defense of homeschooling and condemnation of her own life choices. I'm sure she expected me to answer as confidently and proudly as she had just listed off her own accomplishments: the stores she owned, the magnet schools her children attended, the awards each one had won. But in that moment, in the midst of a real-life Mommy War scenario, I couldn't do anything but stammer, "Because I like it."

Homeschool mom FAIL.

The fact of the matter is I haven't always *wanted* to homeschool. That day I was particularly tired and frustrated with all of it—books, children, papers, messy house, the whole nine yards. Go ahead and be shocked, but I'm not going to say every homeschool day is a bed of roses and tweeting birds and cold Mocha Frappuccinos.

But I've never, not for one minute, regretted any of it. Pretty much.

Several years have passed since my chicken salad inquisition, and I'd like to think I have a better answer to the question now. I've made it past the busy preschool stage (hooray, everyone can use the bathroom on their own!), I've learned how to survive through the tough family trials (maybe even thrive!), and I've seen two of my children make it all the way past graduation (hallelujah, give me a medal!).

So if that confrontational restaurateur asked me the question today, I'd be able to answer her quite simply and confidently (no choking required)— because I know my *why*.

The decade ahead presents an exciting time for students. There is so much to learn, so many facts and applications and philosophies and subjects to explore. And in this generation, the range of educational choices available to parents grows broader than at any time in history. Our children enjoy a bright, shiny future ahead of them full of amazing opportunities to work and to serve.

But the responsibilities loom great, too, for us as parents. We are responsible for who is training our children, and we are responsible for what they are taught. We are responsible for the beliefs and philosophies and worldviews being presented to our children, and we are responsible for protecting the truth for our next generation.

It is that *responsibility* that drove my husband and me to homeschool our children from preschool through graduation. And it's that *responsibility* that drives us to ensure each of our children has the best possible education we can provide—the best spiritual and academic preparation possible for the wide opportunities God will bring in the years to come.

> I can do all things through him who strengthens me.
>
> **PHILIPPIANS 4:13**

That responsibility lies so heavy at times. As parents, we can lose sleep over it. As homeschool moms, we can burn out from it. But this God-given responsibility doesn't have to defeat us. We *can* educate our children confidently, knowing they are compiling the tools they need for a lifetime of success. We can choose homeschooling boldly, knowing we have what it takes to educate our children wisely. And we can live every day guilt-free, knowing God will use our ordinary efforts as part of his extraordinary plan for each family member each day.

Should you homeschool? And if you've already started, should you continue? To answer these questions, you must understand your *why*.

1.1 START WITH YOUR WHY

Way back in the Dark Ages when I was homeschooled—we're talking late eighties here—I actually attended an entire schoolroom in my basement. I sat at a desk with textbooks in it, surrounded by whiteboards and time lines and maps and posters, just like a classroom. It was just in my basement, and my mom was my teacher, and my little sister in the desk beside me was my only classmate. And that's where I graduated. Well, I did come up out of the basement to graduate, but you know what I mean.

So when I started homeschooling my first son, I tried very hard to set up the same scenario. I bought a heavy, expensive box of curriculum with teachers' manuals and textbooks and workbooks and posters and classroom games and flash cards and the whole nine yards.

For my three-year-old. Bless his heart.

And it's not like we were rich, either. We were living hand-to-mouth in a basement apartment (I apparently have a thing for basements), and my husband was working two jobs to keep food in our mouths. We probably ate spaghetti every day for a month, but we had shiny new flash cards and wall posters to remind us what the ABCs were everywhere we looked.

I kept at it like that for a couple of years, obediently buying every single thing the curriculum catalog told me to, convinced that's what a good homeschool teacher did. I schooled that little boy very nearly to death, poor thing, making him copy pages of phonics and complete workbook after workbook of math. Other homeschool moms tried to tell me I didn't need to do all of that, but I wouldn't listen. I was sure those books and flash cards *were* homeschooling.

It wasn't until much later, when I was homeschooling two, then three, young children at once, that I began to recognize my problem. To me, homeschool equaled piles of books and educational *stuff* that I bought and pointed to and forced my children to consume until we were all nauseated from the bloat. As time went on and we added more subjects and more children and more ministry and more *real life*, it all became so tedious. But homeschooling shouldn't be drudgery I check off my to-do list, any more than parenting or marriage, right? It should be a lifetime of loving to learn.

I had to resolve my *why*. Why was I homeschooling in the first place? It wasn't simply because I had been homeschooled; I was nowhere *required*

ARE YOU READY TO HOMESCHOOL?

- Are you passionate about raising your child?

- Is *why* your child learns as important to you as *what* he learns?

- Is his preparation for adulthood important to you?

- Do you (sometimes) enjoy training your child?

- Do you like to both be at home and leave the house?

- Do you make mistakes but sometimes learn from them?

- Can you provide a library card and a pencil?

- Can you attempt to dissuade your child from writing in the library book with the pencil?

- Do you drink coffee or some other nonalcoholic beverage that could possibly endow you with supernatural or natural powers?

- Do you own pajamas or yoga pants?

- Do you love your child?

If you said yes to any of these questions, you are ready to homeschool.

---

to teach my children the same way I was taught. In fact, there were public and private schools that I could enroll them in just fine. I even taught in the school next door for several years, walking back home to teach my own children after class. So I knew homeschooling was not simply the easiest or the most obvious choice. Homeschool parents—all parents, even—need to know *why* they have chosen their educational path.

1.2 WHY THAT SCHOOL?

There are lots of reasons people choose their child's school. I think the default reason is most common. We just do **what comes naturally**. For most parents, that's sending their children to public school. It's similar to how they themselves learned, there's that convenient bus, and there are several locations nearby. Our tax money even pays for it. Public school seems like the obvious choice.

Private schools are the answer for many parents. I went to private Christian schools for all of preschool and elementary, in fact. For parents who want to make sure their child gets a better education within a particular worldview or belief system and who can afford to spend a little more on education, private schools represent a simple solution.

Homeschooling, however, is rarely a default for any parent. It takes some courage, some intentionality, some guts to say, "I think I can do better," and then spend years dedicated to proving just that. Really, hats off to everyone who goes that road less traveled.

Public, private, or homeschool, there are at least five major considerations parents discuss when choosing their child's school.

1.2.1 To instill a deep faith

Many parents choose their child's education because of **religion.** Religious reasons influence the decision for over 50% of homeschoolers, and 16% say this is the most important reason to homeschool.[1] They find a private school that teaches Christianity (or Islam, or Judaism, or another faith tradition) and place the child there. Sometimes that's because passing on their values and beliefs is very important to them, and they want to make sure the teachers are "backing them up" in school.

Then some parents, like my friend Angie, send their child to religious school to teach them the beliefs and practices they themselves don't know. They hope the teacher can fill in all the particulars—the important details of *how the child views the world and himself and his relationship to his God.* When I asked another mom why she chose her son's elementary school, she said, "Because I just don't know those Bible stories. They can teach him."

Christian homeschool parents often choose to teach their children for this very reason—their beliefs are too important to them to delegate to someone else. They are passionate about sharing their walk with God with their children, helping them develop biblical discernment, protecting them from the errors of false teaching, and building the foundation of their future ministry. It's a priority relationship they simply must transmit. They don't claim to have all the answers and the sinless life and the sanctified teachings. But they know they are growing in grace, and they yearn to bring their children along on that journey with them.

1.2.2 To prepare your children academically

In my area, most parents choose their child's school for **academic** reasons. They find the right public or private schools based on test scores, STEM subjects, gifted or special education programs, even arts opportunities. My friend Natalie spends hours every day driving her children across two cities to three different schools and then various after-school programs, all to give them the best academic training she can find.

Over 60% of homeschool parents are motivated to provide academic advantages, and 17% consider this the most important reason to homeschool. Twenty percent of homeschoolers made the decision, at least in part, because of their child's special needs.[2] The superiority of one-on-one instruction and impressive homeschool test score results lures ambitious parents into investing more time and attention in their student's learning. Personalized education and therapy allow parents to give students with special needs invaluable support. And with the extra time saved by staying home, these students often invest more in the arts, sports, and hands-on learning opportunities.

1.2.3 To encourage positive social connections

I know many parents who make a **social** choice to keep their child in traditional schools. They choose to send their child to a particular school district or private school because of income or ethnic demographics. They want their child to learn in a more diverse environment, or they want to protect their child from crime, bullying, and gang elements. They may be

I think parents need to begin with the end in mind. Too often they just send their kids to public schools because that's what you do. But they should be asking what they want their kids to be and then search for a method that will create that. It makes no sense to me to blindly send your kids to public school and hope they turn out the way you want.

With all that said, I'm not someone who pushes homeschool as if it's the only way. Each family needs to choose what works best for them and will get the results they want. But I do believe that whatever they do they should do it intentionally. Don't just send your kids to public school because that's what you do. Make it a choice.

TEACHING HOMESCHOOL DAD CHAD KENT

looking for an educational environment that more closely represents the world they imagine their child living in as an adult.

Even 80 percent of homeschoolers consider public school environment a factor in their choice.[3] They may be pulling their child out of a classroom with bullying. Or they may be protecting their child from growing ethnic unrest in a particular district. Minorities, particularly black homeschoolers, are often reacting against the "school to prison pipeline." They feel they can better train their children to live and work and serve in the real world outside a race- or age-segregated environment.[4] Over one-third of homeschoolers say school environment is the single most important reason to homeschool—the most important reason found in a 2016 survey.[5]

1.2.4 To save money

In addition, many parents make a **financial** choice for where their child goes to school, sending their child to public school because it's free. Some sacrifice to send the student to private schools, working multiple jobs to pay the increasing cost of specialized education. Many feel forced into their choice of school since both parents work, struggling to juggle the demands of managing a two-income household.

Surprisingly, though, homeschool families have found ways to educate their children without the high cost of private tuition. In fact, I have found that the longer I homeschool, the less expensive it is for us every year. Homeschool products and curricula are easier to obtain and more affordable than even a decade ago. And experience has taught me how little a student needs to thrive; I wish I could have my money back from those thick teachers' manuals of years gone by!

1.2.5 To pass on your cultural heritage

Many minority parents also choose to homeschool, at least in part, to **pass on their culture and history.** This is, according to Hispanic homeschool advocate Monica Olivera, the second most common reason for minorities to homeschool, after avoiding the public school environment. The author of *The Latino Family's Guide to Homeschooling* and founder of the Mommy Maestra support blog, Monica says, "Passing on cultural heritage and maintaining bilingualism is extremely important to a lot of Hispanics right now."[6] A CDC study conducted in 2009 indicated that when Latino children were raised to understand and be proud of their heritage, they had higher self-esteem and lower incidence of drug use, aggressive behavior, and social problems.[7] Pier Penic, founder of the Culture at Home support group for black homeschoolers in Washington, DC, cites this as the driving force for around 85 percent of African American homeschool families. "Many of them have said [as parents] that they want to incorporate [into their kids' schooling] the experience and legacy of being an African American in this country. . . . They want their children to understand . . . that their ancestors were beaten, sold, killed just [for] learning to read one letter."[8] Ethnically diverse homeschool parents are often motivated by the prejudiced rhetoric around them, choosing instead to instill cultural pride in their children.

1.3 WHY WE HOMESCHOOL

The reasons laid out in the preceding section are all valid ones for making school choices, but I wasn't even thinking about these things when my husband first challenged me to homeschool. Quite frankly, the decision was made for just one year, at least in my mind. My husband says he always knew we'd homeschool "all the way," but one year was all he could talk me into at first.

His argument became, "Why not? If we can provide an excellent education, if we can train our children to love God and love others, if we can avoid the high costs of private tuition, if we can protect our children from bullying, peer pressure, bad influences, and disrespect, why not do it? What do we have to lose?"

If we can fulfill God's command to teach our children through our lives together, why would we not wholeheartedly follow him?

Here are some distinctives of our family's *why* when it comes to homeschooling:

1. We want to **share God's love** with our children. We want them to know God personally and to know he desires a personal relationship with them. They need to know that even though we all are sinners, that we all make mistakes, that we all fall short of God's glory (Romans 3:23) he still loves us unconditionally. His love for us is so powerful it led him to death, the bloody death on the cross to pay for our sins (Romans 5:8). And we can each know God's free gift of salvation by simply accepting his

love for ourselves (Ephesians 2:8). Then we can enjoy a personal relationship with God. That's the love God wants us to know and to share with our children.

2. We want to **pass on our values** to our children. We want to reinforce, through our day-to-day lives, that we believe what we say. As God helps us live out those principles from his Word, we pray that our children will know him and desire to know more about him. We want to share the love and truths of God consistently through our own lives.

3. We want to **reveal God's plan and purpose through their academics**. No truth occurs in a vacuum; each principle is created and sustained by God. How and why we communicate (language arts), the consistent patterns that hold all of creation together (math), the record of God's dealing with mankind (history), the wonder of God's creative plan (science)—these all reveal the glory of God, and we want to revel in it along with our children.

4. We want to **prepare our children for adulthood**. The schooling years are not only a celebration of the joy of childhood. These are the years to prepare for the rest of their lives. Taking part in this journey, guiding their privileges and responsibilities even in academics, allows us to be a greater part of this transformation.

5. We want to **teach our children through relationships**. Indeed, we will see in chapter 6 that this overriding principle is the basis for every homeschool teaching style. Education itself is a teacher/student relationship, a relationship that can build and solidify over time through learning. We want to strengthen that relationship with God and within our family. We want to demonstrate the most important commandments of God, the relationships he prizes most: love for him and love for others.

In fact, my relationship with my husband is why I started home-schooling twenty years ago. He always wanted me to homeschool our son, but I was skeptical about how it would affect our family. I loved my husband, so for the sake of our marriage, I tried for just one year.

Our relationship as husband and wife has only grown more intimate since then, and homeschooling had a lot to do with it. We are in this together, and we can only succeed by working together. That means a lot of creative problem solving, decision making, and hand holding. It demands late-night talks and early morning planning sessions. We invest not only our funds and my career and all our family vacations but also our time, our date nights, and our long-term goals into making this endeavor work for our family.

> You shall teach [God's words] to your children, talking of them when you are sitting in your house, and when you are walking by the way, and when you lie down, and when you rise.
>
> **DEUTERONOMY 11:19**

Homeschooling has molded my relationship with my children. Obviously, we can't live together 24-7 and not influence each other in a big way. But living every day right with my children, letting them see me in all the ordinary struggles and frustrations and joys and hilarity of daily life, has drawn us together, even as they have grown older. That intimacy and trust built over countless hours and prayers and projects and lessons and apologies and graces pays off in deeper, fuller relationships with my teens. We genuinely enjoy being together, traveling together, running errands together, and working together. And that's in large part because of homeschooling.

But most of all, homeschooling changed my relationship with God. Taking on the responsibility of teaching my children, of guiding them into adulthood, of discipling them to a personal relationship with Christ, I feel keenly the enormous burden of it all. There is no way I could be all that and a bottle of hot sauce for my children and my husband, so I must rely on the Lord every moment of each day.

That relationship with the Lord is also the very reason I homeschool in the first place. I know God gave these children to me as a stewardship, a responsibility to him. He has a specific plan for each of their lives, a ministry and a calling he is preparing them to realize. They may be in the ministry, or they may serve in secular jobs. One dreams of being a business owner, another is studying for a lifetime in academia, another is praying over a ministry in professional sports. Whatever God designed them to do, they must do it for his glory and to the very best of the abilities he gave them.

Homeschooling changes relationships—our relationships with our spouses and with our children and each child's relationships with his parents and siblings. All of us are transformed in our relationship with God as we depend on him for each subject, each assignment, each day. We grow in our understanding of him. We see his love for us every day.

That is my greatest homeschool *why*: transformed relationships, relationships that last for eternity.

• • •

While all of the reasons I've mentioned have become a sufficient rationale for our own homeschooling, friends and acquaintances often push for more. Why should a family go through the expense, the frustration, the drain of homeschooling . . . embarking on a project that, with multiple children, will take decades to complete? And why would one or both spouses sacrifice career, privacy, and *sanity* to take on such a Herculean task? And even, when the going gets tough—the mom becomes chronically ill, the family faces financial setback, the student rebels, real life intrudes on schooling—why would the family continue prioritizing homeschooling? Why this radical lifestyle when there are so many alternatives?

This is the reason why before embarking on the homeschool journey *you must connect with your own why.* You and your spouse must *know* why you are homeschooling and what you want out of it. And you need to know how you will define homeschool success.

> Many are the plans in the mind of a man, but it is the purpose of the LORD that will stand.
>
> **PROVERBS 19:21**

Because if you know what *homeschool success* looks like in your family, if you know what your own unique homeschool *why* is all about, then you can homeschool with confidence. When the learning difficulties emerge, when the character problems arise, when the subject matter gets tough and the days grow longer, you will continue undistracted. Because that's not what you are about. You measure success differently.

Though your own plans may—and probably will—run amok, God's plan for your homeschool will be a success.

Take a few minutes, before you continue reading, and define your own homeschool *why*. Consider the results you want in your relationships. List the outcomes you expect in your children's academics, social skills, and spiritual lives. Then pray about how God will change *you* yourself through the homeschool journey. If you're married, discuss these issues with your spouse, even write down your mutual goals. Come to terms with your homeschool *why*—then pursue it with joy. Filter not only this book but all of your homeschooling through the lens of this *why*, through the expectation of what God will accomplish in your lives.

2

GET READY FOR THE QUESTIONS

AS SOON AS YOU EVEN START *considering* homeschooling, everyone will have an opinion on it—and desperately need to share that with you. Brace yourself, because from now on everyone you meet, from the bag boy at the grocery to the mechanic at the auto body shop, will have opinions on your family's choice of education.

Some days, you'll feel confident and poised, ready to answer everyone's questions with a smile and a joke. But other days—the days your toddler hasn't slept through the night, your preteen is giving you attitude, and the science project has exploded across the family room—you'll have no good reason to give a stranger.

The following are some questions you may be asked and a simple, quick answer you can give. Keep in mind that others' questions are rarely condemnations of your life choices. Most people are genuinely curious, even envious, of your lifestyle. And maybe you look more "with it" than you feel. Take these opportunities to encourage others in your extended family and community to consider homeschooling. You may gain a new homeschool friend!

2.1 QUESTIONS ABOUT SOCIALIZATION

2.1.1 Will your children be unsocialized?

No. I let them out in public. This question—notoriously the most common reaction to homeschooling—is really hard for homeschoolers to answer with a straight face . . . and without sarcasm. It's just too funny. This issue often comes up if you are just starting homeschooling or if the stranger has never interacted with your children. Anyone who knows your homeschool students personally would not ask this because they have held a conversation with them and seen that they can function in the real world.

Many people don't understand what they are asking about. The word *socialization* has two important definitions in the Merriam-Webster dictionary. The first is "the process beginning during childhood by which individuals acquire the values, habits, and attitudes of a society." This is the exact reason many families homeschool—to instill the values, habits, and attitudes of their own family. These parents intentionally choose *which* society or community they want their child to become a part of—Christians, academics, overcomers of special needs, expert underwater basket weavers. Homeschooling is actually intentional socialization.

The second definition (right before socializing an animal) is "social interaction with others." Again, homeschool families intentionally choose the "others" with whom they want their child to interact. As they live intentionally within the church and community, homeschoolers interact with adults and children of a variety of cultures, beliefs, vocations, and ages. Rather than spending the majority of the day interacting with individuals their own age within similar demographics, homeschoolers have the means and opportunity to broaden their social circle.

2.1.2 Will your children be able to face the real world?

Homeschool families do exist in reality. Homeschooling has been proven to produce responsible, reliable adults. In general, homeschool students adjust to college quickly, begin preparing for their chosen career early, volunteer in their community, and stay active in their local church. In addition, many homeschool teens begin working earlier than their public school counterparts, giving them more real-world experience in business, community work, and social interaction.[1]

Sometimes it helps to ask questions about what issues are of concern.

Those questioning you may be worried about cultural ignorance, adult peer pressure, job interviews, or even dating. I've found it helpful to ask for more information before assuming someone is antagonistic to homeschool graduates in general.

2.1.3 Won't your family be weird?
It's true that there are weird homeschool families. There are also weird public school families. Our family is not one of them. Is yours? Homeschool families are aware of the stereotype, and most of us actively oppose it. The average homeschooler today is not isolated, ignorant, stuck in the fifties, or wearing a denim jumper. In fact, you've probably met several homeschool graduates and didn't realize it; they looked so normal.

2.1.4 What if your children miss their friends?
Then we'll invite them over. There is a misconception that homeschoolers have fewer friends than kids in public schools. In fact, there are cliques and lonely teens in the homeschool community just like in public school groups. Parents still have plenty of opportunities to teach yet more social skills of kindness and inclusiveness. One of the clear advantages for the homeschool student and teen, however, is greater opportunity to join more groups, take part in more activities, and initiate more playdates because of the greater time flexibility.

2.1.5 Won't the student miss out on "rites of passage" like crushes, prom, and detention?
Homeschool families don't need to miss anything that is important to them. If dating is a priority, homeschoolers will enjoy more time socializing. If prom is important, they will take advantage of the many large, elaborate formals for homeschool students (check with your local homeschool support group). And if parents want them to experience detention, there is ample opportunity to ground them indefinitely.

2.1.6 Shouldn't the student be a "light" and a "witness" in the public school system?
We homeschool because of the gospel. Gospel living is important to homeschoolers, which is why we concentrate on discipling them intensively before sending them out on their own to confront opposing worldviews.

We all come in contact with differing worldviews every day. A young eight- or ten- or fifteen-year-old cannot have the background and discernment to understand the implications of humanism, New Age philosophy, Eastern mysticism, postmodernism, pluralism, and other anti-God beliefs that permeate secular education. Homeschooling parents have the opportunity to carefully instruct their students not only in their own beliefs but also in the implications and consequences of other beliefs. This helps produce adults who consciously choose their own convictions and are prepared to address the challenges around them.

2.1.7 What if you are lonely?

We can join a support group. In my area, there are so many homeschool support groups, one can't possibly keep up with them all. That's not counting the co-ops, playgroups, park meetups, and book clubs. A quick internet or Facebook search is all it takes to make more friends. I joined a monthly homeschool mom supper club. And you'd better believe I'm having coffee or lunch with my friends a couple of times a month. A girl's gotta eat.

HOW DO I FIND A HOMESCHOOL SUPPORT GROUP?

The website hslda.org has a lengthy list of homeschool support groups by state and county. I found my local group by googling "homeschool support group [city]." You can take your best homeschool mom friend along with you to the next meeting—or join her group.

2.2 QUESTIONS ABOUT TEACHING

2.2.1 Isn't it too hard?
I don't think I could ever homeschool my child.

Yes, you could—one day, one challenge at a time. This is what nearly everyone tells me right after asking, "What book are you writing now?" I want to say this is why I wrote this book. I want everyone to know that homeschooling can be simple.

Many people think that homeschool moms have this rare superpower or weird personality that makes them super-suited to homeschooling.

Don't we wish. Homeschool parents like you and me are just normal people who chose a path God called us to. We dared to take a few uncertain steps toward God's promise for our family, and little by little we gained knowledge and confidence. Well, sometimes confidence.

> Not by might, nor by power, but by my Spirit, says the LORD of hosts.
>
> **ZECHARIAH 4:6**

There is no magic formula for homeschooling. Every day, ordinary people slowly but surely begin to learn within their own family culture, teaching the way they teach best for the way their child learns best. It's a gradual process, but it can be done.

No one needs to know everything all at once. None of us can know all about homeschooling. I definitely don't; this book is a compilation of things I have learned over time by making lots of mistakes, along with things my friends have taught me and things experts have written. We can all keep learning while we're doing this.

If God calls you to homeschool, he will enable you to homeschool. It's not by our strength but only by the Holy Spirit.

2.2.2 Are you academically qualified to teach your child?

I'm more qualified than anyone. Homeschool parents with little or no training continue to successfully teach their children. For students in the public school, success in math and reading scores is directly related to the level of education their parents possess. Yet researchers have found that regardless of a homeschool parent's degree or diploma, average homeschool student test scores are above the national average.[2]

Homeschool success is not affected one bit by the level of parental education. Homeschooling is a success because of the nature of homeschooling itself.

Many homeschool programs walk you step-by-step through each subject and assignment. Many do the lesson planning for you, and some even tell you what to say every day. Of course, books like this one help you realize you can confidently and excellently train your own children.

2.2.3 What if you do not have the gift of teaching?

There are many ways to homeschool. With the availability of video homeschooling, online classes, local co-ops, and even student-directed curricula, each homeschool mom can find the resources that fit her own personal style, as well as that of her children. To tell you the truth, I don't feel I have the gift of teaching myself. But I love homeschooling. It's just plain different. Chapter 6 explores many different ways a homeschool mom can teach much differently than traditional schooling or tutoring.

2.2.4 Who will make sure your children are learning?

That is my responsibility. It's a misconception in today's society that the public school system or other governmental institutions are necessary to ensure children's futures. Homeschool parents strive to raise responsible, hardworking adults by modeling those values in front of their children. And that starts with taking responsibility for their own family, even educationally.

Many people who ask this question, though, are really worried about *graduation* or *college acceptance* or even *job applications* (which we talk about in section 13.3). You can reassure them that homeschool transcripts are accepted at all major colleges and that most employers are eager to hire hardworking homeschool graduates.

2.2.5 Will your children suffer if you can't duplicate the classroom experience?

No, because homeschooling gives students so much a classroom cannot replicate. Public school classrooms cannot duplicate the advantage of the fully customized, one-on-one teaching that homeschooling provides. Homeschool families can spend more time researching, visiting museums and historical sites, and exploring hands-on projects. They can learn from experts in their field and engage in mentorship. Individualized instruction combined with the specialized opportunities creative families enjoy gives homeschooling a clear advantage over classroom instruction.

2.2.6 How can you adequately teach the really hard subjects like high school science, algebra, or foreign languages?

There is nothing a homeschool student can't study. If a homeschool parent feels a topic is beyond her expertise to teach, a variety of alternatives exist, including internet-based classes such as those Khan Academy provides, online interactive classrooms, co-op classes taught by experienced teachers, private tutors, and more. Today's homeschool families have so many options for curricula and classes there is almost nothing a homeschool student can't learn at his own level.

2.2.7 Will your child miss out on sports, music, or art opportunities?

There is a wide variety of extracurricular opportunities open to homeschool students. Homeschoolers can enjoy participating in community sports, music, drama, and art organizations. Musical students often take private lessons and join choirs and orchestras. Homeschoolers have formed their own local and national organizations for student competition, like the National Christian Forensics and Communications Association.

Many public school and extracurricular programs allow homeschool students to participate in their programs as well. And many states have versions of a "Tim Tebow Bill" allowing homeschool students to participate in University Interscholastic League (UIL) sports. Serious student athletes usually join private sports clubs for soccer and other sports not only for specialized training but also for exposure to top recruiters. Many homeschool parents coach teams or attend team practices to stay involved. There is almost nothing a homeschool student cannot get involved in.

2.2.8 What if your child has special needs or is gifted?

By homeschooling, I can meet his unique needs. This is where homeschooling shines—individualized education. Homeschool parents have the luxury of customizing every aspect of the child's learning, routine, and environment. Many utilize a vast range of resources, including private tutors, online classes, co-ops, and master classes to ensure their student remains challenged and engaged. Turn to chapter 16 for more on special needs.

2.2.9 Can a homeschool student get accepted into college, or does she need a GED?

Homeschool transcripts along with college entrance exams are acceptable proof of graduation. The GED (or General Educational Development test) is for individuals who have *not* completed high school, so homeschool graduates do not need it. Because of the rising popularity of homeschooling around the nation, most colleges are familiar with homeschooling and even have clear directions included in their admissions process for how homeschoolers should apply.

2.3 QUESTIONS ABOUT HISTORY AND LAW

2.3.1 How did homeschooling begin?

With Creation. Ultimately, parents have been teaching their own children since Adam and Eve started a family. Throughout ancient history, including the Greek and Roman Empires, children learned at home for years before beginning what we would call secondary education in a small class or with a tutor. In early America, colonists varied between home education, small classrooms taught by volunteer parents, and publicly funded schools. In the 1640s in Massachusetts, Puritans began to establish public schools to inculcate Calvinist and Biblical teaching.

However, compulsory schooling spread widely with the rise of socialism, humanism, and the industrial age, with children taught from young ages in age-segregated classrooms. The purpose of public education has been twofold: to instill modern social beliefs and to train the next generation of workers. By the twentieth century, this form of education became the norm.

Then the rise of private religious schools gave birth to the modern homeschool movement. In 1925, Catholics won an exemption from compulsory attendance laws and established parochial schools based on their doctrinal beliefs, as a result of the court case *Pierce v. Society of Sisters*.[3] Emboldened by their example, Jonas Yoder took his own case, *Wisconsin v. Yoder*, to the Supreme Court to win an Amish exemption to compulsory attendance based on religious liberty in 1972.[4]

Two separate events are recognized as the genesis of the homeschool movement. In 1977, John Holt, an educator, author, and speaker, began publishing and speaking on the failures of the public school system. He advocated child civil liberties—including educational freedom—beginning the secular homeschool movement and the unschooling method, as we will see in section 6.6.

Separately, the Christian homeschool movement took off with a now-famous 1982 radio interview on *Focus on the Family* between Dr. James Dobson and Dr. Raymond Moore.[5] Moore shared his extensive research on

FAMOUS HOMESCHOOLERS AT LEAST PARTIALLY TAUGHT AT HOME

Leonardo da Vinci	Woodrow Wilson
John and Charles Wesley	Pierre Curie
John Marshall	William Jennings Bryan
Wolfgang Amadeus Mozart	Beatrix Potter
William Carey	Orville and Wilbur Wright
Daniel Webster	Winston Churchill
Robert E. Lee	Albert Einstein
Abraham Lincoln	Douglas MacArthur
Charles Dickens	Franklin Delano Roosevelt
Susan B. Anthony	C. S. Lewis
Florence Nightingale	Ansel Adams
Clara Barton	Sandra Day O'Connor
Andrew Carnegie	Whoopi Goldberg
Mark Twain	Serena and Venus Williams
Dwight L. Moody	LeAnn Rimes
Thomas Edison	Tim Tebow
Alexander Graham Bell	Hilary Duff
Booker T. Washington	

the rate of child development in the first ten years, arguing that classroom education harms young children. These children, he pointed out, would quickly catch up academically with their school-aged peers only if they learned life skills and strengthened family attachment first at home. He claimed standardization was the greatest failure of classroom education. Raymond Moore and his wife, Dorothy, had previously written *Better Late Than Early* and *School Can Wait* among many other books to encourage home educators. That one radio interview, though, heard by thousands of listeners, convinced many parents to remove their young children from school to teach them at home.

From this point, the homeschool movement took off in the eighties and nineties. In 1980, Pat and Sue Welch began the first homeschool publication, *The Teaching Home*. From 1981 into the nineties, Gregg Harris helped grow the homeschool movement and taught a delight-directed method.

In 1988, Skeet Savage began the *Home School Digest*, the longest-running Christian homeschool magazine in print.

An important catalyst for the growth of the homeschool movement was the founding of the Home School Legal Defense Association (HSLDA) in 1983 by Michael Farris and J. Michael Smith. The association quickly became active in defending the rights of homeschoolers and lobbying for educational freedom across the country. Farris argued cases all the way to Capitol Hill. Smith first served as vice president of HSLDA and became president in 2001. The late Christopher Klicka joined HSLDA as senior counsel and director of state and international relations. Klicka argued for the legality of homeschooling even to the United States Supreme Court.

Current homeschool leaders include Brian Ray, Mary Pride, and Cathy Duffy. Dr. Ray of the National Home Education Research Institute (NHERI) publishes research on homeschooling and testifies in court as an expert witness. Mary Pride, formerly an outspoken anti-feminist and author of numerous volumes on homeschool methods and family life, founded *Practical Homeschooling* magazine. Since 1984, Cathy Duffy has published many books reviewing homeschool curricula and materials, including the 2015 *102 Top Picks for Homeschool Curriculum*. Her newsletter and website are trusted resources for homeschool product information.

Presently, there are hundreds of state organizations, homeschool publications, homeschool conventions, homeschool curricula, and homeschool speakers. From its humble beginnings in the early eighties, homeschooling grew to over 2.3 million in the twenty-first century; then, when the pandemic of 2020 upset the continuity of public education, those numbers doubled again.[6]

2.3.2 Is homeschooling even legal?

Homeschooling is legal now in every state in America. Each state has its own simple reporting regulations, varying from testing to portfolio reviews to no oversight at all. Many states have compulsory attendance laws, which simply require attendance records. I live in one of the easiest states in the country to homeschool; I don't have to tell anyone anything. Check with the Home School Legal Defense website at hslda.org for your state's regulations.

2.4 QUESTIONS ABOUT MONEY

2.4.1 Can you afford to homeschool?

Homeschooling is more economical than private school tuition and more cost effective per student than public school education. Nationally, the public school system spends over $11,000 per student each year on education.[7] Homeschool parents spend only a small fraction of that on books, memberships, technology, field trips, and other educational expenses. Homeschoolers may choose free curricula or spend thousands of dollars for co-ops, online classes, and

> An investment in knowledge always pays the best interest.
>
> **ATTRIBUTED TO BENJAMIN FRANKLIN IN *THE EVANGELICAL REPOSITORY*, 1849**

private tutoring. It is estimated that the average homeschool family spends around $900 per student per year,[8] though I personally only spend $500 to $1,000 each year altogether for 3–5 students. And homeschooling provides an excellent education in spite of this cost difference.

Cost is rarely an issue for homeschool families. With free and low-cost materials available, including educational internet sites, libraries, and museums, homeschooling provides an excellent education without breaking the bank.

2.4.2 Will you be forced to live on one salary? Would it be better for the student to be in school so both parents can work?

We can work and homeschool, too! Many teaching homeschool parents work full- or part-time in and out of the home. I myself have worked twenty to forty hours a week, both in and out of my home, nearly every year we have homeschooled. Many homeschool moms run their own business, participate in direct sales, tutor, or work remotely. Some work night shifts after homeschooling during the day. Homeschool parents thrive on creative problem solving, and fitting another career or income stream into the family routine is just another way to make homeschooling part of the family culture. I speak directly to working homeschool moms beginning in section 15.5.

2.5 QUESTIONS ABOUT LIFE AT HOME

2.5.1 What if one spouse doesn't want to homeschool?

You need to be unified for homeschooling to work. Homeschooling is a family project. I would never recommend embarking on such a fundamental lifestyle change without the complete agreement of both parents. Marital unity is too important.

But in my own instance, I did not want to homeschool in the beginning, while my husband was determined this was the right path for our family. He wisely asked for a one-year trial period. That was a good compromise because it gave him more time to convince me this was right for us. At the same time, I knew that if things went badly, I could tell him I had tried, but it hadn't worked for us. When I was a homeschool student myself, my father was not completely sure it would work. So, again, my parents tried for just one year and continued to take homeschooling just a year at a time. This is why some couples find a one-year trial works for both of them.

2.5.2 How can you stand being around your children all day, every day?

I love my children, and we are making lasting memories every day. Sadly, one of the biggest reasons moms tell me they don't want to homeschool is because "I couldn't stand being in the same house with my children 24-7." Or they may say, "I don't have the patience to live with my children all day, every day." I think this response bothers homeschool parents more than any other for two important reasons.

First of all, homeschool moms are tired. We want a break. And we have all, every one of us, watched the yellow school bus pass our home with a wistful sigh of fatigue and longing. We don't homeschool because it's easy. But we homeschool because it's more important to us than a break or a weekly coffee chat with friends. Our love for our children drives us to continue on, even on tough days.

Secondly, homeschool moms take personal responsibility for the people our children are growing into. If our children are ill-behaved, arrogant, disobedient, or unkind, then we want to address that primarily—before academics or sports or any other lessons. We don't homeschool because we love being around our children. We homeschool because we value these lessons. We homeschool, praying our young people become adults who love God and love others.

2.5.3 What if your child doesn't listen to you?

Then I need to teach them to listen and obey. This is a somewhat frustrating objection to homeschooling because it implies that parents cannot adequately instill character in their own children, that they need other professionals to do so. Homeschooling provides plenty of opportunities for parents to focus on such issues as obedience, respect, listening, and thoughtfulness. This is not to say that homeschooling raises perfect little angels that hang on to every word parents say and cheerfully do what they are told the first time every single time. But homeschooling does allow more time to work on obedience and character issues. Living together all day, every day helps parents pass along the qualities that matter most to them.

2.5.4 What if you aren't organized?

Fortunately, that is not a prerequisite. The only real necessities are to not lose *all* the books and to keep track of the high school grades. Everything else is gravy. Over time, most moms fall into a routine and an organizational system that fits them best. But the boys still lose the pencils. Just accept it and move on.

• • •

Explaining and defending homeschooling—to others or even to yourself—can seem intimidating. Hey, I dread the questions every time I go to the grocery store, though now the checkout people are used to seeing me with my kids.

"Why aren't you in school?"

"I'm homeschooled."

Then the quizzing of the children and the quizzing of me begins. Fortunately, all these questions have given me practice at giving quick answers with a (somewhat forced) smile.

But you know what? Many times, these are legitimate questions. Once I get past my own awkward defensiveness, I sometimes find the person honestly wants to know. And sometimes, she will even say, "I've thought about doing it myself, but . . ." and then I willingly answer more objections. Over time, homeschooling has grown from just a few thousand to millions of students. All because we answered the objections honestly, showing our neighbors and friends that this really is possible—even enjoyable sometimes.

And each time I do, I remind myself of my own *why*, the reasons I keep going on the hard days and look forward to seeing the progress of my own children:

I love my children and I love God, and that is why I homeschool.

PART TWO

GETTING STARTED

MY FRIEND DIANE AND I connected through soccer practice.

If there is a mom who yells as loudly as I do, I'm sitting next to her. I feel all self-conscious screaming next to a quiet mom. Like, I yell really, really loud, "Yay, Xzavian! Great pass!" every time my son touches the ball. I can't help it. Then I give the side-eye to the serene woman sitting beside me clapping politely, and I feel like an animal. But instincts take over in just a milli-minute, and I'm jumping and screaming again.

So, like I said, I sit beside the passionate soccer moms in my fold-up red chair with the ripped armrests. And on my right sits/jumps Diane. In between yells, she used to describe to me her frustrations with her child's public school experience: the homework, the wasted time, the lack of personal attention. She was fed up with the politics of the PTA. She was burned out over the futility of suggesting, volunteering, meeting with leaders. She felt like she was doing more work behind the scenes and after school than if she taught her son herself.

Yep, she probably was.

Finally, she'd had it. Had it enough to ask me what homeschooling was all about. So I tried to be generally positive about it in just a few words. But she wasn't content with the pat answers—she wanted more.

She wanted to pull her son out and start immediately.

This more detailed conversation had to wait for halftime. I was entirely too distracted by my son's athletic prowess to help a mother make one of the most important educational decisions of her life.

But I finally gave my friend the attention she deserved. Thus began a consistent before-, after-, and in-the-middle-of-soccer-practice crash course on Homeschooling Benefits. Diane graduated to Homeschool Philosophy. Then she progressed to How to Buy Books. Then came her most burning question: "How do I start?"

So I gave her the general you-can-do-it speech, complete with self-deprecating anecdotes of personal failures. But she yearned for more. She literally wanted to know "What do I do at 8:30 a.m. Monday morning?"

I'd never considered that, but she was right. That *is* a tricky question. We spent a little more in-depth time on that one, moving our conversation from mid-soccer to text and Facebook Messenger. That's how you know things were getting a little serious.

That's how I knew you might need a little push in the right direction too.

So in this section, I will literally tell you what to do on the first day. Then we'll move on to some ways homeschooling is distinct from public or private schooling and how to handle its unique challenges. I'll then lift up a mirror for you to see the true picture: you, yourself, are a great teacher.

Next, we'll get into the details of homeschool styles: how different homeschooling parents choose to teach. You will likely resonate with one or more of the homeschool styles and find some inspiration for your own personal best way of teaching. Then we'll look at some of the many theories of learning styles. We'll examine some of these models and how they might present in your student. Finally, we'll get to the stuff of homeschooling—how to buy the books. This is the second most frequent question I hear from new homeschoolers.

I hope that this section will help you overcome each of these "firsts" and enable you to confidently teach the way you teach best and the way your student learns best. Homeschool firsts are always exciting—the first books, the first box of materials, the first day, the first year. Let's celebrate the fun, answer your questions, and enjoy these steps in the chapters to come.

3

READY, SET, GO!

SO YOU'VE DECIDED to try out this homeschooling thing. What next? How do you get started on your first day? After you call the children to the kitchen table, where do you begin?

I remember my first day of homeschooling. The poor guy was only three. I didn't have room in the apartment for a school desk, and I wondered if he would learn anything sitting at the kitchen table. I had purchased this huge, expensive box of curriculum. So I dutifully taped charts and game posters all over the kitchen wall. I tore out the worksheets and set them aside until I could formally tell him, "Pick up your pencil and begin." After starting with pledges and a prayer while standing at attention beside our chairs, we sat down to flash cards. He was less than impressed.

I had taught K3 in a private school four years before. I knew classroom management, how to drill facts, how to lead group games, and how to teach a child to hold a crayon.

My own son hated coloring and was bored of the classroom games.

I pressed on. Bless his heart, he learned patiently—I think he was more patient than I was! It took me years of trial and error (mostly error) to see my problem. I was not beginning the way I wanted him to learn. I wanted my son to love learning but, from day one of each "school year," I sucked all the wonder out of it.

Over the years, I have grown to understand how I teach best and how my children each learn best. This did not come easy to me; I had no one to guide me or even to show me that such a unique and beautiful approach to homeschooling was possible.

So, yes, if I had it to do all over again, I would definitely start differently. For our homeschool culture, we would have begun in the family room. We would have played with his own toys to learn math. We would have read more books. We would have visited more museums. And we would have had very, very little coloring time.

You can have a much better first day than I did. Will it be picture perfect? No! Don't put that kind of pressure on yourself! But can it be a short, relaxed, less stressful event than my own misinformed foray into homeschooling? Absolutely! You can *totally* do this.

First of all, take a deep breath. Your entire homeschool success doesn't rest on the first day or the first week. It doesn't even depend on the first year. This is a learning period for you—even more than for your children. Give yourself permission to observe what works for you and what excites your children, and be flexible with the changes that are coming to your family lifestyle.

So much will change throughout the first year, so just relax and go with it. Nothing is set in stone. You can change style, materials, schedule—anything. Just look at this as a trial-and-error year and enjoy the process.

But you have to start somewhere—and since you do, in this chapter, I've given you a quick-and-easy start guide to some of what you'll face in the first days of your homeschooling journey.

3.1 BEFORE YOU BEGIN

3.1.1 What do I do before I begin the first day?

Gather your basics. Pick out some simple curricula. Don't go crazy buying everything you find. Actually, get just the minimum—probably just language arts and math—at first. As you get into your groove, you can add more. Look at chapter 8 for more ideas. If there are subjects you don't feel confident teaching, you might join a local homeschool co-op (see section 6.8) or use an online course.

Consider joining a homeschool support group (see sidebar in section 2.1.7). The homeschool moms you meet will be an invaluable resource and encouragement when you hit a roadblock or become unsure of your methods.

Be sure to talk with your students. Let them know *why* you decided to homeschool and what your homeschool goals are. Give them some sense of what is to come: what your routine will likely be, what subjects you will mostly focus on, and what you will expect of them. Show off your new materials and take your students shopping for new school supplies. Present the advantages of homeschooling, like increased free time, more field trips, and possibly a shorter school year. Help your students look forward to homeschooling as much as you do.

Plan for fun. Ask your students what their particular interests are and what subjects they enjoy the most. As much as possible, tailor your curricula, lesson plans, field trips, and assignments to excite them.

Sign up for other extracurricular activities that interest your students. They'll make friends from a variety of backgrounds while enjoying their favorite interests. Consider local Little League sports, music groups, children's theater, or art classes.

Check social media, library boards, or your local homeschool support group for playgroups, clubs, and meetups in your area. This is a great way for you and your students to make friends and (can I say it?) socialize.

3.1.2 How do I know what grade level my child is?

Homeschooling is not about grade levels. If your student is coming out of a traditional school, you'll generally start on a curriculum level approximately where the student left off. Be prepared, however, to find some discrepancies. In some subjects, your student may struggle more than you anticipated; in that case, slow down your progress or even find a lower-level curriculum or workbook to help your student gain confidence and understanding. He may work through that level faster than a year (maybe in one semester), so then he will be caught up to where you would like him to be for his age.

But still, keep in mind that there is no such thing as "being on track" or "getting behind" when you are homeschooling. Behind in whose opinion? You are setting your own pace for where your child is right now.

On the other hand, your student may find some material for the grade level she is in to be too simple. In that case, you could consider moving through the book quickly, requiring her to complete only half or a quarter of the questions on each assignment, so long as she understands what she is doing. You might later slow down when she begins to find the material more difficult.

Another possibility is purchasing the next grade level material for that subject and beginning again at that level. Most homeschool students are in several different grades in different subjects for this very reason. Try asking a homeschool student what grade he is in, and watch him stammer to figure it out. His mom may not even know.

To get an appreciation for the wide range of student abilities in each level of learning, look at part 3.

3.1.3 What is deschooling? Do I try that first?

Deschooling is detoxing from institutional school. It is a time for you and your child to enjoy an extended vacation away from studies and to acclimate to being at home all day. Not all families spend time deschooling, but many find it a good way to adjust to the idea of homeschooling. Families who deschool might spend that time going on field trips, playing board games, or reading aloud. They might watch documentaries, spend time exploring nature, or pursue another of the child's interests. Deschooling helps children and adults adjust to life after school, to days at home, to extended time together, and to a new outlook on education. The goal is to strengthen the parent-child relationship while overcoming traditional school expectations.

Many find that instead of deschooling, they would rather ease gently into homeschooling whenever they choose to begin their school year or to begin immediately if the student was pulled out of traditional school midyear. They find this helps the student better understand what home-schooling entails, sets up a comforting routine for the family, and enables the student to retain the knowledge she has already practiced at school. Some feel that extended deschooling might influence both children and parents to develop a lax attitude toward studies. They instead find that beginning homeschooling right away helps avoid laziness, undisciplined behavior, or apathy toward learning.

3.1.4 Do I need a schedule for schooltime, recess, and housework?

Maybe yes, maybe no. If you are a super-planner person like me, it might make you feel better to sketch out what your ideal day might look like. Just remember that you'll be adjusting your expectations and your routine constantly as you learn what works for you and your student. No day—not a single one—will follow your plan.

But for those of you who are more relaxed, who like to see how things come and concentrate on the results more than the routine, a lack of schedule may be just the ticket. Just jump in and see what happens.

As for recess, that's called *free time*, and you'll find your children have more of it than ever before. But if they get bored, there's always more math they could be doing! Young children will need periodic breaks during study time. And of course, there's always second breakfast.

Housework is a dirty word your first week or so. Plan on easy meals, scattered clutter, and exhaustion. You'll catch up later. Or never. Just join my club.

3.2 THE FIRST DAY

3.2.1 What should a typical first day look like?

Who knows? It really depends on what works for you. Here's a general recipe for a good start:

- Find your personal best time of day to begin, the time when you feel most alert, patient, and productive. For me, it's morning, but for some, it's after lunchtime.
- Brew a large pot of coffee.
- Gather your students at the kitchen table, schoolroom, or wherever you've chosen to study.
- Take a picture before everyone is tired.
- Consider beginning with a short family devotional and read-aloud time. If your students are young, they could color or play with math manipulatives while you read. This sets up the day gently and pleasantly for many families.
- Begin with your most important subject, the one that means the most to your family. Complete a short assignment to help you and your students gain confidence.

HOW CAN I MAKE THE FIRST DAY FUN?

- Stay in pajamas all day (go ahead and embrace the stigma!).

- Make an extra-large pot of coffee (but don't share it with the students!).

- Take a picture. Or forget to like I do and take one around Christmas time.

- Eat out for breakfast (maybe in the pajamas!).

- Or bake a cake or cookies, eat everything, and call that breakfast.

- Send the children outside to work off the sugar from breakfast.

- Play a board game before getting started with schoolwork.

- Go to the movies (the theater is empty!).

- Leave for a field trip.

- Go to the park and have a picnic (I'm thinking . . . pajamas!).

- Visit the library (maybe do a worksheet while you're there).

- Celebrate at the beach or at a water park.

- Stay up past bedtime since everyone can sleep in the next day.

- Move on to a subject with which your students struggle. Spend a limited amount of time (fifteen to twenty minutes tops for elementary students and maybe only a half hour for older students) working on a book, discussion, or worksheet together. Congratulate them often on progress.
- Continue working through the remainder of the curricula you've chosen, spending only a few minutes on each subject.
- Aim to complete your first day in just a couple of hours, three at the most. Stop before everyone becomes tired and frustrated, even if you don't feel like you finished everything. Remember, learning *how* to homeschool was the most important lesson of the day.
- Consider taking a special outing (a restaurant lunch, afternoon at the park, etc.) to end the day.

Keep practicing your routine for the first week, maybe the first several weeks, of your homeschool. If studying more than one subject feels overwhelming to you and your students, perhaps concentrate on only one subject for the first week and add another subject each additional week or so.

Continue to make adjustments based on the needs and interests of your students as well as your own strengths and interests. Soon you may find you can finish a quantity of material in a much shorter time than traditional schooling while still giving your students the attention and assistance they need.

Most of all, remember you are not re-creating an institutional school. You don't need to say the pledges, take attendance (unless you are a very large family and your middle child is hiding in the pantry eating potato chips), create bulletin boards, or hang large educational charts. Be you, and do your own thing.

3.2.2 What if I royally mess up the first day?

How can you mess up? You're just barely stepping into homeschooling and figuring out what works and what doesn't. This isn't like baking a soufflé or driving down the highway for the first time—you can't burn down a kitchen or wreck a car. You are just learning.

You may be learning what doesn't work for you. You may be learning what your student doesn't like. You are still learning what is your own teaching style (see chapter 6). You are just beginning to learn about your student's learning style (see chapter 7).

So if you don't enjoy the first day, don't despair. The next day might be more fun. If your student declares she hates homeschooling, ask her what the worst part was and start working on that. Regardless, it will take some time for both of you to find your groove. But you aren't a failure in the beginning any more than your student is.

3.2.3 How do I know the first day was a success?

If you are still alive and breathing, it was a success. Also, if you accomplished just a few of the items on the list in section 3.2.1 on how to get started, then it was a success. Maybe you even served dinner that night or brought home the pizza before it got cold. If so, pat yourself on the back; you are a homeschool overachiever.

If you learned something—what you like or dislike, what your student likes or dislikes—you completely succeeded. Do the exact same thing, with whatever necessary adjustments, tomorrow.

Or if everything felt completely wrong, maybe try it all again but differently. Be flexible.

Be careful, especially in the first year, not to compare yourself with other homeschool families. They may have already found their personal homeschool groove, what works best for those homeschool moms and students. Their homeschool style fits with their own unique family culture. And they may even assume that their way is the single best way to homeschool. That's not true. Remember that you are actively learning what works for your unique student, your unique teaching style, and your unique family culture. You won't find a family who homeschools exactly like you do.

Most of all, get a good night's sleep and set the coffeepot timer. You get to do it all again tomorrow.

3.2.4 What if my student balks at her work at first?

She very well might! Ease her into the work by giving her clear, easy-to-reach goals. Recognize this is a big life change for your student, whether she is starting out as an early learner or she just left a traditional school. Help her make the adjustment by reminding her of the benefits she is enjoying and by making it easy for her to succeed.

- Set a timer she can see or hear for each subject. Let her stop, even in the middle of a page, when her time is up. After the first week or two, you may consider lengthening the time per subject.
- Consider allowing a short break between subjects, especially with her harder subjects. Give her five or ten minutes to run outside, color a picture, or play with a favorite toy to clear her mind. Again, setting a timer can help her understand her limits and give her hope that there is an end.
- Sit with her and set her up for success. Help her do just one problem or read one sentence, then the next, and so on. She may be overwhelmed by everything on the page, so your encouragement over small progress can make a big difference.
- Set an overall limit for homeschooling in general the first week or so. For early learners (preschool through about age six), that should be less than an hour daily of reading and pencil/crayon

JUST FOR DAD: HOW CAN I SUPPORT MY WIFE?

The first year of homeschooling is stressful for Mom, but it is also a big change for you. If your wife is taking the lead on homeschooling, how can you support and help her with the transition? Here are a few suggestions:

- Pray over the homeschooling in front of your children.

- Encourage your wife daily, perhaps texting or calling from work to see how her day is going.

- Firmly support your wife's standards, assignments, and discipline with the students.

- Be the bad cop on irresponsibility and bad attitude to help your wife foster a positive homeschool environment during the day.

- Have an honest discussion with your wife about household chores and be willing to take on household responsibilities she may have carried in the past. And encourage her that, if everything doesn't get done, the pile of dishes and scattered papers are actually evidence of her hard work.

- Rise early in the morning to help set the tone for the day, maybe even bringing her that first cup of coffee and supervising breakfast preparations.

- Ask your children regularly what they are learning and excitedly converse with them on their current topics. If you have no idea about the ramifications of the Crusades on the development of European countries, just ask and listen. Your children may enjoy showing off.

- Help tutor your children if they are struggling with certain subjects. Sometimes a fresh perspective and new voice help students overcome difficulties.

- Bring home dinner when she's having a busy day. So basically every day.

- Attend homeschool events and conventions with her to learn more about what she's doing.

- Read homeschool articles and join homeschool Facebook groups to gain perspective on the highs and lows your wife faces.

- Regularly (each month and each semester at least) meet with her to hear her perspective on what's working, where she and the children are struggling, and how you can support your family's homeschool.

- Don't ask how your children compare with other schoolchildren. Each child is unique. Instead, converse with your children yourself to understand their growth and development over time.

- Regularly take your wife out for dates without the children.

- Encourage her to get away with friends for coffee or dinner.

See also section 15.4 for more discussion of dads and homeschooling.

work (see the pie charts in sections 10.2, 11.2, 12.2, and 13.2). For elementary students, an hour or two at first should be sufficient, working up to three or four hours. For secondary students, they may tolerate three hours per day to begin with. Soon they should be studying a few hours in the morning with a couple of hours of independent work in the afternoon.

Don't gauge your homeschool success by how much time you spend at the table with a pencil in hand. Even as a veteran homeschool mom, I spend ten to fifteen hours total each week physically teaching my children (elementary through high school), and my middle school and high school students spend three to five hours each day on their studies. The longer you homeschool, the more efficient you will be with your schooling time, and your student may improve in her independent learning.

3.2.5 What if my student becomes upset at wrong answers?

Stay calm and help him gain perspective. In traditional schooling, teachers mark all the mistakes in bright red and give bold grades at the top of the paper . . . then move on to the next day's assignments. This can not only discourage students but also leave small gaps in their understanding that grow over time.

Even homeschoolers who have never been in traditional school may have perfectionistic tendencies that make them want to get every problem, every sentence perfect the first time. But perfection isn't possible for any of us, right? This is a great opportunity to teach this important life principle.

As a homeschooling parent, you have the wonderful opportunity to focus on *quality* over *quantity* of work. Consider grading with a soft-colored pencil or a highlighter in your student's favorite color. Instead of simply passing back the paper, sit beside him (maybe waiting until the following day to avoid sudden confrontation) and say something like, "I want to help you better understand this problem. Do you know what your mistake was, or would you like me to help you find it?"

After a time, your student may become more adept at correcting his own errors. Most of all, your calm, encouraging tone while discussing those errors will help your student learn how to take mistakes in stride while still striving to correct them.

If a subject becomes mistake-ridden (commonly a problem in reading, grammar, or math for even the brightest of students), it may be time to slow down the progress. Consider giving smaller assignments and working on them together to increase confidence. Maybe find a new workbook, library book, or even worksheets you create yourself for additional practice. Don't worry about slowing down . . . your student will likely hit his stride and make quicker progress later when these foundations are strengthened.

My eight-year-olds have been working on contractions. They had literally no concept of what I was talking about. What do you mean, put two words into one word? What do you mean, this word actually means two words? How in the world did you get *will not* from the word *won't*?

I worked on it for a couple of days, then I gave up. Why do eight-year-olds need to understand contractions, anyway? They could read them, and they could understand them in conversation. They simply didn't put the concept together in their minds. So I gave up.

The next day, each of them grabbed their own language assignment paper and proudly completed the section on contractions. All by themselves.

Did they get it because I am such a great teacher? I wish. Did they get it because they are the most brilliant students? Maybe. Did I care if they learned it? Not at all. I would have crossed off that assignment for them and skipped it entirely for a few months. But for some reason, the concept clicked when I stopped paying attention to it.

Sometimes, we may need to just pull our child away from the paper or the book or the concept and say, "Maybe later. Let's go on to something else right now." Sometimes, we may skip it entirely (I would have preferred to do contractions when they were ten years old, anyway). Sometimes, the child will just master the concept when she is good and ready.

Regardless of whether your child makes no mistakes or a lot, regardless of whether you finish the entire workbook or only half of the workbook, regardless of whether your child understands the first time or the five-thousand-three-hundred-and-eighty-sixth-and-one-half time, your first year is a success.

• • •

These days, my family often begins the fall with "We're *Not* Back to School" week. The week that local schools start up again, there are few crowds in our favorite places. We spend days at the zoo, at the park, at the museums, and just playing in the neighbor's pool. Our freedom to homeschool our own way is something to celebrate, and we relish every opportunity to push the books away for fun memories.

Whatever I do, I try hard not to replicate that dreadful first day of homeschooling all those mumble-mumble years ago.

Your own first day of homeschooling and first year of homeschooling should be a celebration of your family too! Your success is following God for your child, loving on your child, and pointing your child to your own *why*. So hit the beach or sit back and put your feet up. You did it.

4

WE AREN'T IN SCHOOL ANYMORE

MY ADOPTED TWINS BEGAN HOMESCHOOLING after being in a classroom from preschool through part of first grade. They loved school, but they each felt that learning was difficult. They struggled with reading even though they loved looking at books. They constantly asked questions about patterns and time and amounts but struggled with math. They wanted to know more, but they were addicted to screens.

Coming home to learn *was* a big adjustment for them. The first day, I just set out some math manipulatives called pattern blocks, different shapes to make designs. I let the twins play with them for a few minutes. Then I drew pictures and asked the twins to recreate them with their shapes. They stared at the table, dumbfounded. Slowly, each one began working tentatively on the assignment. Then after a few short minutes, I asked them to put the shapes away when they were done.

Next, I read them a picture book. I then encouraged them to look at some books quietly. They sat on the sofa looking at the illustrations for a few minutes. After that, I again told them to clean up whenever they were done. They pretended to read for a few more minutes before putting the books on the shelf.

Juliana asked me, "When do we start homeschooling?"

"We just did," I answered. "Do you want to celebrate at McDonald's?"

They didn't believe me. They told their siblings and their father that they did nothing in homeschooling that day. They had no idea that I was gently *deschooling* them (see section 3.1.3). I was gradually introducing them to a new way of looking at learning. I began weaving homeschooling into their lives.

Now they understand that homeschooling is completely different from what they knew before. Each day, they race through their breakfast and chores to begin the day with a Bible devotional and a chapter of read-aloud. They reserve chapter books at the library. They beg to go to the museum.

They have turned into homeschoolers.

Homeschooling isn't really schooling your child; it's building a relationship with your child. It's presenting subject matter and assignments in a way that engages both you and your student to learn more. It's inciting a delight for learning itself. It's instilling a healthy appetite for education, an appetite above society's addiction to media. It's an entirely new way of life that will gradually shape your teaching style, your student's learning style, and your unique family culture.

> In order to instill a love for learning and education in your children . . . invest the time to teach this love to your children.
>
> **DR. SOO KIM ABBOUD AND JANE KIM**

Homeschooling is different from traditional schooling in every way. You will learn to homeschool within your own family culture—teaching the way you teach best for the way your child learns best.

4.1 A DISTINCT WAY OF SCHOOLING

4.1.1 How is homeschooling different from traditional public or private school?

Homeschooling is different in every way. It's not a classroom. It's not standardized instruction, lessons for the "average student" (whatever that is). It's not merely following a curriculum or an expert or your friend Lea Ann. It's teaching directly to your own student, teaching the way you teach best for the way your student learns best.

If you think of your homeschool more like private tutoring, you'll be closer to understanding the difference. If you think of it as helping your child fall in love with learning, you'll be spot on.

The big difference from schools is not merely academic, though. Homeschooling is based on relationships: the relationship between spouses, between parent and child, among siblings, and between the family and God. Making these relationships a priority affects how every subject is covered as well as how your day progresses.

4.1.2 How does a homeschool schedule differ from that of public schools?

Completely. Over time, your homeschool days and years will little resemble those of the local school. **First of all, you set your own school calendar—**you decide when each school year begins and ends, even studying year-round if you want to. Some families study in blocks, working for six or nine weeks and then having a break. We studied year-round when my children were little and then in two sixteen-week blocks when I began teaching high schoolers.

You can schedule your weeks differently, as well. Some homeschoolers prefer a three- or four-day school week, especially for younger students. My elementary students only work Monday through Thursday.

Your school days themselves will be scheduled quite differently. You can and should teach at your family's optimal time, which could be morning, afternoon, or evening. Do what works best for your students. Classes

HOW CAN I HELP MY STUDENTS LEARN INDEPENDENTLY?

- Begin having the students read directions aloud to you or explain the first step of an assignment.

- Give them a daily or weekly list of assignments to check off.

- Set a homeschool routine, including what order each subject should be completed.

- Check your students' work regularly.

- Set goals and rewards.

- Use a timer to allow them to end after a few minutes.

- Don't answer every question. Make "Look it up" or "Read it again" your default responses.

likely will not last a full hour, and you can have snack time whenever you want to.

4.1.3 How can I make homeschooling a part of our family culture?

Do what comes naturally. Include homeschool topics in normal conversation throughout the day. Remember that learning occurs in the grocery store, at the park, in the kitchen, and in the minivan. Recognize that your students will remember more from hands-on, experiential learning and conversations with you than they will from worksheets and textbooks.

Plan field trips and even family vacations around learning. Visit historical sites, museums, art shows, and reenactments as a family—and make your outings fun! Take camping trips, hikes, and nature walks. Your students will start learning throughout life rather than only at the kitchen table.

Consider celebrating "We're *Not* Back to School" the week your local public schools begin. Enjoy the smaller crowds at theme parks, beaches, museums, and more.

4.2 YOUR FAMILY'S UNIQUE HOMESCHOOL

4.2.1 Do I stand up in front of my students and lecture, ask review questions, and point to charts?

Not usually. Your students will retain more during relaxed conversations on the sofa, around the dinner table, and in the minivan than through lectures. Some students, especially visual and kinesthetic learners (see sections 7.2.2 and 7.2.5), might even tune you out completely if you wax eloquent. This is not a sign of rebellion but simply their inability to process what you are saying over a longer period of time. If you sit down and learn beside your children, both you and they will enjoy the assignment much more.

4.2.2 Do I need to give tests?

Probably not. Check your state's homeschool regulations (start at hslda. org), though, to find what the minimum requirements for standardized tests and reporting are. Many states require no testing at all.

As you teach your early learner or elementary student, you'll have a good idea how much she comprehends and where her weaknesses lie. Since you are working on *quality* rather than *quantity* of work, you are likely focusing on problem areas anyway. Testing would be redundant.

However, you might want to administer tests in high school for proof of competence and preparation for college study. Though many colleges accept homeschooled students based on your prepared transcript and college entrance exams alone, a few may also require additional proof of work like tests, lab notes, and so on. Testing in high school also helps objectively measure the grades on your transcript (for more on high school testing and transcripts, see section 13.3).

For that reason, you may want to have your middle school student practice taking tests. Most states that require little oversight won't need any grades for middle school students and younger. But if you'll be testing in high school for transcript and college preparation, middle school is an excellent time to begin practicing test-taking strategies: how to study, how to answer questions completely, how to determine the most important information to remember, and how to write complete and grammatically correct essay answers (for more on middle school study habits, see section 12.3.8–12.3.10).

4.2.3 Do I have to do ALL the teaching myself?

Absolutely not. Your spouse, for one, may choose to take on teaching his favorite subjects. This is a great way for him to show support for your homeschooling. You might hire a teacher, enroll in a co-op, take online classes, or even hire a tutor for some or all of the subjects (for more on these topics, see chapter 6). Homeschooling means you as a parent take control of making the best educational decisions for your child.

4.2.4 How do I know what my child should learn next?

Guess at first. If you have brought your child home from a traditional school, you may have an idea of what grade level your child should be in, what subjects she excels at, and what areas she needs to work on.

Whether you work from a packaged curriculum or tailor your homeschooling, follow your child's pace. If a subject is easy for him, breeze through it and move to the next level. If he is struggling, slow down so he can fully understand.

Starting in part 3, we will be discussing the wide range of mental and physical developments that affect your child's learning. Be sure to turn to the chapters on elementary, middle school, and high school for academic milestones your child should experience. This will help you set realistic goals and will reassure you of your child's progress.

4.2.5 What if my student says, "That's not how my old teacher did it!"?

Remind your student gently that this isn't school—it's homeschooling. You are a different person than her previous teacher, and you'll be doing a lot of things differently. Point out some of the advantages: no standing in lines, no raising her hand, fewer worksheets, studying topics she is interested in, and more free time. Most of all, you will be working hard to make her studies as simple and easy for her as possible, though it may take a while to get into that groove. In exchange, you'll need her patience as you find your own best way of teaching her.

• • •

The transition for my twins from traditional school to homeschool wasn't completely smooth. Yes, they missed recess, gym class, lunchroom, and movie day those first few weeks of homeschooling. (Movie day, seriously? Finish your work and maybe I'll let you watch a Disney cartoon!)

So we improvised. Instead of gym class, we found sports they loved. Instead of lunchroom, I let them make whatever crazy sandwich they wanted. Instead of recess, we had snacks and outdoor playtime. Then there was that trampoline accident that ended in a broken tooth and led to a lesson about cosmetic dentistry. Fun times.

Now, they will often look at the clock in the middle of playing and say, "If I was back in school, I'd still be doing work!" or "I'm glad we can go out during the day!" or even "Can we do our schoolwork at the library today?" They have learned how to celebrate homeschooling, too. Apparently, their own homeschool *why* is to have fun!

Homeschool is not school. That may seem awkward at first, but it's a benefit to embrace. Enjoy the differences!

HOW TO BE A
GREAT TEACHER

I HESITATED TO BEGIN THIS CHAPTER. My eight-year-old son just walked by, saw the title at the top of the page, and said, "Tell them to have snack time at ten o'clock." So definitely start there.

Remember what we talked about in chapter 1, our homeschool *why*? Now is a good time to review yours. Why are you homeschooling, and what do you want out of it? You need to know this now, and you need to remember this every day, or you will quit. Homeschooling can be difficult at times, and the challenges may seem insurmountable. But God will sustain you as long as you keep your eyes on him and remember *why* you are doing this in the first place.

This chapter, then, is to help you *not* quit. If you are clear on why you are homeschooling, then nothing needs to stop you. You know how to defend your decision, you know how to start the first day, and you know your homeschool is not just a little school in your house.

Now you need to know you are doing a good job.

Do you know how to fight your own insecurities? And what about those bad days when you want to run from the house screaming?

I do know about the running and screaming. One day, I got so fed up with the stress of it all, the chaos of it all, and the noise of it all, I just exploded. I ran out the front door, stood in the middle of the front yard, raised my face to the heavens, and *howled* a scream with all my might.

Then I heard a car door shut beside me. There in the neighbor's driveway and down the street sat several cars. And beside them, a crowd of people stared at me, mouths open as wide as mine.

> Put more of yourselves into what you can do. But don't think about yourselves.
>
> **CHARLOTTE MASON**

"Well, do you feel better now?" a gray-haired lady huffed.

"Not really." I ran into the house in embarrassment and cried into my pillow. Which, in retrospect, I probably should have done in the first place.

All that is to say . . . we all have bad days. Some of them worse than others. But do we need to lose hope? Do we need to quit? Do we need to scream at the neighbors?

Should we call into question our very ability to teach, our likelihood of hanging on another day, our chance to even *be a great homeschool mom*?

Nope.

You and I, my friend, we can, and we should, be the very best homeschool moms we can be. We may cry or embarrass ourselves publicly, but we'll get up in the morning and go back to being great homeschool moms.

When we focus not on our own inadequacy but on the task in front of us, we will see clearly. When we give ourselves to our children rather than holding back in fear, we will see God grow and change us.

We *are* good teachers, you and I. We should be doing this, and we can do this. And here's how.

5.1 HOMESCHOOL CONFIDENCE

5.1.1 How do I know homeschooling is still the right thing for me?

Remember, you are called to homeschool. You didn't make this decision lightly—whether you plan to homeschool for a few months, a year, or a lifetime. You decided for a reason, and you are called by God to that determination. Since this is God's idea, not yours, why worry?

As you continue teaching—more importantly, building that relationship with your child—you will see changes. Changes in yourself, changes in your child, changes in your perspective. A lot of these changes are really good. But I'm going to be honest here: some of these changes might seem really bad.

And maybe you are there right now. Your child doesn't seem to be learning. He isn't improving in his areas of special needs. Your homeschool projects don't look awesome like everyone else's Instagram posts. He's giving attitude or just plain disobeying. You are tired of it all and questioning whether you made the right choice.

But are you going after your *why*? And do you think you yourself can accomplish it *all by yourself*? If your answer is yes, then stop right now and don't homeschool anymore. Because homeschooling, if nothing else, is an exercise in faith. Not that your child will grow up happy, healthy, godly, and smart. If that is your measure of success, again, stop now, or else stay away from the rest of us.

> He who calls you is faithful;
> he will surely do it.
>
> **1 THESSALONIANS 5:24**

Because the work of homeschooling is getting down in the nitty-gritty, down in the sweat and tears and prayers over our children, night and day wrestling with God to please, please change our hearts and the hearts of our children.

That is success.

If you are crying out to God for him to work in you first and your child next, no matter the physical or emotional or academic wars within your home or with your child—yes, my dear friend, you are doing the right thing.

Clinging to God is the right thing.

Keep going, my friend.

5.1.2 Can my family handle me changing from mom to teacher?

Yes—because your roles as a mother and as a teacher are the same. In both cases, you are training your child through a relationship, and then building from that relationship the knowledge and character you know he needs for life. And honestly, if you stop thinking of yourself as a teacher so much and instead just view all of this as Parenting 2.0, then most of your worries will be solved. Seriously. This is just parenting leveled up.

5.1.3 How will homeschooling affect the rest of the family?

Christian homeschooling solidifies your family like few other experiences. Your family members will work together, learn together, and have fun together throughout daily life. Homeschooling will bring you together because you will have to work closely every day. And that is a good thing.

Homeschooling also changes your relationship with your children. Working together, learning together, surviving algebra together makes you comrades in arms. There will be, at times, clashes of wills. Homeschooling will bring out the spirit of your children, revealing their struggles with you and with God. But in the end, you may see your relationship with your children and their relationship with the Lord strengthened and deepened.

> Many families make the decision to homeschool because they want to tap into their children's highest potentials.
>
> **MARIAEMMA WILLIS AND VICTORIA KINDLE HODSON**

5.1.4 How can I homeschool if I have never taught before?

Actually, experience is not as important as you think. Researchers have found that increased experience teaching does not necessarily result in better learning.[1] In the homeschool community, no correlation whatsoever has been found between the education of the parents and the success of the child.[2] Homeschooling itself makes all the difference.

5.1.5 How do I know if I'm homeschooling correctly?

Success is different for each family, and it is connected to *why* you are doing this. You have to get out of bed every day just because you know you are going toward this *why*. If each morning, each hour, each day you get just a little closer to your goal . . . you are doing it right. If, for weeks and months on end, you see no progress, but you are reaching with faith toward that *why* . . . you are going in the right direction.

Don't look at the grades. Don't look at the projects. Don't look at awards or recognition or who wins the spelling bees. Look at where you want to be in a couple of decades, and dream about the character you want to instill in your child. Keep going there, and you are doing just right.

If doing homeschool the right way means pure academic achievement, then don't I wish I knew a magic formula. This, my friend, is the question that, if I answered it in one sentence, everyone would pay me millions of dollars for, and I would not be writing such a long book. So I don't have an easy answer to that, sorry. Here are a few things I've tried:

a. **Borrow brains.** Use self-teaching textbooks, the kinds that set realistic expectations each day and explain each lesson to your student. Join a homeschool support group and ask other moms what they are doing.

> Neither he who plants nor he who waters is anything, but only God who gives the growth.
>
> **1 CORINTHIANS 3:7**

b. **Find a homeschool mom who loves the subject you hate.** Ask her if your student can sit in on her teaching. She may even hate a subject you love, and you can trade off.

c. **Consider joining or even starting a co-op** (see section 6.8). Moms take turns teaching small classes of homeschool students. Many co-ops are taught only a day or two a week so moms can complete the homeschooling personally at home. It's a win-win situation for many families.

d. **Look into online classes.** There are so many right now. I personally am a very hands-on homeschool teacher, but I cannot understand science to save my soul. And I just don't have time to read and discuss many great works of literature in-depth with my high school students. So I found interactive online classes for each of those subjects. My students learned so much and even enjoyed them.

Get help. Do your best. Then trust God for the outcome. What happens next is completely in his hands.

5.2 HOMESCHOOL PLANNING

5.2.1 How do I set my academic goals for the year?

Each year, look ahead to where you would like your student to be in each subject. Envision *not* what the curriculum covers, what the final test is over, what the publisher's scope and sequence describes. Nope. You are the teacher, my friend. And you know what your child can and should learn through the coming year.

NO, I DON'T, you may be screaming back at me. Go ahead, vent and yell and stomp your feet and throw this book across the room. Then come back, and I'll walk you through this.

I used to think goal setting was really hard too. But as I practiced home-schooling over the years and began simplifying my teaching process, it dawned on me that *I am in charge of this homeschooling, not the bossy curriculum.*

Yes, publishers have a carefully thought-out system of what-to-know-when. And curriculum authors are (usually) experts in the field. So we moms get intimidated about setting our own goals and measurements.

But those authors and publishers have never met your child.

Let that sink in for a minute. Your child is not like my child and not like any of the children in your nearest public school and definitely not like any other homeschooler taught to his own unique ability.

AHA! See what I did there? The other homeschoolers taught to their own unique ability? That, my friend, is where we are going with this.

You know what you want your child to know. Or you may feel fuzzy about it right now. So crack open your nearest subject curriculum and flip through it. See some important stuff? Maybe you also see some things that you feel like, "Nah. I don't care if my student ever gets that." Or maybe for some of them you feel like, "She will pick that up over time or in real life. Totally don't need to make a big deal about that this year." Like I feel about teaching contractions to eight-year-olds. It's totally not on my list of priorities.

You will come to know what you value and what you don't. If you don't feel very confident making value judgments right now, you will gradually over time. As you begin teaching your student, you will notice what seems *very important* and what seems *just fluff* in the lessons. And you will prob-ably find some topics or subject matter that you feel quite strongly should be emphasized. *This is setting academic goals.*

Want to get started with this at the beginning of your academic year? That's great. Sit down with a pencil and paper and maybe your curriculum. Think about *where your student is now* in knowledge and ability. Consider carefully what you imagine she can accomplish this year or this semester. Write some of these thoughts down.

Think about what concepts are most important to you in that subject. Jot those down. Here are some examples I had a couple of years ago for my eight-year-old twins in language arts:

- I want them to read confidently, to enjoy the ability to grab anything off the junior fiction and nonfiction shelves of the library and know they can read and understand much of it with help.
- I want them to learn to read all of the "special sounds" in their phonics curriculum.
- I want them to memorize how to spell nonstandard words by applying their "special sounds." I will *not* expect them to finish one year's spelling workbook, but instead to understand each list they work on.
- I want them to improve their writing skills to correctly spell many of the words they want to use. I want them to learn some comma rules and to correctly use apostrophes. I want them to master most capitalization rules.

Now, those are the goals I set by looking at where they were academically at the time and how quickly they generally progressed. After setting those goals, I felt that reading curriculum was not necessary; they preferred to practice with whatever they found at the library, and I desired to use that enthusiasm to build their ability. However, their spelling was abysmal compared to what grade-level workbooks expected of them. I did not expect dramatic improvement; instead, I celebrated gradual progress. Similarly, I desired less technical ability than the writing curriculum demanded; instead, I focused on gradual progress toward my year's goals. This helped me use the curriculum as a tool, not a dictator.

Again, this is hard to do your first year homeschooling. You don't know what to expect and how to envision progress. *That is okay!* Go ahead and follow the plan your curriculum sets out. As you get into it, you'll likely find what your student's pace is, where she excels, and where she needs more time. In that case, you can adjust your goals as you go.

Remember, you are in charge. You are not a slave to your curriculum. Of course, the publisher does not know what is best *for your own child*. You do, or you will as you move along.

Here are some alternate ways to approach long-term goal setting:

- You may want to complete a workbook in one year. Remember that most school institutions do not complete an entire workbook or curriculum in one year, so you should not pressure yourself to complete every page.
- You may set a goal of covering all the major concepts in your yearly boxed curriculum or workbook. This would allow you to skip some lessons and spend more time on lessons that need more effort.
- You may set a goal of following your student's lead. In this case, you may find yourself fighting some inner pressure to push your student forward. At other times, you may find your student suddenly take off in areas you did not expect.
- You may set a goal of following your special needs student's aptitude. You would then seek to adapt daily to his needs and achievements. If this is your goal, you may need to remind yourself every day of your and your child's progress. (See chapter 16 for more on teaching students with special needs.)
- You may set a long-term goal of preparing for college. In that case, you will have an eye on state institution graduation requirements. Or your long-term goal may be workforce preparation. These goals need not be strenuous if you keep your child's aptitude in mind. We will talk more about these questions in the high school chapter (see chapter 13).

One final consideration is the requirements of your state. If you live in a state that requires more oversight, you will need to follow the guidelines set out by the authorities. If you live in a less regimented state, or even a state like mine with no oversight, you are completely at liberty to set your own goals.

How do you know you have the right goals in your homeschool? Remember, the most important goal to keep in mind is your own homeschool *why*. Remember what your original reason is to homeschool and remain faithful to that calling.

Keep your goals in prayer. You know why you started homeschooling. God will continue to impress on your heart why you *keep* homeschooling. Humbly follow his yearly, monthly, and daily leading. God wants to disciple your students through homeschooling—and he wants to change you through it too.

5.2.2 How do I break down my yearly goals into short-term goals?

You have a choice: you can divide them quarterly, monthly, and/or weekly. Personally, I set weekly goals for my students. This helps me not push them beyond their ability. Sometimes I will write down in my notebook or on my to-do list, "Work on spelling a few more minutes each day this week" or "Keep this review spelling list light. Try games and small rewards."

Sometimes, the goal is just the work I want to accomplish. "Seven worksheets completed" or "Move on to spelling list nine" or "Quiet reading thirty minutes each morning." In fact, I use weekly goals instead of lesson plans much of the time. This helps me remember to keep my students' needs in my focus, not the curriculum assignment. Last week, it was "Spend two weeks on this list, because everyone is confused." Yep, I was even confused how to help them understand it.

That's why you don't need to worry if you don't have a yearly academic goal for your child. Go month to month or week to week instead, keeping your child's ability, rate of learning, and needs in focus. Next week, your goal may be to review what you did last week. Or it may be to pick up the pace. Or you may even choose to skip a topic you feel is unnecessary.

WHAT ARE THE MOST IMPORTANT GOALS TO ACHIEVE IN HOMESCHOOLING?

- faithfulness in your calling
- strengthened relationship with God
- strengthened relationships within your family
- life skills
- service
- love for others

Fear God and keep his commandments, for this is the whole duty of man.

ECCLESIASTES 12:13

5.2.3 What do I do about lesson planning?

Plan the way you like best. Some homeschoolers love to buy a lesson plan book and make copious notes on what lessons they want to teach each day. They list each child and each subject goal and keep track of their progress in detail. There are several print and online homeschool teaching planners listed in appendix F that can help with just that.

Some homeschoolers use homeschool lesson plan books to retrospectively record progress, kind of like a journal. Once a week or once a month, they record what the child completed and maybe what concepts were covered.

Some homeschool states require a review of lesson plans. Families in these states keep track of what the child has accomplished, a grade for each lesson, and maybe a collection of schoolwork to show the authorities. Home School Legal Defense, at hslda.org, lists which states require these. Your own state or local support group will also know what records you need and how to keep them.

Many homeschoolers are not required to keep lesson plans and prefer not to do so at all. Some curriculum providers include simple lesson plans in the beginning of the book to guide the student through the course within a school year. Some online classes keep a student working through a school-year's worth of studies, and parents find no reason to track what is being done.

In my case, I do very little lesson planning. I live in a state with no supervisory review, so I am legally allowed to do as much or as little as I prefer. After several years of using lesson plan books to keep detailed reports of my children's progress, I quite simply got tired of doing it all.

For several years, I kept a simple spiral notebook for each year. I used two facing pages for each week. For my elementary students, I jotted down some extra things I didn't want to forget, but I wrote no real lesson plans. I knew I was simply doing the next couple of pages in their writing and math workbooks and reading about history and science.

I kept lesson plans for my middle school children and grades on their work so they could prepare for their high school years. At the beginning of each school year, I divided any workbooks into 180 days, then those down to 90 days each, then those sections into weekly assignments. I highlighted any quizzes or tests. It took me less than an hour for each subject. Now my student had assignments to complete each week. In my spiral notebook, I wrote extra reading and reminders for other subjects. In the back of my notebook, I divided a page horizontally to keep track of grades. This was only to help my middle school student understand how to study and how much preparation is required to pass a subject.

My high schoolers require a little more detail since I am simultaneously preparing transcripts. For these older students, I divide each section into 45-day (9-week) quarters, then separate those batches into weekly assignments. I may then write more detailed assignments in the spiral notebook. I also keep a list of subjects at the bottom of my notebook so I can check them off at the end of the week. My student shows me at the end of each week that she has completed the week's assignments. I also record the grades for quizzes, essays, and tests in the back of my notebook.

This year, I have decided to go even more simple. Our family calendar mobile app has a to-do list option. I make a list of reading assignments for my students there. I have another list of the things I need to remember, concepts to cover, and read-aloud chapters. My older students know what to do in most subjects without a list. All I need to do then is keep track of grades in their workbooks and/or online.

WHERE CAN WE GO ON A FIELD TRIP?

- museums
- aquariums
- zoos
- art galleries
- farmers' markets
- restaurant kitchens
- cultural events
- festivals
- police or fire stations
- post offices
- historical reenactments
- concerts
- gardens
- lakes
- water or power plants
- libraries and bookstores with rare books
- woodworking demonstrations
- war memorials

So my lesson plans take a couple of hours at the beginning of the year and around a half hour each week. This works for me. I know other homeschool moms with more relaxed methods of homeschooling who do even less or no homeschool lesson plans at all. For more on lesson planning, see section 8.2.1.

5.3 HOMESCHOOL TEACHING

5.3.1 How can I teach in a way my child will understand?

Teach from what you know about your own child. You know your own child better than anyone else—any teacher, any expert, any fellow home-schooler. This is your secret weapon in homeschooling, something no other teacher can match. You know her personality. You know her interests. You will learn to appreciate how she learns. You will find out what she wants to get out of her studies. You know how she prefers her routine, her lunch, her environment, her daily grind. You see when she needs variety to maintain interest and concentration. You know who she is as a person. No teacher can match your knowledge.

Teach to your child's learning style. Your child learns in his own unique way (see chapter 7). How he thinks, how he processes, how he applies, how he communicates are all part of who he is. As you grow to understand his learning style—and help him utilize that style to its full potential—you will open to him the joy of learning his way. You have an edge here: the ability to tailor his studies and his environment so he can be at his best.

Teach at your child's pace. No classroom teacher can pace entire lessons and subjects around one child, but you can. You can skip entire chapters of math that your child understands intuitively. You can spend extra time on a grammar concept he just can't understand. You can stop completely and restructure a curriculum around his learning needs. You can concentrate on the lessons you feel are most important for his growth and gloss over what your child has already mastered. You know what he needs best.

HOW CAN I BE AN EFFECTIVE TEACHER?

- Focus on success, not grades.
- Know how you teach best.
- Teach the way the student learns.
- Change small things at a time, not entire methods all at once.
- Remain available for help.
- Admit you don't know everything.
- Help your student find the answer.
- Remember why you teach.

Teach your way. Every teacher—every parent—has a unique way she teaches best, the way she naturally communicates and the way she loves to learn alongside her children (see chapter 6). Over time, you will begin to recognize where your strengths lie. You'll try new strategies and change up your routine. And as you homeschool your own way, you'll teach the most effective way you can.

Teach in a relaxed environment. Children learn best when calm, relaxed, even happy. So homeschooling should have few rules: listen, learn, work. In contrast, school classrooms need more structure to control a large group of people. Your homeschool caters to one child or a sibling group, so the relationships already in place govern what happens each day. Homeschooling should not, and cannot, be regulated by stiff rules.

That is where consistency comes into play. This is not a rigid schedule. This is not even a firm routine. This is consistency of love, of learning, of demonstrating that learning. No harsh regulations, just consistent love.

> The LORD gives wisdom; from his mouth come knowledge and understanding.
>
> **PROVERBS 2:6**

Teach what interests your child. You know if she likes frogs or books. You know if she runs outside or plays quietly in her room. You know if she's motivated by candy or screen time. You can use her interests as a springboard to learning math, science, literature, history—anything. Why not learn what animals lived on the Great Plains? Why not learn how to calculate the area of the plains, and what *area* means in our lives today? Why not read about the native people who lived in the plains and historical fiction of the settlers? No matter what homeschool methods or textbooks you use, your knowledge of what your child enjoys will change everything about what she learns each week.

Connect learning into one whole. Instead of studying subjects as separate ideas, you can actively integrate some concepts together. No matter what method of teaching you choose or what learning style your child prefers, you can help him appreciate that all details work together to demonstrate God's pattern and plan for the world as a whole. He will see God's glory through it all.

5.3.2 How do I teach a subject I don't know?

Learn the academic material along with your child. Discuss your child's studies at the dinner table and let her show her growing expertise. Frequently ask her about a concept she is studying.

> You then who teach others, do you not teach yourself?
>
> **ROMANS 2:21**

I have learned more about frogs, ancient Mesopotamia, Buddhism, and calculus than I ever wanted to know. And I've forgotten most of it already. But my children appreciate my interest and are motivated to show off to Mom and Dad. And when they need help, we just huddle around the books, chatting and pointing at terms, until we all learn something new.

5.3.3 What if the subject is too hard for me and for my student?

Be patient and stay calm. Remember that a large part of homeschooling is learning alongside your child. It is too easy to become emotional about your own child's struggle, and he is likely already upset about it himself. My daughter became livid at her trigonometry textbook, and I found myself becoming impatient with her. Wasn't she trying? Didn't she realize her older brother had breezed through the same book? Why couldn't she try harder? My husband had to help me remove my emotions from the

---

HOW CAN I MAKE LESSONS EASIER?

- Remind the student of the subject's goal.

- Learn or review one basic step a day.

- Point out repeated steps.

- Set smaller goals.

- Teach shorter lessons.

- Set a timer.

- Shorten the homeschool day or week.

- Teach the student how to study by focusing on
  - bold words,
  - important people,
  - repeated concepts or steps, and
  - chapter summaries.

---

issue so I could calmly understand my daughter is different, she learns differently, and she needs me to help her calmly approach her difficult subjects. Also, maybe trigonometry isn't that important.

Avoid comparison. Don't compare yourself with other homeschool mothers. Don't compare your child to other homeschool children or even other institutionally schooled children. Don't compare your methods or your curriculum to those of others. And don't compare your family with other homeschool families.

Don't assume your child will excel in every subject. Two of my children excel in the humanities but struggle with math and science. One of my students breezed through math and science but pulled his hair out over writing. Another son vacillated in his grades depending on each lesson's level of real-world application or hands-on practice.

Motivate her efforts. We, as adults, need motivation to complete tasks we hate, and your student does too. Negotiate how she will be rewarded for completing work within her ability and on time.

> **HOW DO I FIGHT FRUSTRATION?**
>
> - Don't make frustration a moral issue.
> - Replace mistakes or problem behavior with a correct activity.
> - Become patient with chaos.
> - Stay positive — celebrate small wins.
> - Stay faithful in the little steps.
> - Remember your child loves you.
> - Remember *why* you are homeschooling.

Take it one step, one day at a time. My son struggled with algebra. I immediately went to the worst-case scenario: Was he going to fail an important, transcript-changing subject? How would he possibly pass his college entrance exams? He was destined to fail, and there was nothing I could do about it! Again, my husband had to help me separate myself from the issue and remind me that both my son and I could tackle this subject just one lesson at a time. We didn't need to worry about the entire subject—just one day, one lesson (or part of one lesson) was enough to work on. This completely changed our perspective and even our relationship with algebra and with each other.

Try a different perspective. At first, try not to throw out your curriculum, change your method, cram your child into a different learning style, or reinvent the wheel. Just take a step back, look at the big picture of the subject, and go at the lessons from a different point of view.

Change one aspect of your homeschool method. (See chapter 6.) Again, don't go crazy and join a new homeschool club, buy a brand new "morning basket" filled with routine group lessons, and cram the entire family into a whole new way of doing things. For one, that's probably not who you personally are, and it will not work in that case. And two, your children could become frustrated by a sudden change.

> One who is faithful in very little is also faithful in much.
>
> **LUKE 16:10**

Instead, make one change. Find one thing you are attracted to and that you think will interest your child. Try it for a day, a week, maybe a month. This may be a new adjustment to your own personal eclectic homeschool style.

5.3.4 How do I motivate my child to learn?

Learn the material yourself. Let your child see you read good books of all kinds—fiction, nonfiction, self-help, Christian living. Let her notice you listening to audiobooks and podcasts. She will see that learning is important to you. Show your love for learning and your satisfaction with knowledge.

Make learning fun. Is there a board game that teaches skip counting? Can you use playing cards to learn which numbers are larger? Can you make flash cards of states and capitals? Your child can learn while playing to his heart's content all day.

Reward your child. Does she want more time to play, more verbal recognition at the dinner table, more opportunities to show off her learning, or more charts and graphs to measure her progress? Does she compete against herself, working for greater mastery, more accuracy, or faster computation each time? You can motivate your child in her best way.

Sympathize and set limits. Sometimes a lesson is just plain boring. Or hard. Or even more boring. My children are motivated by an apple slice for each correct section or a Cheerio for each correct problem. Even the older ones. I set a twenty-minute timer for early readers and then let them run and play outside when it goes off, no matter where they are in the book.

Sometimes I have even resorted to extra screen time. Hey, we as moms reward ourselves with a chocolate bar or extra Facebook time at the end of a long day. Our children deserve the same opportunities to blow off steam after strenuous work.

Don't immediately assume your child's frustration or reluctance is a discipline issue. Sometimes, complaining, sloppiness, or reluctance toward work means the child simply does not understand the subject. First of all, she may be completely lost and just trying to live another day. Secondly, she may feel no personal connection to the subject and see no reason to put forth the effort in the first place. If she is lost in the material, try going back and working with her on the basics in a new way, from a different perspective or with new activities. That may be all she needs to move forward at a better pace (in other words, get it done in time to play). If she has lost connection to the material, sometimes a change of activity helps. Look for a field trip or museum about the topic. Find a club or competition in the pursuit. Try to find interesting ways the subject relates to other subjects she is working on.

Remember that it is your child's responsibility to learn. You can teach, but you cannot force your child to want to learn or to make the effort to learn. Some children have learning obstacles to overcome, but most students simply need to decide to learn and then do the work.

> ## HOW DO I INSTILL A LOVE FOR LEARNING?
>
> - Model learning all day, not just during schooltime.
> - Model a love for work.
> - Include everyone in schoolwork and housework.
> - Celebrate achievements as a family.
> - Make long-term goals together in projects and subjects.
> - Prioritize family, not grades.
> - Set clear limits and accountability.

As we move forward in the homeschool journey, especially into the preteen and high school years, we find it difficult to keep this in mind. We want to make learning happen, and we want to force our student to love it, whether he likes it or not! But in the end, this is God's work in his heart, and we need to let the Holy Spirit work in his own time.

5.3.5 How can we homeschool on the go?

It's called carschooling, and it is a real thing. Many homeschoolers study in the car between long errands, while waiting for a sibling's enrichment activity, or during road trips. Carschooling is just like it sounds: learning in the minivan.

Carschooling moms move their homeschool on the road in backpacks or small crates. Frequent carschoolers just leave their materials in their to-go containers permanently. Some moms keep a veritable homeschool library in their van at all times. This may include containers for paper and other school supplies.

Many subjects can be tackled on the road. Young children can practice reading. Older children can read to everyone from their literature assignments. Children can complete math worksheets, grammar exercises, and other written work. Many families listen to audiobooks or play their curriculum DVDs for the whole family to enjoy.

> We will not hide them from their children,
> but tell to the coming generation the glorious deeds of the LORD,
> and his might, and the wonders that he has done.
>
> **PSALM 78:4**

We carschooled before carschooling was cool when I was a student. Growing up, my family often drove for several days at a time, traveling for my father's work. And mean Mom would not give us time off. So we packed up our book bags and carried our homework with us. I was a teen and did most of my studies independently, then Mom graded my assignments in the front seat. My younger sister read aloud and colored papers about her subjects. She had it easy.

What about getting carsick? My mom gave me a cracker and told me to toughen up. But for the truly queasy child, no one wants to clean up a barfed-on textbook. That's why so many carschoolers rely on CDs or digital downloads for their studies. Or else they make the one who does not get carsick read aloud.

Take snacks in the car. Preferably Cheez-Its. Carschooling is always easier with a box of food.

• • •

The questions covered in this chapter may pop up repeatedly. I wonder about most of them at least once a month. I don't think that we as parents ever stop worrying about our children's future, and that includes their educational future. And when we look at the enormity of what we hope and dream for our children, we become aware of our inability to meet every need. We become small in our own wisdom.

And that is exactly where God wants us to be. He wants to remind us of our need for him. We need him for eternity, and we sorely need him today. This is faith, again, in our daily homeschool. The faith that God will determine what our children need, that God will direct our goals, that God will guide our teaching, that God will grow each child's understanding.

If I could teach brilliantly and my children did their work flawlessly, I would not need God. But every day's challenge, instead, brings me right back to where my own heavenly Father wants me to be: at his feet, clinging to him.

Do I cry into my pillow every night? Nope. Not even every week. Actually, I can't remember the last time I cried, which means maybe I will tomorrow. BUT I have hope that God will continue enabling me to humbly teach my children

> As each has received a gift, use it to serve one another, as good stewards of God's varied grace.
>
> **1 PETER 4:10**

each day. Not to create spelling bee champions. Not to raise math whizzes. But—faltering at times—to demonstrate God's grace in my homeschool. To walk in the faith that God can use me—one flawed woman—to build up my children in him. To know God himself through the process of homeschooling each day.

6

THE WAY YOU TEACH BEST

THERE ARE TWO PARTS of the homeschool equation: *parents* and *students*. The equation looks like this:

supportive parents + engaged students = learning

And that's all there is to it. This is why I will keep harping: *teach the way you teach best for the way your child learns best*.

The End.

This could be a very short book. Yet I'll elaborate.

You may struggle to understand how to teach. But what you really need to grasp is *how you teach best*. There are as many ways to teach as there are to parent. And just like you don't parent exactly the same way your best friend does, you won't homeschool the same way I do. (Even though I am your new best friend, right? I come bearing coffee.)

Some moms may try to push their teaching style as the only right way of doing things. Sister, I am *not* going to tell you how to teach your children. I teach my way, and I'll be telling you a little about that, but you'd better not copy off me. Because you teach the way you teach best, and there is no way you are going to teach like I do. (Hint: I teach like a crazy woman.)

I have changed *the way I teach best* more times than I can count. Different stages of my life, different stages of each child's life, and different family situations have all factored into finding my groove. That used to bother me to no end (lots of things bother me to no end). But now I've learned to go with my own flow. And I hope you do too, after you find your best way. That's why I'm going to show you a few popular teaching styles. It's possible you'll find something that fits you to a T. More likely, you'll find ways to bring out your own best teaching.

So are you sufficiently confused yet?

6.1 SOME TEACHING STYLE BASICS

6.1.1 What is a teaching style?

Okay, actually, it's more of an underlying philosophy that influences best teaching practices. There are several different camps regarding which style of teaching helps children learn best. Each one tends to think theirs is the very best, the end-all, the one and only way to produce high-quality, grade A students.

> It is the supreme art of the teacher to awaken joy in creative expression and knowledge.
>
> **ALBERT EINSTEIN**

In actuality, though, just between you and me and the bookcase, each style of teaching appeals to a different type of family. Some moms prefer to read aloud a lot and that brings them closer to their children. They tend to call themselves Charlotte Mason homeschoolers. Others are very hands on, so hands on that their hands are always covered in glitter and teeny scraps of paper. They are unit-study-ers. Some parents love a good workbook and daily instructions—we call them textbook homeschoolers. You've also got your classical homeschoolers with their Latin and trivium, your Montessori homeschoolers with their manipulatives, and your unschoolers with . . . a distinct dislike of being pigeonholed.

Aside from their differences, all homeschool teaching styles have three things in common:

1. All believe homeschooling is based on **relationships**, and that a child will learn best surrounded by the family's love and support.
2. All believe children thrive in an **environment** conducive to learning and exploring—and each family can create that environment in the home within the unique family culture.
3. All believe the family can best achieve their personal homeschool *why* by utilizing this particular homeschool style along with the student's own learning style.

6.1.2 How do I know which style I should use?

You will evolve into your own teaching style after you have experimented and gained some experience over time. Honey, if this is your first year homeschooling, don't even worry about it. Just peruse this chapter when you are relaxed and the house is quiet (yeah, let's share a laugh), and keep these ideas in the back of your mind for the next year or so.

If you have been homeschooling for a while, then you may notice that you naturally gravitate toward some of these educational styles already. You may want to dive deeper into those methods. You may also find that you can incorporate some principles from other styles that you haven't considered yet.

Remember that there is no one right style. Instead, homeschoolers have a variety of ways to relate to a child while creating an atmosphere to learn what is most important to that family. Each homeschool family will use these tools in their own way. You simply need to find the teaching style that fits you and your family culture. In actuality, most families do not strictly adhere to a single style. You may try out one style then completely change your mind next year; I change my mind about *something* every year. As the years pass, you'll find that you take the best of many kinds of teaching and make a homeschool style that is all your own. Then just keep endlessly tweaking it like I do.

No matter what homeschool style you choose, make sure it lines up with your family's homeschool *why*. Don't choose a teaching style in order to produce super-students or to impress the in-laws (they can't be impressed anyway). Choose the methods and materials that best communicate your family priorities and culture. Because that is why you homeschool.

6.2 TRADITIONAL TEXTBOOK HOMESCHOOLING

6.2.1 What is traditional textbook homeschooling?

Using schoolbooks. Textbook homeschooling is what most people think of when they first envision homeschooling. This style was very popular in the early resurgence of homeschooling in the eighties, and this is still how many homeschoolers begin their first year. Textbook homeschooling is simply education from the guidance of a published course or curriculum. Once you have your curriculum picked out, you just follow the course assignments and schedule to complete one year's work.

6.2.2 What are the stages of textbook homeschooling?

Textbook homeschoolers progress through traditional school grades. Students graduate from one grade to the next by simply finishing one year's course. The student completes each level from kindergarten through twelfth grade before graduating.

6.2.3 How do I teach textbook homeschooling?

Just follow the curriculum plan. Parents may choose to follow the local school district's subject recommendations or a publisher's course of study. Then they simply order the courses they wish their child to complete. Materials can be purchased directly from publishers or from a reseller.

> Of making many books there is no end, and much study is a weariness of the flesh.
>
> **ECCLESIASTES 12:12**

You can teach the lesson as outlined in the teachers' manual. Some courses include a completely scripted lesson, telling you exactly what to say to the student and what response to elicit from him. The manual may also include what activities and homework the student should complete each day. Many textbook curriculum providers also schedule tests, describing how to administer and grade each one.

6.2.4 What materials do I use in textbook homeschooling?

Parents can purchase textbook kits including teachers' manuals, textbooks, workbooks, DVDs, online material, and/or tests from publishers or resellers. You could choose different sets for different subjects, or you could order one large box that includes everything that your student needs for an entire year.

RESOURCES FOR TRADITIONAL TEXTBOOK HOMESCHOOLING

Two popular Christian textbook providers are BJU Press (bjupress.com) and Abeka (abeka.com). Both have provided homeschool curriculum for decades. Now there are dozens of publishers to choose from. See appendix F for lists of curriculum providers.

6.2.5 How do I grade textbook courses?

With a grading key. Grading is easy with textbook courses. Each course will usually tell you how to grade assignments and evaluate progress, and they often include answer keys.

6.2.6 What are the pros and cons of textbook homeschooling?

Pros. Beginning homeschoolers often find it easy to begin with textbooks. The courses are preplanned, the assignments prepared, and the lessons scripted. The parent knows how to take each next step. As the child continues through the courses, the parent can easily gauge progress through the homework and tests.

Some homeschool parents wish to make it easier for the student to later return to a classroom. Studying at home from textbooks not only makes the transition back to a school easier but also keeps the student in a traditional school grade level.

Working through textbooks makes independent learning easier for many homeschoolers. An older student can study and complete his homework, for example, then grade his own daily progress with an answer key. The parent can evaluate the student's progress with tests and quizzes. For subjects that parents feel less confident teaching, this feature is especially appealing.

Textbook courses are an easy way to measure high school performance. The student herself may not enjoy taking the tests, but combining test scores with their given course descriptions makes preparing transcripts a straightforward task (read starting at section 13.3 for more on testing and transcripts). Families living in states with more stringent homeschool oversight may find it simple to present the curriculum and tests for portfolio reviews. This test-taking, too, helps students prepare for college entrance exams and higher education.

Finally, textbook publishers represent a wide variety of beliefs, so it is increasingly easy to purchase textbooks to reflect one's own worldview. In the past, the majority of textbooks expressed a secular humanistic viewpoint, but now many Christian publishers produce courses from a biblical perspective. (See appendix F.)

Cons. There are many that you don't need to worry about. In the homeschool community, textbook homeschooling carries somewhat of a stigma. The biggest criticism of textbook homeschooling is the sense of doing "school at home," of attempting to re-create a classroom experience to the detriment of learning and enjoyment. Many homeschoolers, including me, do start out with a school model: desks, wall maps, stacks of textbooks, educational charts on the wall. We might have a rigid school schedule and even follow the public school calendar.

After a while, however, strict adherence to a public school model can begin to feel stilted and artificial. So many of the school practices and even published curricula are ideal for a group setting but less so for individualized learning. The beauty of homeschooling, on the other hand, is meeting the individual student's needs. Young children, in particular, thrive in a more creative and active environment than many textbook publishers prescribe. An education tailored to the child's needs and interests may involve only an hour or two of "school" and a day of play, exploration, family time, and outside exercise, whereas published curriculum is often more structured.

Another criticism of textbook homeschooling is that the textbooks may be dry and uninteresting. Students who are hands-on learners may find textbooks difficult to work with. Some textbooks are useful for a good overview of a subject but do not deal with the material in-depth. The student studying from a textbook with reading assignments and workbooks may find the course more time-intensive than other methods. And textbook learning, by its very nature, is more solitary, while other methods of homeschooling adapt better to the entire family learning together.

Using a textbook need not require a rigid school-at-home manner, however. Families can use textbooks as a tool to meet the needs and interests of each individual student, even finding books and workbooks that appeal to the student's own learning style. Ultimately, most homeschoolers find their own individual learning style and teaching style, amassing a variety of materials and methods that best reflect their family culture. And that includes textbooks. Homeschoolers of all philosophies, even those who prefer Charlotte Mason or classical homeschooling, will at times need to supplement with textbooks or even take entire courses from a textbook curriculum.

6.2.7 How can I simplify textbook learning?

Remember that *you are in charge of your child's education.* It is not the book that educates; rather *you* are educating your child. You know your student best, and you have your own priorities raising him. So confidently tailor your child's learning for his needs.

Courses can be condensed or expanded to meet your student's own rate of learning. Feel free to slow down on the difficult parts and speed through what seems obvious. Also, most textbooks and workbooks are written for a classroom of students, so there are likely more questions and examples than one student needs on his own.

I utilize textbooks for several subjects in my own homeschooling. One of the books I have used for each of my children contains way, way too many questions to complete in each lesson. So for each new concept, I ask my child to complete only ten examples. If he has difficulty with those, I can use the remainder for extra practice. Also, I have been known to skip entire chapters that only review concepts they have already mastered.

Likewise, feel free to edit the course to reflect your own values. You may want to spend longer on a topic or insert some extra resources on aspects that are important to you or that are interesting to your students. And then there may be parts that seem redundant or unimportant to you, and you can feel free to skip those parts. Just use the course as a tool, not a dictator. You can tailor the material in textbooks, just like all of your other homeschool materials, to fit your family best.

6.3 CLASSICAL HOMESCHOOLING

6.3.1 What is classical education?

Classical education is a rigorous, language-centered method of study that progresses through three stages of learning interrelated subjects. It is language centered in that studies revolve around copious reading, writing, and conversation. Its hallmarks are the three stages of learning (grammar, dialectic or logic, and rhetoric) and an emphasis on history, Socratic discussion, and Latin. The three stages of learning roughly coincide with elementary, middle school, and high school.

The word *classical* has two meanings: a fine example of something (like classical music or a classic car), or an example from the ancient Greek and Roman times (like classical literature or classical statues). Both of those meanings apply to classical education. Classical education's unique feature is that instead of teaching individual subjects, it combines the liberal arts so they are understood as a whole. Classical education emphasizes a reverence for great thinkers and philosophies of the past and desires to analyze their ideas as applied to current life.

To frame this learning, classical education focuses on the history and development of Western culture, especially the Greco-Roman advances and the philosophies of the Middle Ages. The fields of literature, languages, theology, even mathematics and sciences are viewed in light of their historical development and expression. For example, students studying ancient Egypt could map the geography and study the impact of the Nile; read literature about and written during that period of time; learn about Egyptian mythology and beliefs; create scale models of pyramids; and visit museum exhibits of mummies and pottery, among other things. They might also learn how to perform intricate math calculations on an abacus. In the sciences, students might also study astronomy and how the Egyptians calculated measurements and distances from the rotation of the stars.

6.3.2 Where did classical education come from?

Guess what? Ancient times. The modern interest in classical education began with a lecture by essayist Dorothy Sayers in 1947 titled "The Lost Tools of Learning." In it, she criticized the education of her day as producing adults who could not speak, write, or think logically on current events.

She urged a return to medieval styles of education, connecting the trivium (or three foundational stages) of grammar, dialectic, and rhetoric to specific child development stages. She further championed a return to vigorous scholarship, insisting that such hard work will build character. Education, she said, should be "not learning, but a preparation for learning."[1]

What Sayers (and many modern classicists) failed to establish is the true historical basis for such an educational model. The outline of the trivium, Socratic discussion methods, and history-based inte-
grated learning points further back than medieval times to the days of Greece and Rome themselves. Going back even further than that, we see evidence of such an emphasis in language-based, history-centric learning with a focus on trivium first, then quadriv-ium (the sciences, theology, and specialty subject matter) in the Babylonian Empire.[2] But before these empires, the Bible repeatedly mentions the trivium subjects of knowledge (grammar), understanding (logic), and wisdom (rhetoric).[3]

> The LORD gives wisdom; from his mouth come knowledge and understanding.
>
> **PROVERBS 2:6**

Before the industrial revolution and the standardization of public schools in America, many students were taught at the grammar level first at home, then at the dialectic level in schools or with tutors. University education frequently used rhetoric methods.

6.3.3 What are the stages of classical education?

There are three distinct stages, or the *trivium*: grammar, dialectic or logic, and rhetoric. These roughly coincide with how we think of elementary, middle school, and high school, though a student does not progress through these stages based on age alone. The student moves to the next stage according to her academic and intellectual development.

The *grammar stage* focuses on the foundations of learning rather than self-expression. A child is taught to read and write and memorize. In fact, memorization is a key component of this stage of classical education. Children in the grammar stage memorize lists of dates, conjugations of Latin verbs, language rules, poetry, excerpts of literature, math tables, science facts, catechism questions, and more. The goal is to exercise the child's mind, filling it with information he will use in later understanding and application.

When the student develops the ability to question—question authority, question facts, question causes (you know, when the preteen becomes unbearably argumentative), she enters what is known as the *dialectic stage*. Her studies now focus on logic . . . and the logic behind her studies. Now the student analyzes what she is learning, finding the cause and effect, the for and against, behind historical events and actions, literature styles, artistic expression, scientific discovery, and more. She learns how to construct a paragraph logically. She begins working on algebra and geometry from a logical standpoint. Her studies in the subject of logic itself are geared toward teaching her to accurately and persuasively express herself without fallacy and to appreciate the sound logic of others (like, listen to her parents).

When the student has practiced the logic of her studies, she is ready to begin the *rhetoric* stage of her education (around age fourteen, or when we typically think of high school). At this point, she is making critical opinions and practicing communicating her views on subjects fluently and eloquently through the written and spoken word. She may participate in formal debate. And she begins to specialize her education in areas of greater interest. Some classical homeschoolers graduate early and enter college at age fifteen or sixteen, some take dual-credit college courses, and others delve into their chosen specialties at home.

6.3.4 How do I teach classical education?
Because classical education is centered on history, this subject is the foundation of most classical homeschools. History is often (but not always) studied in a cycle of three or more years. For instance, in a four-year cycle,

RESOURCES FOR CLASSICAL HOMESCHOOLING

- *Teaching the Trivium: Christian Homeschooling in a Classical Style* by Harvey and Laurie Bluedorn
- *The Well-Trained Mind* by Susan Wise Bauer and Jessie Wise
- classical curriculum publishers like Veritas Press and Memoria Press
- free resources at classicalcurriculum.com

the student may study one year each of ancient history, medieval history, renaissance and exploration, then modern history. The following year, the cycle begins again. If a student began this cycle at age five or so, he would finish three full four-year cycles (one each in grammar, dialectic, and rhetoric stages) before graduation. However, parents may begin teaching on a history cycle at any time. Yet while most classical homeschoolers teach history in a cycle, this is not necessary for classical education.

Students in the dialectic and rhetoric stages usually learn by independent study and by participating in Socratic discussion—a question-and-answer form of conversation—rather than lecture. This back-and-forth between parent and child challenges the student to think critically and to carefully hone his statements.

6.3.5 What materials do I use in classical homeschooling?

Textbooks and materials organized around the trivium. Several curriculum publishers and distributors have put together book lists and kits for classical educators. There are also online schools for studying upper-level classical subjects with live Socratic discussion. See appendix F.

CLASSICAL CONVERSATIONS

Classical Conversations provides structure and support for classical education with weekly meetings where students practice memory work and discussion. Find a local group at classicalconversations.com.

6.3.6 What is Socratic discussion?

Named for Socrates, an ancient Greek philosopher, Socratic discussion refers to learning through talking. Socrates taught by asking a series of questions to help the learner delve deeper and deeper into the issue. Classical educators often practice this discussion-type learning with rhetoric (or high school) students rather than lecturing. Students first read for themselves the history, literature, or other materials. Then they formulate their own opinions and connections on the subject matter. Finally, the student engages with the parent-teacher in a discussion in which the parent asks questions of the student to further engage her mind and help her draw appropriate conclusions.

6.3.7 What's with teaching Latin?

Strict classical homeschoolers often study classical languages, primarily Latin, perhaps along with Greek and/or Hebrew. There are numerous reasons for studying classical languages, including better understanding the construction of Greek- or Latin-based English words, learning medical and/or scientific terminology (for example, the Latin names for animals), and gaining a foundation for learning modern languages. Many classical homeschoolers also find that studying Latin builds discipline for a lifetime of rigorous study.

Some homeschoolers may choose not to study an ancient language. They may even study a modern language. While there is controversy in the classical community over the validity of neglecting Latin, a growing portion choose to follow the other classical disciplines without including an ancient language.

6.3.8 How do I grade classical homeschooling?

Grading in the school sense of the word is less important in classical education, where mastery is emphasized. If you are legally required to keep a record of your student's achievements in the grammar stage, you might grade math papers, evaluate reading, and list memory work. For your dialectic and rhetoric students, you may begin testing in some subjects, especially math and science. You might also grade them on papers and discussions according to a rubric or level of participation. Projects and research can also be documented and graded.

6.3.9 Is there a biblical criticism of classical education?

Christian homeschoolers are often concerned that the humanism inherent in classical studies may lead to pride and a rejection of God's truth. A focus on the history of mankind, particularly the writings and philosophies of ancient history and the Middle Ages, prioritizes the works and thoughts of man. This can and sometimes does produce adults who value human logic and human achievement over faith and God's Word.

However, classical education need not be centered on man as the epitome of knowledge and achievement. Biblical classicists teach the works of God throughout history, the biblical criticism of pagan religions and philosophies, and the modern application of God's Word. Their goal is

WHAT ARE THE PROS AND CONS OF CLASSICAL HOMESCHOOLING?

Pros

- Rigorous study
- Integrated subjects
- Deep understanding of world history and great works of literature
- Concentration in logical thinking

- Training in written and oral communication
- Ability to discern modern philosophies
- Teaching siblings of multiple ages similar material
- Can be focused on God's work and Word

Cons

- Too rigorous for some families
- Strict curriculum may stifle creativity
- Sets an educational progression at a rate not all students follow
- Algebra and geometry may be studied too early, leading to logical thinking but unclear visualization

- Some students don't seem to easily fit the standard classical stages
- References to pagan religion and myths may be undesirable to some
- Families with special needs may find it hard to adjust to their unique circumstances
- Can become humanistic and prideful

to produce adults who are equipped with knowledge, understanding, and wisdom.[4] Parents strive to help their child, through the concurrent study of God's Word and the humanities, to better know and serve God. Biblical classical education starts and ends with the Bible.

So while students of biblical classical education might study mythology, false religions, and humanistic philosophies, it is with an eye toward understanding the errors of mankind. As dialectic and rhetoric students, they will learn to follow the logical conclusion of such teachings and to defend their theology on the basis of sound logic and the Bible, correctly handling the Word of Truth (see 2 Timothy 2:15).

6.3.10 How can I simplify classical homeschooling?

Just do less. You can tailor classical education to fit your own family culture. Since the levels of grammar, dialectic, and rhetoric are not strictly tied to ages, your child can progress at her own pace. You can choose which classic literature and historical resources you want to use. And the historical framework can vary for what interests your family most. On stressful weeks, perhaps you'll concentrate on math and writing and read a few books aloud. Then at other times, you may delve deeply into a topic, reading lots of books and doing more research and projects together. The beauty of classical homeschooling is in the method of building on learning rather than a strict list of must reads.

There are many publishers who provide in-depth curriculum for every aspect of classical education. Others intentionally simplify the process with an easy-to-use format. With any classical provider, you can tailor the suggestions and materials to fit your own needs.

6.4 CHARLOTTE MASON HOMESCHOOLING

6.4.1 What is Charlotte Mason homeschooling?

A method based on the teachings of Victorian-era teacher and education philosopher Charlotte Mason. Emphasizing parents' responsibility to love and train their children, Mason taught that "children are born persons. . . . They are not born either good or bad, but with possibilities for either good or evil."[5] Indeed, this method is as much a child-rearing philosophy as a homeschool method. The goal is to produce a child who loves learning and is a delight to his parents and to others. Mason often wrote that education should stimulate a relationship between the child and the subject matter, creating a friendship with learning. Learning should always bring happiness.

> [The] most important part of education is to give the children the knowledge of God.
>
> **CHARLOTTE MASON**

Three important areas of emphasis for Mason were the atmosphere of the home, the discipline of the family life, and the life of the child. The parents develop this home atmosphere through intentional conversation, training in manners, and daily routines, instilling moral habits such as attention, obedience, honesty, and kindness. Charlotte Mason wished for all students to develop an intimate knowledge of themselves and to understand how God created their own individual nature so as to develop their unique talents fully. She saw no difference between the educational development and the spiritual development of the child, and she speaks of the mother as the most important parent and the single greatest influence in the child's life.

6.4.2 Where did the Charlotte Mason teaching method come from?

From Charlotte Mason herself. Charlotte Mason (1842–1923) was a private tutor and schoolteacher from Wales. In 1880, she wrote a series of geography books. In 1891, Mason moved to the countryside of Ambleside, England, to found what is known as the Parents' National Educational Union (PNEU), where she published resources for parents to teach at home. There she also began a school for governesses and wrote six popular volumes on home education and child-rearing. She continued to write and speak on education and parenting for the rest of her life.

6.4.3 What are the stages of Charlotte Mason homeschooling?

Charlotte Mason divided education into two stages, grammar and secondary, much like the schools in her day. But today's homeschoolers often divide their child's progress into our more common elementary, middle school, and high school. Importantly, Charlotte Mason emphasized play in the youngest years, waiting until after age six to begin formal learning.

Charlotte Mason's educational methods truly shine in the elementary years, offering a gentle introduction to learning and morals. In secondary education, the method adds more classical or traditional learning to delve deeper into each subject.

6.4.4 How do I teach Charlotte Mason homeschooling?

By emphasizing a positive relationship with learning. Mason taught that a child should enjoy learning, gradually becoming self-directed by secondary or high school. Teachers can foster the child's personal relationship with education through engaging literature and other educational experiences. The goal is to ignite the imagination with stories rather than dry facts.

Early education lends itself easily to the Charlotte Mason style. This method uses very short lessons of simple picture books, independent play, art appreciation, crafts, cooking, gardening, visiting neighbors and family, and nature studies. Students may begin keeping a nature journal—a scrapbook with their nature collections, sketches, interesting quotes, and poems. Children are encouraged to spend much of every day outdoors playing and adding to their notebooks.

The most important single subject to Charlotte Mason is the Bible. She repeatedly emphasized in her writings attention to biblical truths and the formation of a child's character. She wrote, "The knowledge of God is the principal knowledge, and no teaching of the Bible which does not further that knowledge is of religious value."[6] The Christian character of the mother was equally important, including how she managed the atmosphere of her home and how she developed the child's personal character.

In addition to daily Bible reading and memorization, Charlotte Mason considered history the foundation of all other subjects. In Mason's method, young children study the history of their own country (for Mason, this was England) for several years. Older children learn world history with an emphasis on Western civilizations. Students also explore geography through travel books and adventure stories.

In a Charlotte Mason education, literature is the most important tool for learning each subject, including Bible, history, and even science. Students read a copious number of books. These must be what is called "living books," those telling a story with description and action, rather than textbook-style facts. The author of real books is not only an expert on the subject but also one who can communicate a genuine interest. Each book also should communicate Christian values such as truth, nobility, and beauty. Only when a real book cannot be found on a subject would the parent substitute with a textbook. Students also learn through copy work—handwritten copies of poems, quotes, and portions of books.

The parent usually measures progress through narration rather than questions and answers. The student narrates, or retells what is read, daily after read-aloud and independent reading, from elementary age through high school. By practicing narrating, the student learns to listen to and to recall details and descriptions. Using the more difficult words from the

---

RESOURCES FOR CHARLOTTE MASON HOMESCHOOLING

- The complete set of Mason's books on education, which includes

  › *Home Education*

  › *Parents and Children*

  › *School Education*

  › *Ourselves*

  › *Formation of Character*

  › *Towards a Philosophy of Education*

- *A Charlotte Mason Companion: Personal Reflections on the Gentle Art of Learning* by Karen Andreola

A free Charlotte Mason curriculum complete with book lists is available at amblesideonline.org.

---

reading develops vocabulary. This exercise in narration trains the memory and enhances composition.

Early science education begins with nature studies, walks through fields or woods with observation and sketching. Mason emphasized observation and recording, saying that a student could not understand and appreciate what he could not replicate. Students who practice drawing what they observe work to improve their art skills and their attention to detail. Older students study science from both textbooks and living books.

Mathematics, in Mason's view, is a necessary discipline but not a critical subject in itself. She encouraged students to fully understand math as it applies to other subjects, such as science, but not to become bogged down in the advanced study to the detriment of their enjoyment of the humanities. If a student excelled in math, he should be given free rein. But a student who struggled with math could learn the minimum and then focus on the humanities. The humanities, in her opinion, were always more important.

Charlotte Mason emphasized the study of fine arts with picture study. She encouraged setting a single print of a painting out for children to study for several days at a time. The student may be asked to describe in detail and to later reproduce on paper what he has seen. This, too, is intended to develop an appreciation for the craft and attention to detail.

Instead of ancient languages, Mason encouraged the student to become proficient in modern languages. As a teacher in Great Britain, she urged students to be fluent in French and to become familiar with German and perhaps Italian.

6.4.5 What materials do I use in Charlotte Mason homeschooling?

Some curriculum publishers and distributors sell Charlotte Mason boxed curriculum kits. There are also free book lists and suggestions available online. Many Charlotte Mason homeschoolers put together their own curriculum from library resources and booksellers.

6.4.6 How do I grade Charlotte Mason homeschooling?

Very little. A Charlotte Mason educator eschews worksheets and grades, preferring to motivate the child through enjoyment and respect. There are as many ways of grading in a Charlotte Mason homeschool as there are ways of enjoying that method. While math and other textbook subjects might be tested, the majority of subjects are evaluated based on narration. Many parents grade the narration using a rubric measuring detail, description, familiarity with the material, and more. For the sake of record keeping, you may even transcribe many of these narrations. You could also require high school students to write down some of their narrations in addition to giving them orally. You can then compare what the child has studied with any state or college requirements to prepare a similar transcript based on hours of study. (See more about high school records in section 13.3.)

Many parents forgo grading at all until the student is high school aged. At any stage, you can save projects, notebooks, and assignments for evaluation and grading. At the higher age levels, many students will utilize textbooks and other courses that lend themselves to testing or written assignments that you could grade with a rubric.

6.4.7 What are the pros and cons of Charlotte Mason education?

Pros. Your reaction to Charlotte Mason's method will depend on your parenting style, but since her educational theories are rooted in a Victorian Christian theology of child-rearing, many Christian parents find this style similar to their own beliefs on rearing children. Charlotte Mason's focus

HOW DO CLASSICAL AND CHARLOTTE MASON EDUCATION COMPARE?

These two styles are so similar that many homeschool families combine the two into their own unique way of learning. By choosing from some aspects of one or the other, these homeschoolers create their own unique humanities-based education.

Classical	Charlotte Mason
Three educational/ developmental levels	Gradual development
Heavy emphasis on the humanities	Emphasis on humanities with nature and art
Latin, Greek, or modern languages	Modern languages
Produce composition and rhetoric	Produce narration
Early rote memorization such as historical dates, verbs, language rules, math facts	Early memorization of poems and Scripture
Disciplined study in grammar stage	Relaxed, creative early childhood learning
Older students demonstrate debate skills and Socratic discussion	Older students demonstrate the capacity for independent study

on whetting an appetite for learning and instilling strong character appeals to many Christian parents.

Charlotte Mason's teaching style is especially popular for early childhood education. As students grow toward high school, however, many parents turn to textbooks and tutoring for a more familiar study of advanced subjects, ease of grading, test-taking preparation, and straightforward transcripts.

Cons. Some families simply do not enjoy this style. Mothers may find it too time intensive, especially if they are working out of the home. Some parents and students find the number of read-alouds and the amount of independent reading to be intimidating. Some children may not even enjoy typical Charlotte Mason activities like nature studies, art studies, or sketching. Some modern families have differing views on traditional family roles and may prefer for parents to take an equal share in homeschooling or for the father to be the primary teacher. And many families whose children have special needs find it easier to follow a more structured plan to gauge their students' progress.

6.4.8 How can I simplify Charlotte Mason homeschooling?

By picking and choosing. While it can seem like a Charlotte Mason day is packed with activity, your family can choose the activities and routines that fit you best. The important principles are the *home atmosphere* and the *child's character*. You can feel free to choose the activities and topics that most delight your child.

6.5 MONTESSORI HOMESCHOOLING

6.5.1 What is Montessori homeschooling?

Montessori homeschooling is child-centered life training in academics and life skills for the purpose of developing delight and exploration. The Montessori method utilizes a "prepared environment in which the child, set free from undue adult intervention, can live its life according to the laws of its development."[7] A Montessori school class includes children of a variety of ages learning alongside each other. This teaching method emphasizes considerate behavior and personal responsibility for learning. Since the Montessori method was developed for classroom use, homeschoolers need to adapt this teaching style for home use.

6.5.2 Where did Montessori education come from?

Montessori education is named for its originator, Maria Montessori (1870–1952). One of the first women in Italy to graduate from medical school, Montessori took a special interest in child development during her work in a psychiatric asylum in Rome. There she trained institutionalized children in self-care and manners and, while doing so, she documented nearly immediate improvement in both their behavior and mental capability.

In 1907, Montessori was asked to oversee sixty young children ages three to six in a tenement building. The adults living in the building worked all day, leaving the children to run rampant and even destroy property. Montessori was tasked with simply containing the problem.

Instead, she hired a teacher and prepared a central room in the building with child-sized furniture. She asked the teacher to teach the children basic hygiene and manners only. As the children improved in these areas, Montessori trained the teacher to slowly add simple lessons in self-care and early academics. The results were dramatic. The students were soon begging adults to come into the room and listen to them read or demonstrate their lessons. Montessori frequently visited the class and trained the teacher to observe the children and allow for their own exploration.

Soon the results of Dr. Montessori's methods were well-known in Rome. From there, her methods spread throughout Europe and America as leaders recognized the benefits of sending children to school rather than leaving them to their own devices or forcing them to work in factories. Montessori spent over forty years lecturing around the world on her methods and training teachers on how to set up a true Montessori school. Those who attempted to begin on their own interpretation or to deviate from her specific process were, in her opinion, not truly Montessori.

6.5.3 What are the stages of Montessori homeschooling?

Montessori education is divided into child-development stages. First, the child goes through the Transformation from baby to young child. This consists of what Montessori called the Absorbent Mind (ages 0–3) and the Conscious Mind (ages 3–6). In the Absorbent period, the child is unconsciously learning. In the Conscious period, the child acquires information through his senses.

The second stage is Uniform Growth (ages 6–12). In this period, Maria Montessori taught, the child follows a herd instinct, learning from peers and solidifying a sense of right and wrong.

The final stage is Transformation to adulthood. The period of Puberty (ages 12–15) finds the student sensitive to her own view of herself, discovering who she is separate from the herd. The period of Adolescence (ages 15–18) is a time for increased independence in learning, work, and finances.

6.5.4 How do I teach Montessori education?

Teach the child how to learn. The goal of Montessori is to train the child to learn by himself, to master the materials through practice and exploration within the carefully prepared environment. The teacher prepares this environment free from the "junk food" of technology or screen learning, though many homeschoolers incorporate high-quality online resources.

Each day may begin with a short meeting or greeting time. After this, the student might choose which Montessori materials to explore to master the concepts previously presented. The parent may demonstrate a short lesson, then the child develops mastery through practice on her own. This time is short for the youngest children, but by age six the child is expected to work with materials for two to three hours before cleaning up the environment. Most critical is that the time is carefully guarded—no other schedules and interruptions occur during the learning period.

For example, for a life skill, the parent might teach the child once or twice how to tie his shoes. Then the parent never helps again. The child masters the process because the shoes become untied numerous times each day, offering plenty of practice. An academic lesson may be presented several times, yet the child will not be corrected as he works on it. Instead, he is given multiple opportunities to practice his new skill. Important skills besides academics include caring for himself, properly using the educational materials, and ordering the environment.

The Montessori teacher would be careful not to interrupt or correct the child but instead would allow the child to learn through her own efforts, observing the child and tailoring the lesson to her needs. The parent may present a new concept briefly at the beginning of the learning time. This presentation might also include a brief explanation of why the child should master that lesson. A parent may also spend several days teaching a unit lesson (see section 6.7) on a concept. But the most important role of the parent is to model appropriate behavior and to keep the environment free of interruption, acting as a link between the child and the environment.

In a true Montessori classroom, learning is aided by the presence of multiple children of different ages. Older children may demonstrate to the younger a challenge they are working on. Younger children may actively try to imitate, or they may just casually observe what the older students are doing. Older children may also help a younger child complete a process. Students then learn from one another as much as from the teacher.

An important aspect of Montessori education is self-discipline. A Montessori principle is that true freedom is achieved through correct, polite behavior. In the case of poor behavior, the teacher could redirect the child to another activity. If this continues, the parent may keep the child close by to work quietly or to rest.

Ultimately, the child is responsible for her progress. She practices the concepts and works to master each. The parent provides freedom within a safe environment and offers guidance as needed.

6.5.5 What environment do I use in Montessori homeschooling?

The Montessori method is built around the environment and the materials. The environment, or room for lessons, must be orderly and appealing. Every book and all material should be displayed in easy reach for young children. The environment is arranged to encourage independence and free movement. The room may be decorated with beautiful household products and plants. According to Maria Montessori, the environment is always a closed indoor space, though many modern Montessori teachers utilize outdoor spaces as well.

6.5.6 What materials do I use in Montessori homeschooling?

Montessori materials are concrete objects. Because the Montessori method emphasizes life skills, the classroom often includes real household materials, not toys, such as real pots and pans and kitchen dishes. There may even be real clothes for students to practice dressing.

Montessori materials also include academic manipulatives. These high-quality objects are developed with a specific teaching goal in mind. Each one eliminates as many variables as possible to teach only one concept. For example, shape blocks come in only one color and size, so the student does not associate any other details with the geometry of shapes. Montessori materials, then, must be purchased from specific Montessori providers or carefully constructed to allow only one variable to learn.

Other important parts of Montessori education are books, research time, and interviews with experts in academic fields or community work. Teachers purchase albums (or instruction manuals) of lessons and guidelines. Some Montessori retailers, but not all, will only sell albums to certified Montessori teachers. Many Montessori homeschoolers carefully construct their own albums according to Montessori principles.

6.5.7 How do I grade Montessori homeschooling?

Evaluate your child's progress based on your observations. In Montessori education, you would not test on the concepts. If your child struggles with any lesson, you can repeat that concept until he masters it. Your child should naturally gravitate toward and excel in those areas he enjoys and masters.

6.5.8 What are the pros and cons of Montessori homeschooling?

Pros. Montessori environments are fun and inviting. Many creative homeschool parents enjoy decorating and stocking their beautiful classrooms with household items, books, manipulatives, and other educational supplies. The Montessori emphasis on caring for the supplies helps ensure the rooms stay clean and orderly.

Montessori education can be fun for the student. Young children in particular are drawn to learning household chores and processes. The Montessori supplies themselves are fun and interesting. And if the homeschool includes other children, the students can enjoy the time with siblings.

Montessori education itself is self-paced. Students may remain on a concept until it is mastered. Review is easier as the children become increasingly confident in the process they're practicing.

Cons. Montessori methods were developed for group learning with children close in age. Homeschoolers have difficulty replicating this environment unless they create a co-op or form group lessons. This adds the variable of having a teacher other than the parent or of learning from several different teachers.

True Montessori teachers are required to be certified by Montessori associations. This principle began when Maria Montessori insisted on personally training each teacher. Homeschool parents are, by nature, not required to be certified or trained to teach their own children. So some, but not all, Montessori organizations would not consider a homeschool a valid Montessori school and may refuse to sell them albums or materials.

However, there are some homeschool Montessori suppliers who have developed products designed for home learning.

Montessori materials are designed to be used only one way. If a child uses the material creatively or even finds the correct answer to a problem differently than through the prescribed method, the process is considered wrong. Montessori homeschoolers, however, often allow their children much more freedom in the use of their materials.

Finally, Montessori education was developed for children from ages three to six. Maria Montessori did have theories about teaching older children and even teens to become more independent and to interact to a greater degree with the outside world. She envisioned a process in which children would enter outside organizations and learn morals necessary for successful living. She also wanted teens to become increasingly independent in their work, their reasoning, and even their finances. Unfortunately, Maria Montessori passed away before she could test her theories. Yet many homeschoolers continue to incorporate Montessori methods through the later years.

> ### RESOURCES FOR MONTESSORI HOMESCHOOLING
>
> Deb Chitwood of Living Montessori Now is a certified and experienced Montessori teacher and homeschool mom. She runs a homeschool Montessori Facebook group in addition to writing and creating Montessori products. You can find her at livingmontessorinow.com.

Some parents object to Maria Montessori's principle that a child will be attracted to learning any new life or academic concept if it is presented through an engaging environment and materials. This seems to go against the biblical teaching of the inherent sin nature in every person. But as a Catholic herself, Maria incorporated spiritual lessons into her life skills. She believed that gentle education and training would bring the child to an understanding of her place in creation.

6.5.9 How can I simplify Montessori homeschooling?
Though the Montessori method was originally designed for a classroom, you can adapt the principles for your own homeschool. Many homeschoolers use household materials and academic manipulatives to teach preschool lessons. Most also set aside a dedicated schoolroom to organize

the materials and keep all the manipulatives within reach. Each Montessori homeschool looks different; parents can design the lessons and environment the way that suits them best. Then as the child grows out of the preschool ages into elementary schoolwork, many Montessori homeschoolers gravitate toward unit studies and independent textbook work.

6.6 UNSCHOOLING

6.6.1 What is unschooling?

Of all the homeschooling methods, unschooling is the most difficult to define. Indeed, experts, authors, and homeschoolers practice unschooling in vastly different ways. So to avoid as much confusion as possible, I will discuss unschooling in as broad terms as I can.

Unschooling is a relationship-centered, child-directed method of learning sometimes referred to as *life schooling*. Rather than directing the daily education of the student, unschooling parents act as facilitators of the child's interests. They base their child's learning on the strong relationships they are building within the home. Children are thus given much freedom to explore their surroundings, their interests, and their environment, learning subjects at their own pace. This method originated among rural families, but it is now growing in urban cities, particularly with families in the technology industry.

> The learner, young or old, is the best judge of what he should learn next.
>
> **JOHN HOLT**

6.6.2 Where did unschooling come from?

The term *unschooling* was at first synonymous with *homeschooling*. John Holt (1923–1985), considered the founder of unschooling, used the term to describe the opposite of institutionalized education. Though Holt held no teaching degree, his classroom teaching convinced him that schoolrooms squash the natural abilities of children.

Holt advocated the *deschooling* of society (an idea borrowed from philosopher Ivan Illich). He desired to abolish compulsory school attendance and to instead transfer all authority of personal education over to children themselves. He believed each child should decide if and when to attend school, that classes should be taught by student peers, and that results should be evaluated by peers rather than by adults.

John Holt never married or had children of his own. His theories on child-directed education began with his observations of his friend's young child and toddler. Holt began to believe young children are more eager to learn than those elementary aged, and that if schooling were reformed, education would flourish.

6.6.3 What are the stages of unschooling?

Unschooling is marked by child-directed academics. A young child is encouraged to explore the world around her and to take part in the daily activities of her family. Reading, math, and other academics are begun as the child shows a marked interest and actively pursues learning on her own. Rather than a gradual progression in each subject, unschoolers tend to learn in sudden spurts. Unschooling is the opposite of scheduling, sequencing, or forcing education.

6.6.4 How do I teach unschooling?

Naturally. Unschooling is based on child development within the relationships inside the home. Babies and toddlers learn many things quickly, such as walking, talking, and feeding themselves. Unschoolers believe this rapid learning will continue throughout childhood if uninterrupted by adults. A student will learn what he needs to learn. An older unschooler may even study subjects he does not enjoy if this leads to a better understanding of his interests or serves his long-term goals, such as an occupation or college.

Unschooling parents build an environment conducive to learning and curiosity, including such things as a large library, a tool set, a science workshop, etc. They strive to expose the student to as many educational stimuli as possible, whether it be museums, lectures, rural farms, businesses, or apprenticeships.

Purely unschooled students even make their own academic decisions. These students, then, cannot be compared with one another since the development of interests and mastery are unique for each one. Some unschooling families allow students to decide when and if they study certain subjects, including advanced math and research writing. Thus the student's workload may be relatively light (developing around his gradual interests) or rigorous (utilizing curriculum and evaluations). A hallmark of unschooling content is allowing the child to choose his classes and resources.

Unschooling does offer a holistic education. If a child chooses one topic to study for months, unschooling parents observe which other related subjects the child explores. For example, a student interested in sharks may read every book on sharks in his library (literature) and make diagrams of the different types of sharks (art and anatomy). The student may study the habitat and eating habits of the sharks (marine biology and ecology). He also may calculate how many sharks have been discovered, their rate of death and depletion, and the long-term effect on the shark population (math).

> I will delight in your statutes;
> I will not forget your word.
>
> **PSALM 119:16**

Unschooling appeals to parents who believe children have the capability of educating themselves and that children are responsible for their own learning. These parents see themselves as facilitators, not directors of their children's education. They believe it is important that the parent not squash children's confidence by demonstrating too much expertise. Therefore, unschoolers often try to not correct their children but, rather, allow them to learn from finding and correcting their own errors. An unschooling education is not handed down from the parent to the children because the children educate themselves. The parents' primary job is to facilitate learning rather than coerce. They guide their children to study at their own pace in their own interests, even if the students are learning subjects at different rates. Unschooling students strive not for grades, awards, or parental approval but to satisfy their own curiosity. This delight, then, drives the students' learning.

6.6.5 What materials do I use in unschooling?

Unschooling students use a variety of materials. Parents may stock their home with maps, books, a computer, and other supplies to stimulate their children's interest. Students may gradually collect science equipment, tools, art supplies, and more as their interests and activities branch out. Their continued interest and investigation will determine what materials they need.

6.6.6 How do I grade unschooling?

Unschooling is not graded. That would be the opposite of unschooling, right? However, some states may require reporting, or your student may need a transcript for college. In each instance, parents may ask the reporting party what they need.

For some school districts, an explanation or example of projects and activities pointing out the many intertwined subjects is enough. You might keep a journal to record activities your child pursues and what subject matter each covered. You could make a grid each week with subject headings and jot down activities your student completed that fulfilled a lesson in each one. One of the easiest ways to document your unschooler is to keep a portfolio of her work.

For college transcripts, students may need to untangle subject matter into different subjects and assign them grades or compile a portfolio. As in the earlier years, your student can log his achievements and milestones in each subject, keeping broad categories for high school credits. By high school, many unschoolers begin studying from textbooks, online classes, or dual-credit college classes to make the transition to college easier. Other unschoolers, however, choose not to attend college and instead go directly into the workforce.

6.6.7 Is there a biblical criticism of unschooling?

Some Christians feel that unschooling, by definition, is the opposite of the biblical principles of child-rearing. A foundational text for Christian homeschooling is Deuteronomy 6:5-9:

> You shall love the Lord your God with all your heart and with all your soul and with all your might. And these words that I command you today shall be on your heart. You shall teach them diligently to your children, and shall talk of them when you sit in your house, and when you walk by the way, and when you lie down, and when you rise. You shall bind them as a sign on your hand, and they shall be as frontlets between your eyes. You shall write them on the doorposts of your house and on your gates.

These verses are often referenced in homeschooling as God's command that parents actively teach their children.

Scripture teaches us that while we are all sinners before God, children are inherently foolish (see Proverbs 22:15) and that, left to their own desires, bring shame to their parents (see Proverbs 29:15). Children then are commanded not to seek their own wisdom but, instead, to listen to the teachings of their parents (see Proverbs 1:8). Likewise, parents are commanded to actively instruct (see Deuteronomy 4:9; Psalm 78:5-8; Proverbs 1:8) and rear (see Ephesians 6:4) children toward wisdom and godliness.

> My son, if you receive my words and treasure up my commandments with you, making your ear attentive to wisdom and inclining your heart to understanding . . . then you will understand the fear of the LORD and find the knowledge of God.
>
> **PROVERBS 2:1-2, 5**

Christians who have chosen unschooling don't see their choice as violating Scripture. They base their beliefs in both Christianity and unschooling on Christ's gentle discipling of his children—not coercive but allowing freedom within safe boundaries. As a reaction against an authoritative and restrictive home environment, they yearn to base relationships and thus teaching on freedom and Christlike love. They apply Deuteronomy 6:7 as commanding relational education, not formal education as others interpret it. Less radical than many secular unschoolers, Christian unschoolers are careful to build broad boundaries based on love and personal responsibility. For them, allowing children to practice this freedom prepares them for a lifetime of living under God's love and care.

6.6.8 What are the pros and cons of unschooling?

Pros. The unschooling philosophy reminds all homeschoolers of important educational points. For example, students do learn and retain more knowledge if they are actively engaged with their subject matter. Forcing them to memorize unrelated or misunderstood facts for the sake of a test or transcript does more harm than good to their education. The parent's job is not merely to require homework or projects but to ignite curiosity and wonder that will cause children to learn not only for an assignment but also for the sake of learning itself. That is, indeed, the purpose of homeschooling.

Cons. To do well, unschooling requires creativity. One of the biggest issues with unschooling is that it is inherently unstandardized. Every unschooling family educates their own child uniquely and applies unschooling principles to varying degrees. Some unschooling experts advocate using textbooks in elementary school. John Holt himself suggested beginning phonics early in a student's life. But many unschoolers believe that early reading and textbooks are contrary to unschooling philosophy.

Another unique factor in unschooling is the geography. Holt himself pointed out that unschooling works better in a rural environment than in an urban home. Farming communities offer, in the opinion of many, more opportunities for nature study and life skills training. Urban unschoolers, however, make up this deficit by attending nearby museums and cultural events.

A bigger obstacle in unschooling remains the study of difficult or undesirable subjects. No matter how much fun it is to build a model of a pyramid, not many students wish to calculate the measurements relative to the sun, determine the size stones needed for each level, and find the exact slope of each side. In other words, many teens hate algebra and science, along with aspects of many other subjects.

Unschoolers overcome this problem in several ways. First, they may wait until the student finds it necessary to use the dreaded subject in some delight-directed project. Secondly, the parent may point out the necessary subjects that must be mastered to achieve the student's long-term goals (college, career, etc.). Finally, the parent may hand the student a list of graduation requirements and allow the student to choose how and when she might fulfill them . . . including those difficult and dreaded subjects.

A serious concern of unschooling is preparation for adulthood. Holt's theories, taken to the extreme, would require a teen to make decisions impacting his lifelong career choices in order to determine his own academic path in high school and beyond. Many unschooling families temper this approach by guiding their teen to prepare for possible college entrance or a supportive career at the least.

The worst aspect of unschooling is its unfavorable press. News reports and tabloid stories paint radical unschoolers as the norm for all homeschooling families. Examples of students who watch television all day and play outside unsupervised for years on end cause the public to question the educational validity not only of unschooling but even of homeschooling in general. The misinformed see unschooling, and by relation homeschooling in general, as a type of child neglect or even abuse. It is critical that radical unschooling not become synonymous with moderate unschooling or with homeschooling at large.

6.6.9 How can I simplify unschooling?

Unschooling is, by its very nature, simple and relaxed for the parent. Yet, as you begin, you will find your child needs copious tools and resources to fulfill her growing curiosity. She will ask many questions for which you may give simple answers or suggestions on how she can find the answers. Most of all, you can step back and allow your child to take the reins on her own education.

6.7 UNIT STUDIES

6.7.1 What are unit studies?

Popular with all methods of homeschooling, these lessons focus on exploring one topic in-depth, seeking to connect subjects within the topic. For example, a unit study based on a novel set during the gold rush might include a history of westward expansion, the geography of the western United States, Native American culture, and a look at how natural resources are mined. By immersing himself in a single topic, the student learns how each discipline fits together as a whole, that academic subjects work together rather than separately.

A unit study may be taken from a topic in a curriculum, or the unit study approach can be used as the homeschool method itself. When teaching students of various ages, each can go into as much depth as their own ability allows. And by taking on a topic of interest, children are more likely to enjoy their homeschool projects.

Unit studies often include projects or crafts. A popular tool in unit studies is a *lapbook*, a folder of what the student has learned. Lapbooks are usually the size of a file folder or can be larger, with several folders attached together. Reports, diagrams, maps, photos, and more can be attached to the lapbook for a creative record of the student's learning. Lapbook materials are available for purchase or may be created independently.

6.8 CO-OPS

6.8.1 What is a homeschool co-op?

A co-op provides classes for homeschool students usually taught by homeschool moms. Membership may require a tuition payment or volunteer teaching. Co-op classes are particularly popular for teacher-intensive curricula or advanced subjects like writing, foreign language, science labs, and advanced math. Moms may choose a co-op for one or all subjects.

Many homeschool co-ops provide excellent teaching. Teachers may include moms with specialized training in a particular field or moms with experience teaching that subject.

A good co-op is not a school. It should supplement—not replace—your homeschooling. In many co-ops, the teacher explains the concept in the class, but the parent helps the child understand and complete homework. Some co-ops expect the student to study independently to prepare for class. By attending class, however, he practices learning in a classroom environment and in conjunction with other students. Group projects may even be included.

Co-ops use a variety of teaching methods and materials. Many co-ops

WHAT ABOUT SHARED CLASSES?

An alternative to a co-op is a shared class. Many homeschool families, instead of starting a co-op, simply share teaching in the home. A mom may love teaching science, for example, and invite friends over to do science experiments. Moms may take turns doing projects together weekly. A mom might even give a crash course in a particular topic over a few weeks. There are many ways to help each other with homeschooling besides a formal co-op.

use classical or traditional textbook methods. You may find a co-op that uses your favorite curriculum, or the teacher may have developed her own.

6.8.2 What are the pros and cons of co-ops?

Pros. Co-ops offer many benefits. Some moms choose a co-op class for a subject they are less confident teaching. Others enjoy the camaraderie with other homeschool moms and want their child to make homeschool friends. Still other homeschool moms may sign up a child for a co-op to free up their own time for working.

Students can greatly benefit from co-op classes. Many classes offer more hands-on and technical activities than your student might experience at home. Taking a class offers opportunity for group discussion and peer feedback. Many classes give students the opportunity to work on projects as a group. Students also learn to receive instruction from an adult outside the home and to patiently learn within a group.

Cons. Co-ops aren't for everyone. A co-op may not align with your preferred teaching method, or the class environment may not work for your child's learning style. It may add too many hours to your weekly schedule. If each parent is required to teach, you may find yourself uncomfortable in front of a class. Most co-ops are somewhat exclusive and may not accept all applicants. You may be too independent in your teaching style and methods to conform to group strategies. Co-op classes just might conflict with your vision of your family's homeschool.

The teacher quality may be inconsistent. Many co-op teachers are moms trained in a certain field, moms who have left their careers to homeschool and are excited to share their knowledge with your child. Others may be experienced homeschool moms who simply enjoy teaching that particular subject. Some homeschool moms, however, may be simply fulfilling their required teaching hours.

Co-op is a commitment. Many will have a cancellation policy that may include payment of the remainder of the contract or fee for unused supplies. A co-op depends on its members, too, so if you leave, it will hurt the entire group. This is why many homeschool co-ops require a signed one-year contract.

Co-op membership takes work. A co-op is not a free class. Some may charge a large fee to cover supplies and pay teachers; these function more as school classes. Most, however, require time as payment. In most co-ops, parents teach classes, tutor students, or babysit the younger children.

6.8.3 How can I find a co-op?
There may be a co-op near you. Your local homeschool support group will be able to direct you to co-ops in your area. Homeschool moms near you may also know of popular co-ops nearby. Or you may choose to start a co-op yourself!

6.8.4 How do I start a co-op?
Starting a co-op is not too hard. With some help from other homeschool parents, you can put one together in no time. Seriously, moms do it all the

THINGS TO CONSIDER WHEN CHOOSING A CO-OP

- Do you agree with the statement of faith?
- Are there clear written policies?
- Is there a contract?
- How is the co-op run?
- Is the co-op drop-off, or do you need to supervise?
- Are there security measures in place?
- Is there a nursery?
- Is it affordable?
- What is the payment schedule?
- What is the training of the teacher?
- Do you like the curriculum choice?
- What is the class teaching style?
- How large is the class?
- Is the class daily or weekly?
- Are supplies provided, or do you need to buy them?
- Does your child do well in a classroom environment?
- How much of the assignments will you teach at home?
- Are you comfortable giving the teaching over to someone else?
- Do you have the ability to fulfill any volunteer requirements?
- What are your teaching commitments?
- Are you comfortable teaching a class, as opposed to just your individual student?

time. You do need help leading the co-op, though. Co-ops work best with support, and two or three moms can share the load and share ideas. This is why you may want to form a governing committee. Also, when disputes arise, it is good to have more than one leader to make a decision. If payment is involved, in particular, a committee of leaders offers protection and greater transparency.

Create a statement of faith. Will your co-op be only for Christian homeschoolers? Will subjects be taught from a specific worldview? Will you expect students to align doctrinally? Set these standards in writing so families know what to expect.

Write guidelines. Who will be the leaders? How will payments be accepted and when? Who will pay for supplies? What students will be accepted? What will parental involvement be like? What will the expectations for students be? How will disciplinary matters be handled? How will disputes be resolved? How can a parent terminate participation?

Determine who will participate. Do you have a close group of friends you want to serve? Do you want to provide classes for many in your local support group? Will you publicize your organization? Do you need a website?

Find a place to meet. Will you meet in a church, a school, a storefront, or a mom's house? Who will you need to contact to find out about getting permission?

Ensure security. Are there locks on the exterior doors? Will you have enough parents to keep two adults in each room? Will you use background checks? Are there windows on all the doors? Will the classes be held in the open? What will the emergency procedures be? Will you be careful with what you share online and on social media? Will parents give consent for photos?

Determine reporting requirements. Will you need to keep educational paperwork? Will parents continue to keep portfolios? Are there even reporting requirements in your state?

Research legal issues. What information do you need from your bank regarding financial requirements? Will you be a nonprofit? Will you need help with tax issues related to income and teacher payment? Will your teachers be employees or independent contractors? Who will keep financial records? What are the insurance requirements, if any? Will there be a teacher contract?

Decide what teaching style you will use. Will this be a strictly classical co-op? Will teachers use textbooks? Will teachers have flexibility to choose their style and adapt to the students during the year? Will the subject be taught completely in class, or will parents continue the lessons at home? How much homework, if any, is appropriate?

Choose the curriculum. Will the teachers choose their own curriculum, or will the co-op leaders decide? Will the teachers have flexibility to deviate from the lesson plans? Could they write their own lessons? Or would you prefer the teachers remain faithful to a published curriculum to keep all the families on the same page?

> RESOURCES FOR
> STARTING A CO-OP
>
> - *Homeschool Co-Ops: How to Start Them, Run Them and Not Burn Out* by Carol Topp
> - Homeschool Mastery Academy's "Homeschool Group and Co-op Leadership Training Bundle," audio training as well as printable planning worksheets, available at homeschoolmasteryacademy.com

Decide what ages will be served. Will this co-op be for only a few classes or for a certain grade range? Will there be childcare or a nursery?

Set expectations for parental involvement. Will every mom need to teach? Could a parent pay a higher fee to avoid teaching? Will teaching be shared? Will parents need to stay on premises, or may they leave?

This probably seems daunting now that I've written out so many issues. But you know what? When you grab a friend and start working through this, it will all come together. And not only will you find a good structure for your own special co-op, but you will also find satisfaction in providing great educational opportunities to families you care about.

6.9 ONLINE LEARNING

6.9.1 What is online learning?

Online learning refers to taking a course through the internet. This option became increasingly popular to homeschoolers as technology provided more learning opportunities. Then restrictions during the pandemic of 2020 necessitated students from all schools around the country remain at home for online distanced learning. Still, many purely homeschooling parents intentionally choose online learning as a supplement to their own teaching culture or even as the basis of all their student's subjects.

Besides online school classrooms, homeschool online learning comes in two forms: prerecorded and live. Homeschool online courses vary in what materials and services they offer. Some include placement tests, attendance records, homework and test grading, and feedback for parents. Others offer merely the class basics while allowing the parent to complete the teaching and grading.

Parents may choose to supplement their homeschool with online courses for a variety of reasons. Online learning frees up time for the parents, allowing more time to teach other siblings or to work. Some parents and students value the opportunity to study with professionals or experts in the field. I chose online learning for select courses for several of my children so they could receive more in-depth training in areas I was unfamiliar with. At other times, I used an online class to give my student the foundation of a subject I could later build upon with my own teaching.

HOW MUCH DOES ONLINE LEARNING COST?

The cost of homeschool online learning varies dramatically due to the different levels of expertise, the variety of services offered, and teacher availability. Find lists of homeschool online course providers in appendix F.

6.10 OTHER METHODS

6.10.1 Are there other methods I can integrate into my homeschooling?

Absolutely! In addition to the comprehensive styles of homeschooling discussed above, other methods exist that may be combined or used alone. Some of these include the Principle Approach and WholeHearted Learning. Many homeschool parents prefer to pick and choose in an eclectic approach.

6.10.2 What is the Principle Approach?

The **Principle Approach** centers on studying God's work in founding the United States and establishing Christian principles of government. This approach teaches that America is uniquely blessed above other governments throughout history and around the world today. This lens of learning focuses on views of education and government throughout history and around the world, portraying others as unbiblical and the American approach as based on God's Word. Key to this view is personal freedom and the evils of centralized power.

The Principle Approach is not a curriculum but rather a method of viewing education. There are materials specifically published to support families attracted to this worldview, but many create their own or adapt another curriculum. Specific principles of this method are based on the belief that every government is the result of education. The Principle Approach stresses that modern education and government is increasingly socialistic and, therefore, anti-God. The method seeks to instill character in the student through self-government and individual freedom.

The Principle Approach is practiced through self-teaching as opposed to group learning. The student studies the 4 Rs of learning: researching, reasoning, relating, and recording. This method is applied to every subject. Teachers of the Principle Approach heavily use Noah Webster's *American Dictionary of the English Language* (1828) because of the biblical examples within definitions, despite the change of word meaning and usage over time.

> RESOURCES FOR THE PRINCIPLE APPROACH
>
> The Foundation for American Christian Education produces the Principle Approach curriculum called The Noah Plan, available at face.net /curriculum.

6.10.3 What is WholeHearted Learning?

WholeHearted Learning is a family discipleship style taught by Clay and Sally Clarkson through their books and lectures. The Clarksons developed many of their ideas from the teachings of both Charlotte Mason and John Holt, applying biblical principles of parenting and family life. Covering education and child-rearing from preschool through middle school, this method seeks to prepare hearts for God's wisdom through gentle parenting styles and wholesome materials. The Clarksons teach that learning occurs through relationships, relationships that are developed primarily toward God and other family members. The parents shepherd the child's heart through child-rearing techniques and the use of "whole books" or "real books," reading aloud to solidify relationships. The Clarksons emphasize that learning be used to build these relationships, not for tests or achievements. They delineate five study areas: Discipleship (biblical teaching), Disciplined (basic reading, writing, math), Discussion (liberal arts, history), Discovery (science, nature study, creative arts), and Discretionary (life lessons in and out of the home).

RESOURCES FOR WHOLEHEARTED LEARNING

Educating the WholeHearted Child by Clay and Sally Clarkson explains their child learning and discipleship principles in detail. You can find this and other books by the Clarksons at Whole Heart Ministries, at wholeheart.org.

6.10.4 What is eclectic homeschooling?

A little bit of everything. Many homeschool families start off preferring one method of homeschooling. It is easier for preschoolers to begin with a Charlotte Mason homeschool, for example, or for a student transitioning from public school to use textbooks. But after a while, most families customize homeschooling to fit their needs.

These homeschoolers who call themselves *eclectic* are referring to their own hodgepodge of methods, their own personalized mix of different approaches to suit their various children or their own unique family culture. A family might teach with a Charlotte Mason style but unschool math. Or another family may study mostly classically except for science unit studies. Eclectic homeschooling is another term for just doing things your own way.

• • •

The purpose of this chapter is simply to open your eyes to the many ways you can be teaching your children. Now that you know more about what methods are out there, you're in a much better place to consider which ones appeal to you and fit your family culture. The important point to keep in mind throughout your homeschool journey is that *there is no one right way to homeschool*. You should homeschool the way you teach best for the way your child learns best. You may be at your best with your own mixture of homeschool methods. Or you may be at your best with a different blend of methods each year. Or you may realize partway through the year that something isn't working, so you switch methods completely.

I said at the beginning of this chapter that I would not tell you what method I use. But you probably figured out that I am eclectic. I started off purely textbook and then gradually began experimenting with different materials and methods. I actually found labels for what I was doing *after* I had already begun teaching that way. Kind of backward. But it all just goes to show you it doesn't matter what you are using or how you are using it. You cannot mess this up—because you are training your child for God. You know your *why* and you are gradually working toward your most important priorities. God will not ask you in heaven if you used the correct Montessori materials or taught your child Latin or read aloud the one hundred best books for children.

He only wants you to teach your child about him.

In the next chapter, we'll find how your child *learns* best and how you can find that sweet spot between your best methods and your child's best learning.

7

HOW CHILDREN LEARN

I HAVE SIX DIFFERENT CHILDREN. They each use different materials in different places all over the house, working at different paces with different attitudes toward their curriculum. They even use different curricula altogether. I used to think my homeschool was about struggling with bad attitudes and bad habits and bad books. But over time, one of the many things I have learned from my children is that yes, each one is a different person. And different people learn differently.

Now, you are one of two types of readers. One, you may absolutely love this chapter and take it as your new religion.

Or, two, you may be a hater.

If you are a hater, I love you anyway. I completely understand. Just skip on over to the next chapter, no hard feelings. I'll meet you there in a minute.

Okay, for those of you left wondering why the haters turned the pages so fast, it's this: *learning styles or modalities are so controversial I nearly deleted this entire chapter out of the book.* But, as you'll see, it's a big chapter, and I put a lot of work into it. And also, I really believe there's something here of value.

Not all scientists agree on this subject. Some admit there are different ways students and adults take in new information but don't believe that they learn in different ways. In other words, the way we enjoy interacting with the world is not the same as the way we remember new things. One popular book asserts that the only difference is in how our male and female brains differ.[1] And then there are studies indicating that learning modality is more about student ability and preference than about brain structure or even the act of learning itself.

> We are his workmanship, created in Christ Jesus for good works, which God prepared beforehand, that we should walk in them.
>
> **EPHESIANS 2:10**

And yet, theories on how we learn (both children and adults) have been around for decades and decades. Scientists and educators have devoted a lot of time and research to explaining why some people learn differently than others. Why didn't God make us all learn the same way since we breathe and eat and sleep kind of the same way?

These scientists differ on how learning styles should be categorized and described. In fact, there are dozens of different learning style theories. (Don't leave yet; I'm only going to look at four of them here.) Whether you love or hate learning styles, believe in this one or that one, maybe we can all agree: *we each have different abilities and preferences, and none of us can be put into a box.*

I have seen firsthand that each one of my children is unique. This is a hallmark of homeschooling: teaching each child the way she learns best. And yet I often struggle to find just the right way to communicate new material and help my child succeed.

Sometimes I have tried a new curriculum. I have even blamed my own homeschool method. Some of my friends try co-ops or tutors. So many of us worry our child has a learning disability because he just does not seem to "get it" like other students.

And then I found that many of my problems can be solved by understanding the different ways my child could be learning . . . and that I learn too. Maybe one of these learning style models could help your child over-come those academic barriers and experience success in every subject like they have mine. At the very least, various learning style models illustrate for us how differently we all take in information and communicate that learning to others.

7.1 LEARNING STYLE BASICS

7.1.1 What are learning styles?

Learning styles are all about how we take in new information. What we often call *learning styles* are in actuality what scientists describe as *learning modalities* because they use these as classification systems. Yet, because in the homeschool community we generally refer to these as learning styles, I will use the terms *learning modality* and *learning style* interchangeably. Let's just remember—these ideas are not proven ways all children learn. They are simply ways different scientists view the learning process.

Indeed, these modalities remind us that, just like our brains are differ-ent, our personalities are different, and our interests are different, and the ways we learn and communicate are different. If you have more than one child, you've seen this and become, at times, frustrated by it. Different children just won't look at and retain information the same way. It's so annoying.

7.1.2 Why do I care about learning styles?

To understand how your child is different. It is always hard not to com-pare your own children with each other or your homeschool to another family's or your homeschooling to an institutional school. That's why I keep reminding you and myself that we cannot be comparing. We need to remember that each child may need a different form of communication from us, whether it be words or images or hugs or freedom. Homeschooling is about strengthening family relationships, and these ideas are yet another tool to help with that.

To find out more about yourself. I am a Reading/Writing, Abstract Sequential, Producing mother (wait for it—I'll be explaining in a few pages). This helps me understand why I teach and parent and write the way I do. And it helps me remember not to force my children (or even my long-suffering husband) into my own mold.

To understand that when a child is struggling to learn, it is not always a discipline issue. My son runs outside in between (and even in the middle of) subjects not because he's trying to kill me slowly but because his brain works differently—he needs movement, or he needs space, or he needs daydreaming to process what he is learning. There is a time and a place for me to teach him how to sit and apply himself and follow a schedule, but understanding how he learns best also allows me to give him grace while he is growing and the space he needs to work through new information.

Understanding our children's differences can go a long way toward protecting against impatience and anger. So many times we as parents chalk up our child's learning issues to sin. And of course, rebellion could be an issue. But usually, the struggle is not between your will and your child's will. The battle is over the child's ability to learn her own way.

> Everyone is able to think in words, everyone is able to think in mental images. It's much better to think of everyone having a toolbox of ways to think, and think to yourself, which tool is best?
>
> **DANIEL WILLINGHAM**

To cut down on your frustration. Isn't it hard to teach a child who keeps disappearing? And doesn't the chatterbox seriously drive us crazy? I don't know about you, but I can easily lose my cool when all of my students are acting in a way consistent with their own learning style but the opposite of my own. I get frustrated, I get somewhat critical, I get a little loud (don't judge). Understanding the source of the friction helps me calm down.

To cut down on your child's frustration. A child may be trying to learn our way, yet the stress of it actually hinders her from understanding. In contrast, being allowed to explore concepts her preferred way, or even a variety of ways, can grow her understanding and her enjoyment of learning.

7.1.3 Are learning style models hard to understand and implement?

Not at all. I have been shocked that understanding my students' learning styles and how they differ from my own can actually simplify my homeschooling. By tailoring the curriculum and teaching to the child's natural strengths, I can help him learn faster and easier, no matter what the subject. I can more confidently teach the way I teach best for the way my child learns best.

7.1.4 Do learning style models provide a legitimate way to label my student?

Learning style models are just that—models. As such, they provide a useful way of thinking about how we learn, though they don't explain all the details of the learning process. Yet by categorizing similar styles of learning, we can see trends that will help our students learn to the best of their ability.

And of course, learning styles are not the only important factor in a child's success. Other variables like health, family culture, environment, or subject enjoyment can influence student learning and retention.

7.1.5 Shouldn't my student be able to learn through any learning style?

Surprisingly, no. Many researchers believe a student's learning style or styles are present from birth: that how she learns is an innate part of who she is as an individual. Every researcher I talked to emphasized using one's *own* learning style, not trying to adapt to another one. If these learning styles are truly innate, then both we and our children will always prefer our inborn method of learning and struggle with others. Finding our best way to learn in any situation becomes a valuable tool.

On the other hand, our students will need the ability to adapt to different learning situations throughout life. In various communication and career problems, our young people will not always have control over how information is presented. As our children grow, we can gently help them understand how they enjoy learning and how to adapt to different learning situations.

7.1.6 Will my child become a genius if I teach to his learning style?

Don't we wish. Scientists supporting the validity of learning styles agree that these categories represent one of many factors for student success. Student aptitude is important, but teacher skill, teaching methods, relationships, environment, health, and many other factors also contribute to student learning. Being aware of learning styles is merely one small way to help you understand student differences.

7.1.7 How many learning style models are there?

There are over seventy. Since we typically focus on one way of understanding learning styles, I was surprised to find out that there are so many ideas about how we take in new information, process that information, and utilize it in real-life situations. Four popular learning style models easily applied to homeschooling are the VARK model, the Gregorc Mind Styles model, Willis and Hodson's Learning Style model, and the Dunn and Dunn School-Based Learning Styles model. Since we don't have room in one book to look at all seventy (no book has tried that!), I chose these four because I liked them the best.

7.2 THE VARK MODEL

7.2.1 What is the VARK model?

The one you've heard of. VARK is an expansion of the more commonly known visual/auditory/kinesthetic model of learning, adding a fourth category: reading/writing. Developed by educator Neil Fleming in 1987 along with colleague Charles C. Bonwell, the VARK model explains learning in greater detail than the older visual/auditory/kinesthetic model.

Fleming found from his research of successful student learning in high school and university classrooms that teacher quality and student intelligence had little effect on outcomes. Less talented students could thrive under poor teachers, while bright students could struggle in the same classroom. Similarly, the slower students might learn rapidly under the best of teachers, while the bright

> [Students are] different, not dumb.
>
> **NEIL FLEMING**

students struggled. The correlation between teacher quality and student aptitude did not match as he expected.

Fleming set out to find what, then, enabled students to learn in any teaching situation. He discovered that rather than teaching methods, the students' preferences for communication modes made the difference. He then grouped these preferences into the categories of Visual, Auditory,

Reading/Writing, and Kinesthetic. Fleming also expanded the characteristics of each category with examples of strategies for optimal learning in each mode. This new VARK model then describes the variety of student experiences.

7.2.2 What are visual learners?

Visual learners take in *symbols*. They prefer graphical representations of new material, and they take notes or interact with materials in a graphic way. Your child may be a visual learner if she exhibits some of the following behaviors:

- as a young child, draws a simple picture or doodles on her worksheets before completing them
- in early math, understands graphs intuitively and makes them easily
- draws pictures, symbols, charts, or doodles to take notes
- uses Venn diagrams to compare and contrast information
- prepares for essays with charts or symbols
- sketches hierarchies of government
- makes royal family trees in history class

Your visual learner will probably *not* enjoy the following activities:
- memorizing lists of words
- discussing what she is learning
- reading more than a minimal amount
- writing essays

My oldest son is a visual learner. Even after he learned to read well, he preferred to look at the graphs and diagrams in books. When he began writing paragraphs, he sketched out drawings or charted his ideas before he began. And he was—still is—enamored of our giant pullout time line that includes royal family trees and graphs of civilizations.

He was not a fan of high school literature, and his history essays contained the bare minimum amount of information. We had both literature and history discussions regularly each week, and his notes were charts while his answers were short and to the point. Geometry, trigonometry, and calculus were his favorite subjects.

7.2.3 What are auditory learners?

Auditory learners love the spoken word. They are the chatterboxes of the family. They prefer to learn aloud and to talk about their knowledge. Your child may be an auditory learner if he exhibits some of the following behaviors:

- asks a lot of questions
- asks the questions again
- repeats back what you just told him
- talks to himself, especially while doing his schoolwork
- memorizes by repeating aloud
- enthusiastically participates in learning discussions
- does well in online classes with live participation
- enjoys co-op classes with discussion or debate
- talks about his different ideas for a project or experiment before deciding
- loves to listen to audiobooks
- is frequently told by his siblings to please stop talking

Your auditory learner will probably *not* enjoy the following activities:

- taking online classes with no participation
- studying in a library
- listening to lectures with no participation
- being told to "look it up" when he asks a question

I have an auditory learner whose motormouth sometimes drives the rest of the family crazy. He loves to impress others with his wide vocabulary. He whispers when he reads his literature, he talks about his math, and he mutters over his grammar. As a preschooler, this son listened to the audio series Chronicles of Narnia repeatedly in his room each afternoon until he could recite large portions by heart. Then he moved on to creating his own fantasy tales, stories with many chapters told with great expression to his younger siblings every time they rode in the minivan. He loves words, and words are how he learns best.

7.2.4 What are reading/writing learners?

Reading/writing learners are lovers of the written word. The reading and writing learners are those students you typically think of as visual learners.

Yet reading/writing and visual learners are not the same. Remember, visual learners enjoy graphics, but reading and writing learners love the printed word. Your child may be a reading/writing learner if she exhibits some of the following behaviors:

- enjoys reading independently
- writes more than required
- seems to take off in her schoolwork once she can read and write unassisted
- prefers to read worksheet instructions and complete the paper unassisted
- enjoys reading and collects her own personal library
- makes lists, and perhaps lists of lists
- keeps a journal or book of quotes
- takes notes when listening to a lesson or lecture
- possesses a broad vocabulary
- enjoys researching
- writes essays and research papers easily, even if she does not enjoy the topic
- appreciates it when an online class utilizes a PowerPoint presentation
- learns best if a co-op teacher writes on a whiteboard

Your reading/writing learner will probably *not* enjoy the following activities:

- making mind maps before writing
- studying geometry
- listening to an audiobook that she could read instead
- doing science experiments (she just wants to read the textbook instead)

My older daughter has been a reading/writing learner since preschool. She taught herself to read after one lesson on phonics. Then she could not stop reading beginner books in the house, then every easy reader in the library. Today, she collects her own library in her bedroom, keeps several different journals, and teaches herself any subject in a textbook. She does, though, try to get her younger brother to do her science experiments for her.

7.2.5 What are kinesthetic learners?

Kinesthetic learners are the active students. The kinesthetic learners are often misunderstood. Many parents believe these children simply have too much energy, are distracted easily, need play to learn, and may have ADHD. But in fact, kinesthetic learners may display some of those behaviors because they are trying to find their own way of learning.

Kinesthetic learners have one important goal: they want to learn what is *real*. Their minds are constantly wondering *who*, *what*, *when*, and *where*. These students take in that reality through their four senses—touch, smell, hearing, and sight. Those sensory experiences help them achieve their goal of learning what is real. Your child may be a kinesthetic learner if he exhibits some of the following behaviors:

- touches things, even if you just told him not to
- prefers to read nonfiction books in the children's section and becomes an expert on dinosaurs, thunderstorms, or frogs
- collects items
- learns math by playing with money, counting days on the calendar, or cooking
- tries to perform science experiments before he even knows what the concept is about
- enjoys history, especially reading biographies and reenacting battles
- asks older friends or community workers about their jobs
- eagerly visits historical sites or excavations

Your kinesthetic learner will probably *not* enjoy the following activities:

- reading fiction
- studying algebra
- reading about science instead of doing it
- looking at models of real places

I have a kinesthetic son. And for all of his elementary and high school years, I thought that just meant he was active and preferred climbing on the table while he wrote. His frog farm and gross collection of sea monkeys mystified me. I knew he had to jump around or arrange toys to understand math, but I thought it was just because he needed to move.

What I did not realize was that my son was trying desperately to connect what I was teaching him with real life. This became apparent when we visited the Alamo in San Antonio. Excitedly, my husband and I pointed out the history of the mission, the artifacts in the rooms, and the video about the tragic battle. It's all very Texan and very exciting, but my son remained bored for the entire tour. I was surprised because trips and tours usually thrill him.

"It's not real," he burst out. "They rebuilt it. See, there are even plaques on the ground where the walls used to be. Most of this is not the original mission."

"Would you rather see the rubble left from the battle?" I asked sarcastically.

"Actually, yes," he answered. "That would be real."

Next, we visited a nearby mission. It was not as historically significant, but the beautiful church and small living quarters remained. And my son was *enthralled*. This, at last, was a real historical site that he could touch and see and smell and believe in. He excitedly peeked into every doorway, walked up and down the worn paths, and caressed the old well. He had found a piece of real history.

So I learned to let him go learn his real studies, so to speak. To let him seek the truth, the reality, the experiences, and the events that make life real. Because when he finds these real things, when he can see them and touch them and hear them, then he knows what life is truly about. And he can show the rest of us that reality too.

7.2.6 When does my child develop her VARK learning style?

While she is growing. Contrary to other researchers, Fleming believes a young child will develop a learning preference as she grows into adulthood, and that one's learning style is not a trait set in stone. Fleming cautions against labeling students as they continue to experiment with learning and developing their own preferences. In fact, according to Fleming, children are more likely to be kinesthetic learners. However, few teachers share that style. It seems adults often grow into different preferences. It is important not to label a child as a certain learning style and teach only through that lens.

My young twins switch modes almost every day. They enjoy experimenting with math in real life, they love to read about animals, and they listen to audiobooks with rapt attention. Most of the time, though, they are touching and talking aloud . . . basically making a mess of learning. Which is very fun for them.

7.2.7 What if my child demonstrates characteristics of a couple of these styles?

Fleming calls such a student *multimodal*. In fact, most students—up to 70 percent—demonstrate multiple preferences. A student may have a mixture of styles or may even enjoy using all four. In that case, the student may learn to prefer one learning mode over another for certain academic subjects and not others. And in other cases, he may use more than one mode simultaneously. Fleming cautions that the child should be given ample time to learn in this situation, as he is spending more time processing how he should take in the information.

7.2.8 Should I train my child to use other learning communication styles?

Not at first. Fleming asserts it is important to allow students to use their own preferences—it is how they learn best! Young children, especially, will enjoy learning and retaining information as they explore different ways to learn and settle into how they learn best.

> The fear of the LORD is the beginning of knowledge; fools despise wisdom and instruction.
>
> **PROVERBS 1:7**

As a student grows, especially in high school, she will have ample time to learn in other ways. She will need to study academic subjects that feel unnatural, or she will use a textbook or online class that employs a different teaching style. Simply support your student as she learns other modes as this will become a useful skill for life.

7.3 THE GREGORC MIND STYLES MODEL

7.3.1 What is the Gregorc model?

A learning style model based on the way we see and remember. Anthony Gregorc, PhD, introduced his Mind Styles Model of learning in 1984. Dr. Gregorc bases his model on his scientific research, as well as his many years as a teacher, principal, and professor.

Dr. Gregorc's model describes how people perceive, process, and organize information. Our differences in these areas, he believes, are not learned over time but rather are inherent qualities. He encourages others to understand their own Mind Style to better appreciate their strengths and weaknesses.

7.3.2 How does the Gregorc model characterize learning?

Through two continuums: perceptual ability and ordering ability. These two major categories of learning, according to Dr. Gregorc, affect how we perceive concepts and how we order our learning.

Our *perceptual* preference can be *concrete*, using the five senses, or *abstract*, imagining ideas and the meaning behind occurrences. The concrete and abstract aspects of learning occur along a continuum; they are not static points.

Our *ordering* preference can be described as *sequential*, in which one prefers steps or logical order. It could also tend toward a *random* state, in which a person thinks in chunks or holistically. These traits also appear as a continuum perpendicular to the line of perception, creating four quadrants of learning styles.

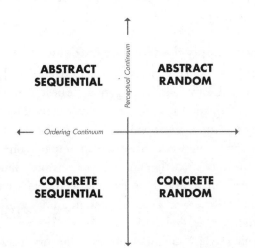

7.3.3 What are the four quadrants of the Gregorc model?

The combination of the continuums of perceptual and ordering ability. The two ideas of perception and ordering combine to form four different types of learners. According to this model, all of us possess each type to a varying degree, but we are created with a dominant style.

The *concrete sequential* learner tends to be very organized. He prefers real-life application and concrete facts. He learns best in a step-by-step method. This learner will thrive on routine.

An *abstract sequential* learner tends to also be organized. She will analyze people and events to learn deeply about them. She loves research and debate. She is a logical, independent learner.

A *concrete random* learner tends to be creative. She will prefer to experiment and follow hunches. She is very intuitive and curious, preferring options and variety. The CR learner finds step-by-step methods stifling.

An *abstract random* learner is also creative, and he will crave freedom in his work. He is a people person with an intuitive sense of the emotions and motivations behind people and events. He imaginatively looks at the whole picture and is sensitive to moods.

According to Dr. Gregorc, every one of us has all four combinations. This permits us to understand each other. It also lets us adjust to different teaching demands. The ability to be fluent in all four categories, however, is extremely rare. Some learners simply cannot or will not adapt. This can lead to frustration.

7.3.4 How can I apply the Gregorc model to student learning?

Through experience. As an experienced teacher, Dr. Gregorc does not endorse testing children to identify their learning style. He believes too many variables could give false information, causing wrong teaching techniques. He cautions against labeling students because both parent and child may make too much of supposed strengths and weaknesses. Instead of tests, he recommends that teachers learn students' strengths and limitations by observation.

Gregorc urges parents also to understand their own learning style with its strengths and weaknesses. This can prevent a one-size-fits-all teaching style. In his studies, Gregorc has found most teachers naturally teach from their own learning style. Sometimes, however, they try to adapt to a different learning style. Long-term attempts to utilize a differing learning style, he believes, can cause frustration and even poor mental health.

If a student has a significantly different learning style from his teacher, Gregorc believes the student should be allowed options for learning. If the student and parent are unable to adapt, he recommends the parent seek help from another teacher.

Dr. Gregorc says, "We are inherently limited so that we can concentrate on what we are designed to do. . . . [Parents] should venture to become lovingly aware of the style abilities of their spouses and family members. A way of doing this is through the lenses of the Mind Styles Model. They will soon learn that adapting to qualitative differences comes naturally and automatically to those with open minds."[2]

In my case, I believe I fall into the abstract sequential quadrant. I carefully organize the schoolbooks and our daily routine. Researching and thinking through this volume for you has been so much fun. Comparing curricula and teaching styles is a joy. And I love to learn alone, curled up on my bed with a few good books. And once I stopped struggling with my abstract random student and gave him the freedom to learn his own way, his academics took off, and I loved homeschooling him again. Recognizing God created me much differently than some of my children has taught me to respect the beauty and complexity with which he has created each of us.

> [My] strongest recommendation for parents is to come to know themselves and respect God's gifts to themselves. This is one of the greatest gifts you can give to your children—an authentic you.
>
> **ANTHONY GREGORC, PHD**

7.4 WILLIS AND HODSON'S LEARNING STYLE MODEL

7.4.1 What is the learning style model published by Willis and Hodson?

An all-inclusive description of learning. Mariaemma Pelullo-Willis, MS, and Victoria Kindle Hodson, MA, have backgrounds in education, speaking, and writing. From their experiences, they developed their own comprehensive model. Interestingly enough, they apply their ideas not only to classroom instruction but also to homeschool education. Their ideas encompass learning *modalities* as well as *dispositions, talents, interests*, and *environment*, all working together as a system to increase learning. All these factors together contribute to the child's unique experiences and outcomes.

7.4.2 What are the five aspects of the Willis and Hodson model?

Five ways to influence learning: dispositions, talents, interests, modalities, and environment. The dispositions are primary, seen in the actions of each student. These five dispositions are performing, producing, inventing, relating/inspiring, and thinking/creating. These are usually expressed as verbs rather than as nouns (performing, not performer) to remind us that we see children *doing* these actions, not being these people. This also reminds us that each individual could display any of these dispositions; they are not held to only one type.

7.4.3 What is the performing disposition?

The key word for the performing student is *action*. These are some characteristics of the performing student:

- moving often
- entertaining and teasing
- behaving in a silly or humorous manner
- using lots of energy

The performing student learns best in the following environment:

- plenty of free time
- unstructured days
- short spurts of work
- plenty of space to move freely
- movement while memorizing
- learning games
- hands-on activities
- opportunities to act out events or processes

My performing son is hilarious. While his siblings are studying hard, he interrupts them with teasing or a joke. History discussions are interspersed with sarcastic comments while he rolls across the floor or throws pillows. I need to put him in a separate room by himself or *no one* in the house will get any schoolwork accomplished. He learns well and is a great student, but I will find, after twenty minutes without supervision, that he has left his books to wander across the house and play with a gadget, to find someone to distract, or even to walk next door and visit the neighbor. He knows every single person on the entire block, and they all think he is a hoot. All his color-coded binders are filled with mixed-up worksheets, tests, and assignment schedules from varying subjects; he has to check every page of them each day to find what he is looking for. Yet if left alone to learn at his own pace, he will accomplish his tasks eventually and accurately.

7.4.4 What is the producing disposition?

The key word for the producing student is *organization*. Other students and teachers admire the producing types, and many who are naturally a different disposition will attempt to become producing students. To allow other students to thrive in their own dispositions, it is very important not to compare them to this type of student. These are some characteristics of a producing student:

- finishing work systematically
- crossing off tasks from a list
- maintaining a routine
- working responsibly
- taking care not to waste time
- disliking change
- needing to be told to take a break
- taking tests well
- setting personal goals
- requiring motivation to work with others
- needing encouragement for creativity

The producing student learns best in the following environment:

- a structured routine
- a quiet area for studying
- drilling
- taking notes and highlighting in books
- filling out workbooks
- classifying and diagramming

I was raised to be producing, so I'm not sure what my true disposition would have been in a less structured environment. I *was* an excellent test-taker; even if I didn't understand the subject matter, most questions seemed to have obvious answers to me. But to this day, I enjoy a routine life with little change, I live by my lists, and I feel guilty about wasting time. While I am working on a project—like writing this book—I become flustered and frustrated if anyone approaches me, even to give me a hug. I'm wearing noise-canceling earbuds alone in my room right now. I have kept the same Bible since I was fifteen because it has my notes in it, and I would be completely lost trying to use a new one.

My oldest daughter has producing tendencies, though I try not to push them on her so she can develop into her own style. She keeps her subjects organized in hanging file folders, outlines her notes for subjects, and races to finish a workbook. She can diagram the living daylights out of any sentence.

7.4.5 What is the inventing disposition?

The key word for the inventing student is *discovery*. This student has many varied ideas and interests, even during one lesson, and this student can also be mistakenly labeled ADD. These are some characteristics of the inventing student:

- asking questions incessantly, especially on irrelevant subjects
- seeming absentminded
- focusing single-mindedly on one project or idea
- enthusiastically making discoveries
- wanting to craft
- preferring to work independently his own way
- enjoying science and engineering
- effectively problem solving
- tending to be serious about his work

The inventing student learns best in the following environment:

- subjects presented from theories or models
- room for experimentation
- opportunities to use inventions
- demonstrations and illustrations
- communication through visualization
- discussion of his own findings
- more projects and less writing
- flexibility with area and time

- a timer to remind him to stop when necessary
- help learning with others
- parental patience
- validation

True fact: I don't have an inventing student in my family. I cannot imagine the mess and chaos, nor the joy of discovery. Many students growing with this disposition are considered bad students, especially when compared with the producing disposition. Yet the world would be so much poorer without Johannes Gutenberg, Benjamin Franklin, Thomas Edison, the Wright brothers, Henry Ford, Bill Gates, and many more who have enriched us all with their own unique gifts.

7.4.6 What is the relating/inspiring disposition?

The key word for the relating/inspiring student is *interaction*. This is the chatterbox student, the one whose mouth you think you may want to tape shut to get any work done. These are some characteristics of the relating/ inspiring student:

- talking and becoming gifted communicators
- demonstrating team spirit
- behaving kindly and thoughtfully
- seeking approval
- possessing social intuition
- giving others personal attention
- caring for the hurting or those with problems
- motivating herself and others to volunteer or contribute to causes
- enjoying studying the humanities

The relating/inspiring students learn best in the following environment:

- read-alouds
- "what would you do" questions about the subject
- group discussion, especially arguing opposing viewpoints
- difficult subjects tackled in a group environment
- subject matter related to how it affects the lives of others
- the chance to help others with their assignments
- constant affirmation

I have three students with the Relating disposition. One will talk anyone's ear off and believes with all her heart that every single person in her life is her best friend. She intuitively finds a "special" Sunday school classmate, usually someone with learning disabilities or special needs, and gently helps him participate in activities and feel welcome.

Another daughter ran for youth group president on the platform of building team spirit and reaching out in the community. She remembers not only birthdays but also significant dates in the lives of every member of her family. She supports a child through Compassion International and has visited him twice. She plans to go into early childhood education or social work.

7.4.7 What is the thinking/creating disposition?

The key word for the thinking/creating student is *creativity*. I know, that's kind of on the nose, but there you are. This student may seem very similar to the inventing student, but she is not really that interested in practical applications. She creates because she has ideas she wants to express.

These are some characteristics of the thinking/creating student:
- thinking quietly and deeply
- possessing imagination
- daydreaming
- seeming to not pay attention to the lesson at hand
- entertaining herself
- spending lots of time in a fantasy world
- pursuing the arts
- becoming moody if interrupted
- developing interests in abstract ideas and philosophy
- excelling in literature and the arts

The thinking/creating students learn best in the following environment:
- plenty of unscheduled time to wonder
- a place to work alone
- help making lists and keeping appointments
- help interacting in group learning
- opportunities to draw maps or pictures for history or math
- materials to make projects or posters for science

- music while doing homework to fill the need for art in the background
- doodling
- alone time after studies

I have a purely thinking/creating son. These lists describe the way he has interacted with the world his entire life. As a preschooler, he had two imaginary playmates and a make-believe wife and children who all lived in his closet. They have moved away, but over a decade later, he still keeps in touch with them.

Today, every time I turn around from giving that preteen boy an assignment, he runs outside in the backyard to twirl around talking to himself and his imaginary soldiers. He makes up lore about a fantasy-land and has drawn several maps to explain where each continent and city is located. He is constantly hiding away from the rest of the family, and he considers it a reward if I send him to his room. He does well in his subjects when allowed to daydream about them and to intersperse his studies with imaginative pursuits. His retention improves if I can find a way to relate a new subject matter to his current imaginary land or friend. After his schoolwork is finished, he spends a good hour writing his fantasy novel.

7.4.8 What do Willis and Hodson say about learning modalities?

The model is incomplete. Willis and Hodson emphasize that the dispositions are only one part of the learning process along with talents, interests, learning modality, and environment. So yes, Willis and Hodson do write that modalities contribute to the student's entire learning style. The modalities they teach in their writing include the visual/auditory/kinesthetic method, though they describe modalities in terms closer to Fleming's VARK model.

7.5 DUNN AND DUNN LEARNING STYLE MODEL

7.5.1 What is the Dunn and Dunn learning style model?

A model which focuses on the conditions necessary for learning. In the sixties, Dr. Rita Dunn (EdD) and her husband, Dr. Kenneth Dunn, developed their learning style model. They were working in special needs education, particularly with students who had visual and auditory impairments. The Dunns discovered that changes to the students' education process greatly helped the students to learn and retain information. These researchers then began applying the same principles in other classroom situations to develop their system. Dr. Rita Dunn brought the model to mainstream use through teacher education, writings, and lectures.

Dr. Dunn emphasized that students do not struggle to learn because of the curriculum. They struggle because of how the information is presented. If the student is taught the way he learns best and is allowed to interact with the new information the way he prefers, Dr. Dunn asserted, he will achieve his learning potential. She believed strongly that learning is not about how difficult the subject matter is, but rather about how the lesson is presented.

Dr. Dunn went so far as to say that not allowing a student to work within his own learning style is morally wrong. She believed that many schools and teachers were frustrating students and preventing them from learning.

7.5.2 What are the five aspects of the Dunn and Dunn Learning Style?

The five areas of learning that affect student performance. Each child, the Dunns believe, is born with environmental, emotional, sociological, physiological, and psychological preferences that impact how she learns. When a student makes the most of her preferences, she learns more easily and retains information better.

7.5.3 What are the environmental aspects of learning?

The student's preferences in regard to the room itself. Each student has preferences in his learning environment, particularly in how his work space affects his five senses. He may prefer bright light or dim. He may work well in a bustling atmosphere, prefer background music, or need complete quiet. He may be sensitive to the temperature in the room. He likely has a preference in how he sits—or whether he does so.

One of my sons, for instance, learns well in a bright, sunlit room; if it's cloudy or dim, he can't concentrate. He likes soft music in the background and not too many distractions from other people. He often grabs a sweatshirt before working on his handwriting. He can sit in a chair if he is doing something easy, but when he concentrates, he lies over the table or stands.

7.5.4 What are the emotional aspects of learning?

How your student connects to learning. This may come out in how independent she appears. She may need a lot of external motivation or rewards, or she may be internally motivated. She may be very competitive in her accomplishments, or she may only compete with herself, trying to do better than previously.

Her emotions also apply to the task itself. She may or may not find it easy to persist when the task becomes difficult. She may or may not connect easily to a sense of personal responsibility for the lesson.

Finally, her emotions play into how she works. Whether she prefers to have structure and routine or to instead work freely depends on her learning style.

My older daughter is internally motivated, unlike most of her siblings. She is very competitive, asking to see the grades her older brother received when he took the same course. She is fairly persistent and takes personal responsibility for completing her work and for getting good grades. She makes her own learning routine, and when the day deviates from her plan she will usually wait until the next day to try again. When a lesson isn't well structured, with step-by-step directions, she easily becomes frustrated. In that case, she looks for another explanation from a different source.

7.5.5 What are the sociological aspects of learning?

How your student prefers to work with others. Your student may prefer to work alone or in groups. Some students work well in pairs but not in larger numbers. Some learn well from their peers while others rely on adult teachers.

I wish all my children were independent learners who work best on their own. But even homeschool students sometimes need a group. My middle son thrives in a homeschool discussion, often starting an argument over a finer point of worldview just to keep the dialogue going. He began understanding chemistry better when he started bringing his younger siblings into his experiments.

7.5.6 What are the physiological aspects of learning?

The sensory way the student learns. Dr. Dunn's description of physiological areas of learning strongly resembles the VARK model. Indeed, the student's visual, auditory, written, and kinesthetic preference of learning plays entirely into the application of her learning style.

The physiological category also includes a student's preference for a certain time of day for studying. The mobility of the student is also included—how much physical activity he needs during and between subjects.

I prefer both learning and teaching in the morning. But one of my children—the one who is always the opposite learning style from me—learns better in the afternoon. And he can't sit still. In the middle of a subject he just wanders off, and he's always finding an activity—even a chore—he *needs* to do before the next assignment. If I make him go right from one assignment to another without stopping, he becomes extremely frustrated and mentally shuts down. I now just let him work at his own pace every day.

7.5.7 What are the psychological aspects of learning?

The child's cognitive processing. Does the child focus on the big picture or the details? Does he wait and think about a new concept, or does he jump in and learn from mistakes? As in other areas of learning, this difference can cause frustration for the parent. Instead of immediately assuming a child's hesitation or failure to understand is a discipline issue, it helps both the student and the teacher to stop and consider how the student best thinks through new concepts.

One of my children does not love details like most tests require. He is a big-picture learner. He can tell me an emotional story about an event in history or a scientific discovery, but he won't remember exact dates or names. However, he clearly understands the relevance to his life, current events, and worldview.

7.5.8 How do the five aspects of learning work together?

In relation to each other. Every individual, Dr. Dunn taught, has multiple preferences within each of these categories. She estimates students and adults have between six and fourteen preferences that should be aligned in order to learn optimally.

That is a lot to know and use properly, right?

Dr. Dunn developed tests to evaluate each student on her own particular learning needs so a classroom teacher could optimize the teaching for each one individually. Obviously, not all schools can implement her program. However, my twins attended public school for one semester during our foster-to-adopt process. One of the teachers gave students a wide variety of options for learning, including standing tables, balance balls, and pillows on the floor. While she taught, students were allowed to move around the room to their comfort, provided they were quiet and did not disturb others. She kept pets and fish in the room so students could look at something interesting while thinking about their work. She also allowed the students to complete their assignments throughout the day using a variety of materials. My son thrived in that classroom, and I learned a lot about giving my child the freedom to learn his own way. Since he began homeschooling for good, I have tried to give such freedoms to my own children and have seen great results.

7.5.9 How can I implement the Dunns' learning model at home?

Through your relationships. Without using the Dunn test, you can start with trial and error, attempting different approaches to environmental and physiological aspects in the beginning. An older student may naturally gravitate toward and even ask for his own unique learning situations.

A strength of homeschooling is the ability to tailor these five areas to each child, a task quite difficult in a classroom environment. As you grow to understand your child's learning preferences, you can allow him to work in the environment he loves best, attacking new ideas from the perspective and methods that come naturally to him. In larger families, you can give each of your children the freedom to learn in his own way.

Dunn gave an example of videotaping a lecture or lesson to allow the student to listen again later; she said this would help auditory learners, those who preferred to take time thinking about a new concept, and students who needed to watch the teacher's face again to understand what she was saying.

Another example was giving the student colored pencils. She said depending on his learning preferences, a student may draw a picture to internalize the lesson or mark up the book to make lessons easier to understand.

In her own classrooms, Dr. Dunn often allowed students to choose their own method of evaluation. They could demonstrate knowledge by taking a test or writing a paper. But they could also give an oral presentation or make a project to show their learning.

Most importantly, Dr. Dunn encouraged her students to find their own learning style and to use it confidently. When a student freaked out about a difficult subject, she would calmly remind him to use his own style to learn it well.

7.6 LEARNING STYLES AND TALENTS

7.6.1 What do learning styles teach us about talents?

Learning style is completely independent of talent. All of these researchers emphasize that their ideas are only one piece of the learning puzzle. There is much more to discover about how we learn, and we will never fully understand how our mind works alongside relationships, ability, background, environment, personality, and more.

In fact, Willis and Hodson emphasize that talent and interest are two very different things. A student may be talented in an area, and yet his interests lie in something completely different. As parents, it is hard to avoid the temptation to push a child to work on a talent to the exclusion of his interest.

> What is most surprising about talents is that we can be very gifted in a particular area and not have the least interest in it.
>
> **MARIAEMMA WILLIS AND VICTORIA KINDLE HODSON**

In my case, I demonstrated a talent in music from a young age. My parents encouraged this through expensive violin and piano lessons and music performance opportunities and competitions all over the country. While I enjoyed the success and attention, as a young adult I began to question *what do I really want to do?* It was nearly a decade before I began writing. And I would certainly have to enjoy it to continue this long book, right? I enjoy playing music, but I love to write and cannot stop.

• • •

So what can we learn from learning style models?

A lot. Through these and dozens more learning style models, scientists and educators describe learning in different ways. Yet all of these models have several findings in common.

No one learning style perfectly describes the mind. God's creation is so mysterious, it has taken decades and over seventy models to even attempt to describe how we learn. No one expert or model can completely describe the complex miracle of learning.

Nature versus nurture doesn't matter very much. Researchers estimate at least 60 percent of learning style is inherent in a child's personality.[3] Though some measure of learning style can and probably will be adapted over time, maximizing his own style helps most. Also, teaching him to appreciate how he learns best will ensure a lifetime of learning.

Teachers need to understand their own learning. How we learn affects how we teach. And furthermore, understanding how we learn gives us insight into how our child learns. This is why some learning style theorists cater exclusively to teachers.

No one is an expert on their child's learning style. Almost every learning model requires a specific evaluation for recommendations. This is not to definitively prescribe how all learning must take place. Instead, it helps eliminate the bias we have toward ourselves and toward our child. Whether we choose to test our child in any one style or prefer to carefully observe his behaviors, we can know this: our child is unique, and only God knows exactly how his mind is created.

Learning styles help our child learn independently. That is the entire purpose of understanding our child's learning style—to use these strategies regularly. Learning style is all about adapting to the student's own strengths. This concept—helping our child learn the way she learns best—is a component of strong homeschooling.

Curriculum is not important. Not one learning style researcher we discussed suggests changing materials to increase learning. Rather, they show us how students interact with new concepts to better understand them. This is a good reminder that we can just relax and teach the way we teach best for the way our child learns best.

Teachers need not be experts. Every model was tested in various classrooms and with different abilities and ages of students. None found that the education of the teacher affected student performance. Instead, every researcher achieved positive results by helping the student himself customize his education.

Learning is an intimate relationship. Teachers need to know students personally, researchers assert. Even those who advocate student learning style testing admit that the teacher's relationship with the student is most important. When a teacher truly knows a student, she will be better able to pave the way for learning.

In other words, learning style models teach us what we already know is true: homeschooling allows us to build the relationship and environment that makes the most of the mind God created.

8

BOOKS AND STUFF

NEW HOMESCHOOLERS usually equate *homeschooling* with *curriculum*. They put a lot of pressure on themselves to choose the correct books so they will "homeschool right." Over time, however, families begin to realize that *books don't teach children—parents teach children*. The most important lessons are not contained in magic books or must-have courses; they are lived out day by day.

So when a scared homeschool mom asks me which curriculum to choose, I tell her to stop panicking and just pick one. Any one. Then get started homeschooling. By trial and error, experience and observation, you'll become aware of what works for your family and why. The more you understand your own unique teaching style and your student's learning style, the more confidently you will choose materials that work for you. You will teach the way you teach best for the way your child learns best (see chapters 6 and 7).

I have changed curricula umpteen million times. And I'll use different things next year. There's one curriculum I use for the basis of everything:

my key history guide. But everything else I change with the student, with the family situation, with the sale I found at the bookstore.

My teaching style factors into what I enjoy working with. My student's learning style contributes to what materials he enjoys most. But for everything that I have tried, I have found ways to tweak it or change it altogether to fit our needs. I have completely given up worrying about what to buy next. I just pick something that looks like it will probably work and then go with it.

Worst-case scenario, you can always throw something out and try something new. I put a science curriculum in storage a few weeks into it; the program didn't work for my child, but I thought I might use it later. I didn't, and then I sold it. Yes, there's this financial pressure to get things right the first time. But like I said, almost anything can be adapted to what you need. Just go with it and try something else next time.

You aren't married to the curriculum. You didn't promise to love, honor, cherish, and obey it; you didn't promise to keep it until death. Don't hesitate to break up with your curriculum.

But you do need curricula.

8.1 BUYING CURRICULA

8.1.1 Where do I get curricula?

Wherever you found this book, homeschool curricula are nearby. You can purchase homeschool resources at many local stores and online retailers. You can do a quick internet search for your specific needs like "third-grade

---

PLACES TO BUY CURRICULA AND OTHER
HOMESCHOOL BOOKS

- Barnes & Noble

- Mardel

- Half Price Books

- Christianbook

- Amazon

- Online direct from the publisher

- Homeschool conventions

- Library book sales

- Used from other homeschool moms

THINGS TO CONSIDER BEFORE YOU BUY A CURRICULUM

- What are your favorite teaching styles (see chapter 6)?
- What ways does your child enjoy learning (see chapter 7)?
- Do you enjoy lecturing, reading, or crafting with your children?
- Does your child prefer listening to stories, reading alone, or doing hands-on activities?
- What books and materials do you already have around the house?
- Is there a homeschool friend nearby who can loan you materials?
- Where and when are your local homeschool conventions?
- What is your budget for the year?
- Can you save some funds for changes midyear?
- Does your first-choice curriculum have free samples available? A low-budget option? A return policy?

homeschool math" or "high school homeschool chemistry" to find more publishers than you can possibly use and more curriculum reviews than you can possibly read.

You can hunt down curricula in other ways. Sign up for mailing lists. Ask homeschool parents what they use and if you can borrow the product to look at. Browse the advertisements in homeschool magazines. Attend your local homeschool convention. There you can meet homeschool publishers, handle their materials, and ask questions about their program. This is a great way to compare different approaches and find what most appeals to you. Look at appendix F to find homeschool resources and materials that may be right for you, as well as lists of conventions to consider attending.

8.1.2 How do I choose my first curriculum?

Just pick something and get started! Many homeschool parents sweat their first choice, spending days and weeks researching curricula and spending thousands of dollars on books only to find those materials don't work for them. And then they are tempted to quit homeschooling altogether.

Instead, recognize that your first year or two of homeschooling is more about *finding what works for your family*. Just like your students, you don't need to know everything in the beginning. Look at a few options and choose something simple and appealing. Then jump in. You will likely change methods and materials as you grow to know your own teaching preferences and your child's learning style.

Most of all, be careful not to spend too much money. The more you spend, the more you will feel obligated to that investment, even if it doesn't work. Instead, set a small budget and enjoy the flexibility. Don't hesitate to try something different midyear.

8.1.3 What types of curricula are available to me?

So many more than your old-school textbooks. When we think of curricula, we usually think of what we used in brick-and-mortar schools. Remember the hardback books wrapped in brown paper bags? Am I the only one old enough to remember mimeographed worksheets? Today, you have many more options from which to choose:

Textbooks. This may be what you are comfortable using at first, because it may feel familiar. There are so many textbook companies available to you, many listed in appendix F. Many come with a teacher's guide, workbooks, and/or tests. Many online classes utilize textbooks, in fact. The downside is that textbooks can seem boring, and the course may be more difficult to customize for your student. However, it is a great way to get started while you are learning how you teach best and how your student learns best. All the beginning homeschoolers I know started with textbooks. I myself use textbooks for math, grammar, and high school science. We talked about how to teach with textbooks in section 6.2.

A boxed curriculum. This is an extremely easy way to get started. You can order an entire set of curriculum that includes everything your student needs for an entire year. No worrying about what to order or if you have enough. Like textbooks, this is a one-size-fits-all approach that is not customized for your student. It does, however, guide you through what to do each step of the way.

Some curriculum companies offer boxed sets for classical or Charlotte Mason–style learning. These include lesson plans to coordinate all the subjects, along with the sets of books the child will read. This can help you put your teaching style together without wondering what book to read next.

Boxed curriculum is more expensive than many other options, but some companies allow you to customize the order based on your budget. Ordering a curriculum set could help you jump in if you are afraid to choose your own products. When I first started homeschooling, I began with a boxed curriculum before I learned what works best for us.

Online courses. This is another extremely popular choice for beginning homeschoolers. It is so popular, in fact, that public school online courses are now available. Most homeschoolers I know use online courses for at least part of their homeschooling. Online classes are especially helpful for more difficult subjects. Online classes are not all created equal. Some include materials, and some require textbook purchases. Some include class discussion and some are lectures. Some are teacher-graded and some are parent-graded. Some include only homework and others require class presentations. Before signing up for an online course, be sure to find out exactly what is included. Online courses can be pricey, so I use them sparingly. I have enrolled my teens in honors science classes. I was particularly impressed with a literary analysis class they took that was graded on both class participation and insight into the material.

Digital classes. Digital classes are similar to online courses except there is no live component. Classes are usually recorded, so you and the student are responsible for the work and grading. This is also useful for difficult subjects or for teaching a busy household. One of my sons has taken both a science and a math course that included digital teaching. He loved his science DVD. The math class was much less helpful, so he switched to studying the textbook on his own. Digital classes are good for that flexibility.

> The things I want to know are in books; my best friend is the man who'll get me a book I ain't read.
>
> **ATTRIBUTED TO ABRAHAM LINCOLN**

While my middle son is living in another country, he is homeschooling almost completely online. His courses are self-paced and mostly self-grading. He reads books and articles, watches videos, takes online quizzes, and prints out tests. His relatives proctor the tests and sign them for me. I grade the essays and keep an eye on his progress, and we discuss his learning weekly. He keeps scans of his tests, screenshots of his online quizzes, and copies of his written work in files we share online. We also share a spreadsheet online to track his progress and grades. Online homeschooling allows him the flexibility to pursue extra-curricular interests and goals.

The library. Many homeschoolers in the eighties started out with no curriculum at all. The parents taught their children with a Bible, a library card, and paper and pencil. And the children turned into geniuses who invented plumbing and the internet. Okay, I kid. But some of them are the smartest people I have ever met. You can trust your instincts and create your own path for learning.

Figure it out yourself. After homeschooling for a while, you may slide into your own unique collection of materials. The longer you homeschool, the more comfortable you will become with buying what you use best and what your student learns from best. That's the beauty of homeschooling.

Remember, you are not chained to your curriculum selection. With the exception of some online courses and co-op materials, you can just throw what you are doing out the window when it doesn't work.

8.1.4 What if I choose the wrong books?

You absolutely cannot mess this up. No matter what you choose, you have the freedom to use it—or only parts of it—the way that suits you and your student best. But to increase your confidence, here are some suggestions:

Try it out ahead of time. Many companies will offer you a sample of several days, maybe a couple of weeks, of their product. If you don't find a sample online, contact the publisher and ask for one. You can not only look it over but even try it out on your student to see if it fits. I began using a major portion of my curriculum after trying out a sample that unexpect-edly blew my mind.

Check out your friend's stuff. Several times a friend has said, "Lea Ann, can I borrow your book?" or even, "Lea Ann, can I come to your house and look at your homeschool bookshelf?" Find a homeschool mom you like a little and just ask. Sharing and comparing can be a lot of fun. Most moms have done it. I know I have.

Go meet the publisher. The easiest way to do this is to attend a home-school convention. The plethora of publishers there will be more than happy to show you their product and how it works. Many offer samples and discounts. Another way to meet a publisher is to actually visit them. I drove to a publishing company once and got a tour of the warehouse. They changed my mind about middle school math and science. Finally, search

A FEW SUPPLIES TO HELP YOU GET STARTED

Early learning (preschool through first grade)
- simple phonics program, letter flash cards, or letter magnets
- small toys to count, shapes to sort
- library card for picture books, audiobooks, and story time
- paper, pencils, and crayons

Elementary (second through fifth grade)
- grammar workbook
- library card for literature and for researching science, history, and other topics
- math workbook
- paper and pencils for writing and/or copying practice

Middle school (sixth and eighth grade)
- grammar or writing workbook
- library card for literature and for researching science, history, and other topics
- math workbook
- paper and pencils for writing and/or copying practice

High school (ninth through twelfth grade)
- English grammar, writing, and/or literature curriculum
- math curriculum
- science curriculum
- history curriculum

See chapters 10 through 13 for more information on each grade level.

for the publisher on social media. They will be giving information on their feed, offering samples and giveaways, and answering your questions.

Stop worrying. No mother has ruined her child forever because she chose the wrong curriculum. Even if you choose something you don't like and don't have the budget to replace that year, you are free to change how you use it. Use it as an outline and fill in with materials you like better. Pick and choose which parts to use. Sell it used and try something else. You don't have to do what the curriculum tells you to do; do what you want with confidence. I have changed curriculum midyear and never regretted it.

8.1.5 How can I save money on curricula?

Stay on budget or you'll buy everything out there. There are many ways to spend money on homeschooling. You will find several useful tools, resources, and planners. There are many beautiful books and specialized curricula. At first, you may want them all.

Be sure to set a conservative budget before you begin shopping. Make a list of what you *need* and another list of what you *want*. Consider saving some funds for midyear changes.

Sign up for email lists from your favorite publishers to stay informed of sales and coupons. Save on shipping by buying from vendors at homeschool conventions. Look for used bookstores and library sales. Ask your local homeschool support group if they have swap days. See if a homeschool friend will allow you to borrow some items. And join online used book sale sites and Facebook groups for great deals.

Most of all, remember that the latest and greatest curriculum will not ensure homeschool success. Your own dedication and loving relationship with your child are the most important factors in learning.

8.2 USING CURRICULA

8.2.1 How do I make lesson plans?

The way you want and only if you want. Classroom teachers need lesson plans to coordinate learning for an entire classroom while ensuring the principal and other supervisors know what is happening during each day. That's not how you roll.

Homeschool teachers only need lesson plans for their own use, to remember if projects are coming up or what assignments to check. In some states, homeschool parents may use lesson plans as part of their state-mandated portfolio. So lesson plans look different for every homeschool mom.

Lesson plans can be as complicated as detailed instructions for every lesson every day, or they can be as simple as a to-do list in a spiral notebook. There are homeschool lesson plan books for listing every assignment each student accomplishes, and there are lesson plan software programs to digitally track student progress and grades. Some curriculum workbooks include a short lesson plan for each day at the beginning of the book. Many homeschool families choose to skip lesson plans altogether and just keep doing the next assignment or worksheet every day. You can find lesson planners and planning software listed in appendix F.

I made detailed lesson plans in my early years, filling the paper planner grid with objectives and assignments in itty-bitty handwriting. As my children grew and I became more confident, I gradually simplified what I wrote.

Now, I am very bare bones. In a spiral notebook, I make a list of the reading assignments for each child. I make short notes about what I want to work on with the younger children and any supplies I might need. Then at the bottom of the page, I list all the subjects we cover. I check off that list when I review my older students' independent work at the end of the week. Most weeks, I spend about thirty minutes lesson planning for five students, elementary through high school.

For subjects my children study from a workbook, like their grammar, I plan the entire year in the workbook table of contents itself (see section 5.2 for more on homeschool planning). First, I highlight all the places where there are tests and quizzes. Then I divide the assignments in half, making two semesters. I divide each of those semesters in half to mark off the quarters. Then I take each section and mark off weekly assignments, trying to make each week more or less equal in work. This way, I never need to make a lesson plan for that subject for the entire year.

> ## LESSON-PLANNING TIPS
>
> There are several ways you might choose to plan your lessons:
>
> - Simplify the assignment given in the teacher book.
> - Jot down the main topic or idea you want to focus on.
> - List reading or worksheet pages.
> - Write down what your child learned after the fact.
> - A combination of all of the above.

Lesson plans are helpful if you live in a state that requires detailed reporting. In this case, homeschool parents may keep retroactive lesson plans, recording what the student completed at the end of each school day. Check with your state homeschool organization or Home School Legal Defense Association online (hslda.org) for your state's regulations.

8.2.2 How often do I make lesson plans?

As often as you want. I used to make lesson plans one month ahead of time. Then I cut back to two weeks ahead of time. Now I usually make plans for the week ahead of me so I can see what is coming up.

In some subjects, I don't need to make lesson plans because the material is already broken up into lessons or has a study schedule in the front of the book. Other subjects I divide into lessons at the beginning of the year.

My friends make lesson plans yearly, quarterly, monthly, or weekly. You can plan your subjects however best fits your teaching style and your teaching schedule.

8.2.3 What records do I need to keep?

Each state has its own homeschool regulations. Some require detailed records and reporting. Many, like my state of Texas, require none at all. Your state homeschool organization can answer questions about your state's homeschool regulations. You can also check with Home School Legal Defense Association online (hslda.org).

8.2.4 Do I need a schoolroom and desks and whiteboards and wall charts?

In a word, *no.* It may be difficult to remember for a while, but homeschooling is *not* like school. You do not need to decorate your home like a classroom to create a learning environment.

Some homeschool families enjoy decorating a study space with wall maps and desks and large bookshelves. This can help keep the mess of learning contained in one area. Pinterest is full of creative schoolroom ideas for homeschoolers.

Most homeschool families study all over the house . . . and all over town. The kitchen table, living room sofa, family minivan, and cozy bed are wonderful places to enjoy learning together.

8.2.5 Where do I store all this stuff?

Anywhere and everywhere. In Luke chapter 12, Jesus tells a parable about a foolish rich man who boasted that he was so successful that he would tear down his barns and build bigger barns to hold all the earthly wealth he had accumulated. This exemplifies the never-ending quest of homeschool moms to find bigger bookshelves at deep discount prices to hold the growing collection of books from discount bookstores. I have six overflowing bookcases, and I'm trying to figure out where to put another one.

Besides bookshelves in nearly every room of the house, homeschool parents find creative places to store homeschool materials. Some families have shelves or storage containers in each child's room. Others have dedicated shelves for each student's materials. Minimalists may limit each student to one backpack of items or even a neat stack under a dining room chair.

After a few years of homeschooling, you will become more familiar with what you need to keep and what you can give away or sell. Whether or not you will *want* to depart with your beloved books is another question altogether.

•　•　•

Several years ago, I drove across town to my local homeschool bookstore for their big sale. Excitedly, I bought big, expensive sets of history and science materials I thought that I would use in six months.

Then just a month later, I changed my mind. I found other products that I thought suited my teaching style. So I bought them. *I didn't even remember the curriculum I had stored in Rubbermaid containers in the garage.*

So, the next school year came, and I pulled out the containers to look for what I already had and what books I needed. And sure enough, I had two history programs and two science programs.

I was wracked with guilt. How could I have spent my meager homeschool budget on these huge, expensive sets I didn't even want? And then I bought more? Argh.

I confessed my sin to my husband. And surprisingly, he was not upset. He's used to my forgetting everything I do. Anyway, he asked me if I could do something with the extra curricula.

Yup. I sold it back to the homeschool bookstore. Then I felt much better.

Books are not your bosses. You can use them how you want. You can still be free to homeschool your own way.

PART THREE

GROWING AND LEARNING

"IS MY CHILD BEHIND?"

I see that question posed on Facebook all the time—followed by the comment "My child is behind in math" (or what subject have you). I groan every time I read that.

Behind what?

What is our standard for "on track"? Is it the public school across town? The curriculum publisher? The homeschool child at church? Another child in our family?

I've been guilty of comparing too. I want to know if my child is doing well, just like you do. We all want to make sure we are good teachers, that our children are quick learners, that our homeschooling is *good*.

My firstborn was a freak as an infant. He did freakish things like talking at four months, feeding himself at five months, and walking as soon as he crawled. He was strutting around the room, speaking in full sentences, at his first birthday party. People stared and pointed when he strolled down the grocery aisles. I was proud of him but, boy, was he a weird baby.

On the other hand, my third-born child wasn't talking after his first birthday. The boy just sat there and stared at you, occasionally grunting and gesturing. My doctor thought he had a hearing problem. Then suddenly, one day, he started speaking in intelligible sentences. He just wasn't going to try until he knew he could succeed.

My children have all walked at different ages, talked at different ages, read at different ages, memorized multiplication facts at different ages, studied algebra at different ages. Does that mean some of them are advanced and some of them are slow? Not at all. They were each within the wide range of regular child development. They were normal and they were themselves.

Is your child behind? Probably not. Is your child gifted? Probably not (don't hate me). My early-talker is not a fluent public speaker; he just got an early start. My first reader is a voracious reader, but her siblings who began reading at a much older age now read for hours each day. The exact year does not matter at all.

So this entire "my child is several chapters behind in math" or "my child is six and can't read easy readers" is just nonsense. Instead of looking at arbitrary standards for academics, we need to keep in mind the broad time line of growth and development.

Children do not grow at the same rate. Their gifts and abilities may vary widely. This is especially true of those with learning difficulties, special needs, or a history of trauma. These children should never be measured by a standard. Instead, we can gently encourage them to continue growing right from where they are, going at their own rate.

In this section, we will discuss how children tend to grow and develop both in character and in academics. In chapter 9, we'll look at what intelligence and grade level really mean and then outline the basic growth stages children go through. Then, in the subsequent chapters, we'll look at every stage in detail, outlining physical and spiritual development. In all those stages, too, we'll list milestones for each academic subject and answer common questions that may arise. These descriptions are generalizations that hopefully will give you confidence that your child is healthy and your teaching is on point.

No matter what your child's strength and background, please hold the following chapters loosely. If they comfort you that your child is doing well, then I'm glad. If they cause you concern, don't hesitate to find a second opinion. Turn to chapter 16 if you suspect your child has special needs. And above all, remember that your child is a gift, a beautiful creation growing just as God intended.

9

WHAT GRADE ARE WE IN?

MY OLDER DAUGHTER told me last month, "Every time we ever changed churches or activities, I didn't know what class to go into. I just tried to find other kids my age and follow them."

My son tried this once, following his best friend into a new Sunday school class. "What grade are you in?" asked the teacher.

"Sixth grade. I'm just a little younger."

"What school do you go to?"

"I'm homeschooled."

"Are you *sure* you are in sixth grade? Homeschoolers don't have grades."

He just stood there, speechless, homeschool logic used against him.

One of the most dreaded questions posed to homeschoolers (and their mothers) is *what grade are you in?* No matter how long we have been home-schooling, we have to stop and count on our fingers and try to picture the front of the language workbook and remember what Sunday school class we're attending and recall what year the child was born (take the square root, multiply by 2, add 5 . . .). It's just too much math. We're *something* grade.

We know what age each child is. We usually know if they are preschool, elementary, middle school, or high school. We have a fairly good grasp of their physical development. But that specific grade number? It just eludes us. And even once a number is settled on, we just shrug it off. Grades are relative around here.

Schoolchildren, however, are strictly defined by their grade levels. Not just Sunday school but academic classes and even sports teams are divided into grades. Then each child is "on track" or "ahead a little bit" or "falling behind." Parents and teachers recognize there is a wide range of abilities within each one-year increment.

This is why grade levels don't work well. All children develop at different rates, so standardizing is not always effective. The strength of homeschooling is not standardizing a child's education, but rather teaching him how he learns best. So my son might be in his second year of prealgebra and in middle school science and high school writing and still call himself sixth grade at church. He pretty much gets to be whatever "grade" he wants to be. It's another perk of homeschooling.

Your child's progress throughout his academics depends on so much more than finishing one workbook and moving on to the next. There's his inborn ability, his natural gifts, his rate of growth, his learning environment. Year-by-year measurements tend to be too myopic. A big-picture view of each stage, however, will give you an idea of his overall progress while eliminating the "Am I behind?" stress. This chapter and the ones that follow will, I hope, change your mind about "grades" and also help you to relax and enjoy your child's growth.

9.1 GRADE LEVEL MEASUREMENT

9.1.1 What is a grade level, anyway?

The basic academic standard of what school administrators have decided the average students of that approximate age in general classrooms across the country should be studying. But on second thought, there is no such thing as an average child (I don't know about yours, but each of mine is uniquely special and uncommonly good-looking). And we all know that every school, every classroom, and every child is different. One of the pitfalls of standardized education is the fruitless pursuit of producing standardized citizens. But *standardized* does not describe you and your child nor me and my child. We are each created by God to be unique.

At first, you may feel it is important to make sure your student "keeps up" in his grade level to ensure he is at least as well educated as his peers in school. And yet that standard quickly falls apart for homeschoolers. We all want the same results in the end—high school graduates who are well prepared for a lifetime of learning, mature adults who can provide a living for themselves, minister to those around them, and communicate the gospel effectively. Yet each of us will achieve these goals in the best way possible for our children within our unique family culture. *We each must teach differently.*

The beauty of homeschooling is *individualized instruction.* Your child can and should learn at her own rate, speeding through what is boring because the content seems so obvious and slowing down on the tricky subjects. Your student can dive deeper into the material she loves, achieve greater mastery in her areas of giftedness, and wait on the skills she is not yet ready to develop. This is why your homeschool student will probably find herself in different grade levels in each subject.

So if you discard public school grade levels, what does that leave you with? It leaves you with a child. A child who will proceed through her own natural physical and mental developmental process, a child who will display her own unique learning style and gifts, a child who will follow her own personal path toward graduation and beyond.

9.1.2 What are milestones?

Typical patterns of development. Though each child is unique, there are some general milestones you can anticipate. God designed your child to grow and mature on a general pattern from birth through adulthood. This is why from the time you brought your baby home from the hospital, you began charting and celebrating those achievements one by one. You knew he would learn to walk before he rode a bike. You expected him to say a word or two before writing sentences. And as you consulted the pediatrician and read child development books and WebMD'd your questions, you became familiar with the general time frame in which to expect many of those new skills to develop. You learned to respect your child's progress in physical development.

These types of growth impact your student's academic development. For example, physical growth determines what tasks your child can accomplish: he needs to grow into the ability to sit for long periods of time and focus on one task. He needs fine motor skills and hand-eye coordination to hold a pencil, to sort small objects, to use a protractor, to adjust a microscope.

But your child's mental growth is even more critical for academic success. You don't expect your three-year-old to accurately chart a cosine wave or to diagram the interior of a cell or to mix chemicals with precision. She needs to develop maturity to manipulate imaginary numbers in her head for algebra and to reorganize three-dimensional objects in space for geometry; she needs to remember multiple facts simultaneously to compare and contrast ancient cultures around the world; she needs discernment, empathy, and abstract reasoning to analyze literature and opposing worldviews. Forgetting these things has caused me so much frustration so many times and, worse, I have frustrated my children. It is important to recognize the stages of your child's physical and mental development so you can challenge him appropriately and keep her learning fun and simple.

9.1.3 How do I assess my child's academic growth?

Tests and quizzes and projects? Maybe. Through the school-age years, some families find these a useful tool to gauge growth. But as our discussion of different teaching styles demonstrates (see chapter 6), these are not always necessary for a quality education. Some parents use projects. Others, learning alongside their child, can just tell when the child has mastered a new concept. Yesterday I gave a spelling test and a prealgebra test, helped the twins with their language arts work and noted they needed to review commas, and listened to my son excitedly expound upon Richard the Lionheart and Ivanhoe before urging him to move on in his history studies.

As a homeschool parent, you look at the broader picture. You know your child will progress on many levels, some of which cannot be measured by tests. You can know that your child may grow academically in spurts. You can anticipate there will be plateaus in development. You can remember that your child is unique. So that is why you can hold academic standards loosely as you gently nurture your child's learning.

9.2 NATURE VERSUS NURTURE

9.2.1 How does genetics (nature) affect learning?

It impacts the child's rate of learning. Most of us, including me, homeschool so we can provide the richest environment for teaching our values at our child's own pace. But sometimes we forget that the rate of learning is at least partially set within the child. We cannot rush God's timetable.

My own children inherited a beautiful tan from their Peruvian father and good-sized hips from their mother. Some of them are blessed with their father's soccer-playing ability, while others are musical like me. Is it just because that's what we do around here? Scientists say that's a small part of it. All of our children studied both soccer and music for at least a few years . . . but the environment and training alone did not create musical soccer stars.

> I praise you, for I am fearfully and wonderfully made.
>
> **PSALM 139:14**

Each of our biological children has some genes from me and some genes from Dad. Our two adopted children have genes from people I've never met. To some extent, my children's talents are prepackaged into their DNA. And more than that, *their timetables are preprogrammed too.*

If I can get personal with you for a minute, I'll use another example. I hit puberty at a fairly normal age. But my husband was on the later side. So some of my sons hit their growth spurts sooner than others. That has become a sore spot since guys love to be tall and manly as soon as possible. Yet I've had to remind them over and over, no matter how much milk they drink and protein they inhale and push-ups they grunt through, they are going to grow when their genes say they are going to grow. And what's more, they are only going to grow as tall as their genes decide.

What does that have to do with homeschooling? Here is the important reminder: *no matter how great and enriching your homeschool environment, your child will learn when he is good and ready.* This is in the genes too! I was an early reader, as were my first two children, who were fluent readers before age five. But my husband didn't read until around age eight, and likewise three of my other children took their own sweet time. They all received the same reading instruction in the same house with the same teacher, but they learned when their little brains were good and ready for it.

Genetics also impacts which subjects our children will gravitate toward the most. When I first tried to learn chemistry, the table of elements made *no sense whatsoever* to me, and the frustration inhibited me from learning any further. My Algebra Hater (the one who hit the wall in frustration over math several times because it seemed too difficult), on the other hand, found a model of a molecule and chased *me* around the house trying to explain bonding or solvency or some kind of science word. Learning a subject his mother was completely unable to comprehend—and even despised—was just the right challenge for his brain to tackle.

Before we get into the nitty-gritty of what our children learn when and how, I just want to make this point crystal clear. Our children inherit hair color, strength, and bone structure from their biological parents, grandparents, and other ancestors. They inherit talents and abilities. They may inherit some learning difficulties or disabilities. Nothing we can do will change that. If you adopt or foster, you may not be aware of inherited neurological capabilities, deficits the child will need to work harder to overcome or learn to compensate for. This means teaching a child from a difficult background requires extra patience and a slower pace.

Learning difficulties can show up at different times. Your child may share his father's late reading acquisition, like my son. She may sail through academics until hitting higher math and suddenly she runs up against her mother's lack of spatial understanding. These roadblocks could just be natural growth glitches completely unrelated to your teaching. Please let that truth roll over you and take the burden off your back. *You are not responsible for your child's rate of learning.* By the way, you can't take credit for it, either, lol! I would love to say that my child could read at age three because I am seriously the single most awesome homeschool mom in the world. But, um, his writing skills prove otherwise. End of bragging.

Who cares? Moms care. Because this reminds us how our child truly learns. Instead of pushing him to "keep up" to an arbitrary standard, instead we should be nurturing safe, gentle learning.

Every child inherits a physical brain structure and a timetable for development as well as chemical and electrical response patterns that strongly influence its functioning. A child's personal tempo— the natural pace of responding and the speed of carrying out activities—also seems to be genetically determined.

JANE HEALY, PHD

9.2.2 How does environment (nurture) affect learning?

It supports the child's rate of learning. Though we cannot accelerate God's timetable, we can help the child make the most of the abilities God has given him. When I prepared for adopting our twins, I learned that children must feel safe and secure, with a full tummy, a secure environment, and consistent love, in order to learn. Neglect in the basics of care inhibits learning. Even if a child's basic needs are met—if he's hurt, angry, confined, stressed, or just plain unmotivated—he cannot learn.

I often forget the importance of these basic needs. My youngest gets hungry every morning at 10:30 on the dot. If I forget it is snack time, we experience frustration and really, really bad reading. I have also learned through repeated trial and error that when my teen crumples up his algebra paper and storms off yelling in anger, my following him screaming, "What you do to one side, you have to do to the other!" is Not. Helpful. At. All. He

> KEY ASPECTS OF A
> POSITIVE LEARNING
> ENVIRONMENT
>
> • good nutrition
>
> • regular exercise
>
> • sufficient sleep
>
> • consistent routine
>
> • emotional support

can't learn until his brain calms down, bless his heart. Also, don't follow my example of yelling, "CALM DOWN SO WE CAN FINISH THIS!" It doesn't seem to help as much as one would think.

These facts also give some insight into children coming out of traumatic backgrounds. When teaching a child from foster care or adoption, you need to be aware that emotional issues can affect learning. The stress of adjusting to a new family and the pent-up emotions of a lifetime of pain significantly impact the pace of learning—perhaps halting it altogether for a time. These children need to feel secure before they can turn to the task of academics.

Similarly, children going through family or life changes might slow down in their learning. As they regain stability, they may recover their academic momentum. These two factors—trauma and life change—are part of our discussion on special needs in chapter 16.

My adopted daughter came to my home deeply depressed. I made the mistake of jumping right into reading and writing with her, assuming that academic achievement would bring her satisfaction. Boy, was I wrong. When I finally pushed the books aside and spent all day focusing on hugs, play, and family outings, she gradually came out of her shell. And a year later, she asks every day if we can work on her math paper.

9.2.3 How does past learning affect ongoing learning?

It provides a network of connections to build on. Our town has experienced rapid growth in the decade since we moved here. There are, last I heard, twice as many people living in this suburb now. So a highway has been built to connect my town to Dallas. Several large roads have been built to take us faster from one side of town to the other. And in the process, several small lanes have been widened, while some have been closed altogether.

My brain has been doing the same thing since I was a little girl. My fifth-grade teacher told me, "If you don't use it, you'll lose it!" Sure enough, I have lost the ability to win dodgeball, play cat's cradle, or even concentrate on chess. But I can make beef stroganoff without a recipe. You tell me which is more important. My algebra-hating son has already forgotten how to draw equations on an axis. But he has amazing, split-second instincts as a soccer goalie. My early-reading son has forgotten every point of ancient literature, but he can "calculus" your pants off.

> Rather than trying to pin responsibility on genes or early experiences, our job is to appreciate her particular way of learning and provide new experiences to enhance it.
>
> **JANE HEALY, PHD**

Your child builds on knowledge she already has. This seems obvious, but again, I forget it easily. A young child more easily learns to read if the simple book is about a situation she has encountered before. She can anticipate what comes next or estimate what the new word might be. Reading about a grocery store trip is easier than reading about the history of Egypt.

Like with my Algebra Hater. One day when I sat to grade his work, it finally hit me: he had no scaffolding to build on. The basic principles of the subject had become lost to him, so he had no idea what was coming next. I expected something from my child that he had no foundation for in his reality. He needed to form a connection to the real world—or at least to how he has used the information in the past—in order to make a new connection.

You can, with gentle assistance and exposure, help your student build the connections she needs for school and life. Your child may not have strong connections in the areas you wish. Instead, she will, with her own free will and interest and genetic blueprint, make multitudes of connections in the areas of her own giftedness. That is good. Over time, she will build new roads in the areas she needs.

9.2.4 How do areas of intelligence affect learning?

This goes back to the natural abilities of the child. Sometimes we can focus so much on keeping our children "on track" that we lose sight of their unique abilities. It is important to remember that there are different areas of intelligence. With my young daughter, at first I pushed her to work on her math when she really wanted to explore reading. With my spatially and socially inclined son, I made him look at letter flash cards way before he was ready, poor thing. Please don't make my mistake. With all our children, but especially those in early learning and elementary years, we do best to let them loose on the subjects they love while slowly exposing them to what they will need later.

In subjects matching the child's natural intelligence, the child may suddenly "take off" in the new content, like when my daughter learned to read at age four. She could not throw a ball or remember a single math fact in her head, but she grabbed every book and cereal box and piece of mail to read every word she could find. If I had then tried to force math facts down her throat, I would have been distorting her natural growth pattern in areas where she is not so strong. She did not intuitively see that the equation $2 + 2 = 4$ had anything to do with getting two cookies, then stealing two of her brother's cookies, and now having four cookies. Math solutions don't always come naturally to her.

> ## TYPES OF INTELLIGENCE[1]
>
> - verbal-linguistic
> - mathematical-logical
> - musical
> - visual-spatial
> - bodily-kinesthetic
> - interpersonal
> - intrapersonal
> - naturalist
> - existential

We cannot force our children to keep the same pace in their areas of strength and their areas of weakness. Attempting to do so might distort their natural growth. One scientist I spoke to calls this kind of pushing so harmful to learning as to signify abuse to the child's brain itself.

Instead of forcing my daughter in math, I needed to encourage my daughter's reading by providing lots of books. And I needed to help her build her math abilities by sending her outside to play and by pointing out the natural patterns around her. She needed to develop her own spatial understanding and physical realities in the world as a whole. Later she could build on that understanding to conceptualize how math works.

Every child of mine is weaker or stronger in certain subjects because of these natural intelligences. As my daughter's brain became really strong in one area (language and reading), she stayed weaker in other areas, like math. Now, that doesn't mean she was unable to study higher math. She did build those connections she needed. If I had pushed her too hard to excel in math at a young age, though, her talents in language arts would probably not have developed so fully. But she never loved and explored and shined in math like she has in reading and grammar.

9.2.5 What is mental age versus physical age?

The difference between the child's mental maturity and his age in calendar years. By the time children enter first grade, their mental ages can vary by *four years*.[2] And I totally see that in my own home. My firstborn behaved and learned like an eight-year-old when he was five. My fourth child, at the same age, was more like three and a half. And my youngest twins are a good three years less mature than my other children were at that age, and a year or so behind them academically. *Four years difference.* If we keep this

---

SUPPORT FOR BRAIN DEVELOPMENT

- open-ended toys with no "right way" to use them
- common household objects
- outside play
- plenty of picture books
- art supplies
- flexible, yet consistent routine
- unstructured free time
- room for mistakes
- learning words for emotions
- few academic drills
- limited screen time

---

idea in mind, the whole idea of "what grade is he in" changes entirely. This is why homeschoolers so enjoy the ability to learn at a natural pace instead of by arbitrary standards.

9.2.6 Is it possible my child has a learning disability?

Perhaps, but don't jump to conclusions. Often, we fear our child has a learning disability when in fact, he may just be too immature. Just because he is not advancing in one or two areas that we expect does not mean there is a serious problem. Only time will tell that.

My adopted son had an informal diagnosis of ADHD when he was placed in our home; he was supposed to start medication to help him sit still, be quiet, and keep pace with his classmates in school. But even before he moved in with us, I asked his caseworkers to hold off on evaluation and medication until I could work with him at home first. I realized within the first week he lived with us that he is very, very smart. But his maturity and his strongest mental connections are in all the wrong places for sitting still. He has great energy. He learns by touching things. He anticipates how objects move through space (he built great marble runs and train tracks). He can sit quietly only if pressed up against me to listen to a story. He remembers what the adult sermon was about in church and can tell me before bed what it meant to him personally. He has his own way of learning, and it is not sitting at a desk.

When he first joined our family, my son had strong connections in some areas and none in others. He needed the freedom to do what he does best, build and yell (outside) and run and climb and listen to audiobooks. He needed gentle, slow exposure to areas he had not yet learned. Within six months of coming to our home, he was able to sit for an hour to learn before running away to snack time. Within a year, his behavior while developing had changed dramatically, and he was rapidly learning to read and calculate mental math.

If I had put my son back in a traditional school, he doubtlessly would have gone back to ADHD territory within a month. There are areas—like sitting at a table while copying spelling words—that are still not his strong suit. But he will talk about fractions and adding three-digit numbers every day of the week. **Sometimes what we fear might be a disability is actually immaturity.**

However, sometimes we don't see the improvement we expect, no matter

┌─ THINGS TO TRY IF YOU THINK YOUR CHILD MAY HAVE ADHD ─┐

- Establish a relaxed yet consistent routine.
- Maintain a consistent sleep schedule and gradually increase sleep time.
- Allow choices in his life (Red shirt, or blue? Ice cream, or cookie?).
- Regulate the noise at home.
- Provide a quiet, private space.
- Limit others' screen time in front of him.
- Provide exercise daily.
- Teach him sports for large-motor coordination.
- Play games and pretend with him to learn problem-solving.
- Gradually increase his attention span in reading and games.
- Frequently show physical affection.
- Make eye and possibly physical contact when giving instructions.
- Give a warning (even set a timer) before changing activities.
- Provide proper nutrition, especially frequent healthy snacks.
- Allow time each day for no activity, just laziness.
- Have him evaluated for any suspected allergies.

how we support and encourage our child. In this case, we may want to seek additional evaluation and guidance (see chapter 16 on special needs).

9.3 ACADEMIC DEVELOPMENT STAGES

9.3.1 What are the four stages of academic development?
Early learning, the elementary years, middle school, and high school. I encourage you to keep these stages in mind while you're teaching. Rather than anxiously checking off monthly or yearly goals for your student, you can prepare each child for each new stage and celebrate the natural progression of the one she is currently in. By keeping this long-term view with each

student, you may reduce a lot of anxiety, competition, and even busy work. As long as your student is making developmentally appropriate progress in her stage, she's doing great. If she stumbles on a skill or concept, you can rest assured that she has more time and growth before she needs to master it.

Classical homeschoolers refer to the four stages as early grammar, late grammar, dialectic, and rhetoric (see section 6.3). And some Christian homeschoolers draw biblical parallels by labeling them knowledge, understanding, and wisdom. The following four chapters will look at each of these stages in detail.

9.3.2 What is the early learning stage?

Early learning is the preschool and kindergarten stage. This stage will last from ages three to six for most children, but it can begin as early as age two and end as late as ten years of age. Developmentally, early learning begins when the toddler age ends. The child can walk and talk, can feed himself and use the bathroom, and sleeps through the night most of the time. He is beginning to assert his independence in opinion, imagination, and personality, and he delights in learning new skills and facts. His favorite words are "why" and "no." But he usually prefers close proximity to his parents and family, learning most rapidly when he feels safe, happy, and loved. He's enjoying being spoon-fed his learning from his close caregivers, usually mom.

The bookend for the early learning stage is reading independently. This is a significant milestone that requires tremendous physical, mental, and emotional growth. To read, a child must recognize that written symbols mean something verbal and carry concrete or abstract meaning, that letters form the building blocks of words, that each letter or group of letters stands for a unique vocal sound, and that these letters and sounds are combined to produce the words we speak. He then must memorize all those sounds and blends and decode the meaning in his mind, remember what the decoded message stands for, and say it aloud. Then he has to recall the previous words he decoded moments (or minutes) before and put it all together to make a complete thought. This is exhausting work!

Some very precocious, highly verbal learners may begin reading at age three, like my oldest did. Most will learn sometime between the ages of five and seven. But one of mine waited until age eight to read independently.

Though we can support a love for reading and drill phonics until the cows come home (*cow begins with C!*), early learning is really all about waiting for that young mind to mature.

But oh, how fun the waiting can be. Early learning is a joyous, low-pressure stage of education when the whole world is new and the picture books are magical and making messes is the name of every game. If you ask any homeschool mom what her biggest regret is, almost every single one will say *not enjoying the early years enough*. These are the carefree picture book days, the relaxing meandering at the zoo, the field trips and baking marathons and insect collections and bare feet and naps. These days are also super exhausting, so those of us with older children look back with rose-colored glasses, forgetting that we were barely functioning physically and mentally during those years.

9.3.3 What is the elementary years stage?

The elementary years are what most likely come to your mind when you think of homeschooling—with activities such as reading *Little House on the Prairie* and learning long division and memorizing the presidents of the United States. Since you prolonged the early learning stage until your child was fully ready to read, your student could be starting the elementary years stage anywhere from age six to ten. And now it's time for reading, writing, and math.

The elementary time is all about learning *facts*. It's about laying the groundwork for the harder analysis and research and investigation of middle school and high school. As a mom, you are just pouring knowledge and facts and lists and names into that young brain every day. Then the next day, rinse and repeat.

So the comforting part of the elementary years is *you don't have to master anything in one year*. Everything you learn in math is reviewed next year. Every rule you memorize in grammar is repeated in the next book. There is nothing so critical that you and your student must die on that hill; you are just getting what you can now, and you'll pick up the rest next time.

Likewise, it really does no good to push your child to achieve in elementary school. No one is giving out scholarships or cash prizes for diagramming sentences in fifth grade. Those math grades won't make it onto any college transcripts. So while we want to teach our students to love learning, to work hard, and to do their best, we don't need to get wrapped up in grades.

What grade are we in during elementary? It doesn't matter. If your child begins the elementary stage at an older age, he may start with fourth-grade or fifth-grade workbooks in math and language. If he starts young, he can just begin at first grade and keep moving up until he's clearly middle school age. If you don't care what grade your student is in, he probably won't either. Knowledge itself should be the primary goal.

The early learning and elementary stages are, together, called the *grammar stage* by classical homeschoolers (see section 6.3). And some Christian classicists call this the *knowledge stage*. Those terms just state the obvious: students are learning the grammar of every subject, the basic knowledge and rules that govern how we learn and communicate learning. No matter what our personal homeschool style, we would all do well to remember the purpose of these years: to instill a love of learning and impart the basic tools of learning to our students. Everything else is gravy.

9.3.4 What is the middle school stage?

Middle school is more than just an awkward time in our lives we'd rather forget—it's a critical transitional period for your student. As his body and mind begin the smelly transformation from child to teen, academics take a sharp turn from basic facts and knowledge to deeper understanding, logic, and integration. Your student has probably mastered the foundational principles of grammar and math, and now he is ready to take more personal responsibility for his learning. He has also begun exhibiting those telltale signs of hormonal changes like growth spurts, moodiness, and argumentative talking back. These all are big indications that changes are a-comin', and his homeschooling will never be the same.

Now your student is ready to delve into the *understanding* or *dialectic* side of learning, as classicists would say. She yearns to develop her own opinion on everything from religion to history to math to writing, but she is unclear how to evaluate these logically and to express her opinions clearly. But she tries, vigorously contradicting every rule and statement made in print or by her parents.

This can be an exhausting stage to homeschool, especially when your oldest child first hits puberty. In her natural, healthy desire to assert her own individuality and opinion, the homeschool student finds herself with only one worthy sparring partner: her parent. Her already exhausted, over-whelmed parent. So the two main purposes in middle school become *learn to be responsible for your work* and *learn how to state your opposing viewpoint with respect*. These lessons take a few years to learn, but they will serve her well for a lifetime. (After teaching her how to be nice when she doesn't agree, let's try to teach all of Facebook, shall we?)

The middle school years can last from two to four years long. Again, it depends on the child. He needs to be ready mentally and emotionally to begin middle school material, and it could take him a while to develop the maturity for high school responsibilities. So just like in the previous stages, you may want to make sure you are looking at what your student is ready for, not what his age is on the calendar.

9.3.5 What is the high school stage?

High school is the last stage of homeschooling and is the time when some parents give up. If the middle school argumentative stage hasn't worn these homeschool parents down, they now assume the subject matter will be too difficult or their student too stubborn to finish education at home. That's far from the truth. In reality, the high school stage is characterized by much greater independence in learning as the student takes increasing responsibility not only for his assignments but also for his own mastery of the subject matter. High school students should attempt to read and study and apply their lessons on their own with feedback and encouragement from online educators and local experts in addition to their parents. Besides academic studies, high school students begin taking personal responsibility for their own lives by getting jobs, serving in ministries, volunteering in the community, planning for their future, obtaining the necessary training in trades or vocations, and perhaps securing entrance into their chosen colleges.

So by high school, homeschool parents have slowly changed their role from primary educator to facilitator, counselor, and cheerleader. These teen years offer the student plenty of practice in making mistakes, making life choices, and making memories. Parents may practice stepping back to allow the student to learn from the consequences of his choices—and to reap the rewards of his faithfulness. The high school years can seem scary at times, but they are the most rewarding by far.

Classicists call this the *rhetoric stage*, when the teen begins eloquently presenting his own beliefs based on his research, experimentation, and practice (see section 6.3). Biblical classicists refer to this as the *wisdom* stage, in which students practice living out their education in deeper ways. Regardless of homeschool philosophy, all high school parents have the challenge to walk with the teen toward adulthood, toward a life of learning and service. And that starts now.

• • •

In the following four chapters, I look at each of these academic stages in detail. I list the character development as well as the physical, mental, social, and emotional development a healthy student should expect at each point. I consider the various subjects he might study in each phase and some foundational, developmental, and advanced milestones a student is working toward. I also discuss some questions you may face in each part of the child's development. Then I end with some benchmarks to determine if your child is ready to level up to the next stage. Every child travels through these stages in his own way, and your child is no different, but we will look at what you can *generally* expect and what you might do at each stage.

I group these developments in large stages instead of year by year for an important reason: your child and my child, as we discussed, are uniquely different and grow at their own special rate. No two ten-year-olds are the same physically, mentally, or academically. We can, however, say some general things about what most elementary students do within those five or six years. This is what I want to talk about—the broad range of what you might see in your child within a huge chunk of time.

These chapters also discuss character development, which, come to find out, is also progressive. Young children do not have the capability to grasp and internalize some of the spiritual issues we value. Watching their character develop naturally can be a great joy.

Now, here's my great, big, honkin' disclaimer: *these chapters are generally descriptive but in no way prescriptive.* I'm trying hard to keep things broad, but of course there are outliers who are just great but not exactly the way I describe. I love that. Keep it up. There are also outliers who are growing at their own patient rate. I love that. Keep it up.

Throughout this book, the physical and academic guidelines I'm suggesting are true for average, healthy children growing in safe, stable homes free from trauma. The physical and mental guidelines are based on those used by pediatricians and childcare workers in America to assess healthy development. If your child has been diagnosed with special needs or adopted out of a traumatic background, you will likely see a different rate of development. In those cases, turn to chapter 16 and consult your child's doctor or therapist for help forming realistic expectations.

I am not a doctor, nor do I star in a hospital series on Netflix. I have, though, personally consulted a published pediatrician about the physical and mental stages, and I have researched these stages extensively. I tried very hard to keep my descriptions general but reflecting healthy development. *Please consult your own pediatrician or learning specialist with any questions or concerns.*

10

EARLY LEARNING:
THE PRESCHOOL AND
KINDERGARTEN YEARS

Approximately ages 3–7

I MADE A BIG MISTAKE with my first child. When he was three years old, I bought all the curriculum I could find from one major publisher—boxes and boxes of books and worksheets and charts and classroom activities. And I made him do it *all*. Bless his heart, that poor boy was at the table for hours every morning, taking a quick lunch and afternoon break before hitting the books some more.

My friend Trish tried to tell me that is *not* how little children learn to love learning. She gave me books and catalogs of fun activities to do with little children. She invited me over to her house to watch her young children learn. And I, the young expert in all things homeschooling after less than a year of teaching, eschewed it all. I thought she was crazy.

I was crazy.

As I added more and more children to my homeschool family, little by little I learned from my own students. I learned from each of them that Trish was right—there is a much better way to excite little minds. By the time I was teaching my third or fourth child, I was finally starting to get it. To

GENERAL GOALS FOR THE EARLY YEARS

- learn through daily life
- explore the world inside and outside the home
- deepen relationships and social skills
- enjoy books and educational topics
- realize that mistakes are part of learning

- develop educational skills such as sharing, inquisitiveness, caring for materials, and attentiveness
- memorize facts and learning foundations like letters, numbers, Scripture verses, and poems
- begin learning how to read

really see the way I should have been teaching from the beginning. (Get over it, Lea Ann. All homeschool moms have regrets. We aren't perfect, but we do our best and move on. And now, back to your regularly scheduled chapter.) I'm a slow learner, but I've also come to see the beauty of *real-life learning*.

A young child's mind, like that of a growing infant, absorbs so much in a beautifully normal day. Actually, this is the lesson Charlotte Mason and Maria Montessori and our unschoolers are trying to teach us: a child left to explore her environment, her tools, and her relationships will learn a multitude every day. It is our job just to stay out of the way.

Young children lead the way through this real-life learning with their constant questions. Those nonstop questions. Those maddening, never-ending questions. Suddenly, they realize they don't know everything there is to know and that the answer is out there. Furthermore, our children discover that we their parents have answers. And the more we answer the barrage of questions, the further we reinforce that *our children can and will learn from us throughout their lifetime*. This is the foundation of homeschooling. We will often say, "I don't know" and help them find out, but we will more often answer their questions and help satisfy their curiosity.

We all want to give our child the best possible start we can. And there is a lot of societal pressure when it comes to preschool. So many parents of young children are prematurely looking down the road at high school and college and worrying, "Will I get her ready in time? Will I give her enough of an edge to be exceptional?" Okay, we all need to calm down—including me.

Early learning is setting the tone for loving to learn and is not the time to prepare for the SAT. During this stage, you will be helping your child begin the learning process. Quite unlike institutionalized preschool, kindergarten, or even first grade, this early learning stage will likely be more gentle, play oriented, and relational. These years could be the most fun of your homeschooling!

There is plenty of time to work on the algebra and the chemistry and the economics way, way, way down the road. And though those college prep preschool programs promise amazing results, *we should never pick preschool activities based on high school objectives.* We can change course, change programs, change styles, change our minds, change our hair color . . . and I did all that multiple times from the year my first child began "homeschooling" at the age of three to the time he graduated. Early learning, however, should be fun, and that's about all.

10.1 THE EARLY LEARNER'S DEVELOPMENT

10.1.1 How might my early learner's character develop?
Like his physical and mental growth, a young child's character develops gradually over the years. There are a few character traits, in particular, that

---

WHAT DO YOU MEAN BY *REAL-LIFE LEARNING?*

Learning in the midst of the everyday rhythms of life. Some examples of this approach are found in the Montessori, Charlotte Mason, and unschooling teaching models (see chapter 6). Regardless of your own teaching preference, young children will learn from the routines of daily life.

For example, she'll learn responsibility from doing her chores and putting toys away. She'll learn math by helping in the kitchen, setting the table, and counting Cheerios. She'll learn reading by looking at picture books with you. She'll learn science and exploring by playing outside. She'll learn history from the books you read and the stories you tell.

You don't need to set up a classroom or make a lesson plan to teach young children. Learning happens in real life.

emerge during these early years. **Young children develop emotional awareness.** If they have not already, they begin using words for their emotions—much to the relief of us parents! One of my favorite things to say to my youngsters is, "I don't know what you want or how you feel about it unless you tell me with your words." At first, they look at me with a blank expression. Then I offer, "Are you saying you want to play outside, and you are frustrated because Mommy won't help you find your coat?"

Well, that's quite a lot for three- and four-year-olds to put into words. But with a little prompting, soon instead of standing at the door screaming (a sure cue for me to start screaming in agony too), they will at least attempt to tell me how they feel.

And *that* is the beginning of empathy. Once a child can describe how she feels, then she can begin noticing, naming, and even anticipating the feelings of others. That is a huge relief to the entire family. A four-year-old may actually say, "I'd better not go in my brother's room or he'll be mad at me." Or at least *think* it, her brother hopes. And much to my relief, my child may actually ask, "Mom, does my banging loudly on this pot make you feel sad? Is that why you are curled up in a ball in the corner, moaning softly to yourself?"

The next stage of empathy after putting words to feelings and anticipating others' feelings is actually feeling someone else's feelings. It's as confusing as it sounds. This is when instead of wondering if banging louder on the pot might be why I am crying in the corner, my child actually feels sad if the house is loud, and she feels happier if things are quiet (quiet-*er*) for her mother's sanity. Empathy is not just sympathizing with her mother's intolerance for noise (and wondering why she had six children if she is intolerant of noise); empathy is experiencing some of those feelings along with me. This is a huge character milestone.

PATTERNS LEARNED IN THE EARLY YEARS

- time
- sequence
- how to estimate why
- filling in missing pieces
- rhyming
- noticing and following rhythms
- building
- how to imagine
- anticipating a story ending
- describing differences in events or people

Learning to empathize is a spiritual milestone we all experience—and continue to develop throughout life. Paul explains this in 2 Corinthians 1:3-11. God comforts us in our own troubles, and as we experience pain in our lives, we are better able to first feel the pain of others and then anticipate how we can further comfort them. Empathy is shown in our prayer lives and in our physical demonstrations of help toward others.

Early learners will also begin to develop a strong sense of conscience. A young child may seem to have very little conscience. I remember telling my husband several times that my firstborn was headed straight to juvie. He could run rampant, create destruction, and out-and-out disobey with little remorse. Oh, sure, he didn't enjoy consequences, but he didn't ever appear truly, deeply sorry until he was caught. And that was so frustrating! CARE, you little creature!

He developed a conscience over time as he dealt with the consequences of his actions. Being forced to clean up his messes. Eating the squashed, less-than-appealing sandwich. Living with the reality he royally created. Soon the consequences became less desirable than the all-supreme desires of his heart, and then he could anticipate consequences of his actions, feeling remorse for making wrong choices. As his empathy increased, he also began to regret the trouble and disappointment he caused his parents. This was the beginning of developing a conscience.

> [God] comforts us in all our affliction, so that we may be able to comfort those who are in any affliction, with the comfort with which we ourselves are comforted by God.
>
> **2 CORINTHIANS 1:4**

Developing a sense of conscience is also closely tied to learning self-control. We adopted our youngest son when he was only six years old. He had never sat through an adult worship service before. He was suddenly thrown into a new environment—after his life of no training in self-control whatsoever—requiring him to sit quietly for nearly an hour. He wanted to get out of the building, or at least to vigorously kick the seat in front of him and crawl on the floor. So he did exactly what he wanted.

He had consequences of varying kinds. During the sermon, he lost first one crayon and then the other and finally his entire coloring sheet for not sitting quietly. He was taken out of the service (you know it, that walk of shame up the aisle) for a firm talking-to. He became embarrassed that his consequences were completely avoided by the rest of the family and other children around him. He no longer wanted this to happen to him. He even started off services with a promise, "Mommy, this time I'm going to sit quietly," and he usually made it through 75 percent of the service.

He had rewards for his good behavior. He could color during the entire—mercifully short—sermon while he sat still with no kicking. He got a mint to suck on, or even a sucker, after the service for being such a well-behaved young man. Sometimes he even got *more dessert than his older brothers!* Oh, the ecstasy!

The young man, in a few short months, developed self-control and his own strategies for success. He sat on his own hands. He folded his legs under himself. He sighed as his urges came upon him, then clutched his own hands tighter and squinted at the preacher. He worked hard to develop his own ways to control his wiggles.

Then he began to develop the beginnings of that conscience. When his feet would start to kick, he looked at me and stopped without my saying a thing. When his arms raised in a fake stretch, he quickly put them down, again with a glance my way. Within a few months, he was talking excitedly on the way home about the pastor's sermon series on Psalm 23 and how he was happy to be a sheep with Jesus. He was passing through the stages of conscience and self-control. And with less attention on training him and more on the service itself, I was on the way to getting some religion for myself!

Rules become increasingly important during this stage. Clear rules like "put your clothes in the hamper" and "LEGOs do not belong under Mommy's feet but in the bin" and "food belongs on your plate, not spread across the table." For a very young child, it can feel like life is full of rules, rules, rules. And it is hard for us as parents to recall that we need to state clear rules and to repeat these rules several times before they are remembered. Then I like to ask, "What does Mommy say about the [dramatic pause for control of vocabulary] LEGOS ACROSS THE FLOOR!" The child can begin to repeat back rules, then eventually remember them without being told. Except for the LEGO rule. That one is impossible for a child of any age.

Without rules, consequences, and rewards, there is no awareness of wrong. This is what the apostle Paul explains in Romans 7. God gave us rules and punishment from the beginning so we would know what is right and what is wrong. That is how we know we are sinners and we need a

Savior. That is how, as Christians, we know we need Christ so we can do good. And that is how we anticipate our reward of a relationship with Christ here on earth and a hope of life in heaven.

Your little homeschooler will begin to develop either prejudice toward or acceptance of others at this age. As your family is active in church, community, and volunteer work, he will be exposed to a variety of cultures and backgrounds. In the beginnings of this stage, your child may not even recognize that people come in different colors. Skin color is no different to her than hair, eye, or clothing colors. Children are born with an innocence of difference. In fact, many young children at the beginning of this stage don't even identify their own skin color; if asked what color they are, they may say their hair color or the color of the clothing they are wearing.

> There is neither Jew nor Greek, there is neither slave nor free, there is no male and female, for you are all one in Christ Jesus.
>
> **GALATIANS 3:28**

Early learners have a natural tolerance for those of different appearance and background. They become curious about other ways of life when they notice different dress (like turbans) or different prayers in public (like crossing oneself before prayer at meals). But they often have little or no judgment for others that appear different. Young children, however, are very observant of those around them. They may notice their parents or others in their social circle distrust those who have a different appearance or lifestyle. If exposed over time to this distrust or disrespect, they will develop the beginnings of prejudice.

FOUNDATIONAL GOALS
- name his own feelings
- notice the feelings of others
- understand right from wrong
- modify his behavior with reminders
- do daily chores with reminders
- respond to rewards and consequences
- play alone for short periods of time
- share with others
- say please and thank you

- engage in relationships with adults and children of other backgrounds

DEVELOPMENTAL GOALS
- name others' feelings
- take turns speaking in a conversation
- feel bad before being caught doing wrong
- modify behavior with one reminder
- remember more than one chore if asked to "do your chores"
- anticipate rewards or consequences
- engage in pretend play
- ask questions to learn more about other cultures

ADVANCED GOALS
- anticipate others' reactions
- adjust behavior to make others more comfortable or happier
- modify his behavior with a look
- remember to do chores without being reminded .
- say please and thank you without being reminded
- confess wrongdoing before being caught

10.1.2 How might my early learner develop physically?

During these early years, gross and fine motor skills develop rapidly. So, too, children begin displaying a widening range of abilities. This is completely normal. Children these ages sometimes develop in spurts—you may see sudden improvement, then little growth for quite a while. You may even see your child regress in some abilities. As long as he generally continues moving forward in his development, he is fine. If, however, you have any concerns, ask your pediatrician for an evaluation.

FOUNDATIONAL GOALS
- dress and take care of bathroom needs
- scribble
- paint
- cut with scissors
- brush his own teeth

DEVELOPMENTAL GOALS
- tie his shoes
- help with chores and cleaning up messes
- recognize left and right hands
- hold a pencil properly
- color inside the lines
- print his name
- draw triangles
- draw a person with six body parts

ADVANCED GOALS
- kick a moving ball
- perform handstands or cartwheels
- jump rope
- use scissors to cut out complex shapes
- begin typing
- gain independence in all areas of grooming including bathing

---
ITEMS TO BUILD GROSS MOTOR SKILLS

- ball
- jump rope
- tricycle
- bat and ball
- Nerf gun
- noise-canceling headphones for you

10.1.3 How might my early learner develop mentally?

Young children vary widely in their mental and academic ability, and their rate of growth can vary widely too. My oldest son, for instance, trucked through my rigid preschool teaching like a trouper, mastering each new concept as quickly as he could. My older daughter virtually taught herself to read and strove to memorize everything I told her, and even what her older brother was doing too.

But my third child, that boy had no interest in his numbers or letters or sorting or shapes. He would sit happily on my lap if I read to him, but he would not look at books alone. I tried in vain to get him to look at a flash card or repeat "A says a, a, a!" So I gave up.

Then I noticed that all day he just wanted to be near me. To play beside me, to hug me, to sit on my lap, to watch me cook. He just craved relationship. That became the key to his learning. He quickly absorbed phonics and reading for as long as my lap could hold him before my legs went numb. He could count and multiply and divide all the food I could cook him. Any subject about people—especially the people he loved—became the most important to him.

Each of my young children learned at their own rate—reading, writing, understanding math all at different ages. And that is completely normal. Be careful not to compare your child to anyone else's. Your child will learn how and when he is ready.

FOUNDATIONAL GOALS
- look at pictures in books
- understand the concepts of yesterday and tomorrow
- identify colors
- follow one-step instructions
- sort objects by one attribute (color or size)
- tell a story
- speak in sentences with both subject and verb

DEVELOPMENTAL GOALS
- play with simple shape puzzles
- ask to be read to and pretend to read
- try to write
- say rhyming words
- count objects
- understand the passage of time by activities (after we eat lunch, we have nap time)
- understand the sequence of common events and if the sequence is out of order
- recognize some letters
- ask for help solving problems
- sort objects by multiple attributes
- put toys and materials away
- pronounce most words correctly and be understood by strangers
- use some irregular verbs correctly ("gave" not "gived")
- tell a story with a beginning, middle, and end
- speak in sentences of more than four words
- ask "why" questions
- memorize his address, phone number, and how to report an emergency or call for help
- understand that slang or profanity are "bad words"

ADVANCED GOALS

- recognize that numbers correspond to amounts
- make an effort to finish a project
- try to solve problems alone
- write his own name
- follow multistep instructions
- identify the problem and solution in a story
- speak in longer, more complex sentences
- tell a detailed story with a clear resolution
- ask how to read
- memorize poems, songs, verses, and jokes
- remind other family members of tasks

10.1.4 How might my early learner develop socially and emotionally?

Real life is the most important tool for his emotional and social development. Your young child goes through a huge transition during this time, from baby and toddler to big child. His relationship with you changes just as much as he learns to do more for himself. He is observing you and his older siblings to learn how to respond and act in a variety of situations. And he is exploring his own emotions through imaginative play and interaction with his family.

You can help him master his emotions and social skills in two ways. First of all, *let him play.* He will explore a variety of situations and reactions in his own imagination. Even his drawings are opportunities to express how he feels and what he wants. Secondly, *take him with you.* Errands like grocery store trips and doctor's office visits teach him how to treat others outside his family. Playtime and parties allow him to practice social skills. And more adult situations like church help him observe mature behavior.

GENERAL GOALS

- give appropriate eye contact when speaking and being spoken to
- answer adults with respect
- show polite manners for eating, meeting new people, and gift giving

---
DON'T BE CONCERNED UNLESS AT THE MIDDLE OR END OF THIS PERIOD YOUR EARLY LEARNER

- cannot jump with two feet or climb stairs
- cannot follow two-step commands
- cannot dress or use the toilet
- does not pretend
- withdraws from family and friends

- has difficulty separating from parents for short periods of time
- shows no progress in self-control
- is overly aggressive
- exhibits anxiety
- speaks in a way that is difficult to understand

- resolve disagreements with peers or siblings (use your words, share, ask a parent for help, etc.)
- share with others
- learn to say "no" respectfully to adults and to peers
- understand personal boundaries like modesty, avoiding bullying, and stranger danger
- display curiosity and exploration about various subjects

10.2 WHAT YOUR EARLY LEARNER COULD BE LEARNING

Academics are the *least important thing you should be thinking about from the ages of three to six.* I cannot possibly emphasize that enough. This is a

---
IDEAS FOR ACTIVITIES WITH YOUR EARLY LEARNER

- lots and lots of reading aloud
- museum and zoo trips
- gardening or caring for houseplants
- exploring maps and globes

- real life: errands, cooking, doctor's visits, church, community celebrations
- imaginative play: toy kitchen, tools, baby dolls, soldiers, cars, etc.
---

wonderful time for exploration and building a love for learning. The young child is still learning just from her daily environment and her relationships inside and outside the home. Besides character development, nothing else is important during this time. If you allow your child to do nothing but play freely and follow your daily life, she will be well prepared for academics to come.

However, if you want to know more about how your child will be developing academic readiness, and if you really, really, really want to lead her along to more, here are some subjects that may be gently introduced into your young child's life.

HOW MUCH TIME SHOULD WE SPEND?

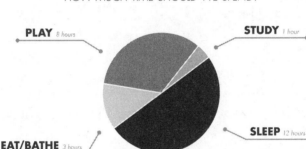

PLAY 8 hours

STUDY 1 hour

SLEEP 12 hours

EAT/BATHE 3 hours

10.2.1 What might my early learner learn about the Bible?

About Jesus, salvation, and major Bible stories. Young children *love* to read Bible stories. These accounts are beautiful and full of action. And best of all, many of the stories star Jesus, the one who loves them the most. A simple yet beautiful story Bible is a great tool for regular Bible reading.

Though each child can be exposed to the basic plan of salvation—we are all sinners, Jesus died to take our punishment, we believe and live with him forever—early learners are usually not ready to make a profession of faith. I encourage my children to wait until they understand more clearly the depth of their decision so they will remain secure in their choice in the years to come. Of course, we never want to discourage a deep love for Christ and a genuine appreciation for all he has done for us.

The single most important Bible lesson in these years is simple: Jesus loves you.

BIBLES AND BIBLE STORYBOOKS FOR EARLY LEARNERS

Many of these Bible storybooks can continue to be used even into the early elementary years.

- *My First Hands-On Bible* (NLT)
- *A Child's First Bible* by Kenneth N. Taylor
- *The One Year Children's Bible* by Rhona Davies
- *The Story Travelers Bible* by Tracey Madder
- *A Child's First Bible: Psalms for Little Hearts* by Dandi Daley Mackall
- *The Lost Lamb and the Good Shepherd* and other flip books by Dandi Daley Mackall
- *The Hurry-Up Exit from Egypt* and other Faith that God Built books by Gary Bower

- *Wow! The Good News in Four Words* by Dandi Daley Mackall (shares the plan of salvation in a way that small children can understand)
- *The Complete Illustrated Children's Bible* by Janice Emmerson
- Bible storybooks in the Arch Books series
- *The Lord Is My Shepherd: The Twenty-Third Psalm*, illustrated by Tasha Tudor
- *Egermeier's Bible Story Book* by Elsie Egermeier

GENERAL GOALS
- gain knowledge of major Bible stories
- understand who Jesus is and that he loves each child personally
- learn that God requires children to obey their parents
- learn that God created the world

WHAT I DO
- regularly read from a Bible storybook with my child
- read this same storybook aloud over and over again until the child understands the flow of biblical history
- discuss prayer and encourage simple prayers during the day
- sing Bible songs

- help my child memorize simple Bible verses and facts like the days of Creation or the Ten Commandments

10.2.2 What reading skills might my early learner develop?

A love for books and perhaps beginning to read. Learning to read is a major milestone in a child's life, marking the end of the early learning stage and the beginning of elementary. Because so much mental maturity is necessary for the task, children will arrive at this accomplishment at vastly different ages, even within the same family or gender. My earliest reader and latest reader were both boys, and they achieved this goal at ages three and eight, respectively. It is perfectly acceptable for a child to read as late as age ten. I learned through the years to allow each of my children the liberty to travel through this subject at his own pace. Please don't rush into reading during the early learning phase. This is best left for later when each child's brain has developed more and his appetite for books has grown. In the meantime, read to your child to your heart's content.

GENERAL GOALS
- listen to and answer questions about a story
- explain her favorite part of a story
- attempt to use learned vocabulary words throughout the day
- reenact stories during playtime
- hold a book the correct way and turn pages
- listen to an audiobook while turning the picture book pages at the appropriate time
- clap out syllables
- identify letters and sounds
- *gradually* develop reading skills

WHAT I DO
- read aloud a lot
- occasionally point out letters and model what sounds they make
- check out an audiobook from the library, lose it, and pay for it
- buy letter magnets for the refrigerator and lose most of them within a month

10.2.2.1 HOW DO I PROVIDE A HEAD START ON READING?

Read, read, read to your child. Before your baby could speak, you did all the talking for him. You talked to him (and even on his behalf!) from morning to night, keeping up a one-sided dialogue about his experiences, his surroundings, his belongings, and his family. Pretty soon, he began babbling back to you, making nonsense noises that you greeted with an enthusiastic response, joining his charade that what he said mattered. Then one day, he said something close to a real word, you called it his most important utterance, and he began trying harder to say more recognizable words and syllables. After he had successfully interjected appropriate words at the appropriate moments in real-life conversations, he began trying to string two or three words

---

STRATEGIES FOR DEVELOPING READING READINESS

- Ask open-ended questions (what do you think?).

- Refer to earlier learning.

- Give hands-on examples.

- Provide lots of playtime with others.

- Provide more opportunities to solve problems while giving fewer solutions.

---

together, eventually even speaking sentences. After that, there was no stopping him. He talked all day to you, whether you wanted him to or not.

Developing reading readiness is much like that process. You are starting off with a one-sided book conversation, inviting your child into a form of communication that is very special to you. You read picture books to him regularly, several times a day, even though he pays little attention in the beginning. But after a few weeks, he begins looking at the pictures, pointing out characters, and trying to babble along with you. Once he can speak recognizable words, he may finish the sentence of a best-loved book or squeal if you change the ending.

Eventually, your child realizes that the words you say were actually symbolized on that very page. He begins pretending to read for himself, making up a story to go with the pictures or reciting his favorite picture book's story from memory. As far as he is concerned, he is reading just like you, and he begins enjoying every page turn.

But one day, a new book catches his eyes, and he's frustrated to make sense of the pictures. He may begin straining to understand the letters on the page, even following along with his finger as you read to him. He has a desire to take a more active role in reading, but the code mystifies him. As he continues to grow, this code of letters and phonics will become clearer to him, and you will notice his readiness to read.

Reading readiness is the biggest goal for many parents during early learning. Most academic learning builds on the skill of reading, and schooling seems to officially begin when the student achieves this milestone. So there's understandably a lot of pressure to get this child reading—STAT! But the number one rule is to stop worrying about pushing your child faster into reading. She will learn to read faster and with less frustration if you let her develop the ability at her own pace.

Simply reading stories aloud every day or even several times a day teaches so much: attention, story sequence, vocabulary, characters, how to anticipate an ending, appreciation of different genres, imagination, art appreciation, and so much more. There is no substitute for reading to your young child. Even a few minutes a day of reading a nice picture book makes a big difference. Besides, it definitely draws you and your child close together.

If I say anything at all in this section, it is this: *no three-year-old should be pushed to read.* Children will develop this ability as they grow over the course of several years, and there is absolutely no reason to rush this process. So take a big breath and let this burden slide right off your back.

I feel it behooves me to say yet again *please don't pressure your child to read early.* Some parents have shared with me that early reading instruction can lead to perfectionism or even reading aversion. Read to your child, talk about letters, read a lot for yourself in front of your child, and treasure the books you own. Then allow your child to gently move through the process of reading at his best pace.

10.2.2.2 HOW DO I TEACH MY EARLY LEARNER TO READ?

Take it slowly and keep things relaxed. Probably no subject causes more homeschool angst than reading. When I set out to write this book, I received more questions about reading than about any other single aspect of homeschooling. But if you remember that learning to read is a lot like learning how to talk, much of your fear will be lifted. You did a great job teaching your child to say words, phrases, and sentences, and you'll be just as successful following a similar pattern for teaching him to read.

Reading requires continued mental growth. A child must grow from purely concrete thinking (*this is a ball*) into abstract thinking (*these markings on a paper all together make the word ball, which stands for my toy that rolls across the floor*). This understanding is a huge leap in reasoning—no wonder children seem to struggle with reading at first. But by slowing down the reading process, you can help your young child naturally develop her ability and love for reading.

The process cannot be rushed and should not be pressured. You won't want to stress out your child by trying to force him to do something he is not ready to do. Here are some simple ways you can help your child along this path.

Read to your child a lot from babyhood throughout childhood (and even into the teen years). Don't worry if you haven't been reading for a while—just start where you are! The six-year-olds we adopted from foster care had attended public kindergarten and were required to take one semester of public school their first-grade year. Because they had no educational support their first six years, they were completely unable to understand the reading lessons in class, let alone do any reading homework. So I contacted each of their teachers and asked permission to start over with their phonics for twenty minutes each day instead of doing their assigned homework. For those months, all I did was read to them, point to the words on the page, and help them with the sounds of letters. When they were able to start homeschooling, they continued to work through the basics of phonics and early reading for at least two more years.

Read a wide variety of good books. The most basic tool for teaching reading is a library card. While you are at the library, grab as many picture books and board books as you can fit in a tote and look at them every day with your child. Even pick up some chapter books you loved as a child and read a portion aloud each day. Finally, don't forget to check out some audiobooks for when your own voice gets hoarse.

Sometimes the children's book section at the library seems intimidating. But choosing books to read to your child can be a lot of fun. Start on one shelf. Grab a book that has interesting illustrations. Choose books with a wide variety of illustration styles (watercolors, pen and pencil drawings, paintings, etc.). Next, read the first page, a middle page, and the end. Does it look like the story might be interesting? Check it out. Find books on a variety of topics from different authors, as well as returning to the authors you enjoy. Expose your child to different styles—rhyming, few words on

USE YOUR TEACHING STYLE: READING

- **Classical:** Collect classic picture books and read each one multiple times. Focus on stories of history and the Bible, especially coordinating these with the studies of older siblings. Encourage drawing pictures or reenacting the stories.

- **Charlotte Mason:** Focus on beautifully illustrated picture books portraying morality tales. Develop art projects based on the illustrations of favorite books. Plan a day's or week's activities based on each book and its themes.

- **Textbook:** Follow a preplanned program of chosen picture books, art activities, and family projects.

- **Unschooling:** Expose your child to a wide variety of books and audiobooks, allowing him to select his favorites.

a page with beautiful illustrations, or longer books on family, occupation, emotions, or social issues. The worst thing that can happen is you get a book that you don't enjoy reading and you return it. It's a risk you can totally take!

While you are at the library, take part in story time, craft time, and puppet shows. Most libraries include a children's area with toys and puzzles, allowing your child to practice his sharing and group play skills. Your child can find that the library is a fun place to visit.

Begin building your own home library of best-loved children's books. We encouraged grandparents to give books for birthday presents. Every Christmas, I give each child at least one book, no matter how old my child is. Growing a library isn't a problem—storing the books is! I keep the picture books on low bookshelves, on dressers in their bedrooms, stacked on the sofa table, and in baskets around the family room.

Read about daily life. Studies have shown that children understand what they are reading better if they are presented with stories about things they have experienced. So a child reading a story about cooking dinner will anticipate that Mom puts the food in the oven, so the word *oven* will not seem so hard for her to read. She may read it without help, even though she hasn't seen it before. And she is more likely to recall facts about the story when she is done reading, because she has a personal connection to it. When I get things from the library, I allow my young reader to help me

STEPS TO LEARNING TO READ

- Understand that books contain stories.

- Recognize that written words on each page mean something.

- Listen to a story for over twenty minutes (maybe while playing with small toys, coloring, or sitting in a parent's lap).

- Recognize that symbols mean something (like the YouTube logo or the McDonald's sign).

- Recognize that letters represent sounds.

- Realize that these sounds make words in a book.

- Memorize the letters and their corresponding sounds.

- Blend letter sounds together (*ta, te, ti, to, tu*).

- Sound out simple words (*tap, tip, top*) and understand what the words represent.

- Read and comprehend a short sentence with simple, one-syllable words (*I pet the dog.*) and still remember what it means by the end of the sentence.

- Learn general rules for short and long vowel sounds.

- Read sentences of words containing three or four letters.

- Read and comprehend a simple story made of short, simple sentences.

- Read and comprehend increasingly longer stories.

- Gradually read words with special blends (*th, ay, wh, aught*).

- Read and comprehend increasingly longer stories containing more difficult sounds.

- Read silently, comprehend the story, and communicate it to others.

choose books on subjects he is interested in, and I grab a few books about everyday experiences, like grocery shopping or playing at the park.

Let him read what he can. When reading together, I try very hard not to expect my child to read every word by himself. Or even most of them. At first, he may read one or two words on the page and I read the rest. The point is, he starts reading a little every day and building up his confidence.

Start with letters. When your child is conversing in complete sentences and noticing the letters and words in his favorite books, you might begin working through a **phonics program** with him little by little. It doesn't really matter which one, or even if you use one at all, just so long as you stay at your child's own pace. You could use a curriculum, or you could buy one phonics book and work through it slowly, or you could create flash cards and practice those while reading easy books together. Keep an eye on his interest level and aptitude, and pace yourself accordingly.

When I start teaching a young child his letters, I set a timer for ten minutes. One very reluctant reader in my house worked hard on his phonics if I set a timer and promised that he wouldn't have to sound out any more words when the beeper went off (but most of the time, he wanted to finish the page he was on, anyway). We gradually increased our reading time to twenty minutes, but no more. Whatever we learned during that time, we learned. When the time ran out, we stopped and rested our brains, usually with a cookie. Setting a timer helps a child learn at his own pace, just doing whatever he can do in a short time. Setting a timer also protects against pushing him to do more than he can or even should, more than he is developmentally ready for. Finally, setting a timer gives that poor child hope that even if he hates letters and sounds, he will only need to work for a few minutes. Going at this slow pace helps us remember that our children's brains are each developing at different rates. Our children will master reading in their own time.

So you can teach your child some letters, beginning with the vowels. After he's memorized a couple, he realizes *letters are everywhere*. He sees an *a* on the refrigerator, on every page of his book, on the remote control, on your phone, in the grocery store, on street signs . . . and he is intrigued. Maybe reading will open up more information than just the picture book!

Move into simple blends and short words. Then all of a sudden, reading becomes more difficult. When your child has memorized all the vowel sounds and several consonants, he's ready to try blending sounds together (*ta, te, ti, to, tu*). This is a big mental leap, and it could take him a few days or several weeks to recognize the new sound the blend makes all together. But once he understands blends, he's ready to add a final consonant to make short vowel words (tap, ten, tip, top, tub). Again, he might understand that process in one day, or he could struggle for a while to make sense of what he's doing.

Many parents who teach phonics start with rhyming ending sounds—*ed, ted, fed, bed, wed*, and so on. They find that a child can get through the word more quickly if they recognize the ending.

When my twins began homeschooling after nearly two years in public school, we began with relearning phonics. We learned the vowels first, then the consonants. We began putting these vowels and consonants together to form words. They had been taught in school to read words by their endings, one-syllable rhyming words (ball, call, fall, hall, etc.). This was difficult and confusing for them. And though many of my friends have great success with this method, my children found it easier to read simple words from beginning to end (pet, pen, pill, pit, etc.). You may find, like us, that students need some time to understand that the consonant and the vowel together make one sound (not p-e, but *pe*). Once that connection happens, though, blends usually take off.

Next they were ready to read single words with a blend and one ending consonant. My children have each needed a different amount of time to master this process, but once they have mastered it, the excitement really begins. *Pen* means an actual pen! *Ball* is an actual toy! We can read real things! Suddenly, my children began trying to read everywhere. Signs, labels, T-shirt graphics, everything! It all means something!

Begin reading short sentences. After your child has figured out how to read small words as one complete idea, he's ready to string them together into short sentences like *Bill can go fast*. It's exhausting; by the time he gets to the end of the sentence, he may have already forgotten what the first word was! He may practice this process for several days or even months, working out his brain to hold all that information at once without forgetting. After this hurdle, he's nearly done with the worst of the process, believe it or not.

Once your child has learned how to read simple three- or four-letter words and string them into sentences, you might take him to the library to get some books intended for new readers. If you are fortunate, the library has a collection of Bob Books. We used to own our own collection, but we lost them all because we are a large family and losing things is what we do best. Next best is making messes, which can also be a problem with books and young readers.

Anyway, the Bob Books are perfect for teaching young readers. These short books start off very, very simple, and subsequent books gradually become more complex over the course of many, many levels of books. And each book is so short, there is nearly instant gratification. I have never heard of anyone who used a Bob Book and had a bad day that day.

Besides Bob Books, your library likely owns several shelves of easy

BOOKS WE LOVE FOR GROWING CHILDREN

- *All Things Bright and Beautiful* by Cecil Frances Alexander (board book illustrated by Katy Hudson)
- The Babar books by Jean de Brunhoff
- *Blueberries for Sal* by Robert McCloskey (and all his books)
- The Carl books by Alexandra Day
- The Corduroy books by Don Freeman or B. G. Hennessy
- The Curious George books by Margret Rey and H. A. Rey
- *Farmer Enno and His Cow* by Jens Rassmus
- *Find the Constellations* and *The Stars* by H. A. Rey
- *Fiona's Lace* by Patricia Polacco (and all her books)
- The Frog and Toad books by Arnold Lobel
- The Gilgamesh trilogy by Ludmila Zeman
- *The Great Elephant* by Nik Ranieri
- *Hansel and Gretel* by Cynthia Rylant (and all her books)
- The Lilly books by Kevin Henkes
- The Little Golden Books by Eloise Wilkin
- *The Little Red Lighthouse and the Great Gray Bridge* by Hildegarde H. Swift and Lynd Ward
- *Moonfinder* by Jay Ryan
- *The Tale of Peter Rabbit* by Beatrix Potter (and all her books)
- *The Snow Goose* by Paul Gallico (and all his books)
- The Winnie-the-Pooh books by A. A. Milne

readers. Unfortunately, some of these are easier than others, and the library grading system for how hard or easy the book is does not fit my definition. I usually check out several that look as easy as I can find, then at home we will read them together or skip them, depending on how difficult we find them.

Memorize additional sounds, blends, and sight words. Once she can read a simple sentence or two with comprehension, your child has taken a leap in reading. Now she just needs to learn extra vowel sounds, consonant blends (like *th, sh, ch*) and special sounds (like *ough, ought, udge*) and sight words. It's a very long process to memorize all this, but she can do it over the next couple of years until she has the basic ideas down.

Meanwhile, you will want to keep reading to her, listening to her read aloud, and talking about books. The more you practice reading with her, the easier and more enjoyable the entire process will be. When my children were prereaders, I read to them at least three times a day: after breakfast, during lunch, and at bedtime. And even now that they all read independently, we still read aloud almost every day.

READING HELPS

- library card
- beautiful picture books
- regular read-aloud time together—perhaps two or three times each day
- letter flash cards, ABC magnets, alphabet picture books
- simple phonics program if it helps you
- easy reader books from your personal library and the public library

Reading street and business signs is so much fun for young readers. When one of my sons began reading signs, he insisted on going to the grocery store with me one day. He nagged and nagged and nearly threw a fit, he was so insistent that he *must go* and he must take his little wallet with one dollar with him. So I relented. On the way there, all he would tell me was that the grocery store had a toy he simply must buy and that he knew it was there because of the sign. I didn't believe him.

When he walked through the doors, he turned to me and said, "Where are the slingshots?"

There are no slingshots in the grocery store.

"YES! There are!" He pointed to the sign.

Shingles shots read the sign next to the grocery pharmacy. I was so disappointed along with him. How could a grocery store sign be so cruel?

A month or so later, the same son dragged behind me as I held his hand walking through the parking lot to the same grocery store. At the door, he stopped and insisted he simply must see something down the sidewalk. We must see the rhinoceros in a cage!

Come on, this isn't a zoo—it's a grocery store!

"No, Mom! I've seen it in the cage, but I've been afraid of it all this time. I think if I hold your hand I can go look and see it now."

He led me to the cages of Blue Rhino brand propane tanks at the side of the store. Again, deep, deep disappointment. Reading is just not all it's cracked up to be.

10.2.2.3 SHOULD I TEACH MY CHILD PHONICS?

For many children, phonics works best. Some people start off with a non-phonics style, like look-say or other methods. These are particularly popular with programs that promise to teach your baby to read. It seems to work because young children do memorize logos, signs, and certain words with ease. Take your child grocery shopping, and at three years old he can "read" most of the cereal and cookie packages! By memorizing the flash cards or book pages, the child learns to read just what is handed to him.

On the other hand, phonics gives your child the tools to decode more and increasingly difficult words without your help for the rest of his life. By understanding the sounds and special blends that are the building blocks of the English language, he can decipher harder words as he grows. Phonics rules will also help him learn how to spell.

Now, there is definitely a place for memorizing very common words or words that don't follow phonics rules. We call them "sight words" here at our house. Any word that a child needs to begin reading but isn't truly phonetic becomes a sight word.

10.2.2.4 WHAT DOES READING INDEPENDENTLY MEAN?

A child who can read independently can tell you about what he read a few minutes after he read it. Just because your child can read a few easy readers doesn't mean he's ready for a full elementary curriculum. Let him practice reading aloud to you at least once a day, and soon he'll be ready to add his own "read to self" time on top of that. He's likely to hit some more difficulties as he struggles to make sense of the weird sounds and sight words in his library books. But by the end of the early learning stage, he should be able to read aloud with near fluency

---

PHONICS METHODS

Two easy-to-use phonics methods are the *Abeka* reading curriculum (abeka.com) and the book *Teach Your Child to Read in 100 Easy Lessons* by Siegfried Engelmann, Phyllis Haddox, and Elaine Bruner. Be sure to take either one at a slow, child-directed pace.

the more difficult of the easy reader books, enjoy twenty or thirty minutes of reading alone (even if it's mostly picture books), and understand most of the easy-reader nonfiction and picture books he chooses for himself at the library. In other words, he should recognize that *he has the ability to read whatever he wants*, even if he finds "big books" challenging at times.

10.2.2.5 WHAT IF MY CHILD IS NOT READY FOR READING?

Then your child just isn't ready! Don't worry about it! When I had a seven-year-old who was clearly not feeling it word-wise, we spent our daily fifteen or twenty minutes reading aloud and pointing to the words or looking at letters and the sounds they make. After a few months, he suddenly was ready and learning to read.

In my family, teaching my six children of different genders and abilities and backgrounds (with adopted children), I have found the number one key to teaching reading is *giving them enough time to grow and develop*. Reading requires abstract thinking about symbols representing concrete things. Wow, it's hard. I can sometimes expect too much too quickly. My child may feel frustrated, but with enough time—a month or a year or more—he suddenly is reading. A child will read when he is good and ready.

Reading is slow learning with so many developmental steps, so many tasks to master. The important thing I learned from teaching reading with six children is to allow each child to set his own pace. Then both my child and I can enjoy the process.

If you are concerned that your child's slow progress indicates a learning disability, you can take a look at chapter 16 for more information.

10.2.2.6 WHAT IF MY CHILD IS READY TO READ, BUT JUST DOESN'T LIKE OUR READING TIME?

Use a timer so you both know there is an end in sight. This is a lesson my middle son taught me. He could look at the timer when he became frustrated, and he was comforted to know that soon the work would be over for the day. Finally, after a few months of short lessons, he began asking if he could finish the story after the timer went off. And soon after that, he didn't care if the timer was set or not. He was just ready to read a story or two each day.

That boy still doesn't love to read, but he has the tools to study and learn. And that is what matters.

10.2.2.7 WHAT IF MY CHILD'S PERFECTIONISM IS HOLDING HER BACK?

Build your child's confidence with low-pressure goals. My son who was later to read was also late to speak. At his well-child visit to the pediatrician, the doctor said, "If he isn't speaking soon, we need to send him to speech therapy."

I said, "Do you have a house full of young children? I'm happy one is quiet!"

Sure enough, one day, my son started speaking in full sentences. He never said single words or even babbled—he just went right to clearly understood sentences. I think he wasn't going to talk until he knew he could best his older brother and sister.

I think many students feel that way. They think they need to read fluently from the get-go, so they are afraid to take those mumbled, fumbled steps forward. There are a few things you can do to build your child's confidence.

Try reading easier books. Like, really easy books. Things she can read fluently. Or letters she can identify clearly or blends that are simple to make. Whatever level she is at right now, go back two or three steps and make reading time so easy she asks for something a little harder.

Find something she really wants to read or a topic she loves. Look through those library shelves with her. Show her where the nonfiction books on her favorite animal are. Sometimes there are even easy readers based on children's movies.

Take turns reading. Sometimes I read the left pages while my child reads the right pages. Or sometimes I will read a sentence and she will read the next sentence. That way we are still having reading time together, but we aren't stuck on one page for.ev.er.

Stay casual about it. Spend less time asking her to read aloud. Keep reading to her, but don't put pressure on her to try reading more than a few short minutes. After quite a while, she will relax as it all comes together in her mind. And, like my son, she may later read circles around everyone else.

10.2.3 What fine motor skills should my early learner develop?

How to manipulate small objects and color simple shapes. One of the biggest challenges of early learning is developing fine motor skills. It's a necessary precursor to learning to write, but with the tremendous mental and physical growth going on, little fingers sometimes have a hard time catching up. And as a child learns to read, we often expect writing skills to develop at the same rate. So it is easy to expect too much from young children in this stage. Don't be surprised in the early years if fine motor skills seem slow to develop.

When my son demonstrated signs of poor pencil control after age five while he was learning to read, I became quite distressed. What was wrong with him? I sat next to him during coloring time, but he hated every minute of it. I held his hand and helped him trace letters while he begged to go play cars. I played games with drawing shapes, and he countered by asking for more read-aloud time. We struggled through this for months (maybe a year), and he began to improve right around the time I realized *I should have backed off*.

Like so many other areas of child development, fine motor skills develop at their own rate. There is a generalization that girls tend to develop these skills faster than boys, but all children are unique and will learn at their own rate (we keep saying that, don't we?). There are some natural daily activities other than pencil or crayon work that can help your child develop in this area. The last thing we want is for the student to hate pencils and paper, so rather than frustrating young students, I'd rather see them doing things they love with their little fingers.

SUPPLIES FOR FINE MOTOR DEVELOPMENT

- crayons, colored pencils, paintbrushes, paints, safety scissors
- coloring books, construction paper
- worksheets to trace, color, and copy
- stencils to trace and color
- fine motor play toys: puzzles, lacing cards, busy books, blocks, building toys, LEGOs, marble runs, toy animals and soldiers

---

GENERAL GOALS
- pick up and sort small objects
- color and trace
- cut with safety scissors
- fold paper
- use silverware

PRACTICE FOR FINE MOTOR SKILLS

- counting Cheerios—and eating them!

- lacing up shoes

- building things with LEGOs

- decorating cookies with sprinkles and small candies

- making shapes out of Play-Doh

- pecking out a tune on the piano

- picking flowers or berries

- dressing small dolls or superheroes

- playing board games with small pieces

WHAT I DO
- ask him to pick up Cheerios and raisins
- provide safety scissors, glue sticks, construction paper, and crayons
- periodically encourage "art time" to practice
- ask him to clean up his scattered supplies

10.2.4 What writing and spelling skills might my early learner develop?

How to copy letters, words, and simple sentences. As in reading, there are several developmental stages a child has to go through to learn how to write words. A young child must memorize the shapes of letters, recall them in his mind, and possess the fine motor skills to replicate them on paper recognizably. Quite frankly, it is a miracle any of us learn to write.

Writing was super hard for my early learners. I tried to pressure my first child to learn to write quickly, and it didn't go well. My six-year-old adopted twins came home from public school completely unable to write. Their words were unintelligible, their letters were unidentifiable or backward, and they had no idea how to create a legible word. I had to start completely over again with their writing.

I finally realized that there is so much real-life learning going on throughout the day, that early learners don't need too much time with the papers and pencils anyway. In fact, after I learned my lesson with my first child, I tried hard to limit how much time my other children sat at the table. For the first several years of their lives, I limited their pencil time to less than twenty minutes a day. Once in a while, they would ask for more, but generally, they were ready to run outside and find a new bug or snuggle on the sofa and listen to a story.

Children sometimes learn to write alongside learning to read. Many reading curricula that come with writing worksheets expect the child to write what they learned to read that day. But with my children, that did not work in reality. It seemed their penmanship and spelling work was usually behind their reading ability. Writing is just hard to learn. Like reading, it can't be rushed.

Most children will go through these steps toward writing at their own pace, depending on physical and mental maturity. Even if you begin at an early age, please don't expect your child to complete this process for several years. And there is no reason not to wait until age five or six or later to begin handwriting in earnest. Even more importantly, spelling work and writing words from memory can wait. An early learner can take just one step at a time: pencil control, then word recognition, then copying, and later spelling.

GENERAL GOALS
- color inside the lines (mostly)
- draw a person with a body, face, limbs, and distinguishing features
- add details to drawings (like a doorknob on a house or a bug on a flower)
- draw illegible handwriting only he can pretend to read
- trace letters
- draw loops, sticks, and circles
- trace a stencil
- attempt real letters
- draw individual letters from memory
- copy words
- write a word from memory
- write the simplest words he can read by decoding the sounds
- write his own first and last name
- write increasingly difficult words that he can read
- write simple sentences

WHAT I DO
- have my child spend ten minutes or more coloring or drawing if he enjoys it
- provide art supplies with no pressure to use them
- provide toys like LEGOs and a buildable marble run
- work on puzzles together
- write a recently learned letter for my child to trace just a few times
- encourage my child to have fun trying to write a letter only when he is developmentally able
- have my child trace his own name and learn how to write it after he has learned most letters
- let him play video games for a limited time—the controller requires fine motor skills!

10.2.4.1 HOW DO I TEACH MY EARLY LEARNER WRITING?

Start with the letter forms. With my twins, I began with cursive because that's what I do. (Most people begin handwriting with printing, but I have taught all of my children to write in cursive first. It really doesn't matter.) We practiced simple strokes at first—loops and wavelike traces up and down the page. Then we learned letters one at a time, first easy strokes like *e* and *i*, *m* and *l*. After they had learned the lowercase alphabet, they began tracing and writing words. Later, they learned how to write their own name. Then every day they copied a few words and a sentence.

It took months—months—of practice before they could remember how each letter was formed. And that is completely normal for a child of any age and any background. Visualizing a letter when thinking of its sound is a backward task from reading, maybe more difficult. So I hung a page of letters in two places near the kitchen table for them to look at while they worked.

Provide words and sentences to copy. Copy work teaches so many things: letter formation, connecting letters into words, sentence structure, and good writing skills. Students can copy common words, Bible verses, poems, and even silly sentences. The goal of copy work is to remember how to make words. Instead of looking at each individual letter he wants to write, the child develops the ability to write an entire word or group of words at a time.

Dictate simple words. After the twins had practiced copying, we began two other steps. First, every day I would say a simple word, a word that was very easy for them to read. They would then try to write it by simply remembering the sounds. For the first time, I told them, "Let's write *sat*. So think 's-s-s' sound and write that. Don't pick up your pencil! Now think 'a-a-a' sound. Again, keep your pencil on your paper! Now, what sound is at the end? Finish your word, and look at it carefully. Are you sure what it says? Let's copy that word again before we try another one." Soon, they could take dictation of increasingly harder words and simple sentences.

Have your children write their own work. After practicing that process until it became easier, the next rule was *write your own work from now on*. Every worksheet, math paper, thank-you note, story, everything. Once my students learned how to form all of their lowercase letters and practiced dictation for a while, they could write anything. All they had to do was look at the chart for any letters they had forgotten and ask for spelling help if they needed it. Every one of my students balked at this, groaning for a week or even a month, "It's too *haaaaaaaaard*!" But with this constant practice, the letters would soon just click in the little mind, and the young person just took off writing nearly as quickly as he could think. It is one of those light bulb moments I look forward to—when a child realizes he possesses the ability to put on paper anything he is thinking, and someone else will understand it.

STANDARD SIGNS OF SLOW-TO-DEVELOP FINE MOTOR SKILLS

- Child can identify several letters of the alphabet but cannot write any recognizably.

- Child can identify shapes correctly but draws an oval or circle when you ask for a triangle or square.

- Child cannot color inside the lines of a picture or resists coloring altogether.

- Child stacks five or fewer blocks on top of each other.

- Child cannot trace letters.

Seek your doctor's opinion if these signs continue after age five or any other time you are concerned.

10.2.4.2 WHAT IF MY EARLY LEARNER IS STRUGGLING WITH WRITING?
Remember that this process takes a long time. Some students will begin putting pencil to paper and scribbling at age three and not possess the fine motor control to form letters for a couple more years. Some students truly want to write, but their brain-hand connection is slower than their visualization of the letter, and the little guys just get frustrated. And of course, some students take off in the beginning, then suddenly make no progress or even regress in their writing.

It matters not a whit when a child learns to write. If he is writing sonnets in cursive when he is three or he just begins sentences when he is ten, it's about the same. Writing itself is important in middle school, and all of early learning and elementary is just working up to that point.

Please, please take your time. I sat back and told my twins to try one-half of a handwriting practice sheet each day. Just one-half. And I didn't care how neat it was. I only wanted to see that the letters were formed correctly and that they stayed pretty much on the line. It took twenty minutes to do two lines at first, but later the children were copying a page or two in much less time. Later we concentrated on staying on the lines and neatening up the work. Writing their language or phonics worksheets was quite a struggle for months, so I kept our assignments short. It took over six months for the twins to begin remembering how to form a letter they wanted to write. Then that lovable light bulb moment let them take off.

And they were older than most early learners. They were nearly eight when that light bulb lit up. If they had started writing instruction at a younger age, I'm not sure it would have made a difference. Because by now, I've learned a much better lesson—let each child take his time. He will learn when he is ready, and not before.

> **USE YOUR TEACHING STYLE: WRITING**
>
> - **Classical:** Have your student copy facts from history lessons and vocabulary words.
>
> - **Charlotte Mason:** Guide your child in copying poems and sentences on character qualities.
>
> - **Textbook:** Provide a handwriting workbook for your student to practice writing in.
>
> - **Unschooling:** Allow your child to copy portions of a favorite book or other material he loves.

Remember, writing is not the most important skill in early learning or even most of elementary. Some students prefer to write little and dictate the rest or answer oral questions. That's perfectly fine.

10.2.4.3 HOW DO I TEACH MY EARLY LEARNER SPELLING?

Spelling goes hand in hand with learning to write letters. For the early years, winning a spelling bee is not the goal. (Forget that whole legend that homeschoolers can all spell well and win spelling bees. I am a homeschool graduate *and* a writer, and I said, "Hey, Alexa, how do you spell _____" nearly once a page in this book.)

Early learners study spelling concurrently with reading and handwriting, even if we don't think about those subjects separately. Which is awesome, because we don't need something else to think about. I have used a beginner's spelling book for half my children and no spelling curriculum at all with the other half of them. It just depends on my mood that year and not necessarily on any strategy. It has made no difference—those who never took a spelling course actually are my better spellers. I believe, though I can't prove, that phonics training gave them what they needed to spell. Not just the simple sounds, but learning the finer points of *tion* in *nation* and *sion* in *television,* and *er* in *verse, ur* in *nurse, ear* in *earth,* and more. Many spelling and phonics programs are set up that way. I taught phonics with simply one old reading handbook and used that to teach all my children reading, writing, and spelling.

> ┌─ USE YOUR TEACHING ─
> STYLE: SPELLING
>
> - **Classical:** Teach spelling of important words from subjects like history and science as well as other vocabulary.
>
> - **Charlotte Mason:** Teach spelling words from your child's favorite books.
>
> - **Textbook:** Use a spelling curriculum workbook.
>
> - **Unschooling:** Correct spelling issues as they arise.

There are so many excellent and fun spelling curricula, too. Don't be dissuaded from spelling if that makes you and your child happy. Just keep in mind that these are still early years—our young children just need to learn to love learning, that is all.

GENERAL GOALS:
- recognize patterns in how words are spelled
- learn to spell simple rhyming words
- sound out the spelling of simple words

WHAT I DO:
- gently correct spelling during writing dictation
- teach spelling patterns while my student is learning to read special sounds and sight words
- maybe use a spelling workbook and occasional spelling tests
- sometimes participate in a homeschool spelling bee

10.2.5 What math skills might my early learner develop?

The focus is on real-world application rather than math facts. We may not think about math much during the early years, and we really don't need to, since a whole lot of math education is going on in daily life. Ever since your toddler learned how to ask for "just one more cookie," and your three-year-old begged for "one more hour" before bedtime, your child has been using math to her advantage.

Daily life provides a great math education. I am shocked by how little I had to teach any of my children about math until the later elementary years because so much came up in daily conversations around the table and while cooking together in the afternoon and while driving down the street. Math is just a beautiful pattern and order with which God created and sustains our world, and our inquisitive children are exploring these principles every day.

It's important to remember most early learners will not master every math skill. They will get a jump-start on many of them, though, before they begin formal math later in elementary. There are many math curricula for early learners. I myself even use one, slowly, for my young learners. The one I chose is hands-on and fun, and for every one of my six children, it has been their favorite subject for those early years.

However, you don't need to use a math curriculum at this level, and it is best to avoid math flash cards or worksheets. Simply learning the ideas listed below is plenty. *Remember that the most important math lesson in the early years is real-life application.* Math facts and worksheets don't help with

MATH SUPPLIES YOU MIGHT WANT

- small objects or math manipulatives for counting and acting out math stories
- real and play analog clocks
- a large calendar for finding the date and counting days until an event
- paper and pencil for writing numbers and simple math problems and for drawing and tracing shapes
- purchased or homemade number line
- outdoor thermometer
- rulers, tape measure, and scales
- shape stencils
- shape puzzles and toys that encourage designing with shapes
- 100 number chart
- play money, especially coins

that and may even distract from concrete math reasoning. Young learners use so much math in their daily lives, and they observe their parents using math constantly. They have all of elementary school to learn math facts and division and fractions. Right now, they can play and enjoy learning what comes naturally.

GENERAL GOALS
- understand the passage of time—anticipating the pattern of daily and weekly life, what a clock and a calendar represent, the order of the seasons and the months, understanding how long until Christmas or a birthday
- tell time on a clock with hands to the hour or quarter hour
- use applied math—anticipate the answer to real-world problems (If my mom cuts my sandwich into fourths and my brother eats a piece, what fraction is left after I deal with my brother?)
- solve math problems using manipulatives like coins or plastic animals (When my brother takes away three of my toy soldiers, how many do I have left to shoot his brigade?)
- understand the symbols for plus, minus, and equals
- begin figuring simple math problems in his head (If Grandma gives me two dollars, how many dollars will I have in my wallet?)

- divide shapes into fractions
- count and write numbers past twenty-five
- recognize ordinal numbers (first, second) up to *tenth* and use them correctly in a story problem or acted out in a game (Jack is fifth in line, and there are two people behind him, so I am eighth in line.)
- compare, describe, and order objects based on size, weight, distance, etc.
- count coins (pennies, nickels, dimes, quarters) with help
- recognize and create patterns (red, yellow, yellow, red)

> Deal with numbers in a concrete and verbal way until age ten. Use actual objects when you can, and when you can't, then use words and names for actual objects.
>
> **HARVEY AND LAURIE BLUEDORN**

WHAT I DO

- casually talk about counting when setting the table or folding the laundry
- talk about ordinal positions while standing in the grocery line
- read stories with my child and listen as she tells the events back in order
- encourage my child to notice the shapes of common objects and draw pictures with shapes
- answer the incessant questions "when is dinner" or "how long until my birthday" with event benchmarks

USE YOUR TEACHING STYLE: MATH

- **Classical and Charlotte Mason:** Have your child memorize and practice the basic math skills listed above; explore math concepts utilizing art, nature, and household activities; play board games; and play with math manipulatives like linking cubes and tangram pieces.

- **Textbook:** Teach math concepts through coloring pages, picture books, and household experiments.

- **Unschooling:** Observe and explore mathematical concepts with your child as they occur in daily life.

10.2.6 What role does memorization play in my early learner's development?

Memorization is the foundation of problem solving skills. A child who rehearses a process or a group of facts repeatedly can begin using them for real-life application. While every child has a different capability in memorization, this skill as a whole is easier during these early years than it becomes later, and it is great to take advantage of this opportunity. Many young learners enjoy memorizing what they can use and show off—they feel important if their memorization contributes to their lives. So as tempting as it is to drill any number of facts with them, it is wisest to focus on learning information they can perform (like saying verses to their Sunday school teacher) or use (like the letters to write their name).

Young minds will memorize something. They are like sponges. This is why Montessori and classical homeschool styles spend more time on memorization in the early learning and early elementary stages. Personally, I prefer to work on Bible passages, hymns, and short poems. But each parent will focus on what she thinks best. I think the takeaway, as we consider all the homeschool styles with their differing focuses, is that many young children will memorize quickly; we as teachers can determine what we feel is most important to emphasize. That could be Scripture or poetry or hymns or conjugations or dates or classifications. Or any mixture of things. We will each choose memorization that fits our own values and our own family culture, and we will each teach the way we teach best.

THINGS TO MEMORIZE IN THE EARLY LEARNING YEARS

- how to spell his name
- his address and phone number
- the Ten Commandments
- the Lord's Prayer
- Bible verses
- short poems
- hymns
- descriptive passages from favorite books
- facts about his favorite animal or machine
- the continents and the state he lives in
- the national anthem and the Pledge of Allegiance

- **Classical:** Have your student repeat the alphabet daily and learn Scripture verses, short quotes of Shakespeare, or lists from the Bible or history.

- **Charlotte Mason:** Help your child recite Scripture verses, poetry on nature and manners, or proverbs.

- **Textbook:** Provide curriculum, which may include verses and poems, that has passages your child can memorize.

- **Unschooling:** Encourage the child to memorize favorite passages of books or verses.

Even though young children are already memorizing things without trying, this is a good time to further develop their memorizing muscles. They will need to memorize dates and facts for the rest of their education, so this is good practice.

10.2.7 What might my early learner learn about other subjects?

Whatever you can teach her about science and technology, history and social studies, health and safety, and the arts in the course of your daily life. Reading, writing, and math are the foundations of learning for the rest of a child's life. The student will be reading texts, writing his understanding of each concept, and using mathematical reasoning for every course in school and beyond. So during the early years, memorizing the periodic table of elements or the names of every president should not be a top priority. Remember, these years are about igniting a love for learning.

Early learning should be light on pencil work and heavy on real-world activity. I cannot emphasize enough how little structure homeschooling should have during these young years. All, and I mean *all*, a young child needs to learn is how to love learning. Keep in mind that no child will learn every area listed in this chapter. Only extremely precocious learners should accomplish a majority of the listed goals.

GENERAL GOALS FOR SCIENCE AND TECHNOLOGY

- the life cycle of humans and animals including birth, growth, adulthood, and death
- animals can be classified into families by similar characteristics
- different animals eat and behave differently and live in different places
- some animals change forms during their life cycle, like a caterpillar to butterfly
- plants have a life cycle that includes seed, germination, growth, flower, and fruit
- plant, animal, and human reproduction ensures the continuation of life
- the process of making and receiving a phone call and proper phone etiquette
- how to navigate a computer or television to accomplish tasks like playing a game or watching a video (yeah, we don't need to teach that, since they are practically born knowing how to find YouTube)

GENERAL GOALS FOR HISTORY AND SOCIAL STUDIES

- special days like the Fourth of July and Thanksgiving commemorate important events in our past
- significant figures from history are revered and memorialized, like George Washington and Martin Luther King Jr.
- history is about things that occurred long ago, including Bible times, Roman times, medieval times, colonial times, etc. (though the young child probably could not correctly put those time periods in order)
- people lived, worked, and ate differently at different times in history
- people live, work, and eat differently in other parts of the world
- maps and globes show where people live
- money helps people trade for what they need or want, and money usually represents work done in exchange for the privilege to purchase
- a state or country flag represents those who live in that land

---
USE YOUR TEACHING STYLE: OTHER SUBJECTS

- **Classical:** Attach people and events to historical periods; create science experiments with your student; encourage arts and crafts; arrange field trips.

- **Charlotte Mason:** Help your child begin a nature journal, create a basic time line, indulge in copious reading, and participate in household chores. Prioritize outdoor time.

- **Textbook:** Take your student to the library to get simple science and history books; join a formal physical activity group or co-op field trip group.

- **Unschooling:** Allow the child to explore his own interests.

- authority figures at home include parents and grandparents, while those in the community include law enforcement, employers, and governmental workers

GENERAL GOALS FOR HEALTH AND SAFETY
- healthy personal habits like sleep, nutritious food, and personal hygiene
- the purpose of the five senses
- that the body works in basic functions like eating, breathing, and blood circulation (though they don't understand the process or details)
- that illness is caused by germs, and that germs can be reduced by washing, covering the mouth when sneezing or coughing, and cleaning
- safety rules like using a seat belt, wearing a bike helmet, and crossing a street with an adult
- being careful with dangerous household items like scissors, knives, and cleaning products
- how to call for help from an adult, who to ask for help in public, and how to dial 911

GENERAL GOALS FOR THE ARTS
- develop an appreciation for art of different styles and media
- draw and make crafts with a variety of materials
- view and describe sculpture and paintings, noting medium, colors, and perspective
- listen to music of a wide variety of genres, including classical, marches, folk, and hymns
- enjoy making music with an instrument like a piano, drum, or recorder
- view movies from multiple genres, including animation, comedy, drama, and older works
- enjoy live performances of music, drama, magic tricks, or puppetry

WHAT I DO
- take my child to the zoo
- encourage backyard play and gardening
- read books to my child about the past and present
- have my child participate in children's activities at the art museum and library
- take my child for walks through the park and arboretum
- cook together
- attend family concerts
- attend children's art museum tours and craft days with my child

10.3 QUESTIONS YOU MAY HAVE ABOUT YOUR EARLY LEARNER

10.3.1 When is my child ready for preschool or kindergarten?
Real life is preschool and kindergarten—so don't worry about fixing an exact age to begin. I avoid using those words at all, preferring to think of my child more generally as an early learner. You can watch your child gradually move through the developmental process as she continues to grow and mature.

Someone might ask you, "Is your child in preschool or kindergarten?" That is an inconvenient question, but homeschooling is full of inconvenient "what grade is he in" questions. You can take the time to explain that you are allowing your child to grow and learn at his own pace. Or you can just say the quick-and-easy "K3" or whatever age he is. I've done both, depending on how much I feel like explaining at the time.

10.3.2 With all the talk of Head Start, isn't it important to get a jump on early learning? My homeschool friend has his child reading and memorizing his math facts at age five. I am afraid my child is going to be left behind. Am I really doing enough?

Stop it. If you are giving your early learner opportunities to grow through real-life learning, you are doing enough. Studies have indicated no advantage and even potential long-term harm from early academic education.[1] Similarly, research on early reading shows that whether a child reads at age five or after age seven, there is no distinguishable difference in reading skill by age eleven.[2] In other words, early reading has no lasting effect on a child's academic achievement. Though our culture pushes early academics, early learners thrive and even excel when set free from these pressures. Allowing young children to learn and play naturally gives them that "head start" many yearn to achieve.

Homeschoolers have become aware of the danger of pushing academics early and thus damaging the child's interest in learning. That is why the Montessori, Charlotte Mason, and unschooling methods were developed. And that is the reason for the resurgence in homeschooling in the eighties.

I myself, with my experience homeschooling six children, have only regretted teaching my older children more formal academics at a younger age. My fourth child had little reading and writing instruction before he was age five, and that was still earlier than I should probably have started. He's been an avid reader and writer since age ten. And I already told you my adopted six-year-olds started over with phonics at their own pace. We just read aloud the easiest of readers for about twenty minutes a couple of times a week. One day when they were well over seven, they both decided to take chapter books to their rooms. Within a few months, they were suddenly reading.

Remember when we were in school and the teacher told us not to look at other people's papers? Stop comparing your children to other people's children, and enjoy these early learning years along with your child.

10.3.3 What curriculum should I buy for my early learner?

I cannot emphasize enough how little you need right now. Early learners need virtually no curriculum, just your real, daily life. Don't buy anything for a few years, and enjoy learning around the house and out of the house with your child. She will learn so much from everyday life with you and from looking at picture books with you. Even just playing will help improve her motor skills, social skills, practical math, and phonics in the back of her head where you don't even notice.

You could buy some extra craft supplies (do it when they are on sale at back-to-school time!) or letter magnets for the refrigerator. Or you could just use everything around the house. Cheerios are my favorite learning product.

When the time comes that she is really asking to read or showing signs she has already passed through the first several stages of reading development, if you want a program, choose something easy, perhaps just one phonics reader. Then take it slow. There's plenty of time and curricula for elementary subjects later. Save your money for that.

10.3.4 How much screen time should I give my young child?

As little as possible. I'm not going to tell you a number of hours or minutes, but rather suggest it's probably less than he has now. I'm always asking myself: *How can I further limit my child's screen time?*

My adopted son arrived in our home screen-addicted. He asked for video games and TV constantly. If he walked by a screen in a store or at someone's house, he was so mesmerized he had to be physically removed before he could hear what I was saying. I had to wean him cold turkey. No TV, video games, YouTube, tablets, nothing for several months. Then we gradually allowed a little more and a little more. But he easily regresses, and when he becomes addicted again, I pull back more.

When I see troubling symptoms in my child, I do become concerned that he is trading his real-world education for mindless entertainment, and I want to take steps to stop it. When everyone seems to be in control of their screen patterns, I do allow screen time. Video games are fun, tablet games can be educational, family films are enjoyable. I don't believe screen time is evil. My rule right now is "screen time after dinner." This works really well because my youngest children have activities after dinner most

---

SIGNS YOUR CHILD MAY BE SCREEN-ADDICTED

- He schedules his day around screen time.

- When a screen is on, he cannot hear you talk to him.

- He disobeys to get to a screen.

- He will fight for more screen time.

- He hides tablets or video games.

- He tries to wake up early to be the first one to the screen.

- He stares over the shoulder of someone else playing on a screen instead of doing something else himself.

- He asks several times a day for screen time.

---

days of the week, and dinner is late enough that less than an hour remains before bedtime. On Saturday mornings, they have to set an alarm to end the video games they play together.

10.3.5 Should I worry about my child's speech patterns?

Probably not. I don't believe there is any reason to be concerned about normal glitches in your child's speech. I had one early learner who stuttered every time he got excited. It went away over a few years after he mastered more vocabulary, but it annoyed his siblings.

I had another child who said "um" every. Other. Word. That habit nearly killed us all. If the poor boy wanted to tell a story, we felt like we were physically pulling it out of him. This habit continued until puberty. I don't know how we survived. But we did, and he overcame it naturally. I helped him overcome it by stopping him. "Stop and think about what you want to say next." That sometimes kept him going for a couple of sentences.

I really believe that most speech glitches are just a brain-mouth disco-ordination. Over time, the tongue finally catches up to what the brain is trying to get out of there. Yet I'm not a doctor, so ask your own physician if a speech issue concerns you.

10.3.6 Should I be correcting my child's pronunciation and English?

I do. But I'm an English stickler. My mother was, and her mother was, and my legendary great-grandmother would not abide incorrect English or incorrect pronunciation. So it's second nature to me to correct English.

I have a friend who even laughs at my crisp, exaggerated inner consonants. I do correct pronunciation in my children from the time they learn to talk. *Except* each one of them has said a mispronunciation that is so hilarious we keep it as family vocabulary. One child always said "I can't like this" instead of "don't like." We all came to appreciate this as a better explanation for most things, so we use that phrase regularly. Also, one son said *breafkas* for breakfast until he was fourteen years old. After so many years, he could not make himself say it correctly until one week he just went around the house practicing it correctly. It was so funny.

But other than that, yes, I do correct pronunciation and subject/verb agreement and pronoun usage and sentence structure. I will say the sentence properly, then ask the child to repeat it before going on. Because I have done that since they learned to talk, they are not generally frustrated by the practice. And the teens do it to each other every day. It's constant English class around here whether you like it or not.

We all have to bite our tongues not to correct people outside the family. That would be rude, but we have each made that embarrassing mistake at one time or another. I thoughtlessly corrected my orchestra conductor once, and then I wanted to *die*. He just laughed, "You really *are* a homeschool mom!"

10.3.7 How much should I emphasize self-care for my early learner?

Regularly—unless you want to wipe little bottoms for years to come. The skills of dressing, toileting, making a simple cereal or toast breakfast, buckling himself in the car, and playing outside safely are arguably more important than academics.

Self-care teaches many things. Children learn responsibility by using the bathroom independently. They learn consideration and the science of germs by washing their hands. They develop fine motor skills by brushing their own teeth and flossing. They develop fine and gross motor skills by dressing themselves, and they learn matching and social appropriateness from choosing their own clothes.

I love that the Montessori method teaches that a child should be shown once or twice how to do something and then left on his own to repeat the process. I wish I had done that for shoe tying, because I simply hate tying shoes several times a day and usually cheat by purchasing Velcro until the child is eight or nine. Seriously, I'm that lazy about it. Please learn from my mistake.

10.3.8 What chores should my early learner be working on for self-care and real-life learning?

Chores can be whatever the child is capable of doing. Choose a few that are helpful to the family and easy to inspect. (Someone once told me "you can only *expect* what you can *inspect*.") As your child grows older, he can take on more and more responsibility. He will probably enjoy getting a "big kid" chore at first until the novelty wears off.

IDEAS FOR CHORES

- Put dirty clothes in the hamper.
- Make the bed.
- Clean up toys.
- Straighten the bookshelf.
- Pick up items left around the house and deliver them to the correct room.

- Fold towels.
- Clear off the table after a meal.
- Empty small waste cans.
- Put clean silverware away.
- Load a front-loading washing machine and put wet clothes into the dryer.

10.3.9 What if my child asks uncomfortable questions about privates or where babies come from? Am I in for sex ed already?

No, stop panicking. I'm chuckling, because this issue is so normal and yet so easy to deal with.

Only answer the question your child asks and don't give more information. Use as few words as possible. "Where do babies come from?" Mommy's belly. "How did it get there?" God put it there. "How will it get out?" The doctor (or midwife) will help me. "Why are boys and girls different?" God made them very different. (Children figure out there is more to that on their own one way or another.)

I was teaching K3 in a Christian school when I became pregnant with my first son. Every one of those thirty children had to ask me several questions about my growing belly and the entire birthing process. And all the other teachers laughed at my skirting the questions. I learned through practice that less is more.

This frank, unembarrassed communication helps as a child grows toward puberty. Because I have always been willing to answer any question, my children have been fairly comfortable talking with me about these things. When the boys begin puberty in earnest, though, I hand the questions off to my husband.

10.3.10 What if my child has little interest in activities like looking at books, playing outdoors, or using fine motor skills?

Introduce these concepts gently. Read short stories before bed (nearly every child likes the opportunity to delay bedtime) or while he eats lunch. Sit with him to color for five minutes at a time. Teach him how to play marbles, make a craft, or line up soldiers and cars. Kick a ball or pass it back and forth while talking to him or practicing counting. Take walks through a neighborhood or park. Feed ducks. Find a nearby playground. You will eventually find something interesting your child can enjoy.

If your child continues to resist using his fine or gross motor skills, maybe take him to the doctor for a checkup and advice.

10.3.11 I don't particularly enjoy playing. How can I encourage my child to love playing?

Not everyone enjoys playing, believe it or not. I hate games and pretending. I would rather work on a project (like this book), read, attend a lecture or concert, or visit a museum. These are my idea of a raucous good time. But play is incredibly important for early learners. They learn social skills, science, problem solving, role-playing, housework, and work habits through projects or playing scenarios.

I have found that starting your child out with some great tools can help her enjoy playing alone and with friends. Children love household tools like pots, pans, measuring cups, and flatware with a copious amount of water. Throwing all that in a kiddie pool makes for easy cleanup.

Messy play seems to be extremely attractive at this age. Some of my friends lay down mats on the table and floor. I banish my children to the garage or outside. For years, they believed the maxim "play dough is an outdoor toy!" But they still love paints, dough, clay, and sand.

RECIPES FOR FUN!

- **Finger paint:** Mix ½ cup cornstarch, 3 tablespoons sugar, and 2 cups water in a pan over low heat. Stir until blended. Divide into 4 or 5 portions, putting them into separate bowls and using a different food coloring for each. Add a pinch of dish detergent to each to make cleaning easier.

- **Play dough:** Mix 1 cup flour, ¼ cup salt, and 2 tablespoons cream of tartar in a small pan. Stir well. Add 1 cup water, 1 tablespoon vegetable oil, and food coloring, and stir over medium heat 3–5 minutes until the mixture forms a loose ball. Turn the dough out and knead on a lightly floured surface. Store in an airtight container.

- **Modeling clay:** Mix 1 cup salt, ½ cup water, and 2 tablespoons vegetable oil with 2 cups flour. Form clay into desired shape. When finished, bake at 250°F for one hour or until hardened. Decorate with paint, watercolors, or fingernail polish.

Board games teach a variety of important skills. Taking turns, sharing, being a good sport, and showing kindness are just some of them. I try to make myself play board games sometimes, but my children enjoy playing them together nearly every day. And one of my children even creates his own board games and card games with elaborate maps, detailed rules, and fantasy backstories.

Outdoor play develops a variety of gross motor skills. My twins had little or no experience playing outdoors when they moved in as six-year-olds. They could not bounce or kick a ball, run for more than a couple of yards, or ride a tricycle. Team sports were entirely beyond their comprehension. With several hours of outdoor play, swimming, or recreational sports almost daily, however, their therapist says they have caught up to normal physical ability. This experience of teaching them has emphasized to me the importance of outdoor play for young children.

Country children and suburbanites like my family have an advantage when it comes to outdoor play. My friends in the big city, though, take advantage of playrooms, parks, and even empty hallways to give their children space to play.

10.3.12 How do I teach my young child to sit still?

Gradually and naturally. In the real world, sitting is a required skill, and I'm needing to practice it right now while I write this book. It's difficult because I keep jumping up to get more water or walk around the room or look in the refrigerator for a snack or see if someone else is doing something more fun.

On the flip side, very little sitting is required of a young learner, I have found. First of all, there's almost no formal teaching going on in early learning, so there's so little reason to sit still. My young elementary son still lies on the floor and climbs on the table to do his math, and he is much more accurate that way. My middle school son can only read with his feet up in the air. And my high school son wanders around the house every ten minutes and still completes an assignment in a surprisingly short time.

And yet the world requires sitting, as my current desk incarceration proves. There's also sitting at church and Sunday school, waiting at the doctor's office, and even eating dinner. We have increased the dinnertime sitting gradually by enjoying a short conversation as a family before the dishes are cleared from the table. Even if the young ones can't take part in the discussion, they can sit for just a few minutes to listen.

Young learners do gradually learn to sit still, sometimes without our trying to teach them. They sit for increasing periods of time while we read them books. They sit while waiting for the pediatrician. They sit for a short lesson in Sunday school. They will, slowly but surely, learn to sit.

Once elementary school begins around seven or so years of age, lessons will still be short, so little sitting will be required. Maybe you'll want your child to sit for a quick lesson or two. My children often prefer to stand while writing. Or wander while memorizing facts.

I would not worry about sitting at all. It will happen by itself. Someday.

10.3.13 What if my child is shy or has few friends to play with?

Get that child a social schedule, lol! This is not a problem unique to homeschoolers; other moms also try to get their children out of the house and playing with others. You may want to intentionally encourage your child to do things away from you. Even as a young child, she is beginning to individuate, to learn who she is apart from you. She will develop an understanding of who she is, what she likes, what her own personality is, and how she deals with others while she is away from her parents.

Your child's social activities need not be for long periods of time. Short play-dates and church programs are fun ways for her to spend time away from home.

10.3.14 How do I teach my early learning child while taking care of toddlers and babies?

Again, focus on real-life learning. If you spend one hour or less "teaching" your child by cooking with him or pointing out letters or even having a short lesson on how to form the letter *p*, you could do that during nap time. Or while you're feeding the baby. Or right alongside your toddler. One thing I learned when my fourth child was a baby was how little time I needed to teach my older children—the basics are so simple and imaginative play so much more important. Read more about this in section 15.3.5.

HELP YOUR CHILD MAKE FRIENDS

- Take your child to Sunday school.

- Invite Sunday school friends to your house to play.

- Sign up for recreational sports teams or play events.

- Take your child to the park regularly when you know school is out.

- Join a homeschool support group that has park days.

- Accept birthday party invitations, and consider having a friend over for a birthday.

10.3.15 How do I keep my early learner occupied while I'm teaching older children?

With a mix of creative strategies. A young learner's day includes so much playtime, yet a slightly older child may need to hit the books. (For a couple of hours, at least.) With some creativity and planning, you can juggle the needs of your children through different periods of your family life.

Let your older children work on things they can do alone while you keep the little ones occupied in the morning. For example, the older children might complete their independent reading or worksheets or projects to the best of their ability for an hour or two while you work with the little ones. Then, in the afternoon, have a Quiet Time. While the young ones nap or play quietly in their rooms, go over what the elementary students have done and teach them a quick lesson. You might also take that opportunity to grade high school work and answer questions. If you don't finish with the older children, you can do more in the evening after the littles go to bed.

Another strategy is to train younger ones to play by themselves for increasing amounts of time in the morning. This might look like a half hour outside for the younger child while you do a math lesson with a sibling. Then, after a snack and some chatting, the young one could play with an educational toy while you help with another subject, and so on.

My favorite strategy is to include the youngest students in the older students' lessons. While we discuss history with teens, the younger ones look at picture books on the same topic, color a picture about it, or reenact a battle with toy soldiers. While we do science, I include them in the experiment. While I work on algebra with one, I let the younger child play "algebra time" by counting small candies or cereals and trying to write the numbers on paper.

My best advice is to keep three things in mind. First off, the young ones are absorbing so much from what you do and say while they are playing and making messes nearby. Secondly, with some creativity and a lot of patience, each day will go differently and you'll survive. Most importantly, this seemingly crazy stage is, in reality, the best fun you'll have homeschooling. Try to enjoy your three-ring circus. Read more about this in section 15.33 and see sample routines in appendix B.

10.3.16 What if my young child doesn't listen to me?

This may or may not be a discipline issue. Unfortunately, throughout the homeschool years, this problem rears its ugly head during teaching time (or in the case of little children, while you are teaching older siblings).

I have two strategies that I hold on to tightly. The first is to **be consistent.** Whatever disciplinary procedure I have explained to my young child, I follow through immediately. For instance, this afternoon I asked my young child to look at books quietly while I explained an assignment to my high schooler. The young boy left the room and went upstairs to play with toys. He was no longer allowed to look at books but now had to sit right next to me and hold my hand while I finished the explanation to my teen.

Another time, I invited my young children to play quietly with soldiers and coloring pages while I discussed relevant history with my older children. The younger ones interrupted repeatedly with questions about the dog, the weather, what's for supper . . . everything I would rather discuss than the ancient civilization along the Huang He River valley. So instead of remaining with us, each went to his room to play alone just as I had promised. They felt left out and didn't interrupt (as much) next time. Whatever I do, I need to be consistent and relevant.

My second strategy is to **have as few rules as possible.** It's easy to remember, then: do your best work, and obey Mommy. So if anything arises amiss, I can say, "Is this your best work?" and they know what I mean. With the interrupting problem, clearly we aren't obeying Mommy. An obedient response is to hold Mom's hand or stand quietly next to her so she knows you need to talk.

My strategy with homeschool training as with home discipline is really the same: be consistent, have few rules. If a child consistently shows disinterest or has trouble listening during a lesson, I may also look for an underlying learning issue. Is she having difficulty understanding? Sometimes taking a step back and simplifying things helps overcome these issues.

10.3.17   When is my student ready for elementary school?

Your child may be ready to move on to elementary school when the following criteria have been fulfilled:

- **He demonstrates a foundational understanding of reading.** Early elementary students may not be reading fluently for a few years. Many subjects, however, require at least rudimentary skills. Before moving ahead to elementary level studies, spend plenty of time practicing short words and understanding simple sentences. You might want your child to read some easy readers independently before moving forward.
- **She has begun writing simple words and sentences.** Elementary textbooks require writing. And even if your style is more classical or Charlotte Mason, you'll want your elementary student copying words or passages and beginning creative writing to a certain degree. Before moving forward, a student should begin writing simple words similar to those in an easy reader.
- **He understands simple math problems in daily life.** Before beginning elementary math, he should be able to figure out that if he has ten cookies and eats three, he has seven left. He may use

manipulatives, pictures, or his fingers to solve problems, but he can visualize what he is doing in basic adding and subtracting scenarios. He also understands the basic concepts of a calendar and can find the date with help.

- **She has the maturity to complete a two- or three-step task.** Elementary schoolwork involves multitasking—reading a sentence, understanding what it means, and acting on it. Or she might hear a story, comprehend what it means, describe what she hears, and take action by drawing a picture or writing simple words about it.
- **He just seems ready.** No one knows your child like you do, so feel confident moving forward or waiting. You can take into account his maturity and comfort level with books, pencils, manipulatives, and attention span to determine how quickly or slowly to make this transition.

And remember, there should be no arbitrary age for beginning formal elementary school academics. Your child grows in spurts, and even if she seems ready, she may not move forward for quite a while. It is always better to wait than to push ahead. The defining milestone of elementary is **reading**. If your child begins to read simple words, write simple words, and understand math with manipulatives, she's probably ready for elementary school. However, it is important to allow your child to develop these skills in her own time. As I said before, I had a child reading and raring to go at age three, but another not really firm until seven. Early learning can last anywhere from ages three to ten. There is no rush to move on to elementary. Your child will do fine long-term no matter when she begins elementary.

• • •

I love the early learning years the most. For one thing, the student is at his cutest. For another, learning is so gentle and natural. Every day is filled with wonder—the child's wonder at God's creation, and our wonder at the child's growth. It is a beautiful time to build the foundations of a lifelong love of learning and a lifelong bond of family. These loves lay the foundation for the largest learning period right around the corner—the elementary years.

11

ELEMENTARY SCHOOL: THE FIRST- THROUGH FIFTH-GRADE YEARS

Approximately ages 6–12

THE ELEMENTARY YEARS are when we begin thinking we are home-schooling. First grade is when many of us start formally teaching our child. Maybe you took your child out of a traditional school—this often happens during the elementary years. So maybe you did not read my last chapter on early learning and flipped right here. That is okay. You may want to flip through that chapter to understand why slow learning and a relaxed attitude toward education is important. Because all of that applies here, too.

Whatever you do, do not start trying to create a school at home. You don't need desks and a schoolroom (unless that helps you concentrate better). You don't need to buy a big fancy boxed curriculum (unless you find that's your personal homeschool style from chapter 6). You don't need to start with the Pledge of Allegiance and recitation of the seven continents. You don't need a whiteboard or posters or bulletin board or border across the top of the wall showing how to write letters in cursive. None of that is necessary, but you can do what you want. Do what makes you happy, *but don't feel obligated to create a public school at home.* This is a time, still, to gently learn the basics in a warm, encouraging environment.

Oh, my word, that's the opposite of the way I began as a child. I had the desk, the flag hanging from the ceiling, the posters, the whiteboard, the clock on the wall, the entire schoolroom. But back in my time, that's what we knew. Homeschooling was generally schooling at home. But gradually, over the next year or so, my mother learned that I, a middle schooler, preferred to work independently and became incredibly annoyed if anyone so much as read the directions on a paper for me. She also noticed that my sister learned relationally, and did wonderfully sitting beside our mother, reading aloud and answering her questions orally.

We always learned from the boxed curriculum, but my parents used *their* teaching style and customized it to *our* learning style. That intersection was the sweet spot of our loving to learn. And that is the single most important part of the elementary years.

The defining criteria of readiness for elementary studies should be a basic grasp of reading skills. Based on their reading readiness, my own children began elementary school at different ages and times—meaning they also completed a different number of elementary years. (Seriously, what does grade level mean when you are homeschooling a specific child? This is why understanding the child's brain and academic development is so important.)

For instance, my first son began elementary studies when he was five years old and stayed in elementary an "extra year" and middle school an "extra year" so he would be mature enough for high school. My third son began elementary when he was nine. My fourth son began elementary when he was six. My twins, who came home from public school when they were six, started over with early learning and did not reenter elementary level studies until they were eight. There is no exact age level for elementary school. Remember, at age seven we are going to see a four-year age range in brain development. There is no reason *not* to wait if your child is not ready.

I cannot stress this enough. The institutional school system would have us believe that every six-year-old should start a formal first-grade program, sitting still at the table with pencil and paper, learning to read fluently from pre-chapter books. But not every six-year-old child's brain is mature enough for this type of work. Since children learn reading and writing at different rates, there should be no arbitrary age for the beginning of elementary.

Elementary studies are simply preparation for middle school and high school. In the elementary years we are laying the foundation for larger thinking, for making connections, for looking at big-picture issues, for forming logical conclusions.

That is why every year in elementary feels like review. If you examine an elementary textbook curriculum, you will find that language arts is the same over and over again. Literature is reviewing the same simple analysis over and over again in slightly more detail. Even a basic science course simply introduces concepts the student will study in-depth in middle school. In fact, for most of my students, I skipped a couple of years of grammar workbooks and just used higher grade levels. The earlier ones were just redundant, anyway. If I did purchase grammar books in order, there was a lot of page skipping.

I am also guilty of not doing much science. It's not a priority for me in elementary school. I tend to focus on the humanities of history, literature, and language arts. And of course, math. In the elementary years, my children tend to explore, experiment, and read up on any science topic that catches their interest. I guess you could say I unschool science (see section 6.6). My children have not suffered in middle school and high school science because of my lax attitude. My oldest son received a near-perfect ACT score in the subject. He gave me the courage to keep unschooling early science with his siblings.

I have a friend who loves science and really sticks with it in the elementary years. But history is not her thing. That's fine; everyone gets what they need later. Don't be intimidated by your homeschool friends' choices and methods. Remember that each homeschool is and should be very different. Thou shalt not covet thy neighbor's homeschool but be content with such homeschool as ye have.

This chapter is just a general discussion of what an average student (whatever *average* is) will learn by the end of his fifth-grade year—around age eleven or twelve. This obviously varies wildly with each child. Take a look at the "General goals for the elementary years" list. Seriously, by the end of this stage, these items are literally all your child needs to begin middle school. But realize that simply grasping these concepts—which may come as early as ten years old—does not mean the child should move on to middle school. Just like the younger years, there is plenty of time for further brain development. Quite a bit needs to change in his thinking and maturity before he is ready to move on.

Beyond what your child is learning, the elementary years are also an important time for you as a homeschool parent. This is when you decide what is most important for your own family's education: your values, your goals, your subjects. It's also a good time to consider how your teaching style (chapter 6) fits with your child's learning style (chapter 7). This is when you learn how to homeschool within your family culture—teaching the way you teach best for the way your child learns best.

In the elementary years you learn more than your student does. You develop confidence in how you teach. You develop a greater understanding of how your child prefers to learn. You begin gradually showing him how he can learn in other ways too. You become more comfortable with his creative experimentation. You encourage him to take risks and help him learn to deal with failure. You begin appreciating his emerging strengths, talents, and challenges. You begin gradually showing him how to examine details and make comparisons. You begin to lay the foundation for analysis in his work. You encourage, throughout the day, enhanced communication skills. You build the foundation of how you and your child will learn together through the later years.

Elementary years are about the basics: the basics of learning for both you and your student.

GENERAL GOALS FOR THE ELEMENTARY YEARS
- gradually increase reading ability
- understand the basic rules of grammar and punctuation
- comprehend the idea of paragraph construction
- recognize the simple construct of literature (problem and solution, main characters and how they change, different types of literature)
- grasp the basic facts of math
- know how to read and write a math problem
- practice adding, subtracting, multiplying, and dividing large numbers
- understand the difference between perimeter, area, and volume of simple shapes
- master principles of time

- understand guessing (hypothesis) and testing in science
- know the basics of vital internal organs
- appreciate a variety of sciences
- understand the difference between ancient, "olden times," and modern history
- be able to identify some concepts of culture in each time period

11.1 THE ELEMENTARY STUDENT'S DEVELOPMENT

11.1.1 How might my elementary student's character develop?

Your child will grow in empathy and the ability to anticipate others' emotions. In the early years, it does little good to say, "How do you think it feels when you hit your sister?" Quite frankly, it felt really good to him to slap her right in the face. Maybe the hitting will lessen with a time-out. Or hard labor. There's always something that needs cleaning.

But in the elementary years, this "how does it feel to others" takes on more meaning. Finally, at long last, our children begin to look at things from the viewpoint of others. They further develop empathy in a real sense—feeling the pain others encounter. Now that empathy rarely extends to fellow siblings in my house. Apparently, the law of the land is *everyone gets what's coming to him.* But outside the home, there may be sincere feeling for the plight of others.

My children are quite attached to our next-door neighbors. And not only because they let us use their swimming pool for free. Daily, my children will visit them or walk their dog or show off a new ability. The neighbors have begun calling my children their godchildren.

For quite some time, the wife in this family took care of her elderly mother. The mother was frail, though, and needed assistance walking across the room, even though she would never admit it. After she fell and broke her hip twice, the neighbors reluctantly moved her to an assisted living facility nearby that could watch her more closely.

Well, that move devastated my children. They nagged me to take them to visit her every week. And if we accidentally missed a week because of appointments or sickness, we were reprimanded by the elderly resident and forced to sit through two hours of gossip instead of just one, besides the update on what happened each day on Game Show Network.

But sadly, our elderly friend's health deteriorated. Quite rapidly, she was approaching death. And as the Lord would have it, we were the last to say goodbye to our adopted great-grandmother.

The burial, held in the pouring rain, was beautiful. And my young empathetic children could barely stop hugging their beloved neighbors, saying, "You must miss your mother so much! We are so sad with you!" And they meant it. Because at someone else's loss, they felt deep grief.

This empathy takes quite a while to fully develop. My eight-year-old daughter still comes home from choir every week upset that she was not chosen Student of the Week. Never mind that her close friend earned it; she simply cannot be happy for another's success. This empathy is a long, hard lesson to learn during these years.

As a child develops empathy, he can also begin to anticipate others' emotions before they occur. My older elementary student can say, "We need to clean up these LEGOs before Mom finds them and is frustrated." Or even show forethought by bringing extra water to soccer practice to make Dad happy. Passing homeless people or seeing someone at church less fortunate will often provoke questions and a desire to help tangibly. Thinking ahead for others' emotions is a great milestone in empathy development. This anticipation enables the child to behave thoughtfully. If only my children—old and young—would anticipate my frustration over mess more often, right?

With this empathy begins the realization that people can experience two emotions simultaneously. With a friend's death, we can be sad he is gone while happy he is in heaven. When a new LEGO building is erected, we can be proud of the achievement but less than enthusiastic about the mess around it. The child himself will notice he is both tired from work yet happy with what he has done. He is learning the complexity of emotions and how to better relate to those around him.

FOUNDATIONAL GOALS
- name others' feelings
- take turns speaking in a conversation
- feel bad before being caught doing wrong
- modify behavior with one reminder
- remember more than one chore if asked to "do your chores"
- anticipate rewards or consequences

- engage in pretend play
- ask questions to learn more about other cultures

DEVELOPMENTAL GOALS
- anticipate others' reactions
- modify behavior to make others more comfortable or happier
- remember to do chores without being reminded
- say please and thank you without being reminded
- confess wrongdoing before being caught

ADVANCED GOALS
- motivate friends to act on behalf of others
- organize a ministry or volunteer project
- practice controlling his temper
- speak with respect to adults and peers
- maintain a quiet voice
- practice conflict resolution

11.1.2 How might my elementary student develop physically?

Sadly, baby fat disappears during elementary school. Those precious round faces and bodies begin growing taller, leaner, and stronger. Boys and girls, though, still grow at roughly the same rate until the end of elementary or beginning of middle school. Since girls generally begin puberty before boys, they may grow taller than boys toward the end of elementary. But boys quickly catch up in height sometime around middle school.

Because of their increased self-awareness and better communication skills, elementary students complain more often of aches and pains. It feels like they have headaches, stomachaches, and sore throats more often, even when their dislike of homework is taken into consideration. Because their bones are growing steadily, they may experience very real growing pains, particularly at night.

FOUNDATIONAL GOALS
- tie his shoes
- do chores
- speak clearly
- form letters properly

- begin typing
- kick a moving ball
- perform handstands or cartwheels
- take responsibility for all areas of grooming, including bathing

DEVELOPMENTAL GOALS
- jump rope
- use a Hula-Hoop
- ride a bike
- play a musical instrument
- write in cursive

ADVANCED GOALS
- learn to take increased care of hygiene, ensuring he smells good
- take a greater interest in healthy habits of nutrition and exercise
- understand the changes of puberty and the basics of human sexuality
- type fluently
- play competitive sports
- perform on a musical instrument confidently

11.1.3 How might my elementary student develop mentally?

At this stage, your child's brain grows rapidly until it is nearly the size of an adult's. The frontal lobe, in particular, experiences a great development. This allows your child to think through a process step-by-step. Now he can begin learning several-step math problems, for instance, or begin applying the writing process. Also, the connections he began building in his early learning years now allow him to think big picture in all of his subjects.

FOUNDATIONAL GOALS
- work on a puzzle
- read independently
- tell time
- know his left hand from his right hand
- understand the sequence of common events and if the sequence is out of order
- learn spelling rules and write paragraphs

- graph objects by same and different characteristics (Venn diagram)
- use some irregular verbs correctly ("gave" not "gived")
- tell a story with a beginning, middle, and end
- memorize her address, phone number, and how to report an emergency or call for help
- understand that slang or profanity are "bad words"

DEVELOPMENTAL GOALS
- write numbers as words and digits
- complete assignments
- try to solve multistep problems alone
- write a multiparagraph assignment
- follow multistep instructions
- identify the problem and solution in a story
- speak and write in longer, more complex sentences
- tell or write a detailed story with a clear resolution
- read chapter books
- remind other family members of tasks

ADVANCED GOALS
- think abstractly
- work on abstract problems like prealgebra
- connect ideas from multiple subjects
- write a compelling explanatory or persuasive essay
- test hypotheses using the scientific method
- take initiative and study most subjects independently

11.1.4 How might my elementary student develop socially and emotionally?

Though your elementary student is becoming increasingly attached to her friends, her family is still her most important relationship. She still defines herself by where she falls in the birth order and how she relates to each parent. She is likely to feel closer emotionally to her same-sex parent.

Your child is also working on controlling her emotions. As her personality develops, so too do her natural coping mechanisms. She will deal with stress her own way—retreating, arguing, bargaining, or even exploding.

DON'T BE CONCERNED UNLESS AT THE MIDDLE OR END
OF THIS PERIOD YOUR ELEMENTARY STUDENT

- cannot read
- has limited vocabulary
- cannot write a simple paragraph of five sentences on a single topic
- cannot complete math addition, subtraction, multiplication, or division with two-digit numbers
- cannot demonstrate fractions with real objects, such as pizza or chocolate bars
- demonstrates several traits of ADHD (see section 9.2.6)

- exhibits anxiety or sad behavior regularly yet cannot share feelings
- resists family activities
- possesses poor body image
- resists leaving the house
- cannot make friends
- is unduly fearful of failure or cannot handle failure
- has little or no self-control or is overly aggressive
- has little forethought or takes unsafe risks
- shows signs of substance abuse

This is a good time to discuss proper ways to handle strong feelings before puberty exaggerates them all.

FOUNDATIONAL GOALS
- exhibit clear personality traits
- take pride in knowledge and improvement
- use words for emotions
- enjoy a wider variety of friends

DEVELOPMENTAL GOALS
- take responsibility for self-care, like spending alone time when overwhelmed, taking a nap when tired, or running outside when frustrated
- have a positive body image
- bounce back well from mistakes
- get along with siblings some of the time (ha!)

ADVANCED GOALS
- understand when to seek help and when to find the answer herself
- understand the risks of substance abuse and inappropriate relationships
- develop problem solving abilities with friendship issues
- resist peer pressure

11.2 WHAT YOUR ELEMENTARY STUDENT COULD BE LEARNING

The point of elementary school is to gradually build on the slow, relaxed culture of early learning. We are simply introducing basic concepts that are important in middle school—but just introducing, not necessarily mastering. Your student will learn many of these basics through the years leading up to his preteen age. He may not excel in them for a while; he may need to wait for his brain to gradually catch up to his passion. Or he may breeze through these concepts and enjoy building on them until the beginning of middle school. He will just learn at his own pace.

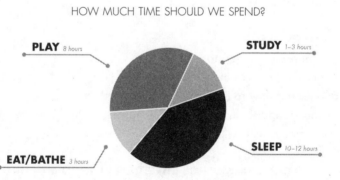

HOW MUCH TIME SHOULD WE SPEND?

PLAY 8 hours

STUDY 1–3 hours

SLEEP 10–12 hours

EAT/BATHE 3 hours

11.2.1 What might my elementary student learn about the Bible?

Important Bible stories and key verses, especially about the plan of salvation. Family Bible reading and prayer should continue during this time. Most elementary students can understand a simple Bible version such as the New Living Translation and even participate in reading it aloud. Many families integrate hymn singing and Scripture memory, as well.

Children in elementary school love Bible clubs and church children's programs. An excellent program will support your training at home with sound Bible teaching, a Bible memory program, and even fun activities to make it enjoyable.

FOUNDATIONAL GOALS
- recall important Bible stories
- know some verses by memory
- understand that morality comes from God
- know that the Bible is God's Word
- know that Jesus loves her

DEVELOPMENTAL GOALS
- participate in a Bible club
- find a verse in the Bible with no help
- fully participate in the adult church service
- volunteer to serve in a church ministry
- memorize the Ten Commandments

ADVANCED GOALS
- take notes on the sermon
- understand how to make a profession of faith
- understand how to publicly declare his faith
- memorize and share the Romans Road of salvation (verses explaining how to know Christ personally)

11.2.1.1 HOW CAN I PASS ON MY CHRISTIAN FAITH TO MY CHILDREN?
The single most important way to pass on your faith is to demonstrate it to your child every day. Since your child is with you literally all day, every day, your personal walk with the Lord is always on display.

Don't hesitate to talk about your personal Bible readings, your prayers, your hope in God. Even difficult times and unanswered prayers can demonstrate your faith through trials.

Many children who are brought up in church will express a desire to

---

BIBLES AND BIBLE STORYBOOKS FOR ELEMENTARY STUDENTS

- *NLT My First Hands-On Bible*
- *ESV Grow! Bible*
- *NIV Adventure Bible*
- *The Big Book of Bible Questions* by Amy Parker and Doug Powell
- *The Story Travelers Bible* by Tracey Madder
- *The Complete Illustrated Children's Bible* by Janice Emmerson
- *Egermeier's Bible Story Book* by Elsie Egermeier

---

make a decision for Christ during these years. They come to understand that God loves them, but they have fallen short of that love by acting in sin (see Romans 3:23). They learn that the penalty of this sin is not only physical death but also an eternity separated from God and heaven (see Romans 6:23). Yet God, in his infinite love for us, died to take the penalty for our sin and that of the entire world (see Romans 5:8). Not only that, but he rose from the grave, demonstrating both his power over sin and death and the new life we can have through him. We can, indeed, accept this free gift, taking this blood payment for ourselves, by simply believing in him (see Romans 10:9). (These, or a similar sequence of verses, are often called the Romans Road.)

WHAT I DO:
- read Scripture regularly with my child and briefly discuss the passage
- get her involved in a church children's program
- encourage regular Scripture memory

11.2.2 What reading skills might my elementary student develop?

Though the ability to read is the benchmark for beginning elementary level studies, reading skills are still developing throughout these years. Students may struggle to read slowly in the beginning, but over the next several years, your child will become increasingly confident in his skills. As he works in other academic subjects, he will learn to read a variety of genres: nonfiction, biography, literature, and even instructions.

245

FOUNDATIONAL GOALS
- read chapter books
- read silently for a period of time and demonstrate comprehension
- enjoy a wide variety of literature, including fiction, poetry, nonfiction, and instructional works
- ask appropriate questions for the story
- identify the problem and solution in a story
- identify the meter and rhyme of a poem
- add increasingly descriptive words to his vocabulary
- learn how to use a computer or dictionary to find definitions, synonyms, and antonyms

DEVELOPMENTAL GOALS
- read aloud fluently and with expression
- identify genres of fiction (historical, fantasy, science fiction, myth)
- understand the difference between the first- and third-person point of view
- understand the difference between direct and indirect quotes
- describe characterization and compare/contrast characters
- identify descriptive phrases and symbolism in poems
- understand the meaning of new words from the context
- understand and use figures of speech

ADVANCED GOALS
- read for enjoyment from a wide variety of genres
- recognize themes and symbolism in stories
- participate in basic literary analysis and make connections after independent reading
- identify changes in characters throughout a work
- discern author's cultural or religious point of view
- discern persuasion and determine the theme's validity
- apply literature knowledge to other media such as movies and commercials
- define words from their similar roots or origins

11.2.2.1 WHAT SHOULD I DO IF MY ELEMENTARY STUDENT STRUGGLES WITH READING?

Go back to the basics. Consider putting all other subjects aside and just work briefly each day on the general skills for reading. Students who struggle with reading may feel rushed through the process and will improve at a slower pace.

Sometimes a student has a true learning disability. Remember, it is completely normal for a child to learn to read as late as ten years old. However, if you feel your child is struggling more than he should, do not hesitate to get an evaluation from an expert. See section 11.3.2 and also chapter 16 for more information on learning disabilities.

Whatever the issue, I would not continue pushing elementary level subjects while working on reading basics. When my twins experienced this issue, I mentally considered them early learners and took a step back from everything. They did well in all their other subjects after growing into this general subject.

11.2.2.2 HOW CAN I STRENGTHEN MY ELEMENTARY STUDENT'S READING COMPREHENSION?

Reading comprehension begins with listening comprehension. While reading picture books or even longer books, stop occasionally to discuss what you are reading.

My twins had very poor reading comprehension, so I read aloud to them quite a bit. And I would stop every few pages and ask questions like "Why do you think that happened?" or "How do you think these two characters are different?" or "What do you think will happen next?" This helped them to practice thinking throughout the story, not just sitting passively and letting it wash over

---

USE YOUR TEACHING STYLE: READING

- **Classical and Charlotte Mason:** Read aloud to your child and let her read to you from various picture and simple chapter books on a variety of topics.

- **Textbook:** Follow a preplanned method for systematic reading progress and literature.

- **Unschooling:** Allow the child to develop increasing reading abilities as she shows interest; allow her to choose books she prefers.

them. After reading and asking questions like this for several weeks, I began asking fewer questions during the story and waiting to ask at the end. "Why do you think that happened?" "Did the character do the right thing?" "What was the problem in the story, and how was it solved?" "Do you like the story, and why?"

When they began to read, I would ask questions after each simple sentence, such as "What did you just read?" Remember, in the beginning, my children were reading barely a sentence at a time. Soon, when they began reading simple books, I could wait until the end to ask what the story was about and what the character's name was. If they could not answer basic questions, we went back to read the book again. We might even switch to simpler books next time.

Just as with the skill of reading, I try not to rush reading comprehension. It will come with time when the child has developed enough to master it. And just like everything else, later reading comprehension is not an indication of intelligence. It is just a growth stage that comes in its own time.

WHAT I DO
- provide a selection of books at various reading levels
- read aloud with my child once or twice a day
- keep a shelf of picture books for my child to enjoy stories and illustrations
- visit the library regularly with my child
- require regular reading of children's classics of a variety of genres, including classic fiction, historical fiction, animal tales, and science fiction
- encourage my child to choose books he enjoys
- set aside time every day for my child to read quietly

11.2.3 What writing and grammar skills might my elementary student develop?

The elementary years are just the beginning of writing and grammar. But like I keep saying with all the subjects, this is just a time to introduce these concepts to your child. In middle school and high school, he will hit these hard. Little by little, you'll begin introducing your child to the parts of speech and basic punctuation rules. Then around mid to late elementary, you may begin thinking about how to teach your child the writing process, beginning with paragraphs and moving to papers. This skill is important in middle school, so exposure in the elementary years is helpful.

FOUNDATIONAL GOALS

- write a rough draft, edit, and polish a paragraph
- write a report on a book or on history
- understand what constitutes a complete sentence
- identify subjects, verbs, adjectives, and adverbs
- use the correct form of regular and most irregular verbs
- use capitalization and ending punctuation in every sentence
- understand plagiarism and how to avoid it

DEVELOPMENTAL GOALS

- construct a five-to-seven sentence paragraph with a thesis statement, supporting sentences, and a conclusion
- write a multiparagraph research essay
- identify all the parts of speech in a sentence
- use the correct forms of irregular verbs
- use commas correctly in most sentences

ADVANCED GOALS

- write a wide variety of pieces including descriptions, instructions, cause and effect, persuasion, and poetry
- utilize a writing plan of brainstorming, outlining, researching, rough draft, multiple edits, and final copy
- write research reports for a variety of subjects including history, literature, and science
- conjugate verbs
- recognize some Greek and Latin roots of words
- diagram sentences
- identify the correct use of most types of punctuation, including commas, semicolons, hyphens, and quotation marks

11.2.3.1 HOW DO I TEACH MY ELEMENTARY STUDENT HANDWRITING?

Practice and more practice. Penmanship may be important to you. I have a moderate standard. As long as the letters are formed correctly, stay on the lines, stay an appropriate size, and are legible, it's fine with me. My elementary student may practice handwriting for a year, more or less, to master the basics. Then I just require that the rest of his work look neat. If it doesn't, then we go back to practice. Some homeschool styles, particularly Charlotte Mason, value copy work quite a bit. This is an excellent way to practice handwriting.

> Writing and Drawing are but Amusements and may serve as Relaxations from your studies.
>
> **JOHN ADAMS TO SON JOHN QUINCY ADAMS**

I personally teach my children to write in cursive from the beginning. This is a controversial decision, and a cursive-first approach is not for everyone. In fact, I don't think anyone should really care whether you choose to teach printing or cursive. I chose cursive because I want my children to be able to read cursive, I believe that writing in cursive helps them to understand how sounds are connected into words, and I hope that forming words all together in one single stroke will enable them to visualize a word as a whole. And I just plain wanted them to learn cursive.

Most of my friends choose to teach their students printing first. I can see great benefits to that. Students learn to form the letters they see when they read, they write the same way the majority of signs, labels, and books are written, and most everyone prints everything these days. Many feel that cursive is becoming obsolete.

I say again, it doesn't matter which you choose. Some people teach their child to write completely in one style, then in a few years teach the other way. Really, it's like anything else in homeschooling—*teach the way you want to do it.*

11.2.3.2 HOW DO I TEACH MY ELEMENTARY STUDENT SPELLING?

With phonics and a lot of reading. There is this myth that homeschoolers are great spellers. Those accursed national spelling bee champions are to blame. They are often homeschoolers, and they have done us all the disservice of propagating this legend that homeschoolers can spell.

But I, for one, hate spelling. I am convinced—you cannot dissuade me—that spelling skills and the enjoyment of spelling are purely genetic. Some people got it, and some don't. If it were not for spell-check, Microsoft Word, and a crack editor decoding my scrambled letters, this book would be entirely illegible. I am a homeschool graduate who cannot spell.

Some people are just good spellers. My husband is a public school, non-spelling-bee champion who speaks English as a second language with a heavy accent, and he can spell anything perfectly. It's a problem in our marriage.

Some of my children inherited my husband's spelling gene. Some of them, like me, care less about spelling than we do chemistry (which is very, very little). This proves my theory that spelling is hit-or-miss.

I do, however, teach my elementary students the rudiments of spelling (and lest you get the wrong impression, the high schoolers do drag themselves through chemistry). Their spelling comes from their phonics studies. As they learn the phonics rules, they learn how to apply those rules to spelling. And as they learn the special sounds or exceptions, they learn how to spell harder words. After a while, the patterns click, and they are spelling with fairly good accuracy.

I have taught half of my students from a formal spelling book and half of them not. It just depended on how I felt at the time. I have not noticed any difference in ability either way, so I just go with my gut every year.

Some parents teach Latin and maybe Greek roots of words to aid their elementary students in spelling and vocabulary. For me, I point out some of these roots to my children in elementary but wait until middle school or high school to really work on those elements of vocabulary.

The best way to learn spelling is to read. A lot. Three of my children taught themselves to spell difficult words simply because they had encountered them so often in novels. My youngest daughter excels at spelling now. I asked her why, and she says that in her mind, she can see the words on a page in a book she has read. She apparently has near-photographic memory. Except when it comes to her chore chart. Regardless, reading expands vocabulary, which thus builds spelling skills.

Your children may turn out to be homeschool spelling bee champions, carrying on that tradition of looking—and being—really smart. But if spelling is a struggle, rest assured that spell-check technology just keeps getting better and better and there are online dictionaries at the tips of their fingers.

11.2.3.3 HOW DO I TEACH MY ELEMENTARY STUDENT GRAMMAR?

Grammar doesn't change over the years. The parts of speech, the comma rules, the sentence structures—they all stay the same. Grammar curriculum just teaches the same things over and over, only in slightly more detail.

If you want, and I really mean this, you could wait until the end of elementary to start grammar. Seriously. And it would make no difference *at all* to your student. If you look at fifth-grade and sixth-grade and seventh-grade grammar books, you'll notice the content is basically the same. It is just drilling the same things, in slightly increasing detail, for increased practice.

When I am teaching my children, I teach grammar to the student's tolerance. If, after learning to point out the subject and verb of the sentence, the student is ready for more, then I will continue. But if grammar is a struggle, I will put it aside and wait another year or two.

Punctuation rules are more useful as the student begins writing. But we don't need to make them complicated. As the student writes something, I show her what punctuation she misses and try to generalize the rules for now. For example, a comma goes after most phrases that come before the subject of a sentence. That is a generalization, but it solves the majority of clause comma problems. I'll teach about how to join sentences with a comma and a conjunction when the student starts writing compound sentences. And when she writes her first story, I can show her how to use proper punctuation during the editing process. Even if a student does not study formal grammar, she can continue building on her writing and punctuation skills.

11.2.3.4 HOW MUCH GRAMMAR DOES MY ELEMENTARY STUDENT NEED?

The basic idea of grammar is more than enough. Your student will study grammar in-depth, reviewing ad nauseam, through middle school and high school. There is little need to torture the poor child too early.

By the end of elementary, a student should know the difference between a complete sentence, a fragment, and a run-on sentence (two sentences incorrectly joined). He should be able to identify the subject and verb—who the sentence is about and what they are doing (or that they simply exist). He should also know that other words describe these subjects and verbs. He may memorize prepositions and identify prepositional phrases, but there will be plenty of time in middle school for that.

Please don't worry if your child does not grasp grammar in elementary. The child has all of middle school and high school to review it every single year.

11.2.3.5 IS IT IMPORTANT FOR MY ELEMENTARY STUDENT TO DIAGRAM SENTENCES?

Probably not. Diagramming shows the purpose of every word in a sentence. Since this knowledge is not critical to an elementary student, I would not require it for all students.

Some elementary students do benefit from the visual discipline of diagramming; it helps them to understand what words are doing and how they interact. Even if a student only understands subjects, verbs, and complements, diagramming can show how these parts of speech work together in a sentence. But an elementary student need not study grammar to that extent. If the student is not prepared mentally, it would actually be detrimental to force the subject. As I said, there are many years ahead to review these skills.

Even if you do have a precocious grammar enthusiast, your student does

GRAMMAR RULES YOUR ELEMENTARY STUDENT MAY PRACTICE

- Capitalize
  - › the first word of a sentence
  - › proper names and titles
  - › the word *I*
- Put a period, question mark, or (rarely) an exclamation point at the end of a sentence
- Use a period for abbreviations
- Use a comma
  - › before *and, but, or, nor, for,* and *yet* when they combine two sentences
  - › between items in a series
  - › in dates and addresses
  - › to set off clauses and phrases at the beginning of a sentence (anything that is almost a sentence and comes before the subject)
  - › where you take a breath in a sentence (sometimes)

not need diagramming to understand how a sentence is constructed. She might label the part of speech above each word, drawing arrows to what the word modifies, and draw parentheses and brackets around phrases and clauses. Some of my students could not understand what a diagram represented but could label, bracket, and arrow a sentence to demonstrate understanding. Whichever works best for your child is fine.

11.2.3.6 HOW DO I TEACH MY ELEMENTARY STUDENT CAPITALIZATION AND PUNCTUATION?

Start with the basics; the nuances of punctuation can wait until middle school. My very general grammar rules (see the sidebar "Grammar rules your elementary student may practice"), especially those about clauses and phrases, get my students through elementary school. I point these out to my later elementary students as I grade their papers, and they pick up quite a bit from that practice. In middle school, students learn what clauses and phrases really are and where exactly commas are needed to set them off. But the "extra words at the beginning of a sentence" and "where you take a breath" tips get even *me* through most of my writing.

These basics of punctuation and capitalization may seem simplistic, but they are truly the hallmark of correct writing. By the end of middle school, I expect my students to have these rules down cold, and they help throughout high school and college. We just begin working on them in late elementary as we begin the simple writing process.

11.2.3.7 HOW DO I TEACH MY ELEMENTARY STUDENT TO WRITE ESSAYS?

A child will develop his ability to write paragraphs gradually. Like everything else, students are ready at different times.

Here are the general steps leading to writing competence:

1. The student will practice writing sentences.
2. The student will understand that a sentence includes a subject, a verb, and describing words. She will continue reinforcing this idea for over a year.
3. The student next learns how to write different kinds of sentences, some with describing words at the beginning of the sentence, some with two sentences put together with the word *and*, some

THE WRITING PROCESS

1. *Identify the topic.*

2. *Write one sentence* that clearly explains the topic. This will probably be your topic sentence.

3. *Brainstorm* and write down everything you can think of about the topic. Everything. Just random words or phrases that have anything to do with it.

4. *Choose the best ideas* and circle them. Cross out the rest.

5. *Organize the ideas.* This could be in chronological order, in space order (front to back, left to right, etc.), or order of importance.

6. *Create a mind map* of the main ideas and details or *an outline* detailing the order of thoughts.

7. *Write the paragraph,* following the plan in the mind map or outline.

8. *Conclude the paragraph* with a restatement of the main idea.

9. *Edit the paragraph* for continuity, detail, and grammar (maybe use an editing checklist like the one in appendix C).

10. *Rewrite the paragraph.*

11. *Repeat editing and rewriting* at least once or until the paragraph is clean.

12. *Present the work* by turning it in.

short, and some long. She needs to practice this skill for a time, as well.

4. As the student learns more grammar, she can write sentences demonstrating the parts of speech she is learning: adjectives, then adverbs, then prepositional phrases, and so on. She can practice putting these parts of speech at the beginning or end of the sentence. This also takes quite a bit of practice.

5. The student begins writing more than one sentence about the same topic, making different types of sentences.

6. In addition, the student may practice writing a few sentences telling how to do a task, putting each step in order.

7. The student then learns what a *topic sentence* is—a sentence at the beginning of the paragraph telling what the paragraph will be about. She practices writing a paragraph with a topic sentence, then five to seven sentences about that topic sentence. She looks carefully back at the paragraph to make sure every sentence is about that topic sentence.

8. The student also learns about the *concluding sentence*—a sentence that restates the topic sentence or gives finality to the paragraph. She now practices the entire process: topic sentence, descriptive sentences, and then the concluding sentence. She is writing paragraphs of perhaps seven to nine sentences, including the topic and concluding sentences.

9. The student now learns how to edit her work. Often using a checklist, she goes back over her paragraph to check paragraph unity, sentence structure, and the mechanics of grammar and punctuation.

10. The student can now practice writing different types of paragraphs: descriptive, instructive, persuasive, and more.

11. It's possible that before middle school the student will begin writing multiple paragraphs on the same topic, but this skill is not really necessary until middle school.

USE YOUR TEACHING STYLE: WRITING AND GRAMMAR

- **Classical:** Teach grammar and writing separately at first. As the child grows stronger in grammar, practice in the context of paragraph editing. Use Latin roots to study spelling.

- **Charlotte Mason:** Study good grammar and writing habits from literature and practice them using copy work and workbooks.

- **Textbook:** Use a grammar workbook that may have writing lessons included throughout.

- **Unschooling:** Encourage your children to write about current interests and perhaps study grammar from a workbook.

Some parents want their child to write longer book reports or research reports in elementary school. I believe there is plenty of time to practice longer-form writing in middle school, and not all students are ready for this assignment by fifth grade. So I do not push this skill until after sixth grade. We'll discuss paragraph writing and essays more thoroughly in chapter 12.

WHAT I DO:
- teach writing concurrently with grammar for the majority of the elementary years
- move to separate writing instruction if the student is ready at the end of this period
- have my child memorize lists like being verbs, helping verbs, and prepositions
- demonstrate how to diagram or mark some parts of speech in a sentence
- study spelling concurrently with reading blends and special sounds

11.2.4 What math skills might my elementary student develop?

Math in elementary school is simply an extension of the exploration begun in the early years. Students continue observing the patterns of time and nature then slowly begin writing their discoveries in "mathematician language," as my family likes to call it. They move from literal thinking very slowly into abstract equations. Everything elementary students study, just as in all the other subjects, simply sets the foundation for later abstract thinking—but only at the rate of their understanding. As in other subjects, progress in math should be unique for each student.

FOUNDATIONAL GOALS
- apply math to real life and answer story problems
- use tools or manipulatives (including coins) to solve math problems
- read and create graphs and diagrams
- understand and write decimals to the tenths and identify their relationship to money or other base-ten groups
- count by multiples (skip count) to find multiplication answers

DEVELOPMENTAL GOALS
- understand the relationship between decimals and fractions
- add and subtract fractions
- memorize multiplication facts
- multiply three-digit numbers on paper
- divide a four-digit number by a two-digit number by hand
- understand negative numbers
- plot positive, negative, and fraction numbers on a number line
- identify *x* and *y* coordinates on a plane
- find the perimeter/circumference and area of simple geometric shapes

ADVANCED GOALS
- multiply and divide fractions, decimals, and mixed numbers
- understand the relationship between fractions, decimals, and percents
- add, subtract, multiply, and divide negative numbers
- correctly solve problems including parentheses and brackets
- understand and correctly apply the order of operations
- solve problems with unknown numbers (prealgebra)
- solve problems and diagram on a horizontal and vertical plane
- memorize and use formulas for surface area and volume of three-dimensional objects

11.2.4.1 HOW DO I TEACH MATH TO MY ELEMENTARY STUDENT?

With exploration of math in the real world, the way you have been. Math in these years is still concrete, things the student can touch and experience. This concrete math is critical. Abstract algebra, geometry, and even calculus make no sense if the student has not sufficiently *experienced* the reality of math, the principles and patterns that higher math is built upon.

I cannot stress this enough. Science tells us that our child's brain does not develop for abstract thinking until after puberty.[1] Until then, the child's brain is designed for reality, for what she can see and touch and hear. This concrete thinking should be the focus of elementary math.

This is also where we sometimes go amiss in math education. While we know that our child may not develop the mental capacity to read until later in elementary, we often do not afford that same leeway in math.

I have experienced this situation with every single one of my children. I want to keep truckin' along with the curriculum, moving forward lesson by lesson, doing what the book tells me to do next, until one day I finally realize that my child is really, truly frustrated. And I should have noticed sooner.

Like yesterday. My daughter was doing her math paper. (Yes, I use math papers, even though I know that real math is way, way more important. My children just enjoy their math papers.) Anyway, she was doing her math paper when she flung down her pencil and said, "If this isn't the right answer, I give up!"

It was not the right answer.

Bless her heart, she was doing two-digit addition, which she understood because she had played with dimes and pennies so many times. She loved adding with money. She even understood exchanging ten pennies for one dime and carrying the one dime over to the tens place. But now the answers were larger, over one hundred. The process was the same, but there were more digits in the answer than she expected.

Her little brain freaked out. Suddenly, she could no longer do any part of the problem—no carrying, no imagining ten pennies, no nothing.

I had moved forward to something I perceived as only slightly more difficult, thoughtlessly turning the page without noticing her weakness. She obviously was not solid on why we make ten pennies into a dime and carry the one. She had never imagined there might be more than ten dimes' worth in the answer. *She needed more literal practice because nothing on paper meant anything to her.*

This is the most important thing I can say to myself and to you about math. Almost all of our difficulties—multiplication, fractions, decimals, long division, all of it—could be so much simpler if we did three things:

1. Always teach concretely what is literally going on.
2. Just stay at the child's own pace.
3. When things get rough, refer to step one.

There is no substitute for these three steps.

There are, however, plenty of shortcuts. We can make our child memorize rote facts. We can teach shortcuts to finish the problem and move on. We can just teach him "the way I've always done it" without explaining what it means. We can make math work by just cramming it into his little brain.

I have tried that way, way too many times.

Yet these shortcuts ignore how God made my child. God made my child to love and explore creation, to glorify him within the world he created. So that means the world of math, too. When I do not allow my child to truly explore what these math principles mean in creation, I am cheating him of the chance to glorify God, even in his math worksheet.

Also, by hurrying past literal math, I'm making algebra and geometry that much harder. Because if my child has not seen—concretely and repeatedly—why and how math principles work in real life, he will not clearly understand how to apply these principles in the abstract. Then he is doomed to a life of just memorizing formulas and taking shortcuts and turning in papers that mean absolutely nothing to him.

Instead, you and I both need to remember *math is to be experienced in the elementary years*. It is not to be rushed through "at grade level" or memorized to move on. Instead, math is an opportunity to get back to our homeschool *why*. This is the time to practice one of the fundamental tenets of homeschooling: teach the child the way you teach best for the way your child learns best.

11.2.4.2 HOW DO I TEACH LITERAL MATH?

There is so much math to experience. God's created order, the patterns with which he made all things, the rules by which he consistently holds the world, time, and our reality together—these are beautiful and comforting. We know, as Lamentations 3:22-23 says, that God's mercy is new every morning—because we can count on that twenty-four-hour day bringing a new sunrise consistently.

Passing through the early years into the beginning of elementary, the student may be ready to write what he has experienced in simple story problems—there were two (2) cookies on my plate, but then I ate one (1), and now one (1) is left: $2 - 1 = 1$. A young child may write the equation, or he may prefer to express it only orally for a while.

The opposite is also true. What does $7 - 5 = 2$ mean? The student can think of a story like this: "There were seven (7) children in Sunday school, and five (5) left with their parents, so now two (2) are still waiting." Asking the child to make a story for a problem helps reinforce this knowledge that "mathematician language" means something that happens in real life.

In another example, concrete thinkers sometimes have a hard time estimating. I have a daughter who hates to estimate. She cannot say "about twenty" if she knows there are seventeen candies in front of her. Her pile of items simply must be sorted and counted. Estimating them first just frustrates her.

But estimating and generalizing answers is also an important skill. My daughter needs to quickly figure out that if there are seventeen (17) children at the party and twenty-seven (27) more show up, there are fewer than fifty (50) people in the house. It is so much faster to generalize, and often in real life, we need to quickly figure out if we have enough hot dog buns for them all. (Side note: we never do. This is why I don't eat any hot dogs until everyone leaves, just in case.)

Generalizing is also important for "check your work" moments. When the student adds 156 and 574 and gets an answer of 431, he should know that this does not make sense, because he was adding less than 200 and less than 600. His final answer should thus be less than 800, not less than 500.

Again, this is an example of understanding the real world of math. Adding always means there will be more, subtraction always means some is going away, multiplication always means groups that make more, and division always means separating groups of fewer things. These rules even work with fractions, since fractions themselves are things divided. These are rules God has built into the world that can comfort us in their *always* nature.

Directional understanding is important in this phase, *up* meaning more and *down* meaning less. Many people use number lines laid across the table to demonstrate this. But I find this teaches more left-to-right reasoning than up and down. This is not necessarily bad, because algebra does use left-to-right for the *x*-axis, but conceptually, young children can sometimes more easily understand a vertical plane. Older children, larger plants, buildings with several stories—they all tend to grow *up*.

So I like to make a number line on the wall or tape a tape measure to the doorway. My favorite is a large thermometer. Thermometers are awesome because they also teach "below 0," which is a difficult concept that is at first taken by faith until a frigid winter.

Besides a tape measure and a thermometer, there are many fun mathematician tools to try out, including rulers, balancing scales, and a bathroom scale (without Mommy stepping on it). I even let my children try out a protractor and compass, though they don't truly comprehend what they are for. I will simply teach them that a protractor can help us draw and measure angles, which are corners of things. And a compass, if you can keep that frustrating needle in the center, can help you draw a perfect circle and measure the distance from the center.

By far the best mathematics tools for early elementary students are manipulatives. My twins just spent nearly a half an hour playing with tangrams. For Christmas, I bought them a magnetic shape manipulative set called Fractiles to help them better visualize how shapes fit together to form patterns and rotate to fit differently. My youngest son's favorite manipulatives are his toy soldiers. Another son preferred a plastic set of four differently colored animals. Anything that can be sorted or put together aids this concrete math.

Manipulatives are a fun way to make graphs. Lining up different-colored or -shaped manipulatives in lines helps children understand bar graphs. We have made yarn circles to re-create a Venn diagram of toys that are cows, toys that have spots, and toys that are cows with spots.

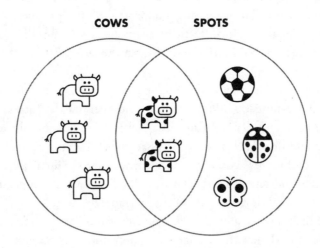

Sorting toys more than one way is useful not only for story problems but also for understanding the concepts of multiplication and division. Eight (8) LEGOs divided into four (4) equal groups of red, yellow, blue, and green means there are two (2) LEGOs in each group: 8 ÷ 4 = 2. Six (6) shapes divided into three (3) types of shapes (circles, squares, triangles) means there are two (2) of each shape per group: 6 ÷ 3 = 2. Three (3) groups of LEGOs—four (4) each of red, green, and yellow—makes twelve (12) LEGOs altogether: 3 × 4 = 12. Young elementary students can make stories like this, then begin learning how to write them in "mathematician language."

[6/3=2]

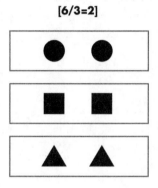

Anything that uses the senses, especially touch and sight, lays the foundation for a concrete understanding of math, which will be invaluable throughout the elementary years.

11.2.4.3 HOW DO I TEACH MY ELEMENTARY STUDENT MULTIPLICATION AND DIVISION?

Make groups of things and skip count. Multiplication is simply making groups of objects and then skip counting by the number in the group. Eight (8) groups of six (6) toy soldiers are forty-eight (48) soldiers: 8 × 6 = 48. In skip counting terms, that would be 6-12-18-24-30-36-42-48.

Sorting the manipulatives into groups of the same number helps the child understand skip counting—counting by twos, threes, and so on. This is very difficult unless the child has something concrete to work with. Pairs of shoes help with twos, groups of manipulatives work with threes, and skipping pairs of shoes works for fours. I love using a calendar to work on sevens. If the student doesn't understand what comes after twenty-one, he can count the days until twenty-eight. Soon he will memorize the pattern he has already visualized.

I teach my children to count by 10s, then 5s, then 2s, then 3s (by whispering, "1, 2, *3!*, 4, 5, *6!* . . ."). Next we move on to 7s (on the calendar), 4s (skipping one of the shoe pairs), 9s (one less than 10 each time, each number's digits adding to 9), then the rest. As they are skip counting, they point one finger for each number they count. They count up to ten times a number, then backward again. After practicing for a while, they can then look at a certain number of fingers and know the multiplication fact. For example, my child will count by threes, using one finger for each new number. Then he can show eight fingers and say, "twenty-four!" or three fingers and say, "nine!"

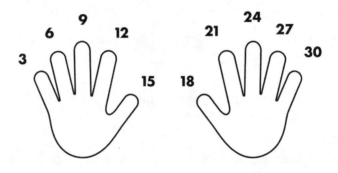

My first son could not understand counting by eight. So I had him make a tower of eight linking cubes at his table. He could see there were eight of them. I sat across the room from him and asked him to bring them to me, telling me how many there were. It was obvious there were eight. I asked him to make another tower of eight and bring them to me. Now, how many are there? Mommy has sixteen. By now he was running to make towers as fast as he could and bring them to me, counting off how many more while he was racing across the room. He used his hands to make the towers, he used his eyes to see the groups, he used his voice to speak the numbers, he used his ears to hear himself say the numbers, and he used his gross motor skills to carry the towers across the room. Eights made sense to him when he could use his senses to work on each group. Using his senses—concrete math—made the multiplication process meaningful. Then and only then was he ready to memorize counting by eights.

Once the child understands that "groups of" means multiplication, division should come naturally. Six (6) groups of eight candies (8) make forty-eight (48): 6 × 8 = 48. Now reverse that: if you separate forty-eight (48) candies into six (6) groups, how many candies are in each group?

11.2.4.4 HOW DO FACT FAMILIES HELP WITH MATH FACTS?

Once a child understands addition and subtraction, he may see that certain numbers just work together. If we have three (3) cookies plus two (2) more cookies to make five (5) cookies (3 + 2 = 5), then two (2) cookies plus three (3) cookies also equals five (5) cookies: 2 + 3 = 5. On the flip side, five (5) cookies minus two (2) cookies equals three (3) cookies (5 − 2 = 3) and five (5) cookies minus three (3) cookies equals two (2) cookies: 5 − 3 = 2. The numbers five (5), three (3), and two (2) go together in those combinations: they are a fact family.

Once the student understands that, memorizing math facts is a breeze. Multiplication and division become automatic. Once the student memorizes one simple math fact, he actually knows four math facts.

Explaining fact families early on, and working with them with manipulatives often, helps the student learn all the math facts. This makes a seemingly huge job of memorizing facts a much smaller task.

11.2.4.5 SHOULD I USE MATH WORKSHEETS WITH MY ELEMENTARY STUDENT?

If she wants to and is ready. After the child is comfortable working with a concept concretely and repeating back what the equation means in real life, then she is ready for the concept on paper. This is where many homeschoolers turn to worksheets, but I think it is important not to use worksheets exclusively at this point. Working on paper too soon takes the concrete understanding out of math education, the concrete understanding the child needs for later math and even science. My children have all needed to go back and forth between concrete play and manipulatives and then showing work on paper.

On worksheets, the student can begin working on more difficult, larger problems based on the concrete facts she already knows. She can add and subtract larger numbers. After practicing with manipulatives a few times, she can multiply and divide larger numbers too.

I don't think there is any substitute for using math in real life and practicing with manipulatives. I make my students do this for all of their math through basic algebra, with rare exceptions. If a student cannot replicate an equation on paper with manipulatives, then certainly she is not applying the equation to real life. Technology further removes the student from the reality of math, and calculators should be avoided until the most abstract of math. And don't even get me started on asking Alexa. I have to keep my ears peeled at all times for sneaky conversations with the machines.

11.2.4.6 HOW CAN I TEACH MY ELEMENTARY STUDENT MULTIDIGIT PROBLEMS IN A CONCRETE WAY?

I love to use candy, but you might prefer Cheerios, coins, or beads. Some students become frustrated by how you and I were taught to work a multiplication problem because it seems like a foreign language. The paper process we all learned as children does not mean anything concrete to our students. The first several times my child tries this type of problem, I will help her act it out with small objects.

We can work on the math problem 4 × 23, reading multiplication as "groups of." So the problem is really asking "What is four (4) groups of twenty-three (23)?" First, we make groups of M&M'S, because who doesn't want more M&M'S? Okay, we are starting off with the *ones* place. We make four groups of three M&M'S. That is so much fun. Once we have our four groups of three, or twelve candies, we separate them into one group of ten with two left over.

Now, if the student is confused at this point for any reason, I stop here and practice this for a while with different combinations of numbers. The student needs to understand making groups *and* then separating the groups into tens with leftovers before we can continue.

When that is clear, we can move the one group of ten to the other side of the table and push the two extras slightly to the other side. Now it is time to work with the *tens* place. We need to make two groups of tens to show the twenty. This is a *lot* of candy, and we aren't even into the thick of it yet. Now we need cups to hold the twenty candies altogether. But what does the math problem say? We need four of those groups of twenty. So we get to work counting out all the candies until we have four cups with twenty in each cup. Then we count it together and find we have eighty candies separated in these cups.

And now we have an extra ten over to the side. We add that ten with the other tens (the cups of twenty) and find we have ninety candies. Then there are the other extra two in the leftover pile. If we put all of those together, there are ninety-two candies.

After trying this several times over several days (or weeks) with different amounts of candy, we are then ready to see how that same equation (4 × 23) works on paper. First we multiply the ones place candies and write the two down. We put the extra ten over in the tens place to save it for later. Then we multiply those cups of twenty by four, and we have eight groups of ten plus the one we set aside, which makes nine groups of ten. We write that nine down and voilà, we have written down the problem in mathematician language. After practicing this a few more times with different equations to make sure it always works, we can eat the candy in exaltation.

Another wonderful way to practice is with dimes and pennies. In the beginning, we have four groups of three pennies which gives us twelve. We trade ten of them for a dime and keep it to the side with the remaining two pennies. Then the four groups of two dimes each gives us eight dimes. We write the two pennies in the "pennies place" or ones place of the problem, the extra dime at the top of the "dimes place" or tens place, and the eight dimes below it for a total of nine dimes or ninety cents in the "dimes place" of our answer. We get the same result: ninety-two cents.

I cannot begin to count how many times we practice this process with money and candy and Cheerios and beads. Multiplying, separating, counting, writing. Over and over and over again until what happens on paper actually means something real in the mind.

Division is very similar. To complete the problem 92 ÷ 4, we can start with a huge pile of ninety-two candies (oh, *that's* a lot of fun to count out!) and then separate them into cups of tens with two left over. Now, first we look at the tens place because division is backward from multiplication. We divide those nine cups into four groups—there will be two cups in each group with one cup left over. We push the four groups, keeping them separate, over to the side of the table. How many groups have we taken away? Four large groups, which make eighty candies altogether.

Now, if this part is confusing the child, I would stop here. It is fine to spend a few days practicing dividing groups of ten into different sized groups until it feels natural.

Now, if the child understands, he should see that he has pushed eighty total candies away by putting them into four groups. He has a cup of ten candies and two candies left over in front of him. That's twelve candies.

Divided into four groups, that makes three each. He puts three candies into each of the four areas.

Now, how many candies are in each area? Twenty-three. Then we are ready to show how to write that on paper. We can do it again, separating candies and working through the paper problem step-by-step. After many repetitions, the child should see what it is he is doing when he divides.

This type of concrete example forms a very important foundation for algebra down the road. When your child begins working on abstract problems, he needs to be able to see what he was doing by separating and manipulating amounts. He will use that understanding to manipulate unknown quantities, and he will see what he is doing even though the amounts remain unknown.

Writing math equations is important by the end of elementary. But nothing is as important as understanding what we are describing in real life every time we put pencil to paper.

11.2.4.7 HOW DO I TEACH MY ELEMENTARY STUDENT PLACE VALUE AND DECIMALS?

Use money. Besides candy, there is no math manipulative my children love more than money. I could say it is because their father is a banker, but we all know that money is just plain fun.

Most sane people buy fake money for math class. I want the real thing. So when my students are in lower elementary, I ask my husband to bring home rolls of coins and a few dollar bills. These go in separate Ziploc bags by denomination and are stored in a hands-off-or-else jar only for math time.

Your child needs to learn what coins are called and how much they are worth. Some learn this in the early learning years, but waiting until early elementary is just fine. Then she can learn how to count coins. She can put the coins in a line carefully in order of value, from quarters to pennies, then carefully touch and slide each one to the side as she counts up that denomination. I start first with just dimes and pennies, then add nickels, then quarters as the child masters each.

Multidigit problems are easier to practice by thinking of them in terms of cents, too. First, we add pennies, then, if we have ten, we make them into a dime and add it to the dimes pile, then add the dimes together. It's fun to see the problem in action and easier to practice than on paper.

Next, it's time to learn how to write dollars and cents. When we write $1.43, we count out one dollar, four dimes, and three pennies. A dime is ten cents. There are ten dimes in a dollar, and that means one dime is one-tenth. That is why we call it ten cents. Similarly, there are ten pennies in a dime. This is why we write money with decimals.

We can practice adding amounts of dollars and cents like $1.43 and $2.52. This is easy to see and easy to work on paper. A few days' practice makes the paperwork easier. Then it is time to practice carrying. That is simply exchanging pennies for dimes, or dimes for dollars. We can play with the money several times, putting the exchanged money into the new piles until the paper way of adding decimals makes sense.

It's the same with subtracting decimals. To begin with, we can use simple problems like $2.95 minus $1.23. That is easy to see. Then we move to numbers that need borrowing, which is simply exchanging money. In $3.43 minus $2.75, we need to exchange a dime for ten pennies, then a dollar for ten dimes. After practicing these problems several times, the mathematician way of writing makes more sense. It took each of my children several days' practice with real money while working the paper way at the same time before it all clicked in their brain.

The important thing about decimals and everything else in math is that the child begins by seeing how they work in real life. We could just teach the rules by rote and get the child to finish worksheets quickly. But truly *learning* the concept takes a little time each day playing with money and eating M&M'S.

11.2.4.8 HOW DO I TEACH MY ELEMENTARY STUDENT FRACTIONS?

Fractions are fun because you can teach them with pizza. There are two ways of doing pizza fractions. First, we can draw pictures of pizza with lots of pepperoni. But my favorite way is to eat pizza for lunch. There are so many ways to divide pizza. And we learn that when we cut the pizza into eight pieces, each piece is called one-eighth (⅛). When my brother ate half of the pizza, he took four-eighths (⁴⁄₈)! That left two-eighths (²⁄₈) apiece for my sister and me. Of course, we need to eat a rectangle pizza sometimes to see how the same things apply to different shapes.

Food fractions work great with young elementary students. They don't need to write them, we can just talk about them every day—parts of a sandwich, pieces of a Hershey bar, and slices of an apple (for those of you who eat healthily and give me your pizza).

To cut down on the carbs, I also let my children make their own fraction manipulatives. We cut out four large circles in four different colors of construction paper. The yellow one we do not cut further. That is a *whole* circle. The red one, we fold and cut in half. That is two *halves*, and we can lay them on top of the whole circle. The blue one we fold in half, then half again, and cut out the pieces. That makes four *fourths*, and they fit on top of the circle too. Finally, we fold our green circle into fourths then each fourth in half to cut out eight pieces, or *eighths*.

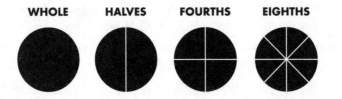

Now we can practice putting the same colored pieces on top of the whole circle. It is important to name the pieces each time. The red one is called one *half*. The green one is called one *eighth*. We play with them a few times, covering the one *whole* yellow circle with all one color, naming how many we put on. "One-fourth, two-fourths, three-fourths, four-fourths! Four-fourths is the same as one whole circle!"

Putting pieces on top of each other also demonstrates what it means to reduce fractions. We can see that two *fourths* pieces cover, or equal, one *half* piece. After trying this a few times, we see the pattern that reducing is simply dividing the top and the bottom by the same number. It's a pattern that always works, so we don't have to worry about working on circles anymore. We can do the fast way of dividing.

After a few times of that, we are ready to cover our yellow circle with different colored pieces. And again we say aloud how we made the whole circle. "One-half, one-fourth, and two-eighths made one whole circle!"

Now we can add and subtract fractions. Usually, we draw pictures of rectangles and color parts of them. One long rectangle divided into eighths. Color three of the parts red and two of the parts blue. Three-eighths plus two-eighths makes five-eighths.

Adding fractions that have different denominators (the bottom number of the fraction) requires more pictures of pizzas at first. We want to remind the student that one-half plus one-fourth is the same as adding two-fourths plus one-fourth, for a total of three-fourths: ½ (²⁄₄) + ¼ = ¾.

Once your child has a good grasp of halves, fourths, and eighths, you can work on thirds and sixths. Suppose you want to add one-half and one-third. To help your child visualize this, make two circles. With a pencil divide one into halves and one into thirds, then color one half and one third. The two circles look nothing alike, so we can't cover the circle together with them to get the answer. We need to divide the circles into pieces of the same size (or find the common denominator, in mathematician language). Two and three both go into six, so let's divide both circles carefully into sixths. When we do that, we see that the colored one half equals three-sixths: ½ = ³⁄₆. And the colored one third equals two-sixths: ⅓ = ²⁄₆. Together, they make five-sixths: ½ (³⁄₆) + ⅓ (²⁄₆) = ⁵⁄₆. Soon, the student can do such problems on paper and visualize what the term *common denominators* means.

This takes a while to visualize. I prefer my students practice making shapes on paper until they start groaning with boredom because it is too easy. Then they are ready to do these problems with pencils.

I made the mistake last month of expecting my twins to write mixed numbers on paper without much explanation. It was a reminder to me that we need to order a few pizzas tomorrow to see what 2 ¾ pizzas look like in real life while we practice writing that.

11.2.4.9 HOW DO I TEACH MY ELEMENTARY STUDENT TO MULTIPLY AND DIVIDE FRACTIONS?

Use more candy (or other small objects). The most important thing to remember when multiplying and dividing fractions is that the multiplication sign means "of." So we can rephrase 6 × 8 = 48 as "six groups of eight equals forty-eight." In the same way, "one-sixth of forty-eight is eight" can be written as ⅙ × 48 = 8. We can use candy to practice talking about this in mathematician language and writing it on paper.

Another important concept to remember is that the center line of a fraction means "divide." Therefore, one-half of forty-eight can be written as ½ × 48 or as 48/2, because a fraction means dividing into sections. And yet another way of writing the same concept is the division problem 48 ÷ 2. There are three ways to write division problems:

$$48 \div 2 = 24 \qquad 48/2 = 24 \qquad 2\overline{)48}^{\,24}$$

It helps my students to practice writing the same problem three ways.

Next, we can try multiplying fractions. That's just taking a part of another part. Take, for example, ½ × ⅓. The answer to this problem rarely makes sense to children at first, so we go back to our colored circles (or a pizza!). We cut the circle into thirds. Then we can cut one third in half and color one of those sections. Cut all the other pieces in half as well and create the circle again. What was one-half of the one third? Now we can see it is one-sixth: ½ × ⅓ = ⅙. And we can write it with a multiplication sign, which means "of."

When we multiply fractions, two things occur over and over:

1. We come up with a smaller fraction—a smaller amount or size.
2. The answer is the two top numbers multiplied by each other placed over the two bottom numbers multiplied by each other.

These two truths hold constant because of God's patterns in math. Once we see that the pattern always works, we can use it to solve more problems in our heads and with our pencils, and we can use the same technique for increasingly difficult problems. Using the fraction circle we see *why* the pencil process works, and we can just memorize the shortcut rule: multiply the top and write it on top; multiply the bottom and write it on the bottom.

Division of fractions can be learned a similar way. If we take two circles and divide them both in one half, how many pieces do we have? Four. Write down $2 \div \frac{1}{2} = 4$ on a piece of paper. Next, take one half of a circle. Divide that piece into pieces that are one-fourth of a circle. There are two one-fourth-sized pieces in one half. So $\frac{1}{2} \div \frac{1}{4} = 2$. We could continue making examples of fraction division with circle pieces to see what happened. Then, to make it easy, show that the "flip and multiply" rule works the same way every time. It's a constant pattern in God's creation.

At this point, the student has seen what it means to multiply and divide fractions in real life. Later he can do it much faster by memorizing the following shortcut rules for what he experienced:

1. Multiply fractions by multiplying the top and bottom.
2. Divide fractions by flipping then multiplying.
3. Many fractions can be divided by the same number on top and bottom to simplify.

The paper fraction-circle trick works for mixed numbers and more difficult fractions, but it is more time-consuming and wearisome to demonstrate, in my opinion. I've only tried going through the whole thing a couple of times. Usually, after a few simple demonstrations with smaller numbers, my children have been ready to simply memorize the shortcut rules and move on.

11.2.4.10 HOW DO I BEGIN GEOMETRY WITH MY ELEMENTARY STUDENT?

Geometry is all about shapes and space. Learning about them in concrete form can be a lot of fun.

I taught my older daughter the concept of perimeter by walking around the backyard with her. We counted how many steps were on each side. Then we knew the perimeter—how many of her own steps it took to go all the way around. Then we learned that instead of steps, mathematicians use feet or yards, a concept she already understood.

If our yard is a square, we will walk about the same number of steps—or measure the same number of feet—for each side. We can add up all four of those sides to make the perimeter. Likewise, we can learn perimeter with the concept of rectangles, noticing the two short sides are the same and the two longer sides are the same.

My middle son had difficulty visualizing area, so I used squares of the kitchen tile to help him understand. I outlined an area for him to count, so he could see *how many tiles were in that area*. That was a hard concept for him on paper, but much more obvious in real life. We could also see that there were rows of tiles, and that we could multiply the number in each row by the number of rows in order to quickly count the tiles in the area. In a couple of days, he could find the area of a shape on paper by imagining the tiles, understand why the answer was called "square feet," and write his own area problems on paper.

$$5^2=25$$

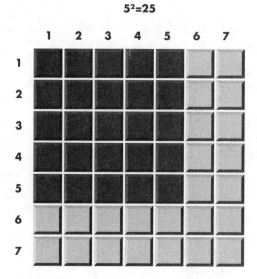

For my other children I drew shapes and had them cover each shape with one-inch color tiles. That was easier when I didn't feel like kneeling on the hard, cold kitchen floor. And when I didn't want to mop.

Learning area teaches a child square numbers, as in 4^2. Filling in an area that is 4 x 4 and then counting how many squares are in the shape demonstrates the principle. Doing this with increasing numbers (5^2, 6^2, 7^2) shows the student how much these numbers grow visually. The opposite, making a square with sixteen tiles, proves the square root of a number. After playing with making square tiles for a long time, most of my children memorized their squares and square roots without trying.

11.2.4.11 HOW DO I BEGIN PREALGEBRA WITH MY ELEMENTARY STUDENT?

I have learned the hard way to let my children take their time with prealgebra. My children have been quick to learn elementary math, but prealgebra moves into abstract reasoning. My first two children could learn the formulas and tricks of prealgebra and even basic algebra without understanding what the equations meant, but that didn't mean they were ready to move on. Advanced algebra and trigonometry are even harder subjects, so it wasn't enough for my children to skim through the foundation of prealgebra without real learning.

A sizable percentage of preteens have not yet developed the abstract thinking necessary for algebra.[2] Experts now caution educators to wait until high school to begin this subject.

With my third student, I worked differently. He took a year of prealgebra in a great curriculum. He got the formulas and tricks down but knew little of what he was doing. The following year, I bought a two-year curriculum on prealgebra. He did each year's worth in one semester. And suddenly, it clicked. This method gave him a review of the concepts when he was a year older. And he read and worked from a different perspective from a different author. By the end of that year, he understood thoroughly what he was doing. This worked so well I'm having my next son take two years of prealgebra too.

USE YOUR TEACHING STYLE: MATH

- **Classical:** Use a math textbook that utilizes real-world experimentation and application; use fact memorization.

- **Charlotte Mason:** Avoid formal math instruction until late elementary; use household activities, exploration, and games until then.

- **Textbook:** Use workbooks utilizing mastery or spiral approach to math education.

- **Unschooling:** Allow the child to learn math naturally as part of her educational exploration; teach each concept as needed.

11.2.4.12 WHAT DO I DO IF MATH IS JUST TOO HARD FOR MY ELEMENTARY STUDENT?

Go back, my friend, go back. Find the point your child does understand and build from there. Find ways for him to practice in real-life application or with objects he can touch and see. Math is hard for all of us when we try to simply imagine concepts that are too abstract. Instead, bring math back to his level.

And if that level means he is not ready for algebra when you *think* he should be ready, or when curriculum manufacturers think he is ready—or when your co-op or friends or local school system thinks he is ready—then so be it. Your child will develop on his own timetable. We cannot rush his brain growth, and we cannot change his capability. All we can do is love him and lead him gently down the path to knowledge.

WHAT I DO
- use a math text that includes manipulative and real-world application nearly daily
- stop lessons and practice new concepts when they are difficult
- talk about math throughout the day
- memorize multiplication by skip counting

11.2.5 What role does memorization play in my elementary student's development?

Elementary school is a great time to memorize the facts, rules, and lists that make middle school and high school studies easier. Some children

---

THINGS TO MEMORIZE IN THE ELEMENTARY YEARS

- books of the Bible
- Bible verses
- poetry
- spelling rules
- preposition lists
- being and helping verb lists
- capitalization/punctuation rules
- math facts
- formulas for perimeter, area, volume
- historical figures and dates
- steps of the scientific method

find memorization easier than others. My oldest son memorized by reciting aloud. My daughter would read something a few times and it was committed to memory. My middle son really struggled with memorizing. He had difficulty with Bible verses, grammar rules, word lists, math facts, anything that needed rote recall. He has tried several strategies over the years:

- walking while reciting
- jumping the squares of the sidewalk while counting by 7s, 8s, or 9s for multiplication
- bouncing a ball while repeating things
- studying, running around the house, then coming back to study again
- sitting at the counter and reading a passage repeatedly to me while I cooked

Surprisingly, that last strategy was one of the best. He is the son that learns relationally, so being beside me and in the thick of family action helped him relax and learn. The second most successful way for him to memorize was jumping the sidewalk squares. Walking outside while he did that gave me a little bit of exercise too. The fresh air seemed to help us stay calm.

Children memorize in many different ways. For more ideas on memorization, see section 10.2.6.

11.2.6 What might my elementary student learn about science?

I have mixed feelings about elementary school science. On the one hand, science is an important study of creation and God's beauty. On the other hand, high school science covers most areas of study in detail.

I take a very relaxed approach to elementary science. With my first two children, I taught no science at all. No science textbooks, no science class. We went on nature walks, we visited science museums, we collected books on nature and animals for our home library. Both of them checked out books from the public library: books on animals, weather, or planets they were interested in at the time. I did not care how much or little science they explored. You could say we unschooled science.

By the end of elementary, both children understood many scientific concepts. Most of their knowledge was from light reading, talking about interests in the minivan, visiting science museums across the country, and experimenting on their own theories. They enjoyed informing anyone who would listen of all the facts they knew about sharks, frogs, fossils, or volcanoes.

My two oldest children began taking science as a homeschool class with a published curriculum when they entered middle school. They both earned As in high school science by taking two years from an online teacher and two years of independent, tested study from a curriculum. They each scored well in science on college entrance exams, one getting a near-perfect score. I felt pleased with my choice of unschooling elementary science before switching to a textbook method.

> Science without religion is lame, religion without science is blind.
>
> **ALBERT EINSTEIN**

With my subsequent children, I taught science class half-heartedly. Children love science, especially experiments, and they are naturally curious about the world around them. Let them go to explore, research, and visit zoos and farms, and they will amass more fun facts about nature than we ever care to hear. With two of my children, I started a great, very hands-on curriculum that was perfect for them . . . and did not keep up with it more than a few months. With my twins, I have a goal to make it further in the book than before.

I have friends who love science so much they could not imagine *not* teaching it regularly to their child. I am friends with authors of wonderful science curricula for homeschool students. All of them would strongly disagree with me about the importance of elementary science education. I admire them so much. This is another example of something you can decide for yourself and not worry about what other people are doing.

FOUNDATIONAL GOALS
- understand and demonstrate magnetism
- recognize the three states of matter (solid, liquid, gas)
- identify thermal, electrical, sound, light, and/or mechanical energy
- understand and describe the water cycle
- understand and use parts of the animal classification system
- identify fossils as formed by catastrophes such as flooding or volcanic activity

┌───┐

USE YOUR TEACHING STYLE: SCIENCE

- **Classical, Charlotte Mason, and unschooling:** Read books on science topics; view science videos; keep a science sketchbook; conduct simple experiments; collect bugs, rocks, or other specimens; take field trips; join the science museum; adopt a pet.

- **Textbook:** Engage in many of the above activities as guided by a preplanned curriculum.

└───┘

- study and model the solar system
- understand Earth's rotation, axis, and eclipses
- use technology such as computers and smartphones to answer questions and to research

DEVELOPMENTAL GOALS

- describe a hypothesis and plan and implement an experiment
- anticipate and apply safety procedures for investigations
- correctly use appropriate scientific tools such as scales, thermometers, magnets, and household chemicals
- accurately explain the existence of dinosaur fossils

ADVANCED GOALS

- memorize and apply the scientific method
- keep a lab notebook
- repeat experiments and variables to test theories
- discuss some differences between evolution and creationism

WHAT I DO

- encourage hands-on exploration in areas of interest
- provide books on science and encourage research
- use a textbook sporadically for areas of interest

11.2.7 What might my elementary student learn about history and social studies?

History should be alive and relevant. There are so many great stories of people, wars, reigns, inventions, explorations, and eras that affect our lives today. Children love learning about ancient people, brave missionaries, and intrepid explorers, and the actions and beliefs of these people have shaped our culture and who we are as individuals. We can't fully understand our current world unless we know where the ideas our society is built on came from. Furthermore, we can't understand who we are as a society without understanding the modern people, institutions, and laws that make up our country and community.

When I first began homeschooling, I bought a beautiful history curriculum with a heavy teacher book. We worked out of such materials for a couple of years. And we didn't enjoy it. Okay, once again, let's remember we all homeschool differently. In my own personal homeschool, though, history is nearly as important as Bible. For us, Bible and history are the lenses through which we see all the other subjects as well as current events. So the fact that we all hated how we were doing history was not acceptable. I got rid of all my history curricula, even some I had bought ahead of time and had never used (remember my mistake from chapter 8?). My used bookstore lady I sold it to thought I had gone mad. Yet those books were what was driving me mad. It is a short trip to madness, and I don't need help.

I have found there are several curricula that help parents teach history from sources other than traditional textbooks. Like fun books. We have begun to really enjoy museums. We look for historical landmarks and museums when we travel as a family. We watch history documentaries and movies from a historical era. We visit art museums to learn about creative expression and artifacts from long ago. We have more fun with history than with any other subject.

When I began having older students in the house, this became even easier. The younger ones began soaking up what their siblings were talking about. They looked through the history books lying around the house. They even enjoyed picture books on the same topic. So this subject has become more and more enjoyable for us as the years go by.

FOUNDATIONAL GOALS
- understand the basic outline of US history from the colonial period to the present
- study the religious, colonial, scientific, technological, and philosophical contributions of specific Americans

---
USE YOUR TEACHING STYLE: HISTORY AND SOCIAL STUDIES

- **Classical:** Focus on a sequential study combining world and American history utilizing real books and time lines; create a history notebook with photos, brochures, and reports on what he has studied; visit historical sites; memorize important facts and dates.

- **Charlotte Mason:** In addition to the above, emphasize reading biographies, reenacting events, and enjoying historical fiction; explore geography and cultures.

- **Textbook:** Utilize a course that perhaps covers world history, American history, and social studies separately.

- **Unschooling:** Encourage the student to participate in many of the projects listed for classical students, while allowing time for researching topics of interest.

- understand the meaning and history of state and federal holidays
- identify symbols of American culture such as the flag and Uncle Sam
- memorize "The Star-Spangled Banner" and understand its history
- identify all the continents and oceans as well as many countries around the world

DEVELOPMENTAL GOALS
- learn principles from the US Constitution and Bill of Rights that outline our federal government
- identify and explain the three branches of government in the US
- learn the history and symbols of his own state
- memorize the fifty states and capitals of the US
- identify many countries in North America and Europe

ADVANCED GOALS
- memorize the US presidents, sections of the Declaration of Independence, and the Constitution
- outline the important events in the history of the United States and world history

- understand the issue of civil rights over the history of the country and how it applies to current political and social issues
- learn the difference between free-market capitalism and socialism
- identify countries and capitals throughout the six inhabited continents
- compare and contrast the US government with that of other countries

WHAT I DO
- let my child study historical topics along with older siblings
- read biographies aloud
- assign several readings from history books and historical fiction each week
- have my child watch history documentaries and movies based on history
- help my child look up places read about and studied on a map
- encourage my child to memorize presidents, state capitals, and excerpts from important documents

11.2.8 What electives might I teach my elementary student?

The elective subjects are less important in the elementary years. Some, such as health and physical education, will be covered in-depth in middle school and high school. And some are just plain optional. But many elective subjects are appealing to students, besides encouraging their love of learning and supporting concepts within other subjects.

Each homeschool family will emphasize different electives at different times. This is another place we all need to be careful not to compare ourselves. We each have different priorities and different homeschool cultures. So take what I say about these subjects with a huge grain of salt. You may completely disagree with me, but I hope we can still be friends. Actually, all the friends I know disagree with me here or there on these. Join the crowd.

Some homeschoolers worry that they need to immerse their child in the arts, or poor thing, he will not be well-rounded. After all, the public school has an hour each of music and art every week, so we need to keep up with it too, right?

And there's foreign language. As the world becomes more multicultural, is it not imperative our child speak more than one language? And can he even understand English if he doesn't know the Latin roots that make up so much of our vocabulary?

One homeschool family we know gives their child drawing lessons, and Gertrude draws beautifully. Another family has entered Bertrand into photography contests. Delores's son plays the harp in the local symphony. Eustace has won national honors in piano performance. Martin's sculptures are so extraordinary that a statue was dedicated in his honor. Stephan speaks to his family and writes his assignments in Latin and only reads the Latin Vulgate at church.

Good for them.

It is definitely great to expose our children to the arts. Look at paintings, go to a couple of children's concerts, make crafts at home. Actually, my children's Sunday school crafts count as art class in my house. Do not feel guilty for not doing more.

If your child has an interest in (or you have a passion for) a particular instrument or artistic expression, go for it. I require my students to take piano lessons from me, and they have the opportunity to learn a stringed instrument. That is just a priority I have to teach my children the fundamentals of music. Only my daughter stayed with the violin, and she plays in an adult symphony. She performs on the piano regularly, as well. But that's her jam. My other children take piano lessons only because I make them. Because I am a mean mom. Do not be a mean mom like me unless you really, really want to.

You do not need to make your child take piano lessons or art classes or anything. Don't feel guilty about it. For every elective, just do what you want to do.

In high school, you can think about electives more seriously (see sections 13.2.7–13.2.10). Now is not the time to stress out about it.

GENERAL GOALS FOR HEALTH AND SAFETY
- study health issues including nutrition, exercise, and hygiene
- learn the importance of different body systems including skeletal, respiratory, and circulatory, and how they work together
- understand the basics of how germs are transmitted and prevented
- learn how to protect himself from harmful situations
- recognize the dangers of substance abuse and experimentation

- learn how to identify harmful behaviors in others, including substance abuse, bullying, and physical and sexual abuse
- learn sex education from the aspect of his own changes in puberty and identify his own internal and external sexual organs

GENERAL GOALS FOR FOREIGN LANGUAGES AND THE ARTS
- study conversational phrasing and/or grammar of a modern foreign language
- learn grammar and vocabulary of an ancient language
- join a book club
- learn to play a musical instrument or sing in a choir
- practice art such as drawing, painting, or sculpting
- look carefully at details of art and compare and contrast similar paintings and sculptures
- participate in a speech or theater club

11.3 QUESTIONS YOU MAY HAVE ABOUT YOUR ELEMENTARY STUDENT

11.3.1 If my child was in the early learning stage for several years, is he behind in elementary?

Not at all. Just like early learning, elementary years can last as long or as little as the student needs. If your child begins elementary at age five, he will likely spend seven or eight years enjoying elementary. But if your student begins elementary later, he may pick up speed and begin middle school just four years later.

All in all, it does not matter how long your child spends in each stage. Homeschooling, remember, is about teaching the way you teach best for the way your child learns best. Let him take his time and learn at his own rate, even in elementary.

11.3.2 Does my elementary student have a learning disability?

Not all learning difficulties are learning disabilities. As parents, we can become concerned about our child's learning, especially when compared to other children or our own expectations. But certain difficulties in learning are completely normal. My daughter is nearly eight and still writes several letters and numbers backward. She can write them correctly when I point them out to her, and she makes mistakes inconsistently. Because she continues to make improvement in this area, I know she will grow out of this phase.

When I was a young child, I could not distinguish between the letters *l* and *r*. When I read words with those letters in them, I understood the words, but I pronounced them incorrectly and sometimes switched the letters when writing. By the middle of elementary, I grew out of that issue. So I can't use that as an excuse for why I can't spell today.

Two of my sons confused special sounds or blends in words. One of my elementary students spent an entire year neglecting to write the final letter of words. He eventually overcame it. I have learned that most children have learning quirks or hiccups they eventually cure in their own time.

Besides these normal speed bumps in learning, your child may exhibit some traits that concern you:

- reversal of letters or numbers after age eight
- complaints of frequent headaches when reading
- slow reading, especially out loud
- poor reading comprehension
- difficulty writing and spelling

If you are concerned your child may have a learning issue, do not hesitate to have him evaluated by a specialist. Two great things could happen: you might be relieved there is nothing wrong, or you may receive tools and strategies to help him overcome his challenge. It's a win-win. Turn to chapter 16 on special needs for more about learning disabilities.

11.3.3 Should I be grading my elementary student's work?

Probably not. When I first started homeschooling, remember, I started with a big box curriculum with all the extras. So from kindergarten, I was testing or evaluating my children in everything. I even kept a grade book.

But as I relaxed and began focusing on real learning and not paperwork, I realized there is no reason to test young children, even elementary students. As I work with them and live with them, I know how much they are learning and when they need more help. That's how I teach my children, anyway. I'll say it again: homeschooling is about teaching how we teach best for the way our child learns best.

So to answer your question, no, I don't think you do need to grade your child's elementary work. Now, some states may require more evaluation and records, so definitely find out your local requirements through your state homeschool organization (you can find it at hslda.org) and stick to them. But otherwise, don't overemphasize your child's grades at this point. Be confident in what your child is learning.

11.3.4 How do I provide my elementary student physical education?

Limit screen time. Most children get plenty of physical activity as long as their screen time is restricted. Again, I'm a mean mom, so I regularly force my children to play outside. (We looked at the dangers of screens and screen addiction in section 10.3.4.)

If you *feel* like it, and only if you feel like it, you could have your child join a recreational sports team. This can provide excellent physical training, as long as you can stay dedicated to practices and games.

Now, as it happens, my husband is not only a children's sports coach but also the owner of his own competitive soccer league. His strong recommendation is to choose one sport and stick with it. The child will then learn the fundamentals within that sport, gain experience with long-term relationships in teamwork, and practice perseverance and responsibility. But this only works with a strong parental commitment too.

Do what works best for your family. And don't feel guilty for not joining a sports team or not even having a homeschool physical education class. Just like in the early learning years, play is the most important.

11.3.5 What if my elementary student is not motivated and will not take the initiative to complete his schoolwork?

I'm not motivated either. Not most days. Honestly, I roll out of bed and stagger to the coffeepot desperate for caffeinated motivation. Then, I shower and do my homeschooling and housework. I am motivated by my love for my children, my duty to my responsibilities, and my relationship with God. If not for those, I would be in bed right now in a TV coma.

Young children do not naturally possess this sense of responsibility. They need to be trained. We need to provide external motivation now so they will take initiative as adults. So don't despair when you find your child does not want to do her schoolwork. She is just being a normal child.

My friends use different motivational strategies. Some have a chart to complete, with a reward each week or month. Others tie allowance to finishing responsibilities in schoolwork and housework. Others view it as a behavioral issue and discipline the child who won't obey and do her work.

First of all, it is important the child knows exactly what is expected. Some parents have posted lists of chores or checklists. We use a combination of tactics. Chores are posted and we give reminders until they are habitual (or nearly so). Practices, lessons, and sports have schedules on the calendar.

We track schoolwork in two different places. Some subjects, like history and literature reading, are recorded in my lesson plans. Other subjects, like grammar and science, I actually map out in the textbook or workbook. I explain more about that in section 8.2.1. I can then check each subject at the end of the day or week to make sure it is all completed.

Some families put everything—all of the schoolwork, chores, and appointments—into one planning system. In fact, many digital homeschool planners are designed just for that. See appendix F for planner options.

Finally, we practice a "work before play" rule. I joke, "No fun or happiness of any kind until your work is done!" Of course, with a large family, many shenanigans go on during work time. But they each know there is no playing, no friends, no screen time until all the schoolwork and housework are completed.

11.3.6 When is my elementary student ready for middle school?

Your child may be ready to move on to middle school when the following criteria have been fulfilled:

- **She can complete an assignment start to finish with little help.** Most preteens are ready to work without your micromanaging every step. Many can simply read instructions or a textbook and complete assignments alone. Some may want a brief explanation at the beginning then will take off. Every student needs help—that's why we homeschool! But middle school is a time to further develop self-teaching skills. A student that needs careful attention for each step of a project or help with most questions on worksheets may benefit from more time at an elementary level to increase confidence.

- **He can take responsibility for his own work.** Preteens generally welcome the opportunity to work without someone looking over their shoulder. They especially enjoy recognition for completing a project or assignment completely on their own. Preteens can usually keep track of their assignments in a notebook or planner or follow a list of requirements each day.
- **She comprehends reading in literature, science, and history.** Middle school students in any type of homeschooling will be reading and digesting more information on their own. Whether they are answering comprehension questions from a textbook or writing a report, preteens should have the ability to consume and then communicate information and ideas. Students who struggle with reading comprehension may spend an extra year working on these skills across several subjects. If they have continued difficulties in reading, perhaps have them evaluated for an academic need. See chapter 16 for more information.
- **He makes connections across subjects.** Middle school students apply their understanding of each subject to other subjects. History impacts literature, science uses math, physical education is related to science, and so forth. Preteen students may begin making connections within the subject matter, applying principles and patterns to other similar situations. Middle school subjects often require this holistic understanding. Students who mentally compartmentalize their subjects may need extra help with this.
- **She shows the beginning of abstract thinking.** Elementary students learn concrete facts about concrete subject matter; they deal with what they can see and touch. Middle school students begin working toward abstract ideas not only in math but also in other subjects. They begin wondering what underlying beliefs cause historical events, or what hidden message is behind their literature. This abstract thinking begins developing during the preteen years, but it continues to grow into high school.
- **He has entered puberty.** I say my child is ready for middle school when I can smell him. Puberty brings with it wild and crazy physical changes, and with them come mental and emotional changes too. This rapidly growing mind helps the young person move into more advanced work and greater responsibility. A child

who develops later physically may also be waiting for that mental growth spurt and may perhaps benefit from an extra year of elementary work. There is no reason to rush ahead before the child is developmentally ready. And it is possible that, like with physical growth, the student could suddenly take off later.

- **You think she's ready.** Don't feel pressured to rush your child ahead. Like we will discuss later in chapter 13 on high school students, there is no firm age for graduation, so stop worrying about that. Each child grows and learns differently; this is one of the reasons we homeschool. Continue to teach the way you teach best for the way your child learns best, whatever rate that may be. Your child can move on in her studies when she is good and ready.

• • •

The elementary years look like a long time on paper, but they really fly by. You'll see your student amass a huge quantity of information. He will probably enjoy showing off some of that knowledge to you. Like, how many facts about sharks do I need to know? How many facts about sharks can I forget each week? And don't get me started on the knock-knock jokes. All of this knowledge comes in handy in our next period: middle school.

12

MIDDLE SCHOOL: THE SIXTH- THROUGH EIGHTH-GRADE YEARS

Approximately ages 11–15

MIDDLE SCHOOL CAN BE INTIMIDATING for many parents. Puberty is scary enough without trying to teach through it. As I write this, I can hear my preteen son yelling, "Go away! Go away! Go away!" to his brother.

Wait, it's quiet.

No, someone else walks through the room and he yells again, "Get out of here, now!"

This is why I am hiding in my bedroom typing. It can become hard to share space with a middle schooler, let alone homeschool him.

I have survived three middle school students, I'm in the midst of schooling one now, and I will have twin middle school children in my future, heaven help me. Let's have a moment of silence for all mothers of preteens everywhere.

[moment of silence]

Homeschooling middle school, however, can be very rewarding. There is so much change and growth during this time. Your student will become such a completely different person so fast, it is exciting to watch.

I wish I could tell you a heartwarming or humorous story about my years homeschooling middle schoolers. But honestly, those years are a blur. I have found that some days are all about patience, some days are opportunities to practice not laughing in your child's face at her foolishness, and some days are a lovely glimpse into the teen God is shaping her to be. All of that is a beautiful haze in my memory, bright and colorful like an impressionistic painting. Blurry enough to cover the weird spots.

Both my oldest son and my oldest daughter could have raced through middle school and started high school early. They were bright, eager to learn, and almost fully independent in their work. Middle school subjects were very easy for both of them. But my husband and I decided not to push them ahead, keeping them in middle school a full three years for several reasons. For one thing, we did not want to rush our children into deeper subjects earlier than they needed, before they were emotionally prepared for it. We also wanted them to start high school studies when their hormones had *somewhat* calmed down. And we did not want them to graduate from high school before the age of seventeen or eighteen so they wouldn't enter the adult world before they were mentally, emotionally, and spiritually ready.

As I have emphasized in previous chapters, it is important to keep brain maturity in mind when teaching our children. We don't want to push students to learn theoretically what they cannot relate to or understand concretely. Education is not about seeing how fast we can get through the material. It is about soaking our children in knowledge to prepare them spiritually and emotionally to live as wise adults.

GENERAL GOALS FOR THE MIDDLE SCHOOL YEARS
- understand the parts of speech
- create a well-written paragraph for different subjects
- appreciate quality literature
- master concrete math and begin abstract equations
- practice the scientific method
- be exposed to different branches of science
- understand the time line of major events in world history
- identify major countries, mountain ranges, and rivers

That is just about it. We'll list some goals for each subject, but there are really only two main ones for middle school: maturing physically and mentally and preparing academically for high school.

12.1 THE MIDDLE SCHOOL STUDENT'S DEVELOPMENT

12.1.1 How might my middle school student's character develop?

In demonstrating greater empathy. Middle schoolers have a lot of raging emotions. This can be stressful for both parents and students alike, but it does mean they can genuinely feel others' feelings. They can now "rejoice with those who rejoice, weep with those who weep" (Romans 12:15).

This developing empathy can now extend to those different from them, whether an opposing team or another culture. This growing awareness enables students to imagine not only the emotions of those around them but also those of another time or place. History and geography may become more personal as students begin genuinely understanding the emotions of others.

This cultural awareness extends to racial and social issues. This is when middle schoolers begin to strongly identify with their own race and notice differences in others. Instead of identifying people by color, they learn the name of their own race and that of others. Middle schoolers have been exposed to their parents' reactions to others for many years; they've noticed prejudice and may have internalized it. They may internalize the prejudice of those around them, or they may openly seek out different perspectives.

Some middle schoolers, especially boys, may become embarrassed by these awakening emotions and try to hide behind tough exterior behavior. Like younger children, they need to be gently reminded to use their words rather than crankiness to describe how they feel.

Some students may begin equating making others happy with being good. Their conscience hurts if they believe they are making others sad or frustrated. This is how they internalize rules now. Rules make them happy and get them what they want, like free time or rewards.

While making strides in empathy, middle schoolers also deal with strong feelings. They may struggle with self-control, particularly at home, while sports and other competitive situations may bring out aggression and frustration. Graciousness and a controlled response are very hard for this age. It takes patience and training to help them with this issue. My husband and I have found a few strategies to help our hot-tempered middle schoolers:

We have clear rules for behavior and words. We can't act out in anger, like destroying property or hurting someone. Destructive or hurtful behavior is disciplined like an obedience issue.

We lighten the mood with humor. One of my preteens struggled with his relationship with his older brother. Every look or comment from the older one sent the younger into a rage of yelling and waving his arms dramatically. I made a joke that he needs to stay out of a fight. He is Switzerland, neutral in a war of siblings. So now, when any tempers begin to rise, the youngest children often start shouting, "Sweden! Scandinavia! South Dakota!" and every place they can think of that begins with the letter *S*. That makes us all laugh and reminds everyone to respond with patience.

We train our middle schoolers how to question an adult appropriately. This takes a lot of practice but is one of the most important self-control skills. When a middle schooler reacts in anger to something we say, I remind her, "Instead, do you mean to ask me 'Can I do this another way?' or 'Would you consider this instead?'" Middle schoolers want to be heard, but they need to be taught how to speak respectfully.

We give our middle schoolers time and space to cool off. Hey, sometimes I need to take a break from my children or to just close the bathroom door and breathe during a rough day. How much more does a middle schooler with strong emotions need some grace to compose himself? Sometimes, I may send a child to his room midconversation when he becomes heated. This is a way we teach our children to remove themselves from unnecessary conflict. Now, my children may race to the backyard when they need to run around and cool off or hide away in their bedroom to relax in privacy.

We congratulate him for a good response. Living with a hot-tempered middle schooler can really wear on me. I need to remind myself to watch carefully for progress and give positive feedback when he responds appropriately or handles a difficult conversation with respect.

FOUNDATIONAL GOALS
- verbalize emotions in a mature way
- speak with respect to adults and peers
- respect cultures and backgrounds different from his own

DEVELOPMENTAL GOALS
- remove himself from heated discussions
- consider opposing viewpoints before responding
- maintain respectful body language when upset

ADVANCED GOALS
- self-regulate emotions
- respectfully negotiate privileges, responsibilities, and compromises
- respectfully confront prejudice in others

12.1.2 How might my middle school student develop physically?

It's easy to notice the onset of puberty. The smell. The hair. The smell. How quickly flee the soft cheeks and high voices of childhood, only to be replaced by the quickly emerging signs of a growing young person. Boys are broadening across the shoulders and hips, welcoming the emergence of muscles and facial hair. Girls accept the gift of periods and curves. And everyone loves the acne.

Some middle schoolers welcome the changes. Girls may feel more grown up. Boys may feel proud of their deepening voice and of starting to shave. Other middle schoolers may feel self-conscious, especially if the growth process begins before or after their peers.

As homeschoolers, we have an opportunity to minimize that sense of embarrassment by stressing how natural and beautiful these changes are, how God designed their bodies exactly this way. The foundations of body image begin with these changes. Girls, especially, internalize their beliefs about how they look and how others perceive them in these years. This may be when they first notice that God created them uniquely, and they may struggle with comparison. Girls sometimes make comments to each other about appearance, not just about what they wear but about how their body looks and their general size. Though their increased interest in how they look may seem vain, part of their changes in puberty include deciding if they like their appearance.

We can help both our daughters and our sons immensely with well-timed compliments. We can try to couch our hygiene lessons in reassurances of our love of who they are. We can show appreciation when they go the extra mile to look nice. We can temper lectures on nutrition with encouragement to keep looking and feeling their best. Our young people are surrounded, especially in social media, with the message that their own unique bodies can never be perfect enough. But at home, we can reinforce the truth that God made each one wonderfully beautiful. We try to compliment our children as much as possible, especially with "I'm so glad you can lift/open/fix this for me!" My preteen has dubbed himself The Ultimate Form of Man and loves to show off his muscles with household chores.

GENERAL GOALS
- learn to take increased care of hygiene and practice healthy lifestyle habits
- understand the changes of puberty and the basics of human sexuality
- demonstrate increased strength and dexterity
- express positive body image

12.1.3 How might my middle school student develop mentally?
Middle school students move from factual thinking to big-picture understanding. They often enjoy putting together what they learn from several subjects into one main idea. One of my children never was good at remembering dates and names. But if you asked him how to compare and contrast different ancient civilizations, he could talk for hours about how their religion, technology, and social habits together created different cultures. Another son revels in learning how beliefs and wars shape the development of nations. Another was interested in how animals, terrain, and technology worked together in the past and present.

Many middle school students even begin developing the beginnings of abstract thinking. In math, particularly, they may excel in prealgebra or even start algebra with a clear understanding of how variables relate to each other. Other students may begin these studies by learning rules and patterns but not conceptualize the problems. Still others struggle with the beginnings of upper-level math. Again, students display a wide range of perfectly normal development.

FOUNDATIONAL GOALS
- complete most assignments with little assistance
- write a multiparagraph assignment
- speak and write in longer, more complex sentences
- read chapter books

DEVELOPMENTAL GOALS
- begin to think abstractly as in prealgebra or literary analysis
- connect ideas from multiple sources
- correctly structure persuasive or explanatory essays

ADVANCED GOALS
- study some subjects independently
- begin algebra
- write persuasive and comparative essays on school subjects
- write and speak about the application of ideas and principles he's studied academically

DON'T BE CONCERNED UNLESS AT THE MIDDLE OR END OF THIS PERIOD YOUR MIDDLE SCHOOL STUDENT

- cannot handle any responsibility for academics
- exhibits academic difficulties in reading and/or math
- otherwise cannot prepare for high school
- is depressed or seems anxious
- resists time with family
- struggles making or keeping friends
- cannot cope with mistakes or failures
- possesses a poor body image
- possesses poor self-control or aggression
- has little forethought or takes unsafe risks
- exhibits signs of substance abuse
- demonstrates signs of special needs (see chapter 16)

12.1.4 How might my middle school student develop socially and emotionally?

Emotional changes happen during adolescence just as quickly as physical changes. Girls experience the ups and downs of PMS, with increased crying, frustration, and craving for comfort food. Boys fight anger, frustration, and even crying as their emotions feel out of control. These battles for self-control affect relationships in and outside the home.

Because, in the midst of this emotional turmoil, friendships become important. Your young person may become attached to a peer group and struggle to maintain acceptance. The strong emotions may cause disagreements and drama within friendships. Peer pressure becomes strong, even in seemingly small areas like appearance and activities. Then the feelings of acceptance or rejection impact your child's feelings about body image and self-worth. This is an important time to discuss the benefits and harms of close friendships.

FOUNDATIONAL GOALS
- practice self-control
- learn how to respond to peer pressure
- develop a positive body image
- articulate the dangers of substance abuse
- learn how to be responsible with time

DEVELOPMENTAL GOALS
- understand when to seek help and when to find the answer herself
- discern positive and negative self-image
- develop problem solving skills in friendships
- become involved in church activities

ADVANCED GOALS
- take leadership in youth organizations like sports or youth group
- establish mentoring relationships with other adults like Sunday school teachers
- actively seek out opportunities to help and be an example to younger children
- look for a job and understand the value of money and work

12.2 WHAT YOUR MIDDLE SCHOOL STUDENT COULD BE LEARNING

Middle school transitions your child from elementary to high school. This is when he learns to study, to research, to write, and to communicate what he is learning. Both you and your student get a glimpse of what high school might be like. And this is your opportunity to prepare for it.

I have heard of parents skipping middle school. Because this is a time of transition to high school, they feel it is easier to skip that transition and get started immediately. And that seems admirable. But there are several reasons I feel this strategy is not in the child's best interests.

First of all, a middle school child's mental capabilities are rapidly developing. As bright and precocious a learner as she may be, her brain is not yet like that of an older teen. There are areas of abstract learning she is physically incapable of comprehending completely until her brain goes through the transformation of adolescence.[1] She may get through the courses and even answer all the questions correctly, but she still may not comprehend the ramifications of what she is studying. This is true not only for higher math, but also for historical and literary analysis.

This doesn't mean that middle school subjects should be fluff. These years of study are crucial not only to solidify the basics but also to build connections across subjects. Students will continue to make connections to religious and philosophical beliefs into high school. Middle school is also when my students begin writing essays and reports. Again, they are practicing and preparing for high school, when these writing skills will be critical. These few years offer plenty of time for learning, feedback, and practicing.

The middle school years are an excellent time for your child to hone the skill of studying independently. He will still need help, but during these years he can likely do more for himself. In middle school, I back off on frequency of accountability. Instead of doing work with my student or checking progress each day, I give her weekly goals and assignments. Then, I allow her the freedom to complete these larger tasks on her own time. My students may, at first, leave much of their work until Friday then learn the agony of spending all day or part of a weekend working. After several weeks or even a year of this, they begin to work ahead more. My daughter even began cutting an entire day off of her week by working ahead. In some subjects, she worked ahead so quickly that she finished an entire month ahead of my family schedule. She continued that pattern through her high school years.

Middle school is the time when my students practice test-taking, as well. In elementary, I don't test; living with my child and teaching her myself shows me clearly what she knows (but note that in some states, elementary testing may be required). In high school, I want to objectively measure my student's knowledge for her college transcripts and reporting. So in middle school, we test and keep grades. This helps my homeschooler learn to study and prepare. It helps her understand what grading is like. It helps her gauge how to earn the grades she wants. And it helps her understand where her own academic strengths lie and where she can improve.

Finally, high school can and should contain more mature subject matter than middle school. In literature, history, and science in particular, high school students wrestle with topics such as rape, the Holocaust, and euthanasia. The content need not be vulgar or explicit, but it definitely should prepare the student to solidify his own beliefs regarding the morality of each topic presented. Most of us would not want an eleven- or twelve-year-old dealing with the same material we would find useful and necessary in high school.

I cannot emphasize this enough: *there should be no race to graduate a homeschool child.* We may read with wonder of the wunderkind who graduated Harvard at age fifteen. But in light of parenting and worldview considerations, such acceleration may be counterproductive. Take your time.

HOW MUCH TIME SHOULD WE SPEND?

STUDY *3–5 hours*

SLEEP *8–10 hours*

EAT/BATHE *3 hours*

PLAY *8 hours*

12.2.1 What might my middle school student learn about the Bible?

Students who have learned Bible stories throughout their childhood are ready for real application. They want to know what these biblical examples mean to their lives today and why biblical passages are important. My preteen son was excited to study the book of Hosea last month; the seemingly obscure book in the Old Testament suddenly meant something to him as he learned about God's love for sinners.

Middle schoolers are also ready to begin studying the Bible in their own time through private devotions. Check out appendix F for some great resources to help your student get started.

FOUNDATIONAL GOALS:
- find a verse in the Bible with no help
- fully participate in the adult church service
- volunteer to serve in a church ministry
- memorize the Ten Commandments, the Beatitudes, the fruit of the Spirit, or other Bible lists

DEVELOPMENTAL GOALS:
- take notes on the sermon
- understand how to make a profession of faith
- memorize the Roman's Road of salvation (verses explaining how to know Christ personally)
- memorize specific Scripture verses related to character issues

ADVANCED GOALS:
- begin having a personal devotional time
- volunteer in ministry opportunities
- memorize Scripture passages
- tell a friend the plan of salvation

12.2.1.2 HOW DO I ENCOURAGE MY MIDDLE SCHOOLER IN PRIVATE DEVOTIONS?

By example. Middle school is a great time to encourage your student to have personal devotions. There are many excellent materials available to help your young person begin this discipline (see appendix F). But you can simply show

USE YOUR TEACHING STYLE: BIBLE

- **Classical:** Study the history, geography, and cultural background of Bible events.

- **Charlotte Mason:** Continue to read Bible accounts along with missionary biographies.

- **Textbook:** Utilize a Bible teaching program.

- **Unschooling:** Learn Bible principles by applying them to current events and daily life.

BIBLES FOR MIDDLE SCHOOL CHILDREN

- *NLT Life Application Study Bibles* (various versions for teen boys and girls)

- *Inspire Bible for Girls*

- *ESV Grow! Bible*

- *NIV Adventure Bible*

her your own method of Bible reading, whether it be a short passage and prayer, or a longer reading and journaling. If your child knows you have a private devotional life, she is more likely to begin such a habit herself.

It is important not to make devotions seem like a burden. A simple five-minute plan is easier to make into a habit than a thirty-minute routine. And of course, we all need grace; not one of us is perfect in this discipline.

The best way to teach God's Word to our children is to read it together. Each morning, we have a short Scripture reading. Then we go around the room, allowing each one to say a few words about what the passage means. Then we read a devotional and pray. Just a few minutes with the Bible together is a great way to start our day.

In the preteen years, a child's spiritual life begins to become a social activity. Young people look for acceptance at church and at home and will follow the most common habits in both. If her friends at church are serious about Bible memory, she is more likely to participate. Christian peer pressure becomes strong in the right environment.

WHAT I DO:
- allow the middle school student to read aloud the Bible passage during Bible time
- ask the middle school student to explain the passage and meaning
- teach him how to take notes on a sermon
- teach him how to have personal devotions

12.2.2 What might my middle school student learn about English language arts?

The middle school student is ready to apply the foundations of English language arts study to literature and writing. He likely can apply his grammar rules while correcting his own writing. He's ready to learn the writing process for short essays and creative writing. And as he reads good literature, he will begin to appreciate plot, characterization, and description in prose and poetry.

FOUNDATIONAL GOALS

- read silently for a period of time and demonstrate comprehension
- identify a fiction book by genre (historical, fantasy, science fiction)
- describe characterization and compare/contrast characters
- identify figures of speech
- construct a five- to seven-sentence paragraph with a thesis statement, supporting sentences, and a conclusion
- identify the major parts of speech in a sentence
- use the correct form of irregular verbs
- use commas correctly in most sentences

DEVELOPMENTAL GOALS

- learn basic literary analysis
- discuss point of view: person, beliefs, and culture
- write a three- to five-paragraph essay with a clear topic and supporting facts
- actively study vocabulary
- diagram sentences
- write three- to five-paragraph essays
- organize information in an outline form
- practice good content and grammar editing

ADVANCED GOALS

- identify Latin and/or Greek roots of words to determine definitions
- identify the theme and author's intent in literature
- perform literary analysis and make connections after independent reading
- discern author's cultural or religious point of view

- apply literature knowledge to other media such as movies and commercials
- write a multiparagraph research report with three sources, notes, rough draft, first edit, and final copy
- write a wide variety of pieces including descriptions, instructions, cause and effect, persuasion, and poetry
- correctly demonstrate the use of all types of punctuation, including commas, semicolons, hyphens, and quotation marks
- understand and identify the construction of complex sentences
- take notes

12.2.2.1 HOW DO I TEACH MY MIDDLE SCHOOL STUDENT ENGLISH LITERATURE?

With exploration. Now that your student has mastered and practiced reading for a few years, he is ready to dive into literature. This is not the time for boring analysis, but it is the perfect time to discover what reading has to offer.

> Whatever is true, whatever is honorable, whatever is just, whatever is pure, whatever is lovely, whatever is commendable, if there is any excellence, if there is anything worthy of praise, think about these things.
>
> **PHILIPPIANS 4:8**

Some homeschool literature programs offer a textbook containing a selection of short stories, poems, and excerpts from novels. (That's how I learned at home, myself.) Or your homeschool curriculum may include a literature program, complete with book lists and discussion notes. But a course of literature study is so easy to create yourself: find a good book, read it together, then discuss. End of lesson.

Keep in mind that literature class is not about training a literary scholar. This subject has very simple goals:

- instill a love, or at least appreciation, of good literature
- develop discernment for good, wholesome, well-constructed works
- train the student to think deeply about not only written works but also other media, including movies and social media
- learn how to wisely differentiate between truth and error in beliefs and worldviews

GOING DEEPER INTO LITERATURE

- What is the genre of the work—is it nonfiction, fantasy, science fiction, historical fiction?

- If it is a poem, what are the genre and structure? How does the structure contribute to the message?

- What is your favorite character? How is he described physically, emotionally, and spiritually? What is his relationship with other characters? How does he change from the beginning of the story to the end?

- What is the setting of the story? How does the author describe it, and how does this setting contribute to the story?

- What is the main problem in the story? Why is it a problem? How does the problem affect each of the characters, and how do they respond? Are there other secondary problems?

- Can you identify some events in the rising action, the climax, and the resolution?

- Do you find the resolution satisfying? Why or why not?

- What is the theme of the story? How do the characterization and plot communicate this?

- What did you learn about the author's culture or beliefs? How is that revealed through the story?

12.2.2.2 HOW DO I TEACH MY MIDDLE SCHOOL STUDENT ENGLISH GRAMMAR?

I really drill parts of speech and punctuation during middle school. My students have a fairly good introduction to nouns, verbs, and modifiers by the end of elementary. But during these three middle school years, I like to completely prepare my student for the rigors of high school grammar. My goals are to make sure he can identify every part of speech by labeling every single word in a sentence and to make sure he can capitalize and punctuate correctly. Those are the two biggies. If my student, with three years of practice, can do those two things with some accuracy, he will do well in high school and on into adulthood.

English grammar does not change from year to year. We just keep repeating the same things every semester. So if my son struggles today, he has plenty of time to practice not only now, but next year too. He will grow into his grammar. A solid start in middle school gives my son a leg up on high school English.

12.2.2.3 IS IT IMPORTANT FOR MY MIDDLE SCHOOL STUDENT TO DIAGRAM SENTENCES?

No. But maybe yes. I do require my own students to diagram in middle school. Right now, my middle school son is leaning back into the pillows on my bed, waving his feet in the air while diagramming sentences. Every few minutes, I hear a soft moan about an indirect object or a predicate nominative. His scribbling is music to my ears. His feet are an assault on my nose.

Diagramming is part of my students' curriculum, and out of three of them who have gone through upper-level English, none of them have had a problem diagramming. My son who is schoolwork-adverse even enjoys showing off his sentence diagrams.

We looked at diagramming in elementary school back in section 11.2.3.5. When my students are in elementary and having troubles understanding diagramming, I have them underline subjects and verbs and label words in the sentence. For words that describe things, like adjectives and adverbs, we draw arrows to what they are describing. Prepositional phrases are in parentheses. By middle school they learn about clauses and can bracket those, underlining and labeling the words in a clause just like the rest of the sentence. Whether a student diagrams or draws all over the sentence, he learns all the parts of speech and what each word in the sentence is doing.

Is diagramming critical? No. The entire reason for diagramming is to enable the student to demonstrate he understands the sentence structure. If my student makes a mistake on his diagram format but he can describe what the sentence part is and what it is doing, I don't count it wrong. It is the knowledge that is important, not the picture itself. He could demonstrate his knowledge any way he wants.

You might just look ahead. If you think your student may later take a course that requires diagramming, middle school is a good time to get some practice. At the very least, it doesn't hurt to show him this weird game we play with lines and words to draw a sentence-picture.

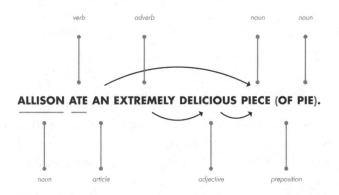

12.2.2.4 HOW DO I TEACH MY MIDDLE SCHOOL STUDENT TO WRITE ESSAYS?

Before learning to write longer essays, students need to master paragraph writing. When it was time to teach my oldest to write paragraphs, I was very confused about where to start. I had a basic idea of how I wrote, but I was pretty sure that I could not just hand him a piece of paper and say, "Here! Now write something!" No, I needed to teach him the basics: choose a topic and write a topic sentence, develop supporting ideas, and write a conclusion sentence.

Here's an example:

1. Topic sentence—explains the superiority of the video game Shooting Zombie Destroyer
2. Supporting sentences—discuss several reasons the topic sentence is true beyond a doubt, even to zombie destroyers
3. Conclusion sentence—reveals that I will only play Shooting Zombie Destroyer

And that, my friend, is how we write a paragraph.

There are many writing curricula for teaching paragraph writing listed in appendix F. The easiest courses I have used with my students have a few things in common:

- clear, concise instructions to make each step seem easy
- short, manageable assignments for each day teaching how to break down the writing process

- plenty of practice on each step before expecting the student to put it all together; for example, several days just practicing writing topic sentences or several lessons just practicing brainstorming on different topics
- simple checklists to help the student edit his paragraph
- easy grading rubric

It is hard to find a curriculum that does it all. So I usually find one that does most things and make up the deficits myself. As long as I know the simple structure and help my student practice each step, she will gradually master the process.

Often the topic our student loves works for multiple paragraph styles, too. We could have an *informative* essay on the significance of Shooting Zombie Destroyer (SZD). We could also have a *compare/contrast* essay with SZD up against Bombs of Aliens (spoiler alert: SZD wins hands down). We could perhaps write an *instructional* essay teaching the basics of how to win the third level of SZD (you know, the level before the total space apocalypse). We could even present a *persuasive* essay to convince mothers that SZD teaches valuable life skills, therefore meriting more playtime.

A good writing curriculum will help guide teacher and student through the writing steps, giving plenty of practice on each. With a basic knowledge of grammar and an understanding of the process, you could teach paragraph writing yourself with only online instructional videos on Shooting Zombie Destroyer and a piece of paper. See the appendices C and D for help with a student editing checklist and a grading rubric.

12.2.2.5 HOW DO I HELP MY MIDDLE SCHOOL STUDENT WRITE IN A WAY THAT IS NOT FORMULAIC?

Don't follow the curriculum too closely. Several homeschool writing curricula do teach a formula for writing: first, write a topic sentence this way, then write one each of these types of sentences, then one of these transition words. The writing becomes very similar in every assignment. Parents will occasionally ask me to look at a sample of their child's writing and to make suggestions on how to teach them better editing skills. Many times, I can identify what curriculum they are using just by how the student composed his paragraph.

Such formulism presents a real danger. If a student carefully follows the

STEPS TO WRITING A GREAT PARAGRAPH

1. **Find an idea.** Any crazy idea will work, like even why the video game Shooting Zombie Destroyer is so awesome.

2. **Find out what is interesting to others about that idea.** Why should anyone care about shooting zombies, and who is this destroyer? Is the destroyer actually shooting zombies, or is there a weapon called the shooting-zombie-destroyer?

3. **Wrestle that idea into one sentence.** "The video game Shooting Zombie Destroyer demonstrates the superiority of zombie multiplayer games compared to other first-person shooters." Wow. Now your mother will wonder what she is missing by not playing SZD! (I would be missing valuable time I could spend reading awesome books like this one, but others may disagree.) Now we have a topic sentence.

4. **List reasons that support your topic sentence.** Just go crazy jotting down everything you can think of. Then circle the best reasons that will completely convert your mother into an SZD fanatic. Scribble them down on a paper, create a mind map, or draw a Venn diagram.

5. **Organize your greatest facts.** Jot your reasons down in order or create an outline so you can see what you are writing first.

6. **Write those best reasons in a few great sentences.** Make the sentences look different from one another. Put the sentences in order from least great reason to the best reason of all, or from greatest reason to okay reason.

7. **Add some connector words** like *also, however, perhaps,* and others to help the sentences at least look like they belong together.

8. **End with a super sentence!** Your conclusion should convince your mother that SZD is *fantastic!* Consider appealing to your mother to purchase SZD from the nearest game store and to allow extended screen time for practice.

9. **Go back and read your work.** Find any factual mistakes in your SZD presentation. Then make sure every sentence is really about SZD being awesome and not about how reading is a better use of your time. And finally, check the capitalization and punctuation.

10. **Give the paragraph to your mother,** who is surely oblivious to the merits of SZD. That is called presentation or publication. Wait patiently for your mother to give your paper an A and your proposition a resounding no.

examples and steps given, then soon all his paragraphs and essays will sound too similar. We can protect our child from this issue by stepping back from the curriculum. Give the child the basics and a good editing sheet. Teach each concept one at a time, then let the student apply it his own way. Be careful not to require your student to write a certain type of sentence, but rather encourage variety and flow. Let natural writing development happen.

Our students do need to learn various ways to construct a sentence. But be careful about requiring a certain number of each construction. Another danger is requiring that every paragraph contain one example of a different structure or a certain number of transition words. Instead, encourage the student to use the sentence structure that best emphasizes his point and help him to gradually add variety. After a few years of practice, he will develop his own mature writing voice. Like my own: complex but informative, encouraging, and sarcastic sentences in paragraphs punctuated by fragments. Can't help myself.

> A word fitly spoken is like apples of gold in a setting of silver.
>
> **PROVERBS 25:11**

12.2.2.6 HOW DO I TEACH MY MIDDLE SCHOOL STUDENT TO WRITE LONGER ESSAYS?

Teach her that long essays are paragraphs strung together. Essays aren't as scary as they sound. If the student understands the principles of paragraph structure, she can learn to write a simple essay quickly and gradually build her skills to write longer ones. Remember that one paragraph in a longer essay serves the same function as a single sentence in a one-paragraph essay.

Students can construct a five-paragraph essay in the same way they constructed a five-sentence paragraph:

1. Topic paragraph
   - a topic sentence that presents the idea that the Shooting Zombie Destroyer multiplayer game is important to play daily
   - several sentences explaining why we must believe this with all our hearts
   - a concluding sentence that compels us to build our own SZD clan and play for several hours each week

2. Supporting paragraphs (three or more)
   - a topic sentence for each paragraph detailing a different compelling reason to convince your mother of the moral and developmental value of SZD play
   - several sentences supporting each paragraph's topic sentence, giving reasons or an example story to support the essay's topic sentence beyond a doubt

3. Concluding paragraph
   - a topic sentence that points back to the beginning of the essay, reminding the reader of the urgency of SZD play
   - an emotional plea that the reader set aside valuable time for video game play
   - a final concluding sentence that irrefutably states the effect this must have on parents and students every day

There are, of course, many other ways to tackle the five-paragraph essay. Your student could construct the interior paragraphs into one compelling story. Or each paragraph could contain a story giving one example. Or any other strategy that completes three good paragraphs that together support the topic stated at the beginning.

Essays, both long and short, often seem more intimidating than they are. With careful, systematic practice, each step becomes easier and the results gradually improve.

12.2.2.7 HOW DO I HELP MY MIDDLE SCHOOL STUDENT IMPROVE HIS WRITING?

Emphasize to your student that editing is an important part of the writing process. Everyone's first draft is going to be worse than their revised drafts and polished draft. But of course this raises the question of how to know if it is a good paragraph/essay or not. How does a student accurately check his work?

First, your student will benefit from an editing checklist. My students loved, honored, and cherished theirs. The list of items to look for helped them know if the piece was ready to turn in for grading. A good checklist may be included in your curriculum. It should include things like "strong topic sentence," "supporting details presented clearly," "uses strong, descriptive words," "uses correct capitalization," "uses correct punctuation," and more. Two sample essay editing checklists are included in appendix C of this book.

Your writing curriculum might also contain a rubric to help you grade your student's paper. This is a fancy word for a chart that tells you how many points to assign for each aspect of writing. For example, assign full points for a clear, detailed topic sentence, two points off for an appropriate yet not detailed topic sentence, four points off for a poor topic sentence, and six points off for no topic sentence. Then the categories go on to help you evaluate each aspect of the work. A good rubric will be very detailed so you can confidently grade your student's assignment. Furthermore, using that rubric for each assignment gives the student solid ways to improve and shows him what to expect each time. I have included a grading rubric in appendix D of this book to help you out.

12.2.2.8 WHAT IF MY MIDDLE SCHOOL STUDENT CAN'T WRITE WITHOUT MY CONSTANT HELP?

Practice each individual step of the process. First, write down the steps for her: choosing a topic sentence, brainstorming, putting ideas in order, writing sentences, developing a concluding sentence, editing and rewriting, presentation. That way the student knows what to do.

Next, allow the student to practice each of those steps individually. Give her a topic and let her write three compelling topic sentences about it. Or let her pick three different topics and write descriptive topic sentences on

---

USE YOUR TEACHING STYLE: ENGLISH LANGUAGE ARTS

- **Classical:** Have your student write essays and research papers on a variety of subjects for writing and grammar practice; work on word structure through Latin studies; practice literary analysis.

- **Charlotte Mason:** Enjoy copious reading on a variety of subject matter; utilize a grammar program; continue reading aloud.

- **Textbook:** Follow a grammar and literature program.

- **Unschooling:** Read books of interest to the student; work on grammar and writing as it applies to current interests and projects.

each. Practice brainstorming on different topics. Practice choosing the best ideas from a list. Practice arranging ideas in order. Practice writing topic and concluding sentences that work together.

Finally, give the student a very short assignment. It could be to do just two or three of those steps on one topic. When her confidence has improved, give her a slightly longer assignment: one paragraph with a topic sentence, three supporting sentences, and one concluding sentence.

Once the student can do that alone, encourage her to look back at how she could vary sentences. Then maybe give her a chance to "find three things from your editing checklist that you can fix."

If you feel overwhelmed teaching writing, just imagine how scared your student is. Keep the process short and easy, and let writing skills gradually develop.

12.2.2.9 WHAT IF MY MIDDLE SCHOOL STUDENT DOESN'T WANT TO WRITE?

Tough noogies. No one likes writing. I don't like writing. As the saying goes, authors don't like writing—they like having written.

Writing is a must, like reading, math, and cooking vegetables no one wants to eat. None of us avoid the scourge. I loathed—*loathed*—writing throughout college. I was a music major, and my English composition teacher tried to get me to change my major. He may as well have told me to stop drinking coffee. Seriously, what a bad idea.

But the fact remained that I, like everyone else, was forced to write for years and years against my will. And worse, with technology, all of us are now writing more than ever before. Badly, perhaps, but we are writing.

I am so sorry to report there is no way around it. We do not all need to succumb to a lifetime of writing lengthy books. But we must learn to communicate via the written word.

And unfortunately, my child, you have to obey me and do your writing homework. Parents make decisions young people do not understand. That is what makes us parents.

WHAT I DO:

- utilize a workbook for grammar
- work through a vocabulary program to study word origins and spelling

- have my child read literature independently and discuss principles of analysis with him
- teach a writing program and use the included assignment ideas
- assign one-paragraph essays in science and history
- continue to read aloud as a family

12.2.3 What math skills might my middle school student develop?

Prealgebra, prealgebra, prealgebra. Most middle school students are ready for prealgebra, but not for the more abstract reasoning underlying algebra and beyond. If your student is precocious, as some of mine are, you will be tempted to push forward into algebra. Beware of this temptation—your child may not be ready.

> He is before all things, and in him all things hold together.
>
> **COLOSSIANS 1:17**

I succumbed to that temptation. My first son was brilliant in elementary math. You cannot accuse me of bragging if it is a fact. He breezed through his math books without even trying and applied his knowledge every which way. He simply lived math.

Then he started prealgebra. Everything was great. He was still cruising along . . . until he started algebra while still in middle school. Suddenly, everything ground to a halt. Nothing made sense to him. Mornings spent hunched over his book with him ended in loud noises and tears. For some obscure reason I will never fathom, my banging on the table and yelling "Write $x = 29$ down! I don't care if you don't know, just write it there!" didn't help matters. Math just wasn't working. Yet we slogged along, him not understanding and me mystified that my genius son could not work a simple xyz problem.

Then, out of the blue, one day he *got it*. He walked down the stairs and said, "Give me my math book!" He sat down and finished his assignment perfectly and with a broad smile.

Eloquently, I asked him, "What in the world?"

"I just sat up in bed, and it all of a sudden came to me!"

And he never struggled with upper math again, even taking calculus (I kid you not) in one week with a perfect exam.

What was the difference? Why did he go from failing basic algebra to suddenly racing through upper-level math?

He grew up.

Children's brains, as we have discussed, grow at different rates. But one thing is for sure: children move from concrete to abstract reasoning later in development, usually sometime around puberty. Until this growth, middle school students studying algebra have two choices:

- get bad grades in algebra and hate it, thinking they will never truly understand algebra
- memorize formulas and strategies, thinking they will never truly understand algebra

There is a third solution: spend middle school solidifying basic math and prealgebra skills. I finally understood this with my third child. He took two years of prealgebra. The first year, he used my usual curriculum and struggled through it, yet prevailed. The second year, he took two years of a more comprehensive prealgebra course, using one year's worth each semester. By the end of that year, he understood the principles and felt ready to tackle algebra.

Most importantly, my son learned how these foundational principles applied to real life. Algebra *is* real-world math, finding an unknown part of a situation. We need to know how many feet are in a meter (converting to different units of measure), how to find what a percentage means in an actual amount (converting, multiplying, and dividing ratios), and how many packages of twenty cookies will give us the one hundred cookies we eat each week (solving for an unknown quantity). We also need to know how many packages of cookies we need to buy to allow our children to eat ten cookies each day if we eat three-fourths of the total cookies ourselves (unknown quantities that enable survival).

My current middle school student is following the same strategy—two years of prealgebra. He is very bright in math and could probably begin

> ## USE YOUR TEACHING STYLE: MATH
>
> - **Classical, Charlotte Mason, textbook:** Study from math textbooks within the child's ability.
>
> - **Unschooling:** Teach basic principles of prealgebra and geometry in conjunction with projects of interest, or use a textbook program.

algebra now, but again, I want to let his brain mature before moving to abstract reasoning.

Most students don't suddenly sit up in bed and declare themselves math whizzes. Instead, we can gradually see our students mature from simple to more complex reasoning, and this will correspond to stronger math skills.

Remember, high school usually requires only two years of algebra and a year of geometry. That is three years of work. The last year is extra—trigonometry and calculus if you want it. My oldest son took both in one year. He entered the university as a math major to discover he had to take calculus again, anyway. Speeding through mathematics did nothing for him at all other than give him more homework.

Now, you may be saying, "Lea Ann, my student is different. She rushed through prealgebra in elementary school, completed two years of algebra in middle school, and started college calculus in tenth grade. She's doing great and now teaching mathematics at Harvard."

Dear friend, I am so happy for you and so impressed with your gifted student. I say that without a bit of sarcasm. Your student is truly exceptional, and I'm glad you were able to provide the quality advanced education she needed and deserved. Sincerely, Lea Ann.

Dear rest of you, Please don't compare your student to any other student. Continue teaching your student the way you teach best for the way your child learns best. With all my heart, Lea Ann.

FOUNDATIONAL GOALS

- understand decimals and fractions and the relationship between the two
- memorize all multiplication facts
- multiply three-digit numbers by hand
- divide a four-digit number by a two-digit number by hand
- add and subtract fractions
- understand negative numbers
- plot positive numbers, negative numbers, and fractions on a number line
- identify x and y coordinates on a plane
- find the perimeter or circumference and area of a rectangle, triangle, and circle

DEVELOPMENTAL GOALS
- multiply and divide fractions, decimals, and mixed numbers
- understand the relationship between fractions, decimals, and percents
- add, subtract, multiply, and divide negative numbers
- correctly solve problems including parentheses and brackets
- understand and correctly apply the order of operations
- solve problems with unknown numbers (prealgebra)
- solve problems and diagram them on a horizontal and vertical plane
- memorize and use formulas for surface area and volume of three-dimensional objects
- complete prealgebra

ADVANCED GOALS
- start algebra
- apply simple algebraic equations to real life
- learn about national economic issues and apply principles to family finances

WHAT I DO
- for some of my students, complete a year of basic math and two years of prealgebra
- for some of my students, complete a year of prealgebra and a year of algebra over a three-year period

12.2.4 What might my middle school student learn about science?

Basics of experimentation and the scientific method. As when they were younger, middle school students *observe* or notice details in the world around them. They *wonder* (question) why it is or how it works. They *guess* (hypothesize) because they believe they are all-knowing. They *assume* (predict) this statement of theirs is the rule for all of the world. They go about trying to *prove* (test) they are right, or they feel forced to prove it by the skepticism of those around them. They either prove themselves right or explain why their declaration did not quite fit the actual truth. They naturally perform the *scientific method*. With a little subtle help, they can continue exploring and learning about the world around them in such a natural way that they don't feel coerced.

You may recall that I am not a science-y person. So while you may totally enjoy doing lots of messy and incredibly exciting science experiments with your student, I prefer to just let things go as they happen. If my student wants to experiment, she had better clean up after herself and not start a fire. If she does not want to experiment, she can read about it.

When I was a homeschooled middle school student, my parents gave me one year of life science and one year of earth science from school textbooks. For my first students, I had them take similar subjects from homeschool curricula. For my middle son (can you tell yet that he received the best middle school education of all of them?), I let him choose which science he wanted to study. He chose a year of life science from a creation apologetics point of view (lots of fossils). Then he took a fun year studying engineering designs from nature. There were experiments, but, again, he just kept them in the kitchen or outdoors and cleaned up after himself. He really enjoyed that year.

Science becomes more structured in high school. Middle school is a continuation of the elementary years' philosophy to *love learning*. So my advice is to keep your students moving forward and get out of the way of fun.

> USE YOUR TEACHING STYLE: SCIENCE
>
> - **Classical, Charlotte Mason, textbook:** Work from curriculum texts, watch videos, and perform experiments.
> - **Unschooling:** Complete any of the above along with research and experiments of interest.

> All things were made through him, and without him was not any thing made that was made.
>
> JOHN 1:3

FOUNDATIONAL GOALS
- describe a hypothesis, plan an experiment, and implement the experiment
- anticipate and apply safety procedures for investigations
- correctly use appropriate scientific tools such as scales, thermometers, magnets, and household chemicals
- study the different perspectives of evolution and creationism

DEVELOPMENTAL GOALS
- memorize and apply the scientific method
- keep a lab notebook
- repeat experiments and variables to test theories
- study fossil layers and theories of their existence

ADVANCED GOALS
- complete two or three introductory science courses (life science, earth science, or general science)

WHAT I DO
- teach science books with workbooks
- have my child complete a study on creation science and evolution
- attend museums with my child and discuss displays
- attend creation science events and lectures with my child

12.2.5 What might my middle school student learn about history and social studies?

A little more of the same from elementary school—with a twist. In middle school, the student keeps studying the past, right? But an interesting thing happens during puberty. Our child begins challenging authority. Trying our patience. Testing the limits.

Those are *great* qualities for history study. The middle school student can begin questioning *why did they do that* and looking for *is that right or wrong?* He begins noticing patterns in history, similar belief systems and struggles that have repeated. He begins challenging his textbooks, his parents, and even his own understanding in order to wrestle out the truth.

Of course, he frequently comes to the wrong conclusions. This is where a good discussion can help direct thoughts toward logical conclusions. Ideally, further study through the teen years combined with this growing discernment will help the student form wiser views even on current events.

My middle son, the one with the better middle school education, was fascinated with false religions during this time. So I bought him a pictorial encyclopedia of world religions. Each lesson in history prompted him to study the religious beliefs of that time and compare them to biblical

Christianity. This enabled him to see how the beliefs of mankind shape their actions and that these actions affect history.

Now, not all middle school students love looking at sculptures of Buddha. My current middle school student scrutinizes maps of major battles to criticize and compare strategies. My daughter compared clothing of the time period and looked for ways women influenced the times for good or bad. Most middle school students will find some aspect of history they can examine and critique. Instead of bristling at this argumentative spirit toward figures of the past, we can allow our students to immerse themselves in the issues that matter most to them.

FOUNDATIONAL GOALS
- identify the causes and effects of major battles in US history
- understand how the Constitution and Bill of Rights form the basis of our federal government
- identify and explain the three branches of government
- understand the issue of civil rights over the history of the US and how it applies to current political and social issues
- identify major countries in North America and Europe
- memorize the fifty states and capitals

DEVELOPMENTAL GOALS
- memorize the presidents and sections of the Declaration of Independence and the Constitution
- outline the expansion of our country and issues related to it
- discuss issues such as colonialization, slavery, states' rights, industrialization, the treatment of Native Americans, the Great Depression, and the civil rights movement
- compare current government and culture with that outlined in our founding documents
- begin studying moral contradictions in movements and leaders of our country
- identify countries and capitals throughout the six inhabited continents
- compare and contrast our government with that of other countries

ADVANCED GOALS
- complete an overview of world history
- complete an overview of American history
- explain capitalism, supply and demand, and economic development throughout US history
- complete an overview of state history

WHAT I DO
- have my child read a lot of history books, biographies, and historical novels about each era
- have my child watch historical movies and documentaries
- hold weekly discussions about what we have learned and/or have my child write an essay

---

USE YOUR TEACHING STYLE: HISTORY AND SOCIAL STUDIES

- **Classical and Charlotte Mason:** Follow a program of reading and discussing history from ancient times to modern over several years with regular discussion.

- **Textbook:** Follow a textbook study of world, American, and/or state history.

- **Unschooling:** Any of the above with emphasis on areas of interest.

12.2.6 What electives might I teach my middle school student?

Unless mandated by your state, you don't need to worry about electives. By their very definition, they are extra studies the student elects to take. But many middle school parents and students want to broaden their education with physical fitness and the arts.

Middle school is a great time to explore these interests. While some physical education and fine arts may be required in high school, a middle school student may have the freedom to choose what activities he wants to add to his weekly studies. In addition to the common sports and fine arts studies, your student may enjoy crafts, home economics, gardening, computer science, mechanics, and other interests.

GENERAL GOALS FOR HEALTH AND SAFETY

- participate in a personal or team sport
- continue to study health issues, including nutrition, exercise, and hygiene
- protect himself from harmful situations
- continue to study how the skeletal, respiratory, circulatory, and other systems work together
- know the dangers of substance abuse and experimentation
- identify harmful behaviors in others, including substance abuse, bullying, and physical and sexual abuse
- learn sex education, including puberty, intercourse, and the birthing process, along with issues such as biblical commands regarding sexual immorality and the harm of sexually transmitted diseases

GENERAL GOALS FOR FOREIGN LANGUAGES, THE ARTS, AND OTHER PURSUITS

- study conversation and/or grammar of a modern or ancient foreign language
- participate in a music or theater group
- study art such as drawing, painting, or sculpting
- study art appreciation and history
- participate in a speech or theater club
- begin computer coding
- learn creative arts such as sewing, baking, decorating, and others
- learn how to read a recipe and practice cooking safety

12.2.6.1 HOW DO I INVOLVE MY CHILD IN PHYSICAL EDUCATION?

Those adolescent emotions are great for team sports. I am always glad when my moody son can take it out on the field. Strenuous, sweaty exercise burns off some of that hormonal energy. My children all participate in team sports in middle school. The training in teamwork and the vigorous exercise are worth the crazy soccer schedule.

If your student is not into team sports, perhaps you can find another way to incorporate fitness. Regular running or swimming are great for conditioning and for improving your child's mood. Lawn mowing and other yard work also provide many benefits.

A common issue during middle school is excessive screen time. Students of this age can become enamored with YouTube and video games. Involving your children in sports and exercise will counter the sedentary nature of these activities and help build important brain connections they may not gain otherwise.

12.2.6.2 HOW DO I TEACH MY STUDENT A FOREIGN LANGUAGE?

Let him speak. If your student has already been studying a foreign language, middle school is a great time to put his vocabulary into practice. He may begin writing sentences and practicing short conversations. If he is studying a modern language and meets a native speaker, he may want to try out his few sentences on him. Middle school students are more motivated to learn conversational than written language during these years. This is fine. If he continues studying a foreign language in high school, he could then learn the nitty-gritty of grammar and formal communication.

Just as with many other things, you should approach foreign language learning on your own terms. If you don't want to mess with it, great. If you want to dive in deeply, more power to you. Whatever speaks to you.

12.2.6.3 HOW DO I HELP MY CHILD APPRECIATE THE FINE ARTS?

Let him take the lead. If your student has begun formal musical training, the middle school years may show marked improvement. For instance, instrumental students will begin putting together the theory of music and understanding how that applies to their pieces. They may be performing larger works from classical composers, popular artists, and hymn writers in public recitals or church services. They could share their abilities with others by playing in rest homes or at community events. Visual art or drama students may likewise broaden their horizons.

Many middle school students, however, balk at practicing and performing during these years. They want to quit, they hate lessons, and they sabotage their own efforts. As a private music teacher for ten years, I learned to expect moody adolescent students. It is just part of the hormones. If the student doesn't hate music in general, she is bursting into tears because her first effort is not perfect.

This is when the parents need to decide why the student is studying. Is music part of the student's education, or was it an interest to be explored? My advice as a teacher is to try to hang on for these middle school years and then decide in high school whether or not to quit. Many adults bemoan the fact that they quit piano lessons. No one says they wish they had never practiced.

In our house, piano is a required course. Any other instruments are optional. If the student never touches the piano again in adulthood, I feel the same as though they had decided to never read Homer again. At least they had the education.

None of my friends require piano. Some require public speaking. Others require some form of visual arts. Most of my friends let their students explore whichever fine arts they want. Just like everything else, do what you want and please don't compare yourself to your friends.

12.3 QUESTIONS YOU MAY HAVE ABOUT YOUR MIDDLE SCHOOL STUDENT

12.3.1 How do I survive puberty?

Give your middle schooler choices. This is one good tip I can give you. As much as your child seems out of control to you, life seems fully out of control for her. She wants to be heard, to grow up, to do things for herself. She needs a way to feel like she can grow. So as much as possible, give her some control. Many arguments can be saved with some negotiation. Negotiate bedtimes, screen time, curriculum choices, fine arts studies, sports activities, snacks, recreational activities . . . everything that causes conflict. Find two or three choices you can live with, then let her choose.

My middle schooler wanted to be treated differently than his younger brother and sister when it came to bedtime. But his dad and I did not feel he was ready to stay up as late as the teens. So I asked him, what did he think was an appropriate bedtime? He said ten. I said nine. We agreed on nine thirty, so long as he always told me good night then and went straight to bed. Weekend and vacation bedtimes were negotiable on a case-by-case basis. If he didn't keep his side of the bargain, I could decide his bedtime. And he knew I would choose 0-sundown-thirty.

Another son bristled at being told what to eat. So I let him decide what he wanted for breakfast. As long as he cooked it and cleaned it up, he could have whatever he found in the pantry or refrigerator. He loves eggs now, and I keep a few dozen in the refrigerator for him at all times.

I am a naturally stubborn person. I tend to draw a line in the carpet and dare any child to cross. But honestly, most things can actually have some wiggle room. Now adolescent parenting has taught me the value of negotiation. After my children graduate, I may negotiate a Middle East peace treaty.

12.3.2 How do I talk to my middle school student about sex?

Quite frankly. This is not the most fun conversation to have, but boy, is it necessary.

Not all families will handle this issue the same way. I can only share with you how we handle it. I know you may make different decisions based on your own beliefs, priorities, and comfort level. That's up to you. Here's what we do:

- **Answer questions as they come up.** My children asked random questions while they were growing up, questions about babies and how they come out and how they are made; questions about how boys and girls are different; questions about how children's and adults' bodies are different. I answered each question as briefly as possible as long as the child was satisfied. By the time each child was a preteen, he had already accumulated quite a bit of knowledge (see section 10.3.9).
- **Have the "big talk" sooner rather than later.** With those first signs of puberty, we know it is time for more information. We explain the upcoming changes in our child's body and the basic reasons why God intended them. The child's subsequent questions usually guide us through what they need to know beyond that.
- **Make sure they get all the info from us.** Before my children become teenagers, we want to make sure they are armed with accurate information—they are sure to get inaccurate information outside the home from friends and media.
- **Go over consequences thoroughly.** For most people, sex works as God designed it to; it often results in pregnancy. And in our family, the genes say the likelihood is quite high. Beyond the risk of teenage parenthood, there can be serious life-changing consequences to having sex. We are quite frank with our children about sexually transmitted diseases, even to the point that we talk about this openly with their doctor as well. And furthermore, there are deep relational consequences that need to be addressed.

- **Display our own attraction to each other without shame.** Whether they like it or not, my children know that I know my husband is hot, hot, hot. And their dad does not make a secret of his feelings, either. Without being graphic, we make it clear how much we love each other *and* how much we love those kisses and hugs. God created physical attraction for our own enjoyment, and as a married couple, we have the opportunity to model healthy physical attraction. Exuberant hugs and kisses are totally awesome, right? Our middle schoolers need to know that married couples have fun, that physical affection within God's design is a wonderful thing.

12.3.3 How do I endure the constant arguing?

Teach her how to argue respectfully. As adults, we argue. We argue more than we realize and more than we care to admit. Much of our arguing is less obvious because we have learned how to argue politely. A little bit.

Each of my teens needed to be taught how to disagree with me. I know they *will* disagree, and I prefer they express their disagreement rather than become bitter over it. Unexpressed disagreement could cause tension in our relationship. So when my middle schooler begins arguing with me, I might try one of the following phrases:

- "Could you say that again politely? Start with 'I would prefer . . .'"
- "We don't use that language. Try it again with better words."
- "I can't hear you if you are yelling. Please tell me again."
- "You are upset at your brother? What do you think he would say about this?"

Often my middle schooler will strongly disagree with a decision or rule I make. I might ask her which alternatives she would prefer or why the rule should be changed. I try to listen to her thoughts and validate her opinion. She can have an opinion, and she will often disagree with me. I want her to know I recognize that.

I also want my middle schooler to know that I know I'm not infallible. I could make the wrong decision. I might make a bad rule. I could even jump to the wrong conclusions and punish the wrong person. I want her to have the freedom to tell me her own side of the story.

I want her to learn how to negotiate. She could present an alternative plan or rule. Or she might ask for other options. These are mature negotiation skills she will use in all of her relationships.

Finally, I want my middle schooler to know that authorities have the final say. She may not always understand my decision. I may not always tell her why I made the decision, either. She does need to learn how to accept the rules that govern her.

Today, far too few adults know how to disagree politely. Our culture has lost the ability to express different opinions kindly and thoughtfully. I hope that by teaching my preteens how to argue responsibly, I will help them to be better equipped to communicate their ideas and feelings as adults.

12.3.4 How do I help my middle school student make friends?

Teach her to be friendly. Friends become increasingly important in middle school. For the first time, perhaps, we begin wondering if we are giving our student enough . . . I can't bring myself to type it. You know, the *s* word of homeschooling: *socialization.*

I have one main principle for my own children: "A man who has friends must himself be friendly" (Proverbs 18:24, NKJV). It is ultimately the student's responsibility to reach out to those around him in the church and community to meet and serve others. Because it is that service—being friendly—that ultimately makes good friends.

Activities outside the home often lead to friendships. My children have made friends on sports teams, at church youth group, and in choir. Many of their friends enjoy relationships in homeschool support group activities and co-ops. Casual friendships in these large groups can turn into closer friendships when we invite our acquaintances to afternoon play, sleepovers, and birthday parties. I talk about this some in section 10.3.13. Service projects can also lead to satisfying relationships. My children have found like-minded friends during mission trips, church community outreach, and town volunteer projects. Again, this is friendly service in action.

Friends don't need to be same-age peers. My preteen's friends include not only his classmates in Sunday school but also the elderly neighbors, the homebound down the street, and the younger children down the block. He has learned to be friendly and outgoing with people of all ages, and this has led to rewarding friendships.

In my opinion, making friends is ultimately the student's own responsibility. Reaching out and forging relationships is a life skill. She doesn't want me to pick her friends for her, and I don't want to be making social introductions throughout her life. Making—and keeping—friendships is a rewarding skill for all of us to practice.

12.3.5 How do I control my middle school student's access to media?

By monitoring and increasing freedom to make wise choices. Our students do—and should—consume media. TV, movies, music streaming, and online videos have become important means of entertainment, communication, and instruction in today's world. And the impact of these is only growing.

In our family, we find it important to actively participate in each of these types of media to engage in the current culture and conversation. So we do watch and listen. In the middle school years, we give our children increased access to these services. While our elementary children have closely guarded and controlled screen time, during these older years we allow more freedom.

Media has much to teach our students through the nearly unlimited reference material available online, including dictionaries, encyclopedias, and instructional videos. My preteen eagerly looks forward to his favorite YouTube history series every week so he can inform the family on the finer points of the Cold War.

Media has much to teach our students through entertainment, as well. My children find literary references in movies and begin to make biblical applications and use discernment while watching. Playing video games helps them not only practice fine motor coordination (I simply cannot work a PlayStation controller) but also improve in group dynamics and social skills during online play.

Yes, we still need to censor the media our middle schoolers consume. Music, movies, video games, and online entertainment should be monitored and approved. Many homes use an internet filter. Our rule is to play video games and use the internet in the family room where the computer is turned so that everyone can see. Online video games usually have the sound turned off to guard against predators and vulgar language. There are steps we can and should take to guard our middle schoolers' minds.

Ultimately, however, these years are the beginning of media training. Just like other areas of his life, my child will not have me staring over his shoulder watching YouTube videos with him when he moves to college.

Several years of monitoring and slow increases in freedom of choice give my children the opportunity to grow their character and to learn how to make the right choices.

One of my children once came across an inappropriate video on YouTube. I overheard his chuckles and looked over to find cartoon girls in bikinis prancing around while a cartoon man told silly jokes. The screen content was obviously not wholesome. After a stern lesson in how to make wise choices, we cut off screen time for a while until he could "grow up and show us you can be trusted." This was another opportunity to learn privilege versus responsibility.

YouTube is my preteen's favorite source of entertainment in the evenings. Besides researching Cold War facts to stump his mother, he is now addicted to a video series I call Stupid Ant Man (SAM). SAM apparently owns the world's largest collection of ants, housed in aquariums in his basement. Besides a weekly soap opera monologue of his ants' activities, SAM gives a daily nature vlog that my son finds fascinating. It has not been confirmed, but I believe SAM is living with his mother. No matter who owns the house, the ants live in the basement in those glass homes with no roofs. Other insects like beetles, flies, and moths crawl into the ant homes and add drama to the insect telenovela. Weekly, SAM narrates with great excitement the latest happenings in his basement. I am waiting for the episode in which the ants figure out they can crawl out and wage an attack on SAM. Stay tuned.

Thus we see that my preteen does not choose high-quality media. I will keep watching over his shoulder while myself perusing the latest home-school parody and maybe an eyeliner tutorial.

12.3.6 Should my middle school student have a phone?

It's up to you. As with most parenting matters, every family is different and will choose different standards.

A couple of friends have pressed me for my opinion, and here is what I say. In our family, which is completely different from your family, we have a "not until you buy it" rule. Our teens may have a phone when they can purchase it and pay their portion of the family's monthly bill. If our teen can consistently live up to this commitment, we feel he's probably responsible enough to handle the privilege with supervision. My first two teens were in high school before they bought their own phones. My third son was working regularly for neighbors from the time he was in fifth or sixth grade, so he bought his phone and started paying his bill in middle school.

We are the only family we know, however, that requires their teens to pay for their phones. Maybe because we are just plain stingy. Or maybe because we want help with the phone bill. I don't know. The plan just works for us.

No matter what the child's age, however, phone use requires accountability. We have found we can track phone calls and text messages on our phone bill. We also have periodic "quick, hand me your phone now!" checks of social media and searches. We're aware this is another privilege that needs responsible monitoring.

12.3.7 How do I teach my middle school student problem solving skills?

Step back and give him the opportunity to make mistakes. When we are overly involved in our student's work, we communicate things we never intend:

- You are not smart enough to do this.
- Your effort alone is not appreciated.
- You can take a shortcut because I want you to get this done quickly.
- You will not be able to think through issues yourself, now or in the future.
- Your grades are more important than learning this thoroughly.

Rather than jump in at the first sign your student is struggling, take the following steps to help him move toward independent thinking.

Wait. Preteens need time to think. Some students need even more time than others. I tend to jump in too quickly or demand an answer too soon. That is totally not helpful. Instead, I'm trying to practice waiting to let my son think through the issue, to consider his response. Not only that, I need to teach *him* to wait, as well. He's impulsive and tends to assume his first thought is perfect in and of itself. In fact, sometimes he may be less than all-knowing. By gently encouraging him to wait on his solution, I can help him think through the options.

Don't validate too quickly. I also tend to jump in with a quick *yes* or *no*. That is not helpful, either. Instead, I'm now trying to say, "Are you sure?" before I tell him my own opinion. Even though I am always right.

Don't ask questions that suggest a correct response. Okay, how many times do we want to say, "Don't you think . . . ?" or "Don't you want to . . . ?" so he knows exactly what we think he should do? "Don't you think Aristotle was wrong about that?" or "Don't you want to measure that angle again?" These questions pretty much tell our student what we want him to say or do. Instead, we should try to ask questions such as "What do you think about . . . ?" or "What would you say to this alternative?" Whenever I ask these types of questions, I can see my student thinking hard, sometimes to change his answer and sometimes to support his opinion.

Assume he can do it. You want to motivate your student, and nothing is more motivating than success. Even if your student has not yet achieved success in that endeavor, knowing that you believe he can will help him move forward. He will see success in your eyes.

Our students often encounter a challenge that is daunting. Believing in them can be as simple as encouraging them to take one simple step, expressing confidence they can make a decision on one right thing.

Let him experience the consequences of his own logic. By experiencing the results of his own choices—insufficient studying, inaccurate math work, poor essay grades, no free time because of goofing off—your middle schooler will learn to look toward the future. This translates into long-term thinking in other areas of his life, as well.

Let him try it himself. Problem solving comes with experience. Leaving the student alone with the challenge forces him to fix his issues by himself. I require my student to read the math lesson and try one or two problems before he can ask me for help. In other subjects, too, he must show effort on his own before requesting help. Even then, he is only allowed one simple question; then, he must struggle through the next step himself.

Our students will take longer to complete a difficult task when we require them to work through it alone. But ultimately, they will learn to think more carefully and confidently by working through these difficult issues rather than being handed the answers.

12.3.8 How can I help my middle school student transition from fun, hands-on elementary work to more difficult high school studies?

Remember that it *is* a transition, and transitions don't always go smoothly. In middle school, we begin preparation for high school. This is the journey from concrete to abstract thinking, from hands-on to book learning, from parent-led to independent learning. It is important for me, in particular, to remember that this is not a sudden change but rather a gradual transformation. My child does not all of a sudden act like a young adult, and he does not all of a sudden study like a teen, either. I forget this for every single one of my middle school children. I'm like, "Good morning, here are your books. Let me know when you have finished the semester. Get good grades on your tests, too."

True confession: that has never worked yet.

The first key to making the transition is to allow your middle schooler to mature. Every time I have a middle schooler, I have to take a big step back and remember that he is still a child. He needs to learn *how* to learn on his own. He needs to carefully study *how* to study. He needs to *work* on how to work out his problems.

This is part of his physical and mental maturation too. (There we go with the hormones again!) Seriously, if this child can't shower reliably, how in the world will he do his math work without my making him sit there and do it? And if my daughter cannot pick up her laundry without reminders, why for Pete's sake am I expecting her to waltz down the stairs every morning whistling on her way to science studies?

For most students, elementary studies are not very taxing. They should not be, anyway. If we are teaching the way we teach best for the way our student learns best, everyone will breeze through every subject.

Not.

But we did learn some valuable lessons, right? We had some shining moments of "Don't I homeschool hard core? Every homeschool mom wishes she were me right now" and some dark days of "Please, please, for the love of dinner WRITE DOWN SEVEN! The answer is SEVEN!" In the middle of that somewhere we have a sweet spot of chugging along every day, teaching and learning and cleaning up a little before dinner.

Middle school suddenly seems *hard*. At least, that has been the case for each of my students. The material goes more in-depth, and now I am grading them on their knowledge of it. QUIZZES! TESTS! EXAMS! Fear and loathing grips young hearts as they consider running away to join the pirates even though there are no pirates around these parts.

So we need to help the young scaredy-cats ease into this. Consider test-taking, for example. One of my children received *a very bad grade* on his first test. He was shocked, but I was sympathetic. He received *a very bad grade* on his second test. He was concerned, but I was showing him how to study better. He received *a very bad grade* on his third test. He was shrugging his shoulders, and I was laying down the law. He received *a very bad grade* on his fourth test, and I was sending him to talk to his father about it.

He received a much better grade on his fifth test. Not stellar but much better. I was encouraging. He was determined. Things trended up after that.

Each of my children went through this process at a different rate. One of my sons did not learn how to master his material until his second year of middle school. But he did great in high school. My daughter jumped right into middle school with no problem. Another was somewhere in the middle. There is no rhyme or reason to this.

How quickly your child transitions to studying difficult subjects independently is no indication of high school success. Please memorize that statement and write it on the back of your hand. Then write it down again when you wash it off in that very, very, very long shower you take to get a break from adolescent hormones.

My students who have taken longer to warm up to middle school—one took all three years—have still done well in high school. I kept forgetting that important truth that my students are still growing. And they keep growing through high school and young adulthood.

The second key to making the transition is to monitor the academics. This is a tricky part. Remember, successful homeschooling is teaching the way you teach best for the way your child learns best. Sometimes middle school material—especially the more difficult curricula available—is not a good fit for you or for your student or for you both. This is just as critical now as in elementary school.

I learned this the hard way. What was *just right* for my firstborn was too lax for my daughter; it didn't challenge her enough to teach her to study. But then my next son did not respond *at all* to any of the same books or methods. He could not understand them, he could not focus on them, they didn't speak to him. He wasn't lazy, it just was not helping him take that next step toward mature studying.

So I changed everything.

I changed curriculum on nearly every subject. I changed where, when, and how he did his homework. I changed how I evaluated his work, gradually working in written quizzes and tests. I eased him into middle school at his own pace. He eased into high school just as gradually, and by his sophomore year he took it all in stride.

Remember to keep teaching the way you teach best for the way your child learns best, even if that means very gradual improvement in the academics you have prepared for him.

12.3.9 How do I make my middle school student more accountable for her work?

This depends on the student. If the middle schooler is ready for independence, then checking her work every week works. Give her daily or weekly assignments then look over things every Friday.

At first, you may want to check in once at the beginning of the day with your student. Allow her to do her work anytime, anyplace, as long as she can show you everything completed by a deadline, like before dinner.

Sometime during middle school, I show my students how to grade their own work. Do not gasp and clutch your pearls—hear me out. In subjects that require regular tests, like math, I let my student grade her own daily work and remind her not only to correct the mistakes but also to study why her answers were wrong. Then she will take the test in front of me, after which I will grade it to see if she has been studying well.

Yes, as you predicted just now, this has gone terribly wrong in the past. One of my children, bless his heart, missed nearly every one of his math problems on his first quiz. Going back to his homework revealed he had not checked one whit of his work. Cue lecture on correctly studying one's math.

Rinse and repeat for three more math quizzes.

Why did I not grade his math myself, you ask? Maybe you would have, and I applaud you. I had a different strategy: let him see how low his grades went and thus how much "trouble" he was in as long as he refused to do his work by the day of reckoning. By the time he got his fourth non-studied test, judgment day arrived. He was, like Nebuchadnezzar, "weighed . . . and found wanting" (Daniel 5:27).

This young man learned the error of his ways and a valuable lesson: one simply must learn from one's mistakes, whether it be mistakes in work, like math, or mistakes in character, like slacking on his studies. Gradually, his math improved. And he even asked me a few questions about difficult problems. He learned to *care* about his work.

One time, the young man in question took a history exam over the empires of Israel, the Assyrians, the Persians, and the early Greeks. He went into the exam all puffed up with his knowledge. By the end of the exam, however, he was weeping and gnashing his teeth. After turning in his papers, he threw himself on my bed and sobbed uncontrollably. "I failed!" he wailed. "I'm so tired of this! I fail, I learn my lesson, I fail, I learn another lesson, I fail again . . . I'M TIRED OF LEARNING LESSONS!"

Bless his heart, welcome to life.

To break the suspense, he did *not* fail the exam. He received a B, to his profound shock. And he learned another lesson: "Always answer something because you just might know more than you think you did. Like maybe you really do know something about Socrates and Plato that you didn't know. You know?"

Checking one's own work over increasingly long intervals teaches accountability. Tests and quizzes provide accountability. But ultimately, allowing our student to fail builds character.

12.3.10 How do I teach my middle school student to take notes?

By reminding him of the principles of paragraph writing. I learned how to take notes by sitting next to my mother in church. She outlined every sermon in her notebook, and I saw how she arranged main points and subpoints. I began carrying my own notebook to services. I would listen hard for the main ideas then check my work against my mother's outline. After a few months, I found I was pretty good at it!

I teach my students how to take notes *after* they have learned paragraph writing. In reality, taking notes is the opposite of writing. To make an essay, a student completes these steps:

- identify a topic
- write a topic sentence
- brainstorm ideas
- organize those ideas
- write the ideas in order

To take notes, a student completes these steps:
- identify the order or structure of the lesson
- capture each main idea
- listen for the main theme of the lesson
- learn the main point of the topic

After the student has practiced the writing method, he is better equipped to take notes. He will understand how individual ideas or facts are put together into a lesson or speech, and then he can differentiate what they are. He will also understand how he prefers to brainstorm, whether through writing down an outline, creating a Venn diagram, or drawing a mind map. His favorite way to organize ideas is also how he will best take notes.

Sermon outlines are a great way to practice note-taking. Our church includes blank outlines in the weekly bulletin and displays each point on the large screen. But like me, my children learn fastest by copying someone else's notes. (My know-it-all daughter just took notes perfectly the first time she tried. It's a good thing she wasn't in a classroom because I'm sure between her test skills and her stellar notes, she would not be popular.)

I instruct my students on note-taking during our history discussion. I will periodically say, "First of all . . . I said FIRST OF ALL! Write number one on your paper!" And pretty soon will come, "Here are five things we should remember about that . . . I said HERE ARE FIVE THINGS! Where is your pencil? Why aren't you writing this down?" I am a very patient teacher of note-taking skills. My teenagers laugh every week at my poor preteen trying to keep up with history notes.

"We went through it too!" his brother scoffs.

"You can copy off of mine," his sister whispers. Too bad for him, she is at college next year, and then he's on his own.

Perhaps you will want to teach your student more patiently. Regardless, note-taking in middle school is great practice for high school.

12.3.11 How do I teach my middle school student to take tests?

Remember that test-taking is not about learning how to take tests. Rather, tests reveal what your student knows well and what he needs to work on in the future. This is where an F is extremely valuable. When your student fails, he is forced to see his own fallibility. He learns how little he knows.

Then he can home in on what he truly needs to learn—including a little humility. We all need to be reminded that we don't know it all, right?

On the other hand, test-taking does teach a student some things about *how* to study better.

Right now, my preteen is learning this. He does great in some subjects like grammar. But others have been very difficult for him—math tests, in particular. Before each test, I remind him to go back and make sure he has learned his formulas, that he understands all the boldface terms, and that he has looked over the mistakes he made in his previous homework. If a test goes poorly, I ask him which of those he did not do. On one test, he didn't memorize the difference between *area* and *perimeter*, terms whose definitions were in bold print in the chapter. On another test, he made the exact same mistakes he had made in his homework; he admitted he never looked over the homework before the test.

Your student will learn to be a good test-taker by taking the time to review what study habits would have helped him perform better on the test.

12.3.12 What if my middle school student is not ready for high school?

So what? Seriously, who said that high school automatically begins at age fourteen? It didn't for all of my children.

If my child were to repeat any grade, I would *totally* choose sixth, seventh, or eighth grade. There is plenty to learn, and there is so much opportunity to increase independence.

Middle school is flexible. We can choose what history to study for another year. We can choose a different science than studied before. We can read new books. We can practice more grammar. We could write a few more paragraphs. We can even repeat prealgebra like my students did! There is plenty to do in eighth grade to fill up another year. Or two.

There are dangers in rushing ahead to high school before the student is ready. For one, just like in elementary, we cannot force skills before the student is mentally and emotionally mature enough. We talked about algebra readiness. This applies also to historical comparisons, literary analysis, essay writing, and scientific methods. You will sense if your student is prepared to move forward to more difficult and more independent work.

We are all tempted to forge ahead following a curriculum timetable without carefully examining where our student is. You know I did that with my oldest in algebra. I was more careful with my next children. And for the younger ones coming up, I'm pretty sure I will add another year of middle school for them. We all want our student to not merely graduate and make it into college or a vocation—we want to give him a real education. We want to *teach* him something, and we want him to *learn* it completely. Homeschooling is not about forging ahead and winning some age-graduation contest. It's about doing what is best for our child.

Some parents balk at this. They are afraid their child will be embarrassed. But homeschoolers are so grade-flexible that many don't even know what grade they are in. The only time this really becomes an issue is if the student is in a co-op, Sunday school, or other grade-segregated group activities. This may cause a slight concern, but giving your child guidance in making and keeping friends may help smooth the first few weeks. Alternatively, the student can stay with the same-age peers no matter what his academic level is.

Other parents might be afraid the student will graduate too late. Whether a student graduates at eighteen or nineteen or later makes little difference. The student could even take some easier dual-credit courses to build up confidence in college-level work. Gentle parenting through this extended graduation process will develop the student's resilience. See section 13.3.16 for more on delayed graduation.

12.3.13 When is my middle school student ready for high school?

Your child may be ready for high school when the following criteria have been fulfilled:

- **He works well independently.** Many teens no longer need or want their assignments spoon-fed to them. They may prefer to work alone or in groups of other teens. All students need monitoring, mentoring, and feedback, but your teen might be ready to take his learning into his own hands. A teen who needs extra oversight, constant prodding, or step-by-step help would probably benefit from an extra year of middle school. High school subjects may otherwise feel overwhelming to him and to you.
- **She reads with comprehension.** High school is heavy in reading, no matter what your style. High school students need to read not only

literature, but also instructions for math, details for science, and heavier books for history. Even online studies often include reading on the screen or in the accompanying material. Reading well is important for independent study, a process you probably want to train your student in throughout high school. If she struggles with reading, has difficulty skimming for important information, or cannot remember what she read, you may want to spend more time in middle school. Also, don't hesitate to test for a learning need (see chapter 16).

- **He understands basic math.** Your child need not have completed a prealgebra course to begin high school. But you may want to ensure he understands the principles of basic math, like multiplication and division, what ratios mean, how to convert units of measure, and the like. If he struggles with math consistently, again, don't hesitate to have his needs evaluated. And there is no need to rush toward high school.

- **She takes responsibility for her mastery.** After spending some time in middle school practicing studying, test taking, and evaluations, your teen could be held responsible for her own progress. She should learn during middle school that she can do well and meet realistic goals in each subject with appropriate steps and effort. If she needs extra help mastering concepts or passing subjects, she might wait for high school until her academics are stronger.

- **He has completed introductory material in each subject.** Your teen will benefit from a foundational understanding in each subject before diving deeper into high school. No matter what homeschooling style you prefer, your teen will need familiarity with the basics of each subject before moving on. If your teen has not completed what you feel are minimal requirements, feel free to spend more time in middle school.

- **She is skilled in preparing for tests, projects, or other evaluations.** Middle school is the ideal time for your student to practice whatever methods of evaluation you will use in high school for her to demonstrate understanding. If a student struggles to recall information, to communicate learning, or to complete a project with reminders, she may prefer working on these aspects with somewhat lighter middle school material.

- **He can critically examine actions, principles, and beliefs.** That adolescent argumentativeness should have helped her pick apart several of her subjects even while driving you completely crazy. Teens will often be questioning not only their parents but also their books and courses. This ability to dig deeper and form independent opinions enables your teen to better apply the scientific method, to more deeply analyze literature, and to more thoroughly detail her writing.
- **She can apply knowledge to life.** Throughout the high school years, you will be training your young person to use what she learns in the real world. As you prepare her for adulthood, you will be preparing her for lifelong learning. Your student may begin connecting her studies to her life now, designing activities around her work, applying history to current events, or analyzing themes in media.
- **He has moved through many of the physical changes of puberty.** Middle school begins with a smell, and high school brings big feet. Though mental and physical development may happen at different rates, you may notice a leap in your teen's growth that corresponds to sudden changes for the better in academics.
- **You think she is ready.** You may just know in your gut if your teen has what it takes to tackle high school. And you should, I hope, feel the freedom to choose whatever timetable is right for your own student. If your teen is not ready, then just wait another year.

• • •

Middle school is another opportunity to teach the way you teach best for *the way your child learns best*. This is such a critical time of mental and physical change. Over the course of these years, he will overcome many challenges and learn from several setbacks. That's all great. And even if he learns best by learning and maturing another year, then rest assured you are giving him what he needs. You can confidently homeschool your middle schooler whatever age, whatever level.

And if that level is high school, then turn the page.

13

HIGH SCHOOL:
THE NINTH- THROUGH
TWELFTH-GRADE YEARS

Approximately ages 14–19

ONE DAY, I WAS HAPPILY WALKING in the grocery store alongside my husband. Somewhere between the tempting potato chips and the illness-required saltine crackers, my husband remarked, "You must be excited to start high school in a few weeks."

I was dumbfounded. High school? Now? I counted the years on my fingers, unsure how my relaxed-homeschooling middle school had so messed up my timetables.

And now the thought of high school was messing up my mind.

I burst into tears. No joke. And not quiet tears. This was full-blown, snotty, uncontrollable sobbing. My unembarrassable husband dragged me wailing up and down the aisles. It was a scene.

(Who hasn't caused a scene in the grocery at one time or another? Employees must come to expect it because not a single one was fazed at all.)

This is what could happen when one casually traipses through middle school, enjoying perusing books and gently discussing prealgebra. One completely loses track of time and might remain in blissful ignorance for years.

But back to the mess in the grocery scene. I was devastated because this stage caught me completely by surprise. And I felt completely unprepared. For one thing, I needed to buy new books. For another, I had to start paying attention and keeping track of things. What and how to keep track? How to know what to do next? I was completely overwhelmed.

My unflappable husband, however, remained convinced that if other families—including my own back in the eighties—had conquered homeschooling high school, there was absolutely no reason that the Garfias family could not succeed, even thrive, through the high school years.

I remained in mourning for over a week.

Then I realized that I had wasted a week of preparation time. I needed to research curricula. I needed to research transcripts. I needed to research dual credit. I needed to research science labs. I needed to research how to breathe while teaching high school.

I had friends who were homeschooling high school. I asked them for options and opinions. I had friends who were just starting high school, or were stuck in the middle of high school, who had just as many questions as I did, or more. No one involved said, "High school is simple."

Now that I have studied, now that I have experience, now that I have actually thrived all the way through graduation twice, I now realize that *homeschooling high school CAN be simple.*

Yes, my friend, it's time to stop public ugly sobbing and start enjoying high school.

I'm sad that many of my friends stop homeschooling during high school. High school seems intimidating to all of us. Your child can, indeed, join the over 30 percent of the homeschool population that are homeschooling high school.[1] I would hope that now I can set your mind at ease, maybe even help you look forward to these years with anticipation.

Because now I do. As each of my children enter the high school years, I know that tremendous changes will occur in their lives and in mine.

In the high school years, our teens rush rapidly toward adulthood. They change from argumentative preteens to truth-seeking teens to adults of conviction. They wrestle with their subjects, not only to master the hard work but also to form lasting opinions on the material. They change their attitudes, change their opinions, and hopefully change their clothes. They perhaps grow more knowledgeable and taller than we are. They give us a glimpse of who they will be and where they are going in life. It is important to remember that *teenage character is not set in stone*.

Character growth and mental development during this period are important. This is why homeschooling is so critical at this stage. This is no time to quit. Instead, continue building on the foundation you laid in the previous years. If you are just beginning to homeschool during this time, this is your opportunity to plant your values in your teen's heart. "Do not be weary in well doing" (Galatians 6:9). Rather, value this chance to help your teen make wise life choices.

To get all technical on you, your teen is undergoing even more brain development. Though this aspect of brain growth will continue into young adulthood, your teen is maturing in decision-making skills and developing his views on identity, morals, and sexuality. He will vacillate between seeking help and fighting for autonomy. This push-pull on your relationship feels both challenging and rewarding, but most of all, it proves the importance of the family relationship.

> A love of learning is imperative to success in any field and should be promoted with enthusiasm despite any objections you might have toward the professions your child wishes to pursue.
>
> **DR. SOO KIM ABBOUD AND JANE KIM**

This relationship may be tried sorely in several ways. As your teen wrestles with his own opinions on a variety of issues, you may also wrestle with your response to his wise and unwise views. As your teen explores options for his future education and vocation, you may fight with your own desires for his future. As your teen makes mistakes in actions and attitudes, you may yearn for different outcomes. His strong feelings may conflict with your equally firm opinions.

Besides this character development, teens have several more needs that homeschooling uniquely meets. Teens have **physical needs**. Because of the tremendous physical and mental growth they are experiencing during this period, they need eight to ten hours of sleep each night, time that is probably not available in a strict school schedule. They also need, in spite of junk food cravings, a healthy diet to promote strong mental development. Teens crave privacy, the time and space to rest and reflect by themselves.

Teens even need time for laziness, some time to think, explore, play, and rest. These needs are difficult, if not impossible, to meet with a busy school and homework schedule. The ability to meet these needs is a powerful benefit to homeschooling.

Teens also have increased **social needs**. As they grow mentally, they may desire more time to think through their response in a difficult conversation. Though they tend to spout off the first thing that comes to mind, they have a greater opportunity in a home situation to go back and change their words. They need freedom to express, within the supportive and private home environment, their conflicted emotions. Sadness, exuberance, and even anger rise to the surface. At home, teens have more freedom to work through these emotions and practice controlling their responses. Family meals provide an opportunity for them not only to get proper nutrition, but also to work on relationships, social skills, and language skills. Many teens become more willing to talk out deep feelings because of these opportunities.

Teens **need to engage with the outside world**. While it is tempting to cocoon them in a safe home environment, this is a time for outside training. By exposing them to news and social issues, we can help our teens develop discernment. By encouraging them to engage in social and community problems, we help them practice identifying and offering solutions. When teens develop relationships outside the home, it reinforces the values taught at home and provides chances to resist outside pressures. This outward engagement is yet another way homeschoolers dramatically impact the world around them.

> We walk by faith, not by sight.
>
> **2 CORINTHIANS 5:7**

Finally, teens **need personal freedom**. They need space and opportunity to explore their own convictions and even to change their views about who they are. They need a balance between rules and freedom, an opportunity to freely experience privilege and responsibility. They need consistent feedback, both parental and consequential, on the choices they make. They need time and space for individualization, not groupthink or peer pressure. They need freedom to develop who they are and what they believe. They need the time and space homeschooling offers.

While the teen years can be a touchy time in our relationships with our children, it is important to remember something: we would experience parenting difficulties even if our teens were not homeschooled. Homeschooling, however, gives the opportunity to demonstrate our support by love, word, and example. No matter what choices our teen makes, we can continually live out the grace of God. And that is the most important value in homeschooling.

I stopped crying over high school within the first two weeks. And soon after that, I fell in love with this stage. My teens became not only young adults but also my friends. Looking back over a lifetime of homeschooling— preschool through high school—I can say to the Lord, "I have done what I could" (see Mark 14:8).

You can do it too.

GENERAL GOALS FOR THE HIGH SCHOOL YEARS:
- correctly use all parts of speech
- write and edit polished essays
- understand the principles of literary analysis
- complete three years of higher math
- conduct experiments and keep a lab notebook
- study three different sciences
- study world history, American history, and government
- prepare for college or career

13.1 THE HIGH SCHOOL STUDENT'S DEVELOPMENT

13.1.1 How might my high school student's character develop?
By learning to apply critical thinking skills to life responsibilities. My eighteen-year-old daughter loves taking care of her younger siblings. And in a large family, the older children get a lot of practice at that. In a family with two parents working four jobs and half of the children in crazy soccer schedules, our daughter has had a lot of practice watching out for little people, and she's pretty good at it.

She often says that one of her favorite days last year was when she played bus driver. My husband had several of his soccer league teams playing in an all-day tournament, with each team changing locations several times throughout the day. It was insane. He was coaching two teams, our son was on a different traveling-around-town team, and on top of that, I was playing the violin in a symphony dress rehearsal all morning in a different city. My husband had one vehicle, so my teen was going to drive everyone else around in the family van.

Then a couple of parents asked if we could give a ride to their players.

Sure, the chauffeur said. She mapped out a plan of how she would crisscross the Dallas area, taking everyone where they needed to be, dropping each one off twenty minutes early and picking up each one within ten minutes of game ending. I looked at her sheet of paper and got chest pains. On top of all of that, she had to watch our seven-year-old twins. All day. In the van.

She did it. She loaded the twins into the back of the van. She picked up players and dropped off players and picked me up and dropped me off to watch our son's game. She told everyone what time and where to meet her for pickups, and she told the right people to get out of the car for their next event (because within a couple of hours everyone was confused—except for her).

By the end of the twelve-hour day, everyone was deposited at the correct home, she was elated, and the twins were asking if they could ride their sister's bus route again soon.

How did she do it? She modeled responsibility. Everyone had to sit still and talk quietly in the van. Every time she stopped at a large service station—which was between every pickup—everyone had to dash out of the van, use the bathroom, wash their hands, and meet her in the front of the store. She bought every child in her van a snack and a drink at every stop to keep them happy. Every child needed to take responsibility for his own behavior. Each child had to obey quickly if he wanted a treat. And it worked. Everyone followed her lead, and so everyone was happy.

High school students know they need to develop responsibility. They are enjoying more privileges, so they are also shouldering more. They may not always enjoy their tasks, but they know that work is an unavoidable part of life. Our teens may experiment with what guidelines they want to follow and what rules they want to break. My daughter is not always the sweet, rule-following, bus-driving angel. I can't share the other stories because she will likely read this soon. However, she always knows that the broken rules come with consequences (even if she hopes to avoid them somehow) and obeyed rules make life easier for everyone.

Teens also develop a deeper sense of public responsibility. During the teen years, 83 percent of homeschoolers participate in community service.[2] And over 70 percent continue serving through adulthood.[3] Homeschool students work in animal rescue, political campaigns, food banks, disaster relief, ministry, and libraries. This commitment to volunteerism stems from their increased consciousness of the needs of those around them.

Along with this growing social awareness, teens become increasingly sensitive to racial issues. Minorities will become aware of how their culture affects how others perceive them and may become sensitive to homogenous situations. My Hispanic son, for example, became withdrawn when joining an all-white youth group, though after a few months he made solid friendships. My teens as a whole grew sensitive to prejudice within their community, especially in local businesses. All teens begin solidifying their views on the social differences around them. They begin to identify, in media and society, those who agree with them and those who do not. They tend to purposefully choose the ethnic diversity in their own close friendships. These decisions will likely affect their beliefs through young adulthood.

Outside their own culture, my teens found others who had also become sensitive to cultural differences, young people taking steps to encourage increased unity in their relationships. When running for choir president in her mostly Caucasian group, my daughter made her platform "let's encourage diversity in our youth group by reaching out to all cultures within our church and community." She not only won but also saw increased discussion and action in reaching out to other groups.

No matter the social issue—societal unity, animal safety, homeless provision, child protection, and others—this is a time many teens become aware of the world around them and yearn to be part of the solution.

GENERAL GOALS
- establish personal convictions for decisions, recognizing that house rules apply only until adulthood
- broaden her community of friends while keeping a few close relationships
- participate in church activities
- be active in community work
- consider how future plans could be used to impact the world for Christ

13.1.2 How might my high school student develop physically?

My teens started looking like adults during high school. Not acting like adults, but taking on physical characteristics. The growth spurt that started in middle school kept right on going through high school (even into their early twenties). Voices deepened. Faces changed from child to young adult. I still see a baby when I look at them, but the rest of the world sees young people who are nearly adults.

I'm not ready for them to be grown up yet, but they are. They are proud to be strong, tall, developed, and sometimes mistaken for someone older. They look in the mirror and see confirmation of their own growing egos—they see young adults ready for the world.

So it's my job to finish preparing them for that. I need to keep them playing sports or at least walking around the block. I need to serve and point out healthy nutrition. I need to oversee that whole hygiene situation.

High school is when I start training my teen to take the lead with her health care. I quit going into the examination room with her at dentist appointments. I sit in the waiting room for eye doctor appointments. And while I may accompany my teen to her doctor's appointment, I expect her to take the lead in answering and asking questions. I want my teen not only to become comfortable having personal discussions with a doctor, but also to learn to take charge of her health care.

Most of all, I want my teen to form solid convictions about how to use and care for her own body. I want her to understand the specific results of casual sex. I want her to know the results of alcohol and drug use. I want her to discuss these things with her doctor, and I want to openly discuss them with her myself.

Teens need to take charge of their physical bodies and decisions regarding them. We as parents have only a few more years to be involved. Right now, we can be a safety net to protect and inform our teens. But very soon they will be making these decisions themselves. We want to prepare them for that.

GENERAL GOALS
- participate in exercise or organized sports
- complete a year of health class or physical education
- learn the principles of good nutrition

- begin taking responsibility in doctor's appointments to ask thorough questions
- understand the dangers of substance abuse

13.1.3 How might my high school student develop mentally?

As teens grow toward adulthood, their abstract thinking moves toward practical application. They are generally dissatisfied with pat answers; they would rather find a thorough reason for the problems and decisions of those around them. High school students consider the philosophical arguments of the decision makers around them and critically decide whether or not they agree. They become interested, then, in global issues like politics, poverty, justice, and other social issues.

As they begin forming their own opinions on bigger issues, they also apply these principles to their life goals. Though they may form idealistic visions for how they can impact the world around them, these visions propel their considerations for life choices. They often argue their own position on controversial societal topics. They may volunteer for a cause they care about. They might even choose their future studies or career based on their newly formed beliefs.

Thus the teen applies his critical-thinking skills to practical issues. This mental development helps him think more deeply about his academic studies, consider the viewpoint of the text or teacher, and apply his learning to his growing personal convictions.

GENERAL GOALS
- debate issues politely
- consider long-term ramifications of viewpoints
- apply beliefs to decisions for now and for the future

13.1.4 How might my high school student develop socially and emotionally?

It's all about respect. Your high school teen wants to be appreciated for who he is. He wants his friends—his close friends and his wider circle of acquaintances—to like him and admire him. And even more, he wants his parents to listen to him and allow him to make his own decisions.

Even if he views himself as a leader, he may be tempted by peer pressure to maintain a certain image. Hopefully, as he matures, he will try to use peer pressure himself to influence others for good. Regardless, he will become increasingly sensitive to how others view him and internalize their opinions into how he views himself.

Most of all, your teen wants further autonomy from his parents. He may push back on rules or argue his own views in an effort to be heard. He wants to make his own decisions—even if he doesn't know his own opinion yet. He may respond to rules better if he has choices in how he follows them or if he is allowed to negotiate. For example, if he speaks and acts respectfully, he can ask for a later curfew on occasion.

During these years, teens learn more from consequences than from parental discipline. They are exploring how the world works and how they will make choices as adults. Though we may be tempted to help our teen out of a jam, we can allow him to learn from a bad experience. By paying that speeding ticket or losing that job, he learns valuable lessons about his future responsibilities.

GENERAL GOALS
- describe his emotions and manage them some of the time
- practice self-control
- practice problem solving with others
- respond maturely to peer pressure

DON'T BE CONCERNED UNLESS AT THE MIDDLE OR END OF THIS PERIOD YOUR HIGH SCHOOL STUDENT

- remains defiant and unable to constructively discuss disagreements over a long period of time

- cannot finish assignments without continuous help

- refuses to participate in family or church activities

- eats to excess, diets restrictively, or exercises obsessively

- exhibits signs of substance use

- exhibits signs of sexual activity

- exhibits signs of depression, undue anxiety, or self-harm

- learn how to be responsible for time and academic deadlines
- exhibit pride in what he is learning
- take constructive criticism
- teach a younger sibling a simple subject or concept
- practice consistently in a competitive sport or performing art
- disagree respectfully and consider opposing viewpoints politely
- develop his own sense of self, including clothing style and entertainment preferences, apart from peer pressure
- internalize personal standards and convictions
- independently consider and take steps toward future education and/or career

13.2 WHAT YOUR HIGH SCHOOL STUDENT COULD BE LEARNING

High school begins transcript season, the time when all of a sudden, the grades count and parents need to keep track of progress. This seems scary—remember my crybaby-freak-out when my son hit high school? But in reality, you can keep high school planning and records quite simple and still be completely prepared for college and career.

Not all students will go on to college immediately after high school. You may look ahead and see your child in a trade school or in a career soon. Yet as we consider what God has for our children, our attempts at prophecy may fall short. We cannot know for sure what the future holds through our child's entire lifetime.

This is why I believe a college-preparatory education is the best syllabus for most students. I don't say all because only you know what is right for your child. Yet college preparation not only leaves the door wide open for university study but also provides excellent training for the rest of life.

How do you know what your student needs to do for graduation and college admittance? First of all, just start freshman year with all the general subjects your student has been taking in middle school: Bible, English, math, science, and history. Add one or two more classes, like a foreign language, a sport, or an art. Keep going for a year or two, then look down the road at what your student might be doing after graduation. If that's college, look up the admissions requirements of a couple of colleges you envision your child entering. Don't feel the pressure to choose her college, just find a sample of possible schools that might be similar to the one your student chooses. After looking at the requirements, you will likely feel really good. Colleges don't require advanced theoretical calculus or fluent Latin. They are just looking for the average, regular high school studies.

What is a high school credit? A high school credit is one year's study of a single subject. One credit is based on one Carnegie unit, which is 120 hours of classroom teaching time. So one credit at an institutional school is based on one hundred twenty class hours of fifty minutes each over one school year (two semesters). Classes including a lab require more hours. This does not include homework time. Remember that a public school will not always finish an entire textbook, either. One completed class, then, is most of the textbook course.

For homeschool records, most parents I've talked to count one credit as one of the following:

- completion of at least 80 percent of one course textbook or course
- completion of over 120 (up to 180) hours of independent study

Completing more than 120 to 180 hours, more than one textbook course, extensive independent work, or a combination of courses could also count as an **honors course**. For example, one year my daughter took a basic online literary analysis course (no written report but multiple oral presentations) and also completed an entire grammar and writing course.

HOW MUCH TIME SHOULD WE SPEND?

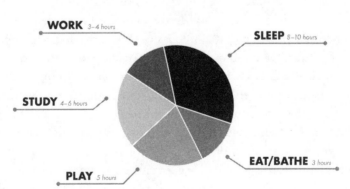

WORK 3–4 hours

SLEEP 8–10 hours

STUDY 4–6 hours

EAT/BATHE 3 hours

PLAY 5 hours

She was, in reality, studying two complete courses for one subject. I gave her one honors credit in English. I'm savage like that. You don't need to be as mean about the honors designation as I am. I would think one and a half times more study than usual would fulfill an honors designation. That is why I count my students' history course—which includes copious geography, church history, and philosophy with some art and music history—as an honors course. They have completed more than a credit and a half of study time and effort. You can find a sample high school transcript and sample course descriptions in appendix E.

USE YOUR TEACHING STYLE: BIBLE

- **Classical:** Engage in conversations focused on the *how* and *why* behind major themes and events described in Scripture. Assign essays and speeches on doctrine and standards derived from biblical teaching with beliefs expressed clearly and defended by scriptural texts.

- **Charlotte Mason:** The same as classical. Families may emphasize reading multiple commentaries, Christian living books, and biographies.

- **Textbook:** Provide textbook or DVD courses on biblical content, both overviews and in-depth on a book of the Bible. Participate in church Bible studies.

- **Unschooling:** Encourage the student to study whom he believes in and what he believes and to become familiar with the major themes of the Bible.

13.2.1 What might my high school student learn about the Bible?

High school is the perfect time for studying God's Word in-depth. Teens can continue memorizing Scripture. They may complete a Bible study. They also could study a course on how books of the Bible fit together. There are many options for a Bible credit, if you choose to go that route.

Because of their emerging skepticism along with their slowly maturing beliefs, many teens also enjoy studying "why we believe what we believe" or a worldview course. My daughter spent a year on this subject. If your family

---

BIBLES AND BIBLE REFERENCE BOOKS FOR HIGH SCHOOL STUDENTS

- *NLT Teen Life Application Bible*
- *The Epic Bible* by Kingstone Media Group, Inc. (graphic novel-style Bible)
- *Nelson's Complete Book of Bible Maps and Charts*
- *The New Defender's Study Bible* (KJV) by Henry Morris (notes from a literal, creationist viewpoint)
- *The David. C. Cook Journey through the Bible* by V. Gilbert Beers (simple illustrated commentary)
- *The Ryrie Study Bible* (KJV or NASB)
- *ESV Study Bible*
- *Holman Study Bible* (KJV or NKJV)

---

encourages conversation around opposing viewpoints, your teens will likely push back on the beliefs and standards you've raised them with. In my opinion, this is great; it creates a space to work through the biblical reason behind doctrine and application within the safe environment of home life.

USUAL REQUIREMENTS
- Bible is an elective. A Bible course or similar program would be counted as one credit.

WHAT I DO
- I have given one credit for completion of a year of Awana memory work (a youth church Bible ministry).
- Each of my teens has completed a Bible survey textbook course for one honors credit. (It was actually two years' worth of material, I learned after they finished it. I probably should have given two credits.)
- One year, my daughter participated in a Bible memory competition for which preparation lasted an entire school year.
- Because we emphasize Bible in our homeschool, I do require my teens to earn one Bible credit each year, though they have input on what they will complete besides my Bible survey requirement.

13.2.2 What might my high school student learn about English?

There are several components to high school English. Most students will study great works of **literature** during high school. These would include classics from a variety of genres and time periods. Students also learn to identify the structural elements of novels such as plot, theme, point of view, characterization, setting, imagery, symbolism, and more. While studying poetry, they would look at the meter, rhyme, stanza structure, and imagery. Students would also read dramas and works from their other subjects. In preparation for college entrance exams, students should also be familiar with reading technical writing.

In **grammar**, many high school students can identify all the parts of speech, but most will need to review these to consistently apply their knowledge. They also might need to work on the differences between dependent and independent clauses and how they function. As students learn the structure of a sentence, punctuation—especially comma usage—will

---

FACETS OF A COMPLEX ESSAY

An essay comparing makeup in ancient Egypt with that used today would contain mature elements like the following:

- a clear, compelling thesis statement

- a compelling introductory paragraph urging us to consider the makeup of their makeup

- supporting paragraphs that each give vital information on the makeup, each paragraph constructed carefully with a topic sentence pointing to the thesis statement and strong supporting sentences

- vivid, descriptive words so we can see makeup all over the essay

- a variety of sentence structures that keep the communication moving forward but don't adhere to a formulaic pattern

- perhaps an interesting story or quotes to further illustrate the beauty of ancient cosmetics

- a persuasive conclusion that makes us want to know more about makeup then and now

---

USE YOUR TEACHING STYLE: ENGLISH

- **Classical:** Have your student study grammar concurrently with Latin grammar; emphasize English rules of writing and punctuation through writing assignments based on other subjects, particularly history and literature; choose literature of different time periods each year for her to study. Classical students often participate in debate.

- **Charlotte Mason:** Have the student write on multiple subjects, with an emphasis on literature.

- **Textbook:** Assign grammar, writing, and literature courses, either studied simultaneously or on alternating years. If literature is studied in only one year, the student may take a world literature class covering ancient works through the twentieth century.

- **Unschooling:** Provide grammar and writing practice through practical application and public communication, such as writing letters to newspapers, participating in debates, and self-publishing novels. Have your student read literature of her choosing.

become easier. Grammar studies will then prepare them to edit their own writing.

Much **writing** in high school will consist of long-form essays and reports. Students will begin learning editorial formats such as MLA for humanities subjects and scientific form for formal lab reports. Your teen will now take the principles she learned in elementary and middle school writing and begin to refine her skills (see section 12.2.2).

An important skill teens need to develop is the use of specific details. Teens tend to generalize. They think their statement is obviously true. Or they are simply soft on facts and need further research. They need to be pushed to answer specifically *who, what, when, where,* and *how.* They also need to explain their own viewpoint clearly, including the consequences of their beliefs.

Your teen may also benefit from a **vocabulary** course. A book that teaches new words as well as the Latin and Greek roots and word parts is helpful. Not only does this better her writing, but it increases her understanding of literature and thus improves her college entrance test scores.

USUAL REQUIREMENTS

- All students should take four years of grammar, writing, and/or literature.

WHAT I DO

- I require four years of combined grammar, writing, and literary analysis for one credit of honors English each year or just one of those for one credit each year.

13.2.3 What math skills might my high school student develop?

High school math includes algebra, geometry, trigonometry, and possibly even calculus—subjects that scare many parents. Teaching long division, explaining ratios, converting measurements from standard to metric systems were all bad enough in elementary and middle school. Who wants to get into algebra—and beyond?

There are, however, several math solutions (ha!) for homeschoolers. First of all, you may choose a self-teaching homeschool curriculum that allows your student to work on simple and then increasingly difficult problems while reviewing the concepts he's already learned. My own middle school and high school students all use self-teaching curricula from different publishers, and they have tested well in each subject. I give help from time to time, but I have found that since the course was designed to be self-teaching, I can look back in the material to find the process if I need to.

> Do not worry about your difficulties in mathematics; I can assure you that mine are still greater.
>
> **ALBERT EINSTEIN**

There are other answers to the math problem (ha ha!). Your student can take online classes. In many of these, the teacher will even grade the student's work. Alternatively, your teen might take a class in person at a co-op or community college. Finally, your student might be tutored one-on-one.

USUAL REQUIREMENTS

- Many students will take three years of higher-level math, including basic algebra, advanced algebra, and geometry.

- If a student is interested in a math, science, or technology degree, he should take four years of math.
- If a student is not on a college track, he may take three years of math, which may include general math, consumer math, and one higher-level math.

WHAT I DO

- I require at least three years of higher-level math. One of my students included trigonometry and calculus. Another dropped trigonometry so it would not affect the GPA, completing the transcript with two years of algebra and one year of geometry.

USE YOUR TEACHING STYLE: MATH

- **Classical, Charlotte Mason, and textbook:** For this subject, many families turn to a self-teaching textbook, an online class, or a co-op course.

- **Unschooling:** Some take classes or use a textbook. Others wait until the student needs algebra or geometry for a project and then encourage the teen to learn more.

13.2.4 What might my high school student learn about science?

High school science (parents' second most-dreaded subject) may include biology, chemistry, and physics. I have used two different strategies for high school science. For two years, my students took an online class. Their assignments were graded by the teacher. Their labs were either simulated online or easily replicated with kitchen products. The classes were very difficult, but my students learned a lot.

At the word *lab*, we all involuntarily shudder. Yet science labs are a great opportunity for our students to learn hands-on and to practice independent learning. Many courses offer lab work using mostly simple household products. There are many labs available online; the dissection videos are especially helpful. And some students take science labs at a co-op or nearby school.

I have also used self-teaching science courses. In these courses, the students read the textbook and completed the experiments on their own. Some of the courses we have used only require basic household products, online dissections, and simple outdoor observations. For one student's chemistry, however, he took a more in-depth self-teaching course. Rather than try to gather all the materials he needed, I found a science equipment retailer that sells boxed sets with everything he would need for his exact course. The large box of materials was expensive, but it completely met our needs and saved me a lot of time and headache. He carefully followed the experiment instructions and replicated fascinating results.

Many of my friends join or even create co-ops just for science labs. They find it much easier to pool resources for science equipment instead of each buying their own. Sometimes you can even find a parent who *enjoys* teaching science. Yes, they exist.

USUAL REQUIREMENTS
- Students may take biology, chemistry, physics, and perhaps one additional science.

WHAT I DO
- After my students complete biology, chemistry, and physics, I let them either choose a fourth science or just skip it. One of my teens took physical science as a freshman and then biology, chemistry, and physics after that. Another only took three years of science.
- I also take my teens to creationism and other science lectures and demonstrations.

USE YOUR TEACHING STYLE: SCIENCE

- **Classical, Charlotte Mason, and textbook:** For this subject, many families turn to a textbook, online class, or co-op course.

- **Unschooling:** Families often allow for personal experimentation and research. They may provide standards or requirements for each science and also may use a textbook as a guide.

13.2.5 What might my high school student learn about history and social studies?

High school history and social studies courses generally encompass American history, world history, and government. There are so many ways to study history and social studies. And none of them have to be dull, either! Students can take classes, read interesting textbooks, do independent study, visit historical sites, and even watch documentaries. There are complete open-and-go textbook courses, but most of my friends use a combination of resources.

Government sounds scarier than it is. When I was homeschooled, I took one short textbook course on government for half a year and another on economics the second half. Since both were written on a simple high school level, I did not need any help completing either course. One of my sons is taking an online course in government and also finds it very straightforward.

USE YOUR TEACHING STYLE: HISTORY AND SOCIAL STUDIES

- **Classical and Charlotte Mason:** Read copious numbers of living books covering a specific time period, often covering all of history within the four high school years. Reading selections will include historical accounts from the time period and histories written over fifty years ago. Many students study art history, government and economics, geography, Bible, and/or philosophy concurrent with history. This course of study also may include a heavy emphasis on persuasive discussion and writing.

- **Textbook:** In addition to the textbook course, students may read other books on history and explore historical places and museums. Tests might focus on memorizing specific facts like dates, names, map locations, and battle details.

- **Unschooling:** Besides reading and writing on historical subjects of interest, many unschoolers visit numerous historical sites. More difficult history projects might include sewing costumes or re-creating a major battle with friends. Students will likely complete projects or reports on their own findings and may use a textbook as a guide.

USUAL REQUIREMENTS
- Most students take four years of history or social studies including American history, world history, and government/economics.

WHAT I DO
- I usually require four years of integrated history. I teach humanities in a semi-classical style, so my students study world and American history concurrent with geography, church history, philosophy, and history of the arts in each year of high school, completing the time period from Creation to current day within those four years.
- A credit of government and economics is included in the integrated courses.
- If my children had graduated from a public school in our state, they would be required to take one year of American history. I indicate on their transcript that this is covered in their world history of seventeenth through twentieth centuries. That's entirely unnecessary, though.
- One of my students, however, studied some years in an integrated manner and some years history or government exclusively.

13.2.6 What might my high school student learn about physical education?

Physical education is an opportunity for creativity. If your student participates in a sport, two semesters or both fall and spring seasons would count as one credit. One summer sport might count as a half credit. In many states your student may participate in homeschool sports teams and competitive leagues. Your local homeschool support group may be able to introduce you to any such programs.

There are a few states that allow homeschool students to participate in public school team sports. They have what is often called a "Tim Tebow Bill," named after the pro football player who, as a homeschool student, began his career playing on a public school team.

Finally, your student may participate in competitive programs outside of school. My husband owns a competitive soccer club that includes numerous homeschoolers on his teams.

Students don't need to participate in organized sports. Swimming, horseback riding, tennis, running, and other individual sports would also fulfill their requirements. Some students choose an exercise class. Or your student might hate sports or be unable to participate in such physical activity. A general health course would also earn one credit.

USUAL REQUIREMENTS
- Most students will take one physical education credit.

WHAT I DO
- Some of my teens became licensed to referee soccer for two years each. Another both refereed and played competitive soccer every year. He then traveled to Peru for training and competitive play. In addition to giving him honors credit, I also listed this as an activity on his transcript.

USE YOUR TEACHING STYLE: PHYSICAL EDUCATION

- **Classical, Charlotte Mason, and textbook:** Have your student participate in at least one year of a sport or take a health class.

- **Unschooling:** Your student could complete either of the above or maybe teach himself a new sport.

13.2.7 What might my high school student learn about a foreign language?

Spanish, French, German, and even Mandarin are popular options for language study. The simplest way to study a foreign language in high school is through an online course. Many parents seek out a native speaker for personal tutoring or a co-op class. Advanced students may take a dual-credit course at a local college. Some students, after studying a language throughout elementary and middle school, take AP tests for credit in high school instead (see section 13.3.7).

USE YOUR TEACHING STYLE: FOREIGN LANGUAGE

- **Classical, Charlotte Mason, textbook, and unschooling:** For this subject, most families turn to an online class, tutoring, a co-op course, or a university course.

USUAL REQUIREMENTS
- For college preparation, some students may take two or three years in the same modern or ancient language, but some may not study foreign language at all.
- If not on a college track, there is no foreign language requirement.

WHAT I DO
- I require four years of online Spanish.
- One of my students studied Spanish in Peru for honors credits.

13.2.8 What might my high school student learn about the arts?

Fine arts credits—choir, orchestra, band, drama, or art—are not hard to find. I would give one credit for any artistic pursuit that fills up the time required for a credit *or* anything that requires regular effort and perhaps public display to demonstrate completion. Examples might be a performing choir, orchestra, band, or drama club. Students could find such a group in a local co-op, community group, or church. Alternatively, private music students might participate in a recital. Visual arts students could present a work in a co-op display or at a public exhibition.

> **USE YOUR TEACHING STYLE: FINE ARTS**
>
> - **Classical, Charlotte Mason, textbook, and unschooling:** Practice a performing art, perform at an event, complete a textbook course, or participate in a visual art display. Save pictures of the project or printed program of the performance for a portfolio, if needed.

If the student prefers not to perform, she might count hours of study. She also could take an art or music history course available in a textbook, online, or at a local co-op.

USUAL REQUIREMENTS
- Most students will take one fine arts credit.

WHAT I DO
- My teens take piano lessons and sing in a choir every year.

NATIONAL HOMESCHOOL SPEECH AND DEBATE ORGANIZATIONS

Check your local homeschool support group for statewide organizations.

- Stoa USA (Christian homeschool speech and debate organization); stoausa.org

- National Speech & Debate Association (secular; open to schools and homeschools residing in a state that considers them a private school; contact for eligibility); speechanddebate.org

- National Christian Forensics and Communications Association (NCFCA) (Christian high school student forensics organization); ncfca.org

- National Catholic Forensic League (Catholic; open to schools and homeschools); ncfl.org

---

- My daughter also plays for a community orchestra, but since she already has a music credit, I just list it as an extra activity on her transcript.

13.2.9 What might my high school student learn about speech?

I have not found a university that requires a speech credit, though one very well may be out there. I waited until my oldest was a senior, then I checked with half a dozen prospective colleges. None of them required it.

In fact, some colleges consider speech part of English credit. Many homeschoolers mark debate and public speaking as part of their honors English credit. If my student *did* participate in speech or debate, I would add it to the activities list on their transcript.

USE YOUR TEACHING STYLE: SPEECH

- **Classical, Charlotte Mason, textbook, and unschooling:** Have your student participate in a speech or debate activity or join a co-op speech class.

However, this is not the only way to handle this subject. Whether you consider speech a "must have" or an elective, your student may absolutely earn high school credit for participation. Use the 120-hour rule to determine credits. You might also look at the dates involved; if the student participates for one semester, you might give him half credit.

USUAL REQUIREMENTS
- Students may take zero, a half credit, or one credit of speech class or debate.

WHAT I DO
- I don't require a speech course.

13.2.10 What electives might I teach my high school student?

With Bible, English, math, history, Spanish, music, and sports, my teens earn seven or eight credits every high school year. By graduation, most college-bound students have earned twenty-four to twenty-six credits. My two oldest teens earned enough credits but not enough requirements to graduate by the end of their junior year. I didn't let them graduate early, and they each took at least six additional credits because, again, I'm savage. For most students taking any two of a foreign language, music, and sports, they won't need another elective.

But . . . so many students want or need the fun electives. Home economics, business, computer programing, agriculture, carpentry, and others are useful *and* enjoyable. If your student wants to take a subject in addition to the required courses, then let him at it!

A word of warning: I would not advise calling housework itself *home economics.* Yes, we homeschoolers learn so much about keeping a home. By graduation, many teens have basically completed a course in cooking, cleaning, yard work, and household finance. But colleges may look at a home economics credit as padding the transcript. And personally, I don't want to do anything to make my homeschool transcript look less than aboveboard.

Many homeschoolers disagree with me and have successfully included

> **USE YOUR TEACHING STYLE: ELECTIVES**
>
> - **Classical, Charlotte Mason, and textbook:** Allow your student to choose a subject of interest for further study.
>
> - **Unschooling:** Finally give your student some credit for all those extras he has worked on.

home economics on the transcript. I don't much care either way; home-schooling is about doing our own thing, right? Some families add a text-book course in home economics, as well.

USUAL REQUIREMENT
- Students may complete four to five credits.

WHAT I DO
- I don't require additional electives.

13.3 QUESTIONS YOU MAY HAVE ABOUT YOUR HIGH SCHOOL STUDENT

13.3.1 How do I grade my high school student's work?

During high school, we need to keep grades. Up until this point, you may not have graded or averaged your child's grades. But now, for the transcript, each course needs a measurement. How you give grades will depend on your teaching style:

- **Classical, Charlotte Mason, and unschooling:** Grade humanities on quality, often using a rubric. (I have included a sample essay grading rubric in appendix D.) Many parents choose to grade without a rubric, but I really need one. Otherwise I take WAY too many points off for little things.
- **Textbook:** Most textbook courses come with daily homework, quizzes, tests, and/or exams. That doesn't mean you have to use them for grading. But personally, I find these quizzes and tests a quick-and-easy way to measure my student's work. Also, I like that my student is preparing for college test-taking.

Another decision you need to make is your **grading scale.** You should decide on your style at the beginning because later it is hard to adjust and explain on the transcript. You need a grading scale because the transcript that colleges expect is based on a 4-point system. An A earns 4 points, a B earns 3 points, a C earns 2 points, and a D and below earns either 1 or 0 points.

Also, you will want to type your grading scale at the bottom of the transcript. (See appendix E for a sample transcript.) This will help the admissions department understand your grading system. I grade on an easy 10-point scale. A grade of 90 to 100 gets an A or 4 points, 80 to 89 earns a B or 3 points, and so forth. I do not give plus or minus grades. Hence, the most dreaded grade in my home is the tragic 89. My oldest son nearly cried over such a grade once.

Not everyone uses the same scale as I do. Some use a 7- or 8-point scale. Others give plus or minus grades with partial points assigned. For example, an A- earns 3.67, a B+ earns 3.33, a B earns a 3, and so on. Others might use a weighted GPA, giving more than 4 points for completion of an honors course. That's too much work for me. And I'm hard core. Thus, the tortuous 89 percent with only 3 points.

Your transcripts should include an explanation of the grading scale you use. To make things even easier to understand (or more complex?), I do include the percentage points on the transcript, as well.

13.3.2 How do I make a transcript?

Transcripts are so easy. Yet this is the second most frequently asked question I get from high school homeschooling friends, right after "How do I teach science and math?" The word *transcript* sounds so dark and mysterious. And then there's the pressure to make sure our teens get into the school of their choice.

I was afraid of the big, bad transcript, too . . . until I started one. Then, lo and behold, I found the process was so simple I laughed. Out loud. (My family always wonders about me.)

I have two transcripts for my oldest son. One is the one I kept all through his high school. The other is the one-page simple document the university actually wanted. Yet again, I made the process a little harder than it had to be. In case you don't believe me that it is simple, I'm including a sample transcript in appendix E. This is the only one I use now.

You will want to *keep your transcript current as you go.* Every semester, I type in each course my student studied and his grade. That's it. Next semester, I do the same thing. It's that easy. I am careful to keep this running transcript in a Google Doc so it is easy to find and a little harder to lose.

There are many great benefits to a running transcript. For one, if you worry your teen needs an elective, you can find out easily without counting classes on your hand. For another, you won't forget (like I *totally* would) what your student studied and what her grade was. I share the transcripts with my teens as read-only documents (another great advantage of using Google Docs). They can easily calculate their own grade average to see what grades they need to get to maintain the GPA they want. My daughter used her transcript to check her English grade against her GPA. She discovered that she was getting a B in the class but that an A would not change her college scholarship level. So she declined to take the final exam and just kept her grade (remember, a class is usually complete when over eighty percent of the course is finished). That took some pressure off her mind.

13.3.3 How do I include combined classes on my high school student's transcript?

There are two ways to handle this. One is to separate them as different classes. For example, my teens' curriculum combines history, geography, and government class. This could count for one credit of history and half a credit for each of the other two, especially since the students spend an exceptional amount of time on those two subjects and are particularly evaluated in those aspects. This is a similar strategy to giving a half credit of speech separate from a full credit of English.

I prefer, though, to keep the subjects lumped together. My teens receive one honors English course for separate literature and grammar curriculum taken simultaneously. I similarly combine history, geography, and government into honors history. In the course descriptions on a separate page of the transcript, I offer an explanation, but no college has even asked to look at the course explanations.

Choose either way for your teen's transcript. Feel free to either separate the courses out or to combine them for one, big honors credit. It is completely up to you.

13.3.4 Can I count classes taken in middle school on the transcript?

Surprisingly, yes. I actually did this for my daughter. She took basic algebra in middle school, then advanced algebra and geometry in high school. I listed Algebra 1 as freshman math and the others in her sophomore and junior years since they were actually classes appropriate for those years' studies.

If your teen takes a high school course in middle school, definitely give him credit in high school. You may choose not to if he will keep moving forward into harder subjects. Use whatever high school courses best fit your teen's achievements.

13.3.5 Should my high school student's transcript include course descriptions?

Maybe. I have heard tell of some colleges out yonder asking for course descriptions. None of the private schools I looked into even wanted to see them. They all wanted a simple, easy-to-read, one-page transcript. So that's what I gave them.

There may be a college that wants to know more. I did keep course descriptions for my oldest son just in case. I haven't worried about it for the others because (a) I have most of them saved already from that first

---

SAMPLE COURSE DESCRIPTIONS

Bible 1: Scripture memorization weekly on topics of doctrine and Christian living. Old Testament (first semester) and New Testament (second semester) overview course. Texts: Awana's *Trek*; Meade's *The Most Important Thing You'll Ever Study*, vols. 1–4.

Honors English 1: English grammar and composition for two semesters. Combined with World Literature III, which includes reading and analyzing *Pride and Prejudice*, *Les Misérables*, *Great Expectations*, *The Scarlet Letter*, and *Crime and Punishment*. Shorter works from authors such as Goethe, Twain, Dickens, Stowe, Crane, Melville, Ibsen, Conrad, Tolstoy, and Wilde, as well as other short works of poetry. Texts: Abeka's *Grammar and Composition III*, Ryken's *Words of Delight*, Strand and Boland's *The Making of a Poem*, and classic literature listed above.

Honors Music 1: Private study in classical technique and repertoire for piano and viola with mandatory once-per-semester performances. Study of music theory and music history. Evaluation of classical form and composition. Regular choral training and performance. Regular handbells training and performance.

---

transcript, and (b) it would be straightforward, if time consuming, to go back and re-create descriptions.

How do we create a course description, you may ask? If you look, it may be already done for you:

- Many homeschool curricula give a course description or product description on their website or in their catalog.
- If not, you can make up a course description including
  - the name of the course,
  - two sentences describing what the course is about, and
  - the main textbook or list of the major books or other materials used.

13.3.6 If the college my high school student is applying to wants a broader portfolio, what else might I include?

Save some of your student's work. Since you don't know for sure at the beginning of high school what your child will study later and what the colleges might want to see, it's nice to keep some examples from the beginning. Again, I did not find that any of the private schools I researched even wanted a portfolio. But I have heard of exclusive schools using portfolio content for scholarship consideration. You might choose to save some of your student's best work in each of his subjects.

13.3.7 Can my high school student take AP or CLEP exams?

Yes, if she wants to. These tests are very similar. AP exams may cost more, can only be taken in high school, and must be taken on specific dates. On a transcript, these are sometimes more impressive to an admissions department if you are hoping for more scholarship money. A CLEP test, from the College-Level Examination Program, may cost less, can be taken in high school or college, and can be taken at several different places.

Many students are ready for these exams after a rigorous study in that particular subject. A student wanting to take an AP exam should try to do so before her senior year so it shows on the transcripts sent in the senior year. But at the same time, she might not be ready until her senior year to take the test.

There are businesses that specialize in helping homeschool teens plan their AP and CLEP tests throughout high school. Some go so far as to help

POSSIBILITIES FOR A PORTFOLIO

- Writing
  - › any award-winning works
  - › examples in a mix of genres
  - › an entire research paper
  - › an excerpt from a novel
- Literature
  - › a reading list of nonfiction works
  - › a reading list of award-winning or classic works of fiction
  - › Note: take care to list very few current popular books
- Arts
  - › award-winning examples of visual arts
  - › programs from performances or a list of performance awards
- Science
  - › a description of a science fair project
  - › photos of presentations
  - › lab reports
- Math
  - › award-winning work
  - › an advanced math sample
- Electives
  - › photos of activities
  - › a list of awards or achievements
  - › any other documentation

teens achieve an associate's or even a bachelor's degree at the same time as high school graduation.

13.3.8 What are dual-credit courses? Should my high school student enroll in one?

Dual-credit courses count for both high school and college credit. Dual credit involves your student taking courses from a college or university and counting those credits on both high school and college transcripts.

Many homeschoolers do choose to take these classes from online universities or local colleges and graduate early. When I was a homeschooled teen, I worked year-round to finish high school in three years. I don't know why. If dual credit had been available to me, I totally would have taken that route. On the other hand, this option has not been right for my own teens so far.

To decide whether dual credit might be right for you and your teen, consider the following questions:[4]

1. **Does dual credit complement my homeschool style?** I think dual credit would particularly appeal to textbook homeschoolers. The style would be very similar to the format the teens are used to. For classical or unschooling students, however, taking a classroom course would be much different. This would be an adjustment for you since you have less input into the teen's learning. Of course it would also be an adjustment for your teen to learn from a different format.

2. **Does dual credit fit my teen's learning style?** If we think about VARK styles (see section 7.2), reading/writing learners who are strongly independent take well to dual-credit classes: it's in their nature. Auditory learners will appreciate the lectures, as well.

DUAL-CREDIT HELP

- Homeschool Counselor: homeschoolcounselor.com
- Dual Credit at Home: dualcreditathome.com
- Homeschooling for College Credit: homeschoolingforcollegecredit.com
- Your own local colleges

Kinesthetic learners will need to be creative in applying their learning to real life and their own actions. Visual learners may find there are too few diagrams and pictures. In another way to look at it, producing students would do well in a classroom environment (see section 7.4). With effort, relating and thinking students could adjust to working within a class. Performing and inventing students would likely find the classroom stifling.

Don't all college-bound students need to learn how to learn in a classroom? Absolutely. But high school grades count for college admittance and financial aid. Which brings us to the next question . . .

3. **Will dual credit affect my teen's GPA?** It very well could. College courses are obviously much more difficult than high school work. And in a college course, you cannot offer extra work or a makeup test; she takes the grade given to her. A lower score than usual would impact her high school GPA, which is important to college admittance.

> ## QUESTIONS YOUR TEEN SHOULD ASK WHEN CHOOSING A COLLEGE
>
> - Do I want to attend a Christian or a secular school?
> - Will I attend a university or a community college?
> - Does the school offer the majors I am interested in?
> - What can I afford, and how do I feel about debt?
> - How far do I want to live from home?
> - What kind of housing do I want?
> - What size school do I prefer?
> - What extracurricular activities are important to me?

Also, if your student starts a course and decides it is not for her, she is in a hard place. Dropping out of a class affects the overall completion value—the way the university looks at the totality of dual-credit work. Dropping out is definitely against her, so she might need to struggle through and get the best grade she can.

Now, many students are completely ready for the challenge of dual-credit courses. I know several homeschoolers who have enjoyed great success in their chosen classes. The answer to this question is definitely not the same for everyone.

4. **Might we be tempted to value the *credit* more than *learning*?** Some families are so anxious to rack up credits that they don't think about how much the teen is actually learning. We know as homeschoolers that there is a difference between passing a class and being changed by that class. I took many difficult courses myself that didn't change my mind or my heart; I just did what I could to make it through with a good grade. On the other hand, classes taught to me one-on-one with my needs in mind impacted the adult I am today.

    One of the reasons we homeschool, an aspect of our *why*, is to teach our own child for a specific reason. And that reason is probably not just to pass a class.

    Again, most dual-credit families have answered this question in their hearts; they know why their teen is in the class and that this is the right place. This question, like everything else in homeschooling, is answered differently for each of us.

5. **Will this class save me money overall?** Obviously, dual-credit classes cost tuition. And if the tuition paid for the class is less than the cost of the course later in college, that's a great value. If your student earns enough credit to graduate a year earlier, you may reap an immense savings.

    In some cases, the cost is not worth it. If tuition at a private school is paid yearly, you will not save per class. So you would still be essentially paying for a class your student didn't take.

    Another financial consideration is whether or not the credits will transfer to the college your teen attends. You might check with the college he is interested in attending to make sure this will work.

6. **Does a dual-credit course fit our family's homeschool *why*?** No one can answer this question for you, and there is no one right answer. But unless the answer is *yes*, you should not be pursuing dual-credit courses.

    There are Christian and secular universities offering dual credit online, as well as many institutions in your own area. You have many options to consider. Whether or not your child takes dual-credit courses is completely up to your family. You need only to follow how the Lord leads you.

13.3.9 Will my high school student succeed on his college entrance exams?

Homeschool students generally do quite well on college entrance exams. On average, homeschool students earn a higher score than their publicly and privately educated peers combined. A 2014 study found that compared to average college-bound students taking the SAT test, homeschoolers scored an average of seventy points higher in reading, eight points higher in math, and forty-eight points higher in writing.[5] The odds are definitely on the side of your student!

I'm of the opinion that our teens should be more afraid of the SAT and ACT than we are. Yet so many women I meet are sweating profusely over their teen's grades. I think it is easy to have this anxiety, but we can check our hearts, remembering two key truths:

First, we cannot grade our homeschooling by the numbers on these tests. Listen, then repeat after me: *My homeschool is not measured by these tests.* Keep repeating that until you believe it. Back in the day—way, way, way back in the first generation of homeschooling resurgence—these tests *were* considered important proofs of homeschool success. Homeschool students and parents faced tremendous pressure to do well, to validate the decision they had made.

But friend, that is not the case today. We now see homeschooled young people well prepared for adulthood, succeeding in college and excelling in their careers. We don't need a test score to validate what we are doing. The homeschool movement does not need our defense.

Besides, we don't homeschool for grades, Ivy League schools, and scholarships, do we? Let's get back to our *why* of homeschooling. If you, indeed, are in this for the grades, Ivy League schools, and scholarships, then I don't know why you are still reading this book. Maybe you just want to see what a slacker I am. But for the rest of us, *we are homeschooling for eternity. No test measures God's favor.*

Second, we cannot measure our child's future by these tests. Seriously, just think about it. Would you appreciate first being pressured to concentrate your very hardest and to do your utmost best for four hours and then being evaluated for the rest of your life based on that one effort? I would fail. Utterly. Please don't judge me by the last four hours of my life. I just ate too many cinnamon rolls.

My young person, your young person, they each are so much more than a Scantron and percentiles. God has a bigger plan for every one of us, much greater than a score and academic standings. And our heavenly Father's favor is so much more than the bulk of all the scholarships in the world— how do we measure infinity? Not on those tests.

No test measures God's favor.

Now, I do agree there is a lot of pressure. My teens lose sleep, and I feel a little nauseous on the test day. But when it is over, it's over. We can move on.

The scholarships and the academic awards and the early admittance? Yeah, that's all fun. And sometimes we financially *need* those scholarships. I know that feeling, trust me. But at the same time, we need to walk by faith that this test may well be either one small portion of God's provision or an indication of his different plan for the future.

My encouragement is to fight against this stress for yourself and for your teen.

13.3.10 How do I know which college entrance exam my high school student should take? How can she take it?

If you have a few colleges in mind, take a look at their requirements. Many will accept either the ACT or the SAT or both. Look carefully, though, to see if they require the ACT essay. If they don't, it is a waste of time stressing over that portion. So far, none of my teens have needed to take it.

Next, let your teen take a sample test of each exam online. Some believe that science-minded students should take the SAT and that humanities-loving students should take the ACT. I don't really see that myself. I think rather that each test makes more sense to different teens. Once she has tried a sample test of each, let her choose which one she's most comfortable with. So far, my graduated teens, even the science-minded one, preferred the ACT.

Next, sign up. The SAT and ACT test websites give information on how to sign up and how to find a testing place. Leave your teen plenty of time for test preparation when you schedule the test. This means you should sign up for the test way ahead of the time your teen wants to take it.

Your teen may want to take the test more than once. Many students

COLLEGE APPLICATION TASKS A HIGH SCHOOL STUDENT COULD DO HIMSELF

When your teen takes charge of his own application process, he sends the admissions office and the professors with whom he communicates two vital messages:

1. I am serious about my education.
2. I am equipped to handle the responsibility of adulthood.

Consider requiring your teen to handle all or part of these tasks himself:

- fill out applications
- communicate with the admissions office
- pay for all or part of the bill
- fill out at least part of the FAFSA to learn about family finances
- request a list of more scholarship opportunities from the admissions department
- research scholarships near him, including sources such as an employer, church, and community
- apply for scholarships or other sources of financial aid
- communicate with department deans and professors

see their scores rise a couple of points the second time around. One of my teens took the ACT a second time because the first time he missed the next scholarship level by one point. It doesn't matter how many times your teen takes the test; colleges only care about the highest-scoring result. In case he will want to repeat the test, consider having your teen take it first during his junior year.

When he registers, your student can choose which colleges will receive the results. We just guessed three places off the top of our heads. You aren't setting the future in stone. Mostly, you are letting the test administrators know which colleges you want to hear from first. You can always have the scores sent to any other college you want later (for a small fee).

As a result of this test, you will hear from other colleges in addition to your preferred choices. These schools will send junk mail; they will call; they will mail swag. My daughter is bemoaning the fact that her second-choice college won't stop sending her gifts long after she told them no. One son was inundated with phone calls from another school he continuously told he had no intention of attending. Everyone wants your student's money, so you will see a lot of marketing in the next few months.

After registering, it is time to get crackin'. Break out the test prep books from the library, do more practice tests online. Create vocabulary flash cards and bone up on algebra. I purchase study materials from the ACT website. When I was a student, I took a test-prep class, and it really helped.

Encourage your teen to study well, but remember again that these tests are no measure of your homeschooling nor of your teen's success in life.

13.3.11 How should my high school student prepare for his college entrance test?

His entire life up to this point has been preparation. All of homeschooling has led your child to this moment. He has been reading and discovering and thinking and exploring and studying for years. That's what the test wants to know.

Sadly, the test asks these things in a secret code. Some students understand the secret code intuitively; it's how their brains work. I was one of those students. I just immediately understood what each question wanted and which answers could never possibly be correct, even if I had no idea about the subject matter. So I many times chose the correct answer without knowing what it was about. But that is only because I speak test language. It's the way my brain works.

I don't, however, speak common sense language, which is vastly more useful in real life. This is yet another way to see that tests do not measure the talents and abilities of each student. We are forced to take the test, but it's really not that useful. It's sad that this is the game we play to go to college, but it is.

My two oldest did well on the test, but not knock-your-socks-off well. They scored very, very high in their areas of giftedness and scooted their way through the rest for a respectable overall grade. They did their best, and their universities could see they were uniquely prepared for the fields each of them wanted to enter. This is an important thing to remember—your student will likely shine where her talents lie. This is valued in admissions offices just as much or more than her overall average score.

So those two students, my relatively good test-takers (reading/writing learners, if you want to use VARK, or producing, if you want to use Willis/Hodson), needed little help studying. I purchased the online test course from the ACT website, and they worked on it as they saw fit.

My next son, a kinesthetic or performing student, is far from an intuitive test-taker. Paper questions and answers are not how he receives information nor how he communicates answers. He needs to have a conversation or demonstrate the answer in the real world. Sadly, there is no college entrance exam for practical application. So for him, I have decided on an ACT prep course. I want a tutor other than his mother to teach him the logic and tricks useful to students like him. My pointing to the answer and yelling, "*C!* The answer is clearly *C!* Why can't you see that?!" has proven to be a less-than-effective teaching strategy for him. This is why he seeks out his own way of learning each subject. So he needs a little help finding his own way to take this test.

Math preparation is straightforward. Students need a grasp of algebra and familiarity with geometry. Advanced math is helpful, but the emphasis is on the basics. Students studying trigonometry and calculus may want to review prealgebra and basic algebra, in particular, to remember the faster way to solve each problem.

The best preparation for the reading tests is reading. Reading a lot. Students who are accustomed to reading deeply in all genres—nonfiction, fiction, journalism, technical works—will better understand and complete the test. The reading questions are difficult because they require analysis and "behind the words" thinking. Your student may want help preparing for this section. Even though my student is an avid reader, she still spent a lot of time taking practice reading tests until this section made sense.

Again, your student may or may not need to take the essay portion of the test. Check with the universities he is applying to first. None of the colleges my teens were interested in would even look at the essay, so they didn't need to bother with it.

13.3.12 What if my high school student is preparing for a trade instead of a college career?

He will do great! Increasing numbers of homeschool students are going directly into a trade after graduation. There is a high demand in many of these fields, and starting salaries are often quite competitive.

High school years are an excellent time for apprenticeships and on-the-job training. With a flexible homeschool schedule, your teen has a leg up on the competition in this area.

In my opinion—and this is not law—it is quite difficult to discern an entire life career at the age of fifteen or even eighteen. So many of us have experienced dramatic career changes over our own lifetimes (good-bye church music director, hello author!). Our college education—or lack of it—may or may not have prepared us for all the turns in the road.

So for our family, we would prefer to err on the side of too much education than not enough. A career in trade work could change to a new job in business or education or vice versa. In the event of these changes, it is good to be prepared.

This is why, again, I would rather give my students the best college-preparatory high school education that I can, so if my teens change their minds, they are ready for the challenge. And besides, no one ever complained they were too educated. Except for high school students. However, this may not be the best route for your student. You may discern that a more accessible course of study is most beneficial to your child's learning style or academic ability. That is great. You are the expert on your individual child, and you make the wisest decision with the knowledge you have. Be confident in your choices.

13.3.13 How should I commemorate my high school student's graduation?

In any way that makes your child feel special. There are some co-ops and support groups that stage beautiful graduation ceremonies. I attended one that was quite moving. I had my own homeschool graduation back mumble-mumble years ago. My parents reserved the church sanctuary, I invited everyone I had ever met within driving distance (a few came), and I performed a violin and piano recital. Then my parents each made a speech. A state senator we knew gave me an official proclamation of graduation. I think maybe that counted as graduation.

QUESTIONS YOUR TEEN CAN CONSIDER WHEN THINKING ABOUT FUTURE CAREER OR COLLEGE STUDIES

- What are my best academic subjects?

- What are some of my abilities?

- What are my spiritual gifts?

- What do I love doing right now (besides playing video games or staring at my phone)?

- What do others compliment me on?

- What do I dream about?

I don't have graduation ceremonies, per se, for my own students. My oldest son forbade me, for one. He would only allow a party, so we had people over for a cookout. It was crowded and crazy, but he loved it. My daughter wanted more formality, so she had a recital and reception. She bought a formal dress and everything. I love that each of my young people can choose to celebrate their milestone the way they want.

I still think I should be presented with my own medal at each graduation, but that hasn't happened.

13.3.14 Where can my high school graduate get a diploma?

From an accredited program or from your printer. Most institutional schools, public and private, are accredited. This means they are certified to meet certain academic requirements. Your homeschooler might receive an accredited diploma if she graduates from an accredited homeschool distance education, an online academy, or a private umbrella school.

On the other hand, most homeschools are unaccredited. So if you are not participating in distance or online learning, you can issue your teen a nonaccredited diploma. It's probable she won't need one—she has graduated and has a transcript, and she's good to go. But if there is a university, employer, military personnel, or someone else who demands to see a diploma (though that rarely happens), you can make one yourself. You can order an official diploma from Home School Legal Defense Association (hslda.org) or some support groups. Include the name of your student, a statement that she met the requirements for graduation, the date, and your signature. Some people go so far as to have it notarized. If I were to issue a diploma for my teens, it would be unaccredited.

If you do have one of those fancy homeschool graduations with your co-op (which might be from either an accredited or unaccredited curriculum), your teen will likely be presented with a diploma then.

As a homeschool graduate, I do not have a diploma, and none of my teens do, either. We've never needed one.

13.3.15 Should my high school student take the GED test?

No. The GED, or General Educational Development test, is actually comprised of four tests that complete an *unfinished* high school education. Taking the GED test gives the impression that your student did not finish high school—but he did. Adding a GED would say something about your teen that is not true.

13.3.16 What if my high school student is not ready to graduate at age eighteen?

Then let him graduate when he is good and ready. Remember how when we looked at each stage of your child's development, we emphasized not moving on until the child is ready? (See chapter 9.) This still applies to your teen. An arbitrary age does not mean all teens of that age are prepared to graduate. The eighteenth birthday does not magically bestow all knowledge and wisdom. Instead, growth happens at the rate of the child's ability, according to the conditions under which the child is growing, and in line with the progress God intended. You already know this in your heart. That's why you have educated him at his own pace.

Your child may understandably graduate later for several reasons: illness, moving, family issues, trauma, learning disabilities, and more. Colleges and employers are not legally allowed to discriminate against your student based on his age at graduation, so he doesn't need to feel pressured to explain anything.

You may wonder how to prepare a transcript for a student whose high school experience lasted five years or more. The transcript could delineate each year what the student learned and what grades he received. It might show six consecutive years of work, with each year documented separately. Alternatively, you might label four "years" just as "freshman work," "sophomore work," "junior work," and "senior work." Then place each subject as completed in the correct slot, no matter what year the student finished it.

There is no cutoff age for finishing high school. Your student could graduate at age nineteen or twenty or what have you. The important principle is that your student continued learning until he was finished with the material.

13.3.17 Can I homeschool driver's education?

Yes. There are two options. Many students take an outside driver's education program through a driving school. Classes are for students of any school background, as well as for adults. Instruction is usually held in the evenings, on weekends, or during summertime.

My teens actually *did* homeschool for driver's ed! In our state, they can take the classes online. Then they go to the Department of Motor Vehicles to take a brief written test and show their paperwork to receive the learner's permit. Once they had their learners' permits, my husband took them out driving (not me! I'm not risking life and limb!), and they tracked the hours on a chart given to them by the DMV office. After logging enough hours, they scheduled the driving test. Only then would I risk riding with them.

> Never lend your car to anyone to whom you have given birth.
>
> **ERMA BOMBECK**

When applying for the learner's permit, your teen may need proof of education. Each state has different ways to prove your homeschooling. In my case, I showed my lesson plans for my oldest. But after that I got lazy, and they took my word for it and just had me sign a form. In your case, contact your motor vehicle department. Find out your own state's policy on its website or from your local support group.

13.3.18 Can my high school student work while homeschooling?

Sure thing! And in my opinion, he probably should. First of all, a job looks great on a transcript. You shouldn't give class credit for it, but mentioning it at the bottom of the page is a huge plus. This shows universities that your student is a hard worker, that he can manage multiple responsibilities at once, and that he is serious about the future.

EVERYTHING YOU NEED TO KNOW ABOUT HOMESCHOOLING

Second, a job teaches valuable life skills. There is nothing like working hard for minimum wage to open a student's eyes to the value of labor. It is hard to get a job, it is harder to keep a job, it is even harder to excel at a job, and it is unbearably difficult to move up in a job. These principles motivate a student to study hard in college and to work hard in other responsibilities.

Third, a job plus bills instills responsibility. There is nothing like working really hard for a small paycheck, then losing most of it to taxes and bills. It is a huge spending wake-up call.

In our home, a child can have a mobile phone when he can buy it himself and pay his portion of the monthly bill, including any overages. Anyone who wants to drive needs to buy their own car (or purchase a portion of a parent's car) and pay their own gas and a portion of the family car insurance. Not only do these expenses motivate our teens to find a job, but they also teach them early that everything costs money and most things cost a *lot* of money.

Not everyone agrees with our family's labor laws. Actually, no families near us have similar rules. The neighbor parents look at me like I've sent my teens to the workhouse. And my teens' friends feel sorry for them. But we are hard-core around here.

Here are some tips to guide your teen in finding a job:

1. **First, encourage your teen to take advantage of daytime hours.** Homeschool teens enjoy flexible work hours. Provided your state does not have a daytime curfew, your teen can take advantage of the school hours. My oldest son worked full time in the afternoons when students were in school. My daughter worked afternoons, as well. My third son did lawn work in the mornings. It was simple for them to do their schoolwork around their work schedule. And it taught them how to juggle a busy schedule.

2. **Second, help him to be creative in finding a job.** Homeschool students have a variety of jobs to choose from. Besides the usual fast-food and cashier jobs, they can take advantage of the skills they have enjoyed concentrating on in homeschooling. My son loved math, so he tutored high school and college students. My daughter loves piano, so she taught homeschoolers during the day

and public school students in the evenings. My middle child, in his lawn care business, kept the landscaping and handyman work to himself and hired other teens to work with him mowing on the weekends.

3. **Teach him the basics.** You might help him fill out his first application and make a resume. It may feel like the resume is pretty empty, but he can include volunteer work, ministry, and tutoring. List strengths like computer software knowledge, opportunities in which he developed people skills (like babysitting, lawn mowing, etc.), any second languages, and character qualities. Otherwise, let him just be honest that this is his first job and he doesn't have work experience yet. Regardless, remind him to offer to provide personal references. You can also give interview tips and help him pick out professional or business casual clothes that make a strong impression.

4. **Finally, leave it to your teen.** Again, I'm probably the meanest mother ever. I never help my teens find a job. If they want nice things, they need to pay for them, so they need to find money. I figure that's enough motivation. Two of my teens applied at businesses and fast-food restaurants within walking distance (remember, no car until he can pay for it?). My daughter put her talent to use tutoring and teaching piano once she had her own wheels. Before he was old enough for hire, one of my teens literally knocked on doors around the block looking for any yard work. One of my children now bemoans the fact that he has no money, and his older siblings will have none of it. "Go out and find a job!" they yell at him.

> Far and away the best prize that life offers is the chance to work hard at work worth doing.
>
> **THEODORE ROOSEVELT**

I feel like if a teen is old enough for a job, he is old enough to get it and keep it. Don't go to the interview, don't even talk to the employer. I usually need to drive my teens to an interview, but I stay inside the car. A teen's job is literally not my business. This is his turn to step up and learn to be responsible for himself.

I think that last point is crucial. We know a teen who lost her job over this very mistake. The mother stood at her side and answered questions in the interview. The mother called to set the schedule. And when the teen was corrected by the employer, the mother marched in to express her disapproval. No one was surprised that it was a short-lived job.

Let your teen have his job for himself. It's his chance not only to build his resume but also to build his reputation.

13.3.19 How can I teach my high school student to be more independent in her schoolwork?

Gradually introduce new responsibilities. When I dropped my son off for college, I stood in his dorm room with a list of reminders. "Don't forget to write down your schedule. Go ask your teachers when you have a question. Keep your notes organized so you can study . . ."

"MOM! You taught me all of this already! Stop nagging me!"

Lots of things were hard for him in college, but being responsible for his work was not one of them. For four years, he had been training for this moment.

My daughter cut me off preemptively. "I don't want any reminders, Mom! I've got this!"

While homeschool families actively train their teens to take responsibility, this is far from the norm for the majority of students in America. According to a recent poll, teens are reminded of assignment deadlines in 76 percent of families. Surprisingly, 15 percent of parents are still calling college students to wake them up in the morning.[6] Homeschool teens, in contrast, have a tremendous opportunity to take charge of not only their schoolwork but also their personal responsibilities, including work.

To help your teen develop independence, let her know that she needs to learn to be responsible for the following areas:

- **Her calendar.** She can be responsible for putting her own activities on the family calendar and make sure they don't conflict with others' appointments. She can manage her own work schedule. She can keep her own calendar to remind her of appointments. We are so mean that we have a policy that whoever is first to schedule an activity in a particular time slot gets to do it; anyone who later wants to schedule something at that same time needs to resolve the conflict (though we parents sometimes veto an activity previously scheduled).

- **Her deadlines.** Test and project deadlines are also her responsibility. As soon as she knows when something is due, she can put it on her calendar to keep track of it. And if we as parents hold our teens accountable for those deadlines, they will be well-prepared for college and work deadlines too.

- **Her process and routine.** During middle school and the beginning of high school, teens often develop a preference for how they work. My daughter is definitely a reading/writing learner. If a subject comes with a DVD, she will toss it out and study extra books if she needs to. One of my sons is a kinesthetic learner, and he will listen to audiobooks or YouTube videos on his subject while he does something else. We can teach our teens to break down a larger assignment into segments. Soon, they can practice vocalizing how they plan to tackle their project. After some practice, most teens can be left alone to work their own process the way they see fit. Many appreciate breaking a project down, but my daughter would still prefer working all day on a long assignment to keep her work unified. As our teens become more comfortable with their own learning style, they can adapt their curriculum and assignments to accomplish their best work.

- **Her routine.** One of my teens liked to get up early in the morning, tackle one subject, relax the rest of the morning, then finish in the afternoon (I thought that was crazy). Another preferred to only work in the afternoon, when the house was quiet. One would complete an entire week's worth of work in a single subject each day. She also tried to do two weeks' worth of work as often as possible so she could finish early in our school year. As our teens experiment with their own best way to work while keeping to their deadlines, we can allow them freedom to do so.

- **Her place to study.** Your teen likely knows where she works best— in the midst of the family homeschool, or off by herself. She may set up her own work space in her room. Or, like my teens, she may prefer to homeschool all around the house. This seems risky, but with some consequences when it doesn't work out, most teens will become more responsible. I flat out refuse to look for a lost book or assignment.

- **Her outcome.** Your teen may appreciate setting her own goals for each subject, what she wants to accomplish, and what grade she would like to achieve. This gives her a standard to work toward with less nagging (hopefully) on your part. Negotiating these outcomes helps both you and your teen maintain realistic expectations.
- **Her finances.** She can start working, managing her bank account, and paying some of her own bills like gas for the car and her portion of the mobile phone bill.

HOW INDEPENDENT SHOULD HE BE?

It's up to you and him. You:

- Do you want to lecture or discuss and then have him complete assignments on his own?

- Do you want him to research on his own and then discuss his findings with you?

- Do you want him to grade his own homework while you grade only tests?

- Do you want him to complete his courses completely on his own?

Your teen:

- Is he capable of studying on his own, or does he need oversight?

- What kind of accountability does he best respond to?

- How does he prefer to complete his course—the way it is laid out, or tailoring it to his own unique style?

- How does he demonstrate his knowledge to you?

The answers to these questions will help you find the right strategy for your family.

13.3.20 What should I do if my high school student is not studying up to his potential?

First of all, my husband reminds me, I need to be reasonable about what his potential really is. All of us think our students are geniuses, but remember that each one has individual strengths and weaknesses. Am I expecting perfection when my student is actually doing his best? Am I holding him to the standards of his siblings, or myself, some other homeschooler, or some curriculum author? Am I really paying attention to how my student learns and communicates his knowledge? I need to accept that he might be doing his very best while barely passing the test. He may be truly struggling to succeed.

Next, I need to find out why he is not doing better. It's possible he may lack motivation—teens generally do. Hey, my own laundry needs to be done, and I lack motivation. I'm not ironing up to my full potential. When my teen is doing half-hearted work, I call it being "lazy-brained." The student is not using his brain when he barely mumbles one-word answers or doesn't do his homework or writes sloppy essays or doesn't follow directions. It drives me crazy.

But there could be other reasons: Is he not feeling well? Is he under pressure in other parts of his life? Is there a change in the family? Is he discouraged by past failures? Does he not understand the foundations of the subject, and now the lessons are moving past his ability? Does he need to go back and repeat some lessons? Have I left him alone to be independent when he actually needs more help? Would he benefit from a different perspective, maybe even a different curriculum? Could a short-term tutor help him get over the hump? I may need to just sit with him once in a while to answer his questions, even help him make a cheat sheet of formulas or rules or facts in the back of his notebook to help him remember what he is learning.

Maybe I need to include my teen in the process. Have I welcomed his input on the course and materials, within reason? Am I giving him options about the course, the curriculum, or the assignments? Have I helped him make goals and expectations for his coursework? My daughter's science grades vastly improved when I let her help me choose the curriculum. My son saw tremendous improvement when I let him determine how he communicated his learning.

Also, I need to look at whether I am being clear enough about my

expectations. Maybe he doesn't know what I expect out of the essay or how I expect a math proof to look. Sometimes clarifying the process makes a big difference. Personally, I expect my teens to read my mind way too often.

Finally, I need to be careful not to be critical. Nothing is as demotivating as being criticized for every assignment. One of my sons was taking prealgebra, and I was adamant he was not doing his best. My husband had to cool me down one night when I was ranting to him about it. Was my son really trying hard, but I didn't notice? Could he use a gentler touch? I started saying to him, "This part of your test is really good! Keep it up! I know you missed many problems, but I think you can make progress next time. Let's think about just this one thing. Let's concentrate on that, and then do our best on everything else." Every test, no matter the grade, I tried hard to demonstrate cheerful confidence that each assignment was improving and would continue to do so. I praised and rewarded his *effort*, not his grades. Sure enough, he gradually raised his test grades a couple of points each time, just by concentrating on one new test skill at a time. And you know what? Now he likes that class because he can prove to himself and to everyone else how smart he is every time he takes a test.

13.3.21 What do I do if my high school student hates his studies and refuses to do them?

That's his tough luck. In life, we all have to do things we don't want to do. I am typing the answer to this question when I really would rather eat the entire package of Slim Jims under my desk. Wait. I'm going to do both. Bad example.

Okay, we can—and probably do—lecture our teens on "You will always have to do something someone else makes you do even though you hate it" and then list off job requirements, household chores, errands, and taxes. This list of things is something we don't enjoy thinking about, but we need to anyway.

We also get to play the "When you're the mom, you get to make the decisions" card. For obvious reasons, my sons hate it when I say that. But as long as they are dependent on us for food, clothing, and shelter, they have to obey the rules that come with those privileges. Even more than that, our teens need to know they are part of the family unit. What they do impacts everyone, and each of us has a responsibility to each other.

Mom and Dad have a responsibility to provide for, protect, and love their children. Teens have a responsibility to respect and obey and to do their very best work for the family. Because we all do our very best for each other. Other times our reason is as basic as "You need to finish this so you can graduate and do what you want to do." I encourage my teens to keep dreaming of their lives as adults, then work right now even in their schoolwork to reach those goals. It helps a little.

> Whatever you do, do all to the glory of God.
>
> **1 CORINTHIANS 10:31**

There are several reasons your teen may be lax in his work other than laziness. Perhaps he is intimidated by the subject. Maybe he is discouraged by criticism or bad grades. Probably he does not understand the purpose of what he is studying. Sometimes the root of the problem is obvious for everyone. Other times, it takes some digging to get at it. Regardless, this will be an issue in the teen's life until graduation—and beyond. High school is an opportunity to struggle through this and learn from it.

How do you make him do his work? I make my teen's life miserable until he does. No screens—including phones—no going out with his friends, no happiness of any kind until the work is caught up. When the work is going especially slowly, I resort to micromanaging: the lazy one gets to sit right next to me all day wherever I go, working on his homework the entire time. No teen loves his mother so much he wants to be glued to her.

Raising stubborn teens is never easy. We all know that. But these lessons of responsibility and consequences are invaluable. Better to learn in misery at home than to cause misery as an adult when the consequences are oh, so serious.

13.3.22 How do I handle the argumentativeness, stubbornness, and hormonal outbursts?

Duck-and-cover drills. Seriously, though—this takes so much prayer and grace. Here are some things I try:

1. **Model patient behavior.** Oh, my word, this is *so hard*, especially when my teen is pushing all of my buttons. I'm also trying to replace a loud, angry voice with a quiet but firm voice. It doesn't always work, but it cuts down on the sore throats.

2. **Apologize often.** Everyone loses their temper, and going through the teen years can cause both teens *and* parents to lose it nearly every day. We set the example of what is and what is not acceptable behavior when we take responsibility for our own mistakes.

3. **Separate from anger.** When I am angry, I often run to my room or even walk around the block to cool down. My teens need the same space. I often ask them to retreat to their room to cool down or move on to a physical activity like music practice or mowing the lawn or even running around the block to work off some of those emotions. Many conversations can be tabled until a later time.

4. **Offer solutions.** It is instinctive to dictate the resolution of the conflict—but these situations can cause teens to feel out of control. Remember that there are often options to consider. Involving teens in these decisions gives them back a sense of control, while also helping them practice decision-making skills for adult life.

5. **Remember this is normal.** Okay, this may not be a lot of comfort in the midst of a really bad day, or week, or year, but these rough times are typical for teens. They are growing into adults and desperately want respect and independence. The constraints of home life and schoolwork and responsibilities get in the way of freedom, and this can cause an underlying frustration. Then other obstacles easily set them off. For most teens, things will calm down in a few years or as they grow and experience the consequences of their own decisions.

6. **Pray fervently.** For many teens, this explosive period will end over the next few years. The patience we need in the meantime is only supernatural. This is the wisdom, indeed, that we need to ask of God, who promises to give it to us generously (see James 1:5).

13.3.23   When is my student ready to graduate?

Your child may be ready to graduate when the following criteria have been fulfilled:

- **He has completed the minimum number of credits.** You can double-check the requirements your state uses for graduation and/or the requirements of colleges she is interested in.

- **If heading to college, she has the ability to complete assignments and track deadlines independently.** She will have a lot to juggle in higher education, and you won't be able to hold her hand through it. After several years of practice through high school, she should be generally comfortable handling her academic responsibilities.
- **He possesses basic life skills.** Whether he lives at home, leaves for college, or moves out of the house, it's time for adult responsibility. He should have experience or at least knowledge about how to get and keep a job. He should understand the value of money and perhaps pay some of his own bills. He should know how to take care of himself around the house, like how to prepare his own food and wash his clothes.
- **She should be almost an adult.** No eighteen-, nineteen-, or twenty-year-old is as mature as she thinks she is. But graduation represents a transition from the basic training of childhood to the greater personal responsibility of adulthood. Before embarking on this new stage, she needs time and training to start off strong.

• • •

You will do great homeschooling your teen through the high school years. You literally cannot mess this up. You love your student. You sacrifice for your student. You give your student the best possible education you can. And you trust God to grow him into maturity. In the end, you are starting a process that God will continue into your teen's adult life—a process of drawing a young adult to himself. If you're feeling like you're overwhelmed, just go back to a few basic things:

> Know that wisdom is [sweet] to your soul; if you find it, there will be a future, and your hope will not be cut off.
>
> **PROVERBS 24:14**

First of all, remember your *why*. Why are you homeschooling? Is it to get your teen into an Ivy League school? Is it to better his college entrance exams? To get him started on a high-paying career? To prove your homeschooler is better than their honor roll student? To say "nah-nah, nah-nah, nah" to the other homeschoolers?

Or—for the glory of God?

Are you headed for your *why*?

Second, remember how you homeschool. By now, hopefully, you are on your way to understanding how you and your student work. You are homeschooling the way you teach best for the way your teen learns best— no matter what the situation, what the course, what the outcome. You and your teen are doing your best and representing who you are.

Finally, remember your God. Who sustains you? Who provides for you? Who gives all wisdom? Who evaluates you? And who finally says, "Well done, my good and faithful servant"?

PART FOUR

OVERCOMING OBSTACLES

I LOVE HOMESCHOOLING. I love homeschoolers. I am passionate about this one fact: *you CAN homeschool, and you can homeschool well.* But just because we are homeschooling doesn't mean we are dancing through the meadows with birds tweeting around our heads and flowers singing a cheerful tune. Come to find out, I am not a Disney Princess. And just because we are homeschooling doesn't mean we live a holy life every day. We make mistakes. We get overwhelmed. We sin.

Homeschooling has its own unique challenges. We not only face questions and discouragement—we meet roadblocks and pitfalls. Some of these are easy to stumble over without even noticing it. That's my fear. I could become blind to how I am sabotaging my homeschool. I could be harming my family.

I wrote this section with two purposes in mind. **First of all, I love the homeschool movement fiercely, and I want to help that community avoid some common mistakes I see.** That is my driving force in talking to you today. There are areas in which, as we have grown in numbers and visibility, we have become lax. There are seemingly insurmountable obstacles we each face. And there are even sins we may commit in the name of homeschooling. So, in the next chapter, I hope to help you avoid those errors and difficulties.

This is my own personal challenge to myself as well as to you. I regularly struggle with so many of these weaknesses. Some of them are bad habits I need to fight. Some of them are serious, and I may neglect to repent of them as sin. I beg God today that he will continue to convict me when I am wrong.

Second, I want you to homeschool and to love it too. You may be facing discouragement. You may be facing trials. You may be facing overwhelming tasks. You may be facing special circumstances and special needs. *I want you to not only make it through each day but even love what you are doing with your children.* The final two chapters in this book will help you navigate those challenges.

Regardless of the pitfalls, the discouragements, and the challenges, we can live and homeschool triumphantly. We can know God's power every day. We can glorify God and know the fruit of his Spirit in our homes.

We can homeschool for God.

14

THE DANGERS OF HOMESCHOOLING

HOMESCHOOLING IS ALL ABOUT having the perfect family every perfect day. If you are doing this right, your children will have good grades and do most of the chores. You will bounce out of bed every single morning, excited about the day's assignments. You will always look amazing, and your counters will sparkle.

Actually, it's never like that. Stop dreaming.

Many days we have problems. Maybe big problems. Most often, however, these aren't problems so much as fears, fears that we are going crazy (probably true) or fears that we are messing up (probably not true).

The single most important principle to remember, as I keep reminding you, is *why* you are homeschooling. Are you homeschooling because you feel God has called you to this? Because he desires that you impart your faith to your children? Because he wants you to train your children from his perspective? Because you love your children and sometimes even want to be around them? If yes, then have no fear. "He who calls you is faithful; he will surely do it" (1 Thessalonians 5:24).

Homeschooling, however, does have some inherent dangers. There are

397

things we struggle with more than our public school friends, and there are unique areas in which we can stumble. Let's take a look at some of those.

14.1 DANGERS FROM WITHIN

14.1.1 What if I face burnout and hate homeschooling?

We all do constantly, and if anyone says they don't, they're lying. When I asked my friends to share some dangers of homeschooling, the number one answer they gave me was *burnout.* Burnout is like a bad virus that keeps coming back and makes our eyes tear up and our nose run and sends us to our bed indefinitely. It is contagious, spreading to our spouse, our children, and even our friends. There is no way to perfectly inoculate ourselves. And it can be completely debilitating. Nothing else can upset our homeschooling faster and more completely than burnout.

Why is the disease of burnout so prevalent in our homeschool society today? It is because the germs are everywhere. We—yes, you and I and your homeschool friend—we face the seemingly impossible task of completely training a child in every facet from childhood through the teen years. We feel the responsibility of turning out a mature adult. And we are stuck in the house with that germy little creature all day, every day, with no end in sight.

We are trapped with our burnout.

14.1.1.1 WHAT CAUSES BURNOUT?

We take responsibility for too much of the results. We try to become the be-all and end-all in all subjects and all behaviors. We even want to train our student's little mind to think right and her little soul to believe right. We take on every aspect of our child completely.

We take on too much of the teaching. We are overwhelmed by the thought that our child may never understand every single concept in every single subject. We are determined to cram everything into that little mind all by ourselves.

We are overwhelmed by difficult subjects. Ever try to teach a young child phonics, when the *r* sound is spelled *er, ir, ur,* and *ear*? And get them to read *where* and *were* or *stair* and *tear*? And then to understand the different *ed* sounds in *looked, played,* and *wanted*? It is well-nigh impossible. Then we get to high school math (anyone remember the formula for the surface area of a cone?) and science (What is the chemical compound of literally *anything*? I'll settle for just one thing!). We don't even understand the textbooks. The instructional DVDs may as well be in a foreign language.

We are frustrated with our child's limitations. He can't sound out the incomprehensible words. He can't ever remember the formula for the surface area of a cone. He can't understand the gibberish on the instructional DVDs. He cries out to burn the books.

We may not be teaching to the child's learning style, we think. If we could somehow engage him with the material, if we were more creative, if we had chosen a better curriculum, if we were a better teacher . . . it's all our fault he hates diagramming sentences.

He may have a learning disability; we just aren't sure. We fear that we aren't able to give him the special support he needs because we don't understand exactly what is going on. Is he lazy? Is he going through a rough patch? Is he unable to understand chemistry anytime in his lifetime? Does he have a special need?

And if he does have a special need, can we meet it? Are we able to help him overcome his weaknesses? Are we teaching to his unique strengths? Are we overwhelming him? Are we pushing him enough? Are we tailoring his curriculum?

We take on too many activities. Co-op, extracurriculars, and tutoring. Therapy, counseling, and physical education. Bible, math, science, history, literature, grammar, music, art, government, economics, church history, philosophy, worldview, read-alouds, test skills, AP classes, dual-credit classes . . . we take on responsibility for way too many subjects at once. Then we jump in the van to drive all over kingdom come to classes, tutoring, and enrichment activities. For each child. Sitting in the waiting room. Where we will grow old and die.

We have to take care of housework. We spend all day working hard around the kitchen table then jump in the van to shuttle our student to other activities. We cram cooking, grocery shopping, cleaning, and laundry into the overflowing schedule. Some weeks, we suffer through starvation, squalor, and nakedness (yes, that happens to all of us, don't lie). We simply do not have fifty hours a day and ten days a week to accomplish it all and still have pressed slacks and a smile at church on Sunday. (I can't remember the last time I pressed the slacks.) We make our children practice duck-and-cover drills in case someone knocks on the door.

We have bad, bad children. Okay, they aren't *actually* bad, we just feel that way sometimes (tell the truth!). They aren't criminals, but they drive us crazy. They do, indeed, burn their books. They threaten to kill their siblings and come near to pushing them down the stairs. They crumple their papers, they break their pencils, they "lose" their math books. They argue, they complain, they dig in their heels, they don't do their chores. We fear they may go to jail. They make us lose our ever-loving mind.

We face criticism. People look at us funny. Because we are aliens from the planet *weird family*. And they say thoughtless things to us at the grocery store, like, "Shouldn't you leave your child's education to the professionals?" Then you say that you are an unpaid professional who works overtime ensuring the education of one individual. So they turn around and ask your child, "What is 4 + 4?" and act shocked that your ten-year-old can do kindergarten math. And they back away when your child then lectures them on how he was just learning about the Incan empire and how the people recorded their financial transactions and maybe their history on these funny strings with knots on them that no one has ever deciphered and perhaps he will grow up to be an archaeologist isn't digging and learning at the same time so interesting?

We are afraid that if our children play outside during school hours that the neighbors might call child protective services.

Our parents have never been on board with this whole homeschooling thing. They keep asking, "Are you *still* doing that? How much longer?" until holiday meals are quite awkward. Even though our children won't shut up about the Incan empire. (Why, why, why did we have to study ancient South America? What will happen when we study the Civil War, and they start arguing with everyone over the cause and long-term effects? Will we have to move to a different state and change our name?)

Then there's the self-criticism—the inner voice that questions our teaching styles, learning styles, discipline styles, cooking styles, fashion styles. We wonder about curricula, educational toys, craft products (will our children be in therapy because we didn't allow glitter?).

We don't have enough support. We feel like our spouse or other loved ones don't understand the pressure we face. They don't know what it is like to homeschool, let alone to juggle the rest of life along with it. We wistfully watch our spouse walk out the door for work, and we long for an eight- or ten-hour day. We try to tell a parent what is wrong, what we struggle with,

THE DANGERS OF HOMESCHOOLING

why we are crying, but words fail us. Unable to communicate our needs, we become frustrated that others aren't helping.

We don't have time for friends. We hear about coffee dates, long lunches, shopping trips, and errands alone, all enjoyed by stay-at-home moms of school children. Yes, they even *go to the grocery by themselves!* And our working-mom friends, again, get out of the house. We know they have their own stress, but we secretly wish we could trade. We want the frequent comradery of other women. We want to walk out of the house when we want to. We want to wear clean clothes and mascara. We want to laugh and complain over coffee and let our friends and coworkers make us feel better.

Instead, we find ourselves all alone at home. Alone with a child or multiple children all day every day, minions we cannot get rid of. Alone in our struggles. We are addicted to Facebook and Instagram (Pinterest is from the devil) because our fellow POWs are there.

We are flat-out exhausted. One week of this life kills us. Thirty-six weeks of a school year grays our hair. (Yes, my friend, this is the cause of the forehead wrinkles too.) We sleepwalk like zombies. We are addicted to coffee and soda. We buy dry shampoo and slap on deodorant with a wish and a prayer. We stay up late making lesson plans, soaking dishes in the sink, and setting up the coffee pot. We wake before dawn to snap a shot of our Bible for Instagram and still not have time for a shower. Don't say the word *nap* in our presence or we may burst into tears.

We are burned out. But even so, we need these things. We need to teach our children day in, day out. We need to train them in academics—even the hard ones—and biblical truths. We need to meet our children's limitations and needs. We need to enrich their lives (i.e., *socialize*) with special activities and extracurriculars. We need to discipline our children. We need to clean the house once in a while and feed the masses three times (maybe twice and a banana) each day. We need to face criticism with grace. We need to remember our purpose and give it all to God. We need to find support for ourselves and give it to others.

14.1.1.2 HOW, THEN, DO I SURVIVE THIS SCOURGE OF BURNOUT?

Most importantly, you need to plan for it. Burnout *will* come because we are weak human beings. We forget—God, remind us—that we truly *cannot do this of ourselves.* God did not call us to homeschool because we are all-powerful and all-knowing.

God called us because *he* is.

When we try to homeschool in our own strength, in our own wisdom, we quickly find ourselves insufficient for the task. When we, instead, lean on him for provision, we find his grace (see James 4:6). But as humans, we still do try to work this all out on our own. There is such a fine line between *doing our best* and *doing it ourselves*. This tightrope we walk finds us falling into burnout itself. This is why we need to recognize our tendency to burn out, to be "weary of doing good" (Galatians 6:9), and to plan for refreshment. We need to consciously create opportunities to return to God's grace, to his perfect rest.

You can plan for seasonal breaks. Literally put rest on the calendar. My friends have chosen many ways to do this. Some schedule to homeschool year-round so they are less likely to become overwhelmed at any one time. One friend teaches for six weeks then takes six weeks off. Another plans ten weeks on, three weeks off. Still another takes time off every nine-week quarter.

For several years, my family homeschooled year-round. My children were middle school and younger, so I took things fairly casually. We could take off whenever we wanted to, and we took our time on some subjects and sped ahead on easier things. The relaxed pace was so much fun; I miss those years.

Now, I take breaks every semester. After about sixteen weeks in the fall, we take a month or so off for the holidays. Then we tackle second semester after the New Year. Having long breaks to look forward to really motivates me.

You can plan for daily breaks too. You can build several opportunities to breathe into the day. After a busy morning homeschooling, I enjoy an hour to eat lunch and rest alone in my room, a routine I have kept since my children were infants. Cooking dinner is actually relaxing for me most days, but I really look forward to eight o'clock. After the clock strikes eight, I put away everything until the next day, whether it is done or not. Having these moments to look forward to keeps me going on a tough day.

I most look forward to—and fiercely protect—my Sunday Sabbath. I need that one day off to replenish my soul *and* my body. That means an easy dinner after church. That means not leaving the house after noon. That means spending some quality time in my recliner and on my bed.

God did not make my body nor your body to work hard for seven days. We simply must have one day of rest.

You can take a break from some of the teaching. You might look for a tutor or a co-op to ease the load. We can share the emotional burden with our spouse or our homeschool friend (hello, Facebook!). We can find a homeschool mentor, someone to take an objective look at our homeschooling and help us find ways to simplify.

I have eased my homeschool burden by finding some self-teaching curriculum. My older students use a very explanatory science course that even lays out their daily assignments. Just giving them a weekly check-in and proctoring their tests has vastly decreased my homeschool stress. You can also consider online courses, DVD courses, or a co-op for this very reason.

You can find a change of scenery. When my children were young and overactive, I frequently took them for walks in the park. Sometimes we even took their books along with us to practice reading under a tree. The outdoors refreshed my children too.

One of my friends schedules playdates, even for her older children. She found other homeschoolers in her area and invites a mom for coffee so the children can play in the other room. Another of my friends walks down the street with her kids. She just puts on her sneakers and off they go. Fresh air rejuvenates her and her children.

You can go to the movies. You can go on a field trip. You can do studies in the library. You can just pile into the car for ice cream. Simply stop what you are doing and shake things up to clear your mind.

You can take care of your physical health. Get some exercise with your children. Or thrust them on your spouse and run—literally run—out the door. Just moving increases those good chemicals in our brains to relax and refresh us. They help us sleep better too.

Which brings us to sleep. It is too easy to neglect those seven or eight hours. Yet we cannot be our best if our bodies are depleted of physical rest. Sometimes chores will be undone. Sometimes even the homeschooling needs to be cut short. But if Mommy is tired and cranky, nothing is going to go well.

That brings us to the not-so-fun topic of nutrition. Moms need to eat healthy too. I'm on a diet right now, but I purposefully *wasn't* a couple of months ago. I was stressed by too many other things, many responsibilities that demanded my attention. Being hungry or managing a food program was not another thing I needed to put on my plate. Now, however, things have settled down, so I can focus on my nutritional health. I don't want to yo-yo diet, but I do want to make the most of good opportunities to retrain my appetite. So my encouragement to you is to definitely eat healthy, but do not let dieting become another contributor to your burnout.

You can take care of your mental health. This is a much-neglected priority among homeschool moms. Meaningful friendships can offer needed encouragement for the daily stresses. Talking to a friend or your spouse about your frustrations will help you work through them, often diminishing the stress itself. Even writing in a journal can help you clarify your thoughts.

Anxiety, depression, and/or clinical mental illness could be weighing you down. You might be afraid to seek the help you need. Not doing so not only causes pain and suffering in your own life but also can affect your relationships with those around you. It is time that we all get over the stigma, disregard the ignorance of others, and just get help. You can reach out to mental health professionals for counseling or therapy. There is no reason to suffer in silence.

You can reevaluate your methods or priorities. Maybe you haven't quite found your own teaching style. Or maybe you aren't quite in sync with your child's learning style. Sometimes I find myself pushing ahead and not paying attention to what isn't working. I just barrel through. But when I stop and spend some time reflecting on what is going on with my child and in my home, I usually find something that needs to be changed for the better. You could try looking objectively at what you are doing to find a way to simplify.

Maybe it is your child who needs to be reevaluated. He may be struggling with a subject or even stuck on a concept. There may be a reason to sweep all the other subjects and responsibilities aside for a time and just focus on one need, gently but carefully going through the difficulties. This is so much more important than pushing forward through the material. Remind yourself that homeschooling is much more than just finishing a book or getting a good grade. It is about *teaching the way you teach best for the way your child learns best*. And that may mean spending quality time on one thing. Tailoring studies to your child is an important aspect of homeschooling.

You need to keep your family first. Besides seeking God in your homeschooling, loving your family passionately is your top priority. Burnout happens when we lose touch with this important value. Rekindle your love for your spouse (kissy-kissy time!). Enjoy your children. Relish your family. Stop and look at what you have built inside your home. Things may be tough; your marriage may be difficult; you may be struggling with your child. But as a mother for God, you can find evidence of his working through you. Find those bright spots, write them down, and actively look for family happiness.

Put homeschooling aside to work on your family. If your marriage is on the rocks, make it more important than math and history. If your child is becoming wayward, spend more time loving and shepherding him than lecturing on science. If God is truly the center of our homeschool, then caring for the family he gave us is time well spent. Never feel bad about stopping what you are doing to care for your family.

My twins were adopted from a hard situation. They came to us wounded and afraid. Sitting at the kitchen table to write spelling words was the last thing that they needed. For months, we focused on cuddling on the sofa with a good book, playing at the park, and just living life together at home. As healing slowly began, we were able to gradually begin academics.

You can just say no. No to volunteering. No to taking meals. No to watching someone else's child. No to helping at co-op. No to teaching Sunday school. No to extra ministries. Saying no—or worse, quitting—is one of the most difficult things for us homeschool moms. When I talk about burnout, this is the single most discussed aspect. Because we all have a hard time with this. We want to help out. We want to be needed. And we feel guilty for not doing more. What if we don't do it? Who will?

Someone else. God will provide someone else. Or it won't get done, and the rest of the world will live. Sometimes saying *no* or quitting requires faith—faith that God will supply that need that we cannot.

To write this book, I had to quit things. I quit playing my violin in three—three!—orchestras that I loved. I felt very sad about that, even guilty. I even quit volunteering at church and some special church services. At the insistence of several trusted people in my life, people God had given me for wise counsel, I finally gave up being the end-all of everything. And you know what? After about two months, I got over the guilt. I opened my eyes to the breathing room God had given me. I now relish my time to rest, homeschool with more joy, take better care of myself, and spend more time with my family outside of homeschooling. Finally, I have time to enjoy what God has blessed me with while putting him and his calling in my life first.

Stop sacrificing yourself on the altar of homeschooling. Just say no. If you have the courage, it will change your life.

You can rest. Yes, you can sleep. You can find breaks in your day and in your year. But ultimately, you can *rest in God*. He promises us—no, he *commands* us—"Come to me, all who labor and are heavy laden, and *I will give you rest*. Take my yoke upon you, and learn from me, for I am gentle and lowly in heart, and *you will find rest for your souls*. For my yoke is easy, and my burden is light" (Matthew 11:28-30, emphasis added).

> We don't homeschool for ourselves. We homeschool for God.

Coming to God is our command, finding his rest is our reward.

"I will give you rest . . . rest for your soul."

You can give your burden to Jesus and just collapse into his arms. You don't need to do it all, to be it all, to work on it all. You need to rest. To accept Jesus' gift of rest today.

You can focus on your *why*. What have you already accomplished? What has God already done through you? Stop and number those things.

Why are you homeschooling? What are you praying God works through you? Stop and remember those things.

Because that is why we do it all. We teach, we train, we drive, we clean, we discipline, we endure, we strive, we struggle, we forgive, we love . . . because we are called to do it. We cherish our children, we adore our God because he has created us to glorify him. And this glory is worked out through our weakness in our home life, even in our homeschooling.

We have a *why*. We know how and why we started this journey of homeschooling. We are committed to teaching the way we can for the children we have because God called us to do so. We know we are, each and every day, living out God's love before our family. We cannot stop, because God moves us along.

We don't homeschool for ourselves. We homeschool for God.

Never forget. Never become distracted. Never stop. Return to your *why*, and continue in God's grace.

14.1.2 What if I suffer the worst day ever in the history of homeschooling?

No, you didn't. I did last week. There were moanings and groanings. There were crumpled papers and thrown pencils. There were math manipulatives on the floor, and I stepped on them and had to bite my tongue lest I say what I really think about tangrams. There were ripped workbooks. There were lost library books. There were failed tests. There was some shoving and some thrown insults. There was—you guessed it—cold coffee. I thought that hour would never end.

Then we got to continue all of this for three more hours before lunch.

Homeschool moms say there'll be days like this (sing along with me). The days that make us question our sanity. The days that even make us question our homeschooling.

Do you know what I do? I quit. That day. Not every day, but when I am having the-worst-day-ever-in-the-history-of-homeschooling, then it's time to pack it up. Sweep all of the books off the table, rake the clutter on the floor into a heap, scrap the homeschool schedule, and just be done with it. I might go to the park or visit a friend. Usually, I'll hide in my room with a fresh cup of coffee and let my children run rampant with their toys. A day off can really help to reset us, and we'll likely do better the next morning.

> We do not lose heart. Though our outer self is wasting away, our inner self is being renewed day by day.
>
> **2 CORINTHIANS 4:16**

Most importantly, don't judge your homeschooling based on your bad day. Or your bad week. Or month or even year. We all go through rough patches, and that is not a measurement of our homeschooling success. Right? Rather, success is God's work in our lives.

14.1.3 What if I don't homeschool right?

There is no such thing as the right way to homeschool. Are you working toward teaching the way you teach best for the way your children learn best? Are you doing so with faith by the grace of God? Then you are homeschooling right for your own family.

Your flesh, though, is not always strong. You will grow tired, and you will grow discouraged. That does not mean you are out of God's will; it means your own body and mind are tired. This fatigue is completely normal. It's simply time to rest in God.

Your enemy, Satan, wants you to stop. He lies to you (see John 8:44). He wants you to think God has forsaken you. He wants you to believe what you are doing does not count for eternity. He wants to incapacitate you. He wants to steal your peace. "Be sober-minded; be watchful. Your adversary the devil prowls around like a roaring lion, seeking someone to devour. Resist him, firm in your faith, knowing that the same kinds of suffering are being experienced by your brotherhood throughout the world. And after you have suffered a little while, the God of all grace, who has called you to his eternal glory in Christ, will himself restore, confirm, strengthen, and establish you" (1 Peter 5:8-10).

Are you homeschooling right? That's the wrong question. The right question is *Is God in my homeschool?*

TRUTHS TO ENCOURAGE YOU IN HOMESCHOOLING

Rather than worry about whether you are homeschooling right, choose to focus on these truths:

- **God called you to this task.** "These words that I command you today shall be on your heart. You shall teach them diligently to your children, and shall talk of them when you sit in your house, and when you walk by the way, and when you lie down, and when you rise" (Deuteronomy 6:6-7).

- **God owns this work, not you.** "It is God who works in you, both to will and to work for his good pleasure" (Philippians 2:13).

- **God always keeps his promises.** "He who began a good work in you will bring it to completion at the day of Jesus Christ" (Philippians 1:6).

- **God works through you when you are unable.** "He said to me, 'My grace is sufficient for you, for my power is made perfect in weakness'" (2 Corinthians 12:9).

- **God determines what is success.** "I know the plans I have for you, declares the LORD, plans for welfare and not for evil, to give you a future and a hope" (Jeremiah 29:11).

14.1.4 What if I overschedule?

Then find ways to cut back. I run a tight schedule. I have one student teaching piano and tutoring full-time and homeschooling and playing the violin. The other students are on different sports teams and involved in church activities that pull them every which way every night of the week. Then I'm homeschooling, writing, performing, and speaking. My husband works full-time and owns a large soccer club.

We are entirely too busy. Family dinner happens on Sunday.

This should not be the norm. And I try to make sure it is not the norm for us, either. Go, go, going all day, every day not only wears each of us out, but it pulls at the unity of our family. We simply cannot sustain the constant separation. It sucks our joy. It crushes our spirits. It burns us out.

Co-op. Sports. Music. Enrichment. Church. Volunteer. The list goes on and on. Our children want these fun activities. We feel guilty for not providing the opportunities. So we pile on more and more. Until we simply *cannot* any longer. We can't drive that van one more hour one more day.

Enough is enough.

We each, myself included, need to take back our days and our weeks. We need to actually schedule *just be home* time. We need to say *no* to the good so we can focus on the best. We need to learn to say *maybe later* or *I'll think about it for next time.*

I told you earlier I quit orchestra and church activities for a time. I also quit driving my children to events; if they want to do it, they can get a ride from a sibling or a friend. I quit scheduling anything after seven o'clock at night. I just focused on three things: homeschooling, writing my book, and breathing.

I said *maybe later* to everything else. Yes, some people tried to talk me into what they wanted me to do, but I learned five words that changed my life: *I just can't right now.*

I am an overachieving people pleaser. But if I can learn how to say *no,* I know you can too.

What is more important than being there for our family? Not just being there physically, but being available mentally and emotionally. Can we give our family our love and peace if we have none ourselves? I'm not going to tell you the cliché about the oxygen mask. I'm just giving you my bad example that I am overcoming.

Do this with me. Help me create a new homeschool culture of calm. Say no to busy.

14.1.5 What if I push my student too hard?

I have to constantly guard against this myself. Consistent grading and teaching about responsibility—while completely necessary—can easily lead to perfectionism in myself and in my children. Not all children achieve the same levels. And our children each have different giftings and abilities. Some are naturally studious, and academics come easily. Some struggle to find their best learning style. Others are talented in other areas of life, like people skills and/or hands-on tasks. Some may have special needs and learning difficulties.

Which abilities are the most important in life? God says that he gives each of us different abilities and different purposes (see 1 Corinthians 12:12-27). I am a writer, and my husband is a natural leader. My oldest son is analytical and logical, and my daughter is creative and sunny. One son is a people person, while his brother is a visionary. The world needs all of these qualities and more to work the glory of God. As parents, we can easily forget this while we focus on academics.

Pushing your child to achieve—whether in academics, sports, or the arts—is dangerous. Your child could become perfectionistic, demanding ever more from himself and from others. This could lead to a bitter, resentful, unforgiving spirit that damages his relationship not only with those around him but also with the Lord.

Pushing too hard can also backfire in your relationship with your child. When a child or teen feels there is nothing he can do to please you, he could eventually quit trying. Instead, he could seek that affirmation from others, becoming needy to those outside the family. Or he could even seek attention by acting out or engaging in dangerous activities.

Finally, pushing too hard could hinder your teen's relationship with God. When you teach your teen that authority expects ever more perfect work, he can grow to expect that attitude from God. He may lose sight of God's grace and forgiveness, instead viewing his heavenly Father as a vengeful tyrant.

You can guard against this by giving your child the grace you also need for yourself. Encourage rather than scold over difficult assignments. Help to understand rather than ridicule for confusion. Patiently repeat rather than ignoring frequent questions. By learning of God's love and forgiveness toward us, we learn how to extend these qualities toward our loved ones. We can then teach our child not only to accept this grace for himself but also to forgive and cherish others.

14.1.6 What if I complicate the education process?

It's the fault of the fancy curricula. I really believe it. There are some companies that make money selling really difficult ways of teaching so we have to buy lots of support materials and a special DVD to train us how to teach our children their way. That's ridiculous.

Don't believe the hype.

It's really simple. You find what you want to teach your child, then you show it to him.

That may sound overly simplistic. And maybe it is a little. But honestly, if you know the basic outline of what your child needs to know, then you can work with basic, simple materials. Then you lovingly communicate those truths to your child.

This is why we talked in chapter 5 about understanding how teaching works. And this is why we talked in chapter 6 about finding how you most enjoy teaching. This is why in chapter 7 we considered how your child might learn best. And this is why, in chapters 10–13, we looked carefully at what your child will learn each step of the way. All of those are not to complicate the process but rather to show you the basics of how you do

> Homeschooling is simply communicating God and his truths to your child.

what you do. The goal isn't to set up some intricate system of homeschooling. It's to help you see how *you* can simplify how you teach best.

Homeschooling is simply communicating God and his truths to your child.

You are communicating the principles of math. You are communicating the facts of history. You are communicating the structure of literature. You are, most of all, communicating the awe-inspiring character of God. That is simple, and that is lovely.

If one subject requires a tableful of materials and an hour a day every day to go through, you may have complicated the process. If it takes you hours every weekend to learn every subject you need to teach the following week, you are definitely complicating the process.

My friend, be free. Simplify. Get back to the basics and enjoy them again.

14.1.7 What if my homeschooling doesn't seem to be making a difference?

Remember that your homeschooling is about your child's relationship with God. Why are you homeschooling? Is it to instill a love for God and others in your child? Then you are achieving what you set out to do. Is your child growing in the Lord? Does he love to go to church, serve others, work in the ministry? Is he memorizing Scripture, applying it to his life, talking about it with you and others during the day? Does he understand that the Word of God set the standard for right and wrong, including obeying his parents (see Ephesians 6:1) and doing his best work (see 1 Corinthians 10:31)? Is he learning how to read God's Word and pray? Does he listen when you talk of God and his works throughout the day? If yes, then you are helping him grow his relationship with God. You are accomplishing the single most important measure of success for all eternity.

What if you don't see those signs? What if your child is walking away from God and you? Are you a failure? *No!* You are raising an autonomous human being, a young person with a free will and independent character. You *cannot* make him love God and others. You *cannot* force him to serve the Lord and your family. You *cannot* make him become a Christian.

You can, however, rest in faith in God's work. Maybe you will see the fruit of your labors later. Maybe you will see them in eternity. Maybe your fruit will be a simple "well done, my child."

Maybe it is your own relationship with the Lord that is changing.

Remember that your child's academic progress may be slow and irregular. You may feel like your student has made no headway in his work. Yet if you look further back from the past month to the past year, even two years, you can see small growth. He *has* learned something, even if it is less than you wish.

Every student's learning is uneven. He will plateau for a while, then make a jump, then plateau again, and continue the cycle. During those dry periods, both you and your student can become discouraged. *This doesn't mean you aren't making a difference.* This means you are helping your student persevere during a difficult time. And over time, even if it is a longer time than you wish, you will see improvement.

Consider how homeschooling is impacting your children's health and family life in positive ways. I never want you to think my own house is conflict-free. To the contrary, my children wage wars constantly. But like their academic progress, their relationships have grown over time in spite of difficult periods. Children who fought constantly with each other for a few years have grown closer as they matured. And two that never saw eye to eye finally found peace. Bickering is normal, but homeschooling offers ample opportunity to work through these difficulties.

In fact, stronger sibling relationships are a direct by-product of homeschooling. Spending all day, every day with siblings helps your children develop a better understanding of others. Your children begin to appreciate the differences and similarities among themselves and even to notice each other's strengths. These relationships will last through adulthood, making that family bond even stronger.

> I know the plans I have for you, declares the LORD, plans for welfare and not for evil, to give you a future and a hope.
>
> **JEREMIAH 29:11**

After the priority of training our child in godliness, the goal of parenting is to rear healthy, happy children. Caring for your child every day ensures you meet his physical and emotional needs on a consistent basis. Children who have endured trauma or who have special needs in particular benefit from this constant care. No matter your child's background, his health and happiness should reassure you that you are loving him well.

In addition, through your homeschooling, you are building memories every day: memories of field trips, family projects, inside jokes, and simply living together. Many moms keep a homeschool journal for this reason. Some jot down incidents in their homeschool planner. Keeping track of these moments gives you something to look back on when you (incorrectly) feel like a failure. You are making great memories for everyone in your family.

Consider how homeschooling is helping you grow thoughtful citizens and empathetic community members. Another great opportunity you have as a homeschool family is to continually apply lessons to the world around you. Your students will become well aware of hot-button topics like racial inequalities, immigration, wars, federal and local budgets, environmentalism, and more. By applying the Bible, logic, and historical background, your children will become better prepared not only to vote thoughtfully on the issues of their day but even to enact change in their world. When you encourage thoughtful participation in these discussions, you are passing along lasting values to your children.

You can also encourage your children to embrace true diversity. As an active homeschooler, you have the opportunity to prove wrong the stereotype of isolationism as your homeschool expands outside into the community, libraries, museums, festivals, and cultural events. Your family might participate in charity work in your community and in needy areas. You can expose your children to a wide variety of different cultures and backgrounds.

In your more academic work, you may spend time studying different cultures and how they interact and enrich your own. As you study history, literature, and the arts, you can include comparative religion, cultural studies, and lifestyle differences. You might seek opportunities for your children to regularly interact with experts and communities to enrich their understanding. Your children may then grow to appreciate the wide variety God has created in the world and to love people of all backgrounds.

Don't undervalue the growth homeschooling will bring in your own relationship with God. There's nothing like watching God do the impossible through us to draw us to him. Homeschooling day in, day out is too grueling, and doing it all is unattainable. Your homeschooling is the greatest success if it brings you away from self-sufficiency to the grace of God.

Will you see all these differences every day? Every month? Each year? In your lifetime? Maybe not. Perhaps you have been laboring toward your *why*, and you see no measurable success. Your child is wayward. Your family life is a battle. Your child struggles with learning. Your relationship with God is hanging by a thread.

Are you, then, a homeschool failure, making no difference at all for eternity? No! Rather, you are fighting a spiritual war that you can barely see. You, my friend, may be struggling for the heart and soul of your child and praying for God to move . . . and seeing no results. But you *are* praying. You *are* clinging to God. You *are* following his plan for your life, your family, your homeschool. Your measure of success is not results—it's what you do.

It's who you are.

You can glimpse in your heart the difference you are making when you remember why you are homeschooling in the first place.

ACADEMIC SIGNS YOUR HOMESCHOOL IS GOING WELL

Your student may exhibit some (but not all) of the following:

- Your student is usually engaged in his subjects.
- You overcome difficulties over time.
- You are slowly finding your own homeschool style.
- You are starting to adapt to your student's learning style.
- Your student has made progress over the last month or year.
- Your student applies his learning to other subjects and areas of his life.
- Others remark on your student's growth.
- Your student answers strangers' quizzing admirably.
- Your student achieves modest test scores.
- Your student graduates.
- Your student adapts well to college.
- Your student finds a job.

14.1.8 What if I become lazy?

There is a difference between *independent learning* and *mom doesn't know or care*. Remember what I said about burnout? Rest is vitally important. Work is also important. When things get tough, we need rest. But we may be tempted to make hiding in the closet or vegging out in front of Netflix documentaries the norm, not the exception. Life could be so good at home, too, that we are tempted to rest and relax a little too much. There is a time to unwind and take it easy, but this is not every day.

God created us to work ever since he commanded Adam to tend to the Garden of Eden. And he continues to encourage and strengthen our work (see Deuteronomy 15:10; Psalm 90:17; Proverbs 14:23; Ecclesiastes 9:10; 1 Corinthians 15:58).

We may become lazy in our schedule or routine. It is tempting for me—especially on those sleepy, rainy days—to drag my feet and skip over some tasks. But having a daily routine (not a strict schedule!) keeps me and my children moving forward. We can work on one thing after another if we just continue walking through our usual plan. Continuing in spite of difficulties or lack of interest teaches our children to be consistent and responsible.

> To this end we toil and strive, because we have our hope set on the living God, who is the Savior of all people, especially of those who believe.
>
> 1 TIMOTHY 4:10

When the long winter turns to sunny spring, it is tempting to throw the books out the window and declare everything done. Or at least the hard subjects. This is even more true since we know that traditional schools, and even some curricula, are designed to finish only 80 percent of the course. However, most homeschool curricula are written thoroughly to the end. The author includes critical information all the way to the finishing chapter. If we end too soon, we may cheat our student out of valuable information. Even more dangerously, we could be teaching that it is not always necessary to finish a task we begin.

Another symptom of laziness is a lackadaisical grading system. Giving a student an A for everything, or even just for effort, is not teaching the value of studying nor the quality of work. By grading on a consistent scale, we train our children and teens to work hard for mastery and to measure their own outcome as well as the work put into it. When they enter adulthood, our children will not be graded in college for effort, but for outcome. They will not be rewarded in their careers for how much they put into a project, but rather for the outcome itself. We can train them to work hard by how we grade their work now.

You can guard against laziness by keeping a routine or schedule. Continue on in the bad days and press forth on the good days. Don't get discouraged—trust God to strengthen you. When I am tired and overwhelmed, I give myself just three things to do that day. On days I am in a funk, I challenge myself to do one thing each hour. Usually, those two strategies turn my day—or maybe slowly, my week—around.

14.1.9 What if I limit my student's possibilities?

There is another side of the coin. Are we giving our student the opportunities he needs to grow in his own direction? Or are we homeschooling for the least effort, the easiest path, the quickest way to a high school diploma?

There are many ways to gloss over homeschooling. We could make it easy to learn more, or we can make it easy to learn little. It's a fine line we all walk.

Have we prepared our homeschooler to pursue God's will for his life?

- What if our young adult could reach athletes for Christ as an athlete himself?
- What if God called our young person to be a musician or artist?
- What if God wants to use our child as a doctor, engineer, airline pilot, or businessman?

Yes, God calls us to homemaking, trade work, and small business ownership. But how well do we know the entire future of our young person when he is only ten, fifteen, or even twenty-one?

Sometimes, we see God limit possibilities and abilities to show his grace in more specific ways. But for many of us, he calls us to prepare for the future while we walk in the dark, by reaching out each day by faith.

We don't know the future. So we must prepare for whatever God has for us.

14.1.10 What if I use our co-op as school?

Co-op classes can easily become a good thing gone wrong. Many families begin attending individual co-op classes for all the right reasons: they want to supplement their courses, they feel intimidated by calculus, they need help editing essays, their child wants to participate in a drama (besides just causing drama). But maybe one or two or three classes lead to five or six or seven . . . and soon the student is spending all morning, every morning at co-op being taught by other moms. A co-op that has become a very small private school. Which is fine, if a small school is what you want.

I love co-ops. I've never used one, but I adore the possibilities. My best friend started and ran a co-op that I would attend to make her teach my children science if only she lived in my state.

But I fear that for many homeschoolers, co-op has become a school. Moms are no longer involved in their child's education other than making sure the homework is done. And that's fine, but it's not homeschooling. Homeschooling is teaching our own children our own values. Co-ops are a useful tool to supplement that. But if God has, indeed, called us to homeschool our children, then our primary responsibility is to communicate his truths to our children within our own family. Co-ops, then, should support, not run, our homeschools.

14.1.11 What if I am nothing more than a homeschool mom?

Hi, I'm Lea Ann, and I'm a homeschool mom.

Blech.

Hey, I love homeschooling. I love spending (some of the) days with my children. I get thrills when the Amazon box brings me new homeschool books. I spend hours every week mentoring and encouraging homeschool moms.

But God made me so much more than a homeschool mom. You, too.

Think down the road a decade or two. When you are all done homeschooling, who will you be? Not just a former homeschooler, but a woman. A woman God created to love him and to love others. A woman who enjoys her family. A woman who serves God and her community in many different ways. A woman with her own talents and abilities.

We have to be careful not to become so homed in on homeschooling that we lose sight of whom God created us to be. My own mother remarked after her divorce from my father, "I just forgot who I was other than a homeschool mom." She forgot she was a wife and a woman in God's image. My husband was aware of this danger before I was. He encouraged me to find other outlets in addition to homeschooling. He supports my music career. Writing this book was his idea.

When you meet someone, how do you introduce yourself? Hi, I'm an awesome woman, and I _____. Fill in the blank with five or six different things. And identify yourself not only as a homeschool mom, but as a uniquely gifted woman.

14.1.12 What if I make homeschooling my god?

Homeschooling is not the reason for our existence. Homeschooling is important. Our homeschool *why* is to teach our children to love God. We do this because we know God has called us to teach our children every day, to lead them to him.

But there are no guarantees.

We often hear these guarantees implied, if not declared: "Homeschool to raise godly children for Christ." "Train them to be the next generation of Christian leaders." "Prepare him for his own special ministry." But God does not guarantee our child will follow him, God does not call every homeschooled child to work in full-time church ministry, and God does not tell parents the exact path our child's future will take. He belongs to God, and his future is in God's hands alone.

We cannot determine the future of our child by following the homeschool god. The homeschool god will not save our child from sin, it will not keep him safe from the temptations of the world, and it will not ensure he lives for Christ as an adult. Homeschooling will not save our child.

Homeschooling will not save us, either. Homeschooling does not ensure we are right with God. Homeschooling does not give us special favor from God. We do not earn our salvation, our fruit of the Spirit, or our peace with God by homeschooling our child.

We make homeschooling our god when we trust it to do what only God can do. When we trust homeschooling to save our family, to make our child believe in God, or to determine the life choices our young adult makes, we give homeschooling honor and power it never has.

Then when our family struggles, when our child questions the faith, when our young adult walks away from the church, we are left with broken promises. The project we began in spiritual pride falls apart in the realities of free will.

We as a Christian homeschooling community need to be very careful. We cannot let our pride in our decision for Christ blind us to what only God can do. We do not homeschool because we are omnipotent. We homeschool as weak mothers and fathers dependent on the omnipotent Creator for each day's grace.

We all need to guard our hearts. Homeschooling cannot be our god. There is one so much greater.

14.1.13 What if I become spiritually prideful?

We homeschool because we believe we teach our children best. And that includes spiritually. We believe we can best train our children to know God and love him forever. This is good.

Sometimes, however, we take this charge so seriously that we commit two prideful errors: we become disrespectful of the spiritual leaders around us, and we become legalistic in our spiritual application.

We should not be the only spiritual influence in our children's lives. God gave them pastors, Sunday school teachers, church friends, and others to teach and show them biblical truth—and we need to learn from others as well. We must demonstrate to our children a soft, teachable spirit so we and they may continue to grow. Conversely, an attitude that suggests "I know best for my family in all situations" stunts our spiritual growth and that of our family. Hebrews 13:17 tells us to obey those ruling over us—meaning our Christian leaders who have taught us God's Word. This assumes we will humble ourselves to submit to others' teaching. It is an imperative for us as well as for our children.

Pride in our own individual understanding of God's Word leads to legalism. By legalism I mean elevating rules and standards that are derived from Scriptural teaching to the same level of importance as the explicit commands of the Bible. There are many areas of life in which the homeschool community struggles with this, including dress, music, entertainment, dating, higher education choices, employment, Bible versions, and theological viewpoints. All of these areas impact our lives. As Christians, it is indeed important to apply biblical truth to our daily lives and worship. That means each of us must discern how to apply God's principles. But at the same time, we must agree that the Bible does not do any of the following things:

- give a dress code
- contain a music manuscript
- talk about fiction books, movies, or television
- list ten rules for finding a spouse
- prescribe a specific career, nor how to train for it
- mention Arminianism, Reformed theology, Bible translations, church style, flat-Earth theory, or essential oil brands by name

We each come to our own convictions in these areas based on the teachings of the Word of God and with much prayer. But I should not make standards that God did not explicitly state a rule for my sister in Christ.

What does this have to do with homeschooling?

We as homeschoolers can become judgmental toward each other when we have different standards and lifestyles. We separate rather than support. We judge rather than unify.

What is worse, we teach these extrabiblical rules to our children as God's Law. As children, they usually accept our rules as the way we live in our family. But as teens and young adults, they begin thinking for themselves. We as homeschoolers have taught them to critically evaluate everything they come in contact with. When they realize that God didn't say "no NIV" explicitly, they begin to question more and more of what we have taught them. And the teachings begin to unravel. We run the risk of harming or even losing our relationship with our grown children when we value principles more than people, rules more than love.

Having grown up in a legalistic home and church, I understand this struggle. As a young adult, I questioned everything I had been taught about the Christian life because so much I had heard was not contained in the Bible. It has taken me years to peel back the layers of man's opinion versus God's teachings.

How can we guard against spiritual pride in our homeschool and family? Here are some steps we have taken as parents that we pray will protect us from this error:

- We regularly sit under the preaching and teaching of God's Word as a family.
- We learn from a variety of teachers.
- We speak of our spiritual leaders with respect in front of our children.
- We encourage our children to love and respect their church leaders.
- We help our children become involved in the youth ministry, including youth group gatherings and service opportunities.
- We teach our children what we believe and how we apply Scripture to our lives.
- We are honest with our teens and young adults about how we come to our own standards and acknowledge they may draw different conclusions.
- We tell our young adults where we disagree, but we do not badger them or make it an issue in our relationship with them.
- We allow our young adults and teens to see us cultivate friendships with Christians who live by different standards than we have personally set.
- We value love for one another and love for our church family more than extrabiblical issues.

We must continue teaching our children in the light of God's Word. We must continue applying Scripture to our academics and our lives. And more than any other rule, we must love God and his people.

14.1.14 What if I don't ask for help when I need it?

Sometimes we don't seek help because we are embarrassed. What will others think of us if we have a child with special needs? Or worse, what if she needs special tutoring or—gasp—the services of a public school system? Perish the thought!

So we don't want to admit we have problems. Our family doesn't have problems. There's no reason to hold back or coddle our child. She's fine, she just learns her own way and takes her own time.

And that may be true. She may be in a plateau or waiting to fully understand or still maturing.

Or maybe she needs help.

Waiting too long is sad. We just postpone the inevitable. We become frustrated with studies. Our child becomes frustrated and loses her excitement about learning. We neglect taking care of our child, even.

In each chapter on academic development (chapters 10–13), I include a list of signs your child may need help. I talk more about learning issues and other special needs in chapter 16. But even more importantly, *if your gut tells you that you could use support, reach out immediately.* You may simply get assurance that you are on the right track. Or, if you do need support, you will find relief that makes all the difference for you and for your child.

Whom should you talk to? Call your pediatrician. She will have a list of specialists in your area. Call your insurance company to see what is covered; many offer benefits. Call your local public school system to learn what programs are offered nearby. Reach out and find the encouragement you need.

I have not faced learning difficulties yet. But I did worry that one of my children was not developing gross motor skills appropriately. I called my pediatrician, who gave me referrals to clinical therapists in my area. After a two-hour consultation, the therapist assured me that, though my son was immature in some areas, he was within the normal range for his age. She also taught me exercises to help him grow in areas he found difficult. That gave me peace of mind and assurance that I could parent him through this glitch in his growth.

So, see? Even if you just have a small worry, make the call. You will either find assurance or you will get help. It's a win-win situation.

14.1.15 What if I become lonely?

You might feel isolated, so take steps to combat it. Staying home most of the day for most of the month for most of the year can feel lonely. Talking to children and teens all day—not actually stimulating conversation—can wear one out. Quite frankly, we need to get our words and emotions out. And maybe some of the whim-whams, too.

I asked my friends to share with me how they keep from becoming too lonely. They came up with several ideas. I am a true introvert; making new friends stresses me out, and I must set up a wingman for any party. I do use some of these suggestions in an attempt to appear friendly. You might want to try a few of these ideas yourself to increase your girl-time.

Invest in one or two close friendships. It's not the quantity, it's the quality. Spreading our efforts and time into a dozen relationships is exhausting, if not impossible. While we all can develop many nice acquaintanceships and casual friendships, we will find our close friendships more meaningful and rewarding. I'm talking about those one or two people you can text for prayer, send memes for laughs, compare homeschool foibles with, and call late at night for a good cry. Those are the friends you can count on.

Reach out to find and keep your friend. I recently made a great friendship from Sunday school for one reason—she started texting me all the time. She sent me jokes, inspirational quotes, funny stories from her day several days a week. Then she started a video message with "if you are going to be my friend, you need to know this about me" and spilled the beans. This girl made me her friend, and I am loving her ever since. I want to be that proactive friend from now on: just find a quality gal and friend her to death until she loves me. Or moves away because I'm psycho.

Make an effort to keep in touch with that friend every week, if not every day. Besides my local friends who keep the conversation and the laughs flowing, I keep in touch with my childhood friend who lives on the other side of the country. We text and video chat throughout the day, and once a year we spend a week together. She's like a sister to me.

I have another local friend who is even busier than I am (and I consider myself overcommitted). We struggle to keep in touch regularly, but once every couple of months we drop everything to have breakfast. I say we drop everything, which in our case means rescheduling half a dozen times but making it happen eventually. And we both agree it is worth the effort.

Schedule a moms' night out. A meetup with several moms builds comradery. You can simply send out a group invite "Let's have supper on Tuesday" and make it happen. In my area, a homeschool mom has taken it upon herself to organize a monthly homeschool moms' dinner. She makes a reservation and creates a Facebook event to invite dozens of us; whoever can make it comes. When I go, I have a riotous time. The Christmas gift exchange alone is insanely funny. We aren't the closest friends, but we have a great time eating and dishing homeschool info with each other.

Married moms, work on your marriage. It sounds cliché now, but our spouse should be our closest ally and friend. He's the one to lean on, share our struggles with, and celebrate our wins with. Staying on the same page not just in marriage but in life fills our hearts and emotions with strength to meet the family challenges. Yes, we yearn for a good girl chat. But our marriage upholds us through the ups and downs of life.

Join a co-op. The main reason for a co-op is purportedly to provide better homeschool teaching. But a great by-product is building friendships. My friends who join co-ops are always talking about the fun they have getting together outside classes and keeping in touch during the summer. I'm a little jealous.

Stay busy. Sitting around the house is not exciting. And truly, homeschool moms don't have much time for that, anyway. If we have a spare hour, though, we can stay occupied with something meaningful. Run errands, visit the library, walk in the park. I will nap if I can. I also try to read a novel once in a while. Browsing Target is dangerous fun. Maybe, maybe if I'm really, really desperate, I might clean something. But keeping myself occupied helps me not feel sorry for myself.

Get involved. We meet friends *and* do good when we get involved in our church and community. Join a ministry or committee. Teach Sunday school class. Participate in a Bible study. Every single church in the world needs nursery workers. I play in my church orchestra and occasionally teach at ladies' retreats. One of my friends teaches Sunday school and helps out at VBS. When we reach out to help others, we build new relationships that matter.

Build relationships across the town. We touch the lives of people all over the community without even realizing. We can stop and intentionally build relationships right where we are. I built a friendship of several years with my favorite cashier at the grocery store; he confided in me about his health issues, and I shared with him my faith. Now I'm working on the meat man; we discuss what I'm cooking that week, and he lets me know if he approves. My family visited the same library for over a decade; the staff knew my children and me by name, what books we liked to read, and so much more about our lives. We see these people around town regularly. It sounds old-fashioned, but we can have small-town relationships even in the big suburbs.

> Let your light shine before others, so that they may see your good works and give glory to your Father who is in heaven.
>
> MATTHEW 5:16

Have fun on Facebook. Social media gets a bad rap, but guess what—it's social. There are dozens of homeschool mom groups on Facebook, active online parties of commiserating and encouraging. In fact, I run some, myself, just to meet and have fun with other moms. We can meet home-school moms all over the country, moms of many different styles and cultures who show us we can do it. Even more, I keep my personal profile as honest and open as I can. My Facebook friends do bring me joy and help. Quite frankly, I could not have written much of this book without their help.

Get professional help if necessary. Sometimes deep feelings of loneliness and isolation can come from a darker place of anxiety or depression. I know that well, my friend. When life becomes too dark and difficult, please reach out to a close friend and even more to a counselor or therapist. God wants you to enjoy life (see Ecclesiastes 8:15) and will give you hope and help to find it.

14.1.16 What if I struggle with depression?

Mental pain happens to everyone—so reach out and get help. Anxiety, depression, and other mental illness affect homeschool moms, too. And in our efforts for family and faith, these issues are often pushed to the back; we are afraid to admit we are struggling for fear of judgment. What if my friends think I'm just unspiritual, guilty of sin, selfish, or lazy? What if no one understands, or if they make things worse? We forget that mental illness in all of its forms is just that: *illness*. We are sick for a time, and we need care to get better.

How do I continue homeschooling, let alone get out of bed in the morning? How do I parent effectively, not only meeting my children's needs but giving them the training and support of a godly home? How can I be an adequate—let alone great—mother if I can't even take care of myself? Why am I homeschooling when life has no purpose for me anymore? I know these kinds of thoughts, my friend, because I occasionally walk dark valleys myself. I do know the depths of despair.

We homeschool moms who are struggling with emotional or mental issues hide our pain from others. We crawl into our hole and pull the hole in after us. We try to become invisible so no one will judge us or hurt us more. We pull back from relationships. We lose friendships to neglect. We lose all perspective, not just on homeschooling but also on life.

As we pull back further and further, falling deeper and deeper into anxiety and depression, the cycle worsens. We may feel like no help is in sight, that there is no hope for recovery.

But this is not the end of the story. God does want us to recover not only the peace and joy of our relationship with him but also our enjoyment of our family and homeschooling. We can take steps out of the hole toward the sunlight. Let me share some tips that help me:

Married moms, talk to your husband. Tell him what is going on. Repeat yourself if necessary. Tell him how hard homeschooling and parenting are for you while you are struggling to hold it together. Let him know how much you hurt. Use words like *depression* or *severe anxiety* to clearly delineate how you are struggling.

Discuss together how much housework, cooking, parenting, even homeschooling is a necessary minimum at this time. In this season of healing, what can you let go or cut back on that won't greatly impact your family? Your husband likely expects much less than you do, and for a time you can let some things go while you work on your health.

Reach out to a friend. Time to call or text your best buddy and say, "I'm struggling right now. I think I'm depressed. I need your help." That's what she is there for. Let her comfort you. Tell her what you need: help with the children, a meal, a visit, an errand. Ask her to check on you regularly for a while. She may not have been through depression herself, so she may need you to frankly tell her what you need.

When you get better, have this conversation with her again. Say, "You know what? I really struggled, and I might go through that again. Next time, could you please . . ." and honestly give her a couple of things to do. Remind her to check on you. Tell her what tangible actions meant the most. And thank her for being there for you.

I have a close friend who did not know what I meant by "I'm feeling bad." So when I was better, I did tell her what I really meant and what helps me the most. And now when I struggle, she eagerly reaches out to show me love.

Don't hide. The biggest temptation we have when we are depressed is to isolate ourselves. But this backfires, keeping us from getting the support we need. Instead, we need to be honest. "How are you?" *I am really struggling.* "Why haven't I seen you much lately?" *I am so overwhelmed it is hard for me to keep up. I need help.* Some people may not be equipped to help you. But many will reach out in support.

Think on better things. Depression and anxiety attack the mind, continuing dark thoughts of despair. During this time, it is never more important to allow God and his Word to renew your mind. Spend time in Scripture, if only five minutes. Put handwritten verses around the house that you can cling to. Find a small phrase like "God is love," "I will never leave you nor forsake you," or "Cast your cares upon him for he cares for you" to repeat to yourself. Try to pray. When words fail me, I use a devotional of prayers I can read back to God.

Rest. Depression and anxiety are exhausting. Sometimes it is difficult to sleep, as well. Make time to sleep, time to just sit, time to stare out the window. Prioritize napping. Take a slower pace. Allow your body and your mind to slowly heal.

Minimize homeschooling. This is not a time to be super-homeschool-mom. Indeed, taking care of your health—especially your mental health—is a priority. Step back and allow your homeschooling to relax. Watch educational videos. Have the children play board games. Read aloud or use audiobooks. Let older children help younger ones. Stick to the basic subjects of English and math.

If your illness continues for a while, find homeschooling support. Join a co-op that allows you minimal involvement or even lets you pay for classes instead of working. Hire a tutor. Use online classes. Or just take a few months off; you can homeschool more when you are well. Read more about homeschooling during depression in section 15.2.3.

Minimize commitments. Whatever you are doing, you should probably stop. Ask yourself, *Would I be doing this if I had the flu?* If your response is *no*, then you have your answer: step back. We often say to ourselves, *But I promised to do this* or *There is no one to do this if I quit.* I used to say those things too. But someone told me that life will go on even if I am not holding things together in my weak, human hands. And you know what? It is true. Life goes on without my power.

Instead of worrying about doing other things for other people, take the time to be concerned with healing from your mental illness. There will be plenty of time to work when you are healthy. Now is the time to step back and rest.

Go back and read this section a few times, because I know you don't believe it in your heart.

Make a list of ten things. A list of ten things you can and might even do. Arrange them in order from easy to a little more effort. But make sure none of the actions are too strenuous or take too much time (less than an hour at most). Start with something simple like *take a shower*, which is NOT simple when we are depressed. Work up to *eat a nutritious breakfast* or *read a verse from the Bible* or *read a small picture book to my child* or *take a walk*. Post the ten things on your wall. On a difficult day, try to do the first one. Then maybe the next day, you can try for two. Slowly allow yourself to work up the list, gradually gaining strength at your own pace.

I have asked my close friends to ask me about this list when they check on me. Working on this exercise does a few great things for me. First of all, it gets me out of bed. On a really bad day, that can be hard. Second of all, it tells me what to do when my mind is not working. Third, I can gradually see myself doing a little more, and that tells me *I really am getting better! I am healing!* Finally, seeing me get out of bed and do the little things helps the entire family breathe easier; they can see improvement, and they know how to support me to keep going.

Get professional help. This is the hardest point, but it is the one you need to hear the most. You might be afraid to admit you need that much help; I was. You might be skeptical that a counselor, therapist, or mental health professional could even make a difference; I was. You might believe that if you only trust God more, you can *will* yourself better; I did. You might be afraid of what other people would think if they knew you saw a therapist, or worse, found medical help for your illness; I was deathly afraid.

But "God has not given us a spirit of fear, but of power and of love and of a sound mind" (2 Timothy 1:7, NKJV).

HOW TO HELP YOUR DEPRESSED FRIEND

- Be present for her.
- Check on her at least once a day.
- Tell her you are not afraid of her mood.
- Listen. Listen. Listen.
- Read online about depression, severe anxiety, or her particular mental illness.
- Tell her that she will live and she will recover.
- Allow her space to feel sad.
- Tell her to stop trying harder and working longer.
- Encourage her to minimize her commitments.

- Help her find a way to simplify her homeschooling.
- Offer to tutor her child or drive him to co-op.
- Bring her a meal and/or easy snacks for her child.
- Buy her paper products and plastic utensils so she doesn't need to wash dishes.
- Take her laundry if she lets you.
- Take her children out to the park or for a sleepover.
- Help her find help—a counselor, therapist, or mental health professional.

If you had an infection, you would rush to the doctor to get medicine so you would feel better and be back to caring for your family and homeschooling as soon as possible. *If you have depression, anxiety, or other mental illness, get help so you can feel better and be back to caring for your family and homeschooling as soon as possible.*

Most importantly—STAY SAFE! Ask yourself if any of the following points are true of you:

- You have reoccurring thoughts of death.
- You wish you were dead.
- You fear harming yourself, your children, or others.
- You are engaging in risky or self-destructive behavior.
- You eat to excess or stop eating altogether.
- You sleep all day or rarely sleep.
- You make a plan to hurt or kill yourself.

QUESTIONS YOU MUST ASK YOUR DEPRESSED FRIEND

Ask these questions when you first find out she is depressed or struggling with severe anxiety—or if you suspect she is experiencing either. Repeat these questions often through her struggle. It may feel awkward, *but you could save her life.*

- Are you safe?

- Are you afraid you may hurt yourself?

- Are you afraid you may hurt your child or others?

- Do you have suicidal thoughts?

- Do you have a suicide plan?

If she answers yes to any of the above, or if you feel she is unsafe for any reason, act fast. Stay with her or ensure someone is with her assuring her safety. Call her doctor if she is under psychiatric care. Take her to the emergency room if she is in imminent danger (they are equipped to help her stabilize her emotions). Call 911 for immediate assistance, if necessary.

If so, *then call your medical health professional immediately*, and tell your husband and/or a close friend right away that you are not safe. (If you don't feel comfortable with these options or can't get to someone nearby, please call the National Suicide Prevention Lifeline at 800-273-8255, or call 911.) Keep yourself safe because God loves you, your family loves you, others love you . . . and I'm writing this to you because I love you.

As I write this to you, dear friend, I am praying for you that God protects and heals you and restores to you the joy of your salvation (see Psalm 51:12).

14.2 COMPARISON DANGERS

14.2.1 What if I compare my homeschooling with someone else's?

This is the second biggest struggle my friends complain about, after burn-out. And I think, don't you, that comparison actually *leads* to burnout. At the very least, it adds tremendous pressure in our homeschool.

Remember, you are teaching the way you teach best for the way your child learns best.

But that school around the corner, it just doesn't disappear. We hear, or we remember from childhood, what school is like inside. We remember the desks, we remember the charts, we remember the lines in the hallway, we remember gym class and field trips and science experiments.

And we feel so inadequate.

We come face-to-face with the hard reality: school is different from homeschooling. *But that doesn't mean school is better than homeschooling.* Yes, that teacher with the hard-earned degree shows children wonders with fancy educational instruments, and the children enjoy group activities. At your homeschool, you have a hard-earned expertise in your child and teach your child the wonders of love and God's grace.

Which is more valuable?

Is the academic education better? You know by now that is not necessarily so. And if academic quality, those super-challenging advanced classes, is important to you, then you have several options for curricula, tutoring, co-ops, and online learning. *There is nothing academically you can't do.* And the statistics indicate your student will be better educated than one in a traditional school, public *or* private.[1]

> Not that we dare to classify or compare ourselves with some of those who are commending themselves. But when they measure themselves by one another and compare themselves with one another, they are without understanding.
>
> **2 CORINTHIANS 10:12**

But if we don't care about other schools, we *do* worry about the other homeschoolers. That mom is brilliant, or that other one does *so many* activities. That one is a science whiz, and the other one knows absolutely everything about every time period in history and how that applies to our spiritual lives today. We try not to hate her and everything that comes out of her mouth, and at the same time we envy her encyclopedic knowledge.

Here are my guilty confessions:

- I can't science. Seriously, sciencing is beyond my capability. I cannot replicate most experiments, I can't summon excitement for the subject, and I can't find the spiritual application other than

"This is how we know God created the world." My best friend, on the other hand, has a nursing degree. She *loves* to teach co-ops on science, and experiments make her giggle with glee. She sees God's voice everywhere. If she lived in my state, I would make her science all my children every day of the week. This is one of the many reasons she lives far away from me, so she doesn't have to raise my children.

- I cannot craft. You don't think this sounds bad, but just consider early learners. Within our home, glitter, Play-Doh, and liquid glue are forbidden. How much crafting can you expect from that? I have finished a lapbook only once in nearly two decades. My idea of art class is visiting the museum and saying *oooh, aaah*. You probably have more than crayons, colored pencils, and glue sticks in your house, so you are out-arting me.

There are lots of other things that I don't do that I don't want to tell you about. I'm just going to keep the rest of my many inadequacies to myself. But let me assure you that there are always areas in which each homeschool mom is not perfect and aspects in which God has given her talents. Here is where my strengths lie:

- I love the humanities. History, literature, and writing are very awesome to me. Are my children geniuses in these subjects? NO! But do I teach my little heart out on them? Absolutely. That's my thing.

It's cliché to say, "You do you." But I can't emphasize enough *you homeschool you*. You teach *the way you teach best*. And leave your homeschool mom friend alone. If you keep staring at her, you'll make her feel self-conscious about her own imperfections. Don't we all need grace?

14.2.2 What if I copy off other people's work?
Keep your eyes on your own homeschool. First of all, we are tempted to copy schools. My childhood homeschool was like that. We had school desks, maps and handwriting charts on the wall, a schedule with a bell on the hour. For the first year, we even stood for the pledges. My mom stood in front of us and taught the lessons from a teacher's manual. We turned in our assignments in a basket and got back our graded papers every day.

There was even a twenty-minute outdoor recess. She rang a little bell when it was over.

It was totally a school, but with fewer classmates.

Gradually, my mom realized that method wasn't working. My eyes glazed over while she was lecturing, and I worked ahead to finish my homework while she was talking, which frustrated her. I read the wrong assignments in my literature class and just skipped around the workbook. Finally, after several months of this, she just dropped the books on my desk and told me to have at 'em. I was thrilled to finish my work faster and have more fun doing it.

But you know what? I made the exact same mistake when I started homeschooling. The desk, the charts, the rigid schedule, the endless work-sheets. And that was when my son was just three years old. It took so much convincing from my relaxed homeschool friend to at least loosen my grip on the phonics flash cards.

But was that the end of copying? Oh, no! Next, I had to copy other people's homeschooling. I read one book and tried to do everything that one said. Then I found another, better book, and that was the new ideal. Then I met a homeschool mom who was so "with it" that I had to be just like her so my children would be just like hers.

Can you even imagine?

It took years before I finally got the picture: I had to stop copying and look at my own homeschool. I actually remember what year it was. 2009. I bought another "perfect history curriculum" but, lo and behold, it was a flexible teaching tool. It did not tell me what to do each day. It didn't tell me what words I had to say to my children and what they should say back. It simply provided information and ideas to teach my children to love history.

It. Blew. My. Mind.

My homeschooling was never the same. Finally, I started looking at my own children and stopped copying other homeschoolers or even other homeschool curricula. Not even that mind-blowing flexible one. I no longer copied the subject schedule of my local elementary school (good-bye social studies, hello world history!). I finally learned how to teach my children the way I teach best for the way they learn best.

Don't take as long as I did to learn the fundamentals. Start now. Look at what God has called you to do with your own family. And go forth with confidence, my friend.

14.2.3 What if I worry about other people's judgment?

Stop comparing yourself with others. So often, we think other people's thoughts for them. We assume others are judging us, thinking things like *How could she do that?* and *Why is she teaching them so badly?* and *I homeschool better* and *My child is more godly because I homeschool them in a more holy way.*

Okay, first of all, I would bet you a Starbucks Venti almond-milk Cinnamon Dolce Latte that she is *not* thinking those things. Tell your mind to shut up (you know that *that woman* would never say "shut up").

Do you want her to think that you are judging her? Then stop it. I love you, but stop it.

And if she actually is—let's pretend that you are right for a moment—if she actually is judging you, then *so what?* Is she the boss of you? Did God give your children to her? Did God give her your unique challenges and children? Did God ask her to judge your homeschooling on a scale of one to ten? No? Well, then, that is a *her* problem, not a *you* problem.

I know it is really, really hard to keep other people's voices out of your head. I hear them often too. (I hear lots of voices in my head.) Especially while writing this book—I've been overthinking everything I'm doing in my own homeschool. But I need to pray every day—every, single day—that God will lead me to teach and shepherd these children that he gave *me* and no one else. No one—no one—can fulfill that mission but me.

Let others have their own opinion. You have your own mission.

If anyone ever says anything critical (which happens only once in a blue moon), then say to her, "You can have your own opinion. I have my own mission."

What about those people after high school, the ones who meet our young adult in college and the workplace? Will they make fun of him for being homeschooled, ridicule him, diminish his work before he even begins? Maybe.

There was a short—very, very short—time that I worked out in a small gym. I hated every moment of it, but I went because my husband had bought me a membership for Christmas (yes, he now knows he picked the single worst Christmas gift available). Anyway, one day when I was on the stair machine, a woman nearby started railing about homeschoolers to the friend beside her. Homeschoolers are irresponsible, homeschoolers are ignorant, homeschoolers are neglectful, homeschoolers are child abusers. On and on and on. It raised my heart rate higher than the stair-climber usually did. I prayed (not trying to sound all super holy, but I was desperate for help), I prayed that God would calm me down and help me to not push the woman off her machine and gently punch her in the face.

Instead, I waited for the verbose woman to take a breath. Timidly, I asked, "Have you ever met a homeschooler?" No, of course not. But they are obviously all like that. "I am a homeschool graduate who received mumble-mumble score on my college entrance exam. And I have home-schooled my children their entire lives. We love learning at home and around the community. Actually, they are involved in volunteer work around here, maybe you have met them. And," I chuckled, "No one has called CPS on me . . . *yet*. Would you like to meet us at Starbucks sometime? You might find homeschool children much different than you thought."

She sputtered some kind of "never in a million years" while her friends giggled. Then they began asking me questions, the typical "How do you socialize?" and "Where do you get your books?" and "What do your children enjoy studying the most?" It was a delightful conversation with some really pleasant ladies.

After working out for a while, I realized that Prejudiced Lady wasn't around, so I asked her friends where she was. They pointed to the parking lot. I hightailed it out there and found her getting into her car. I stuck out my hand for a shake. "It really was nice talking with you and your friends. I hope there are no hard feelings." She nearly ran over my foot.

Critical people? Yeah, we'll meet them. I think back on my gym misunderstanding with humor now, though. People don't know the truth about each unique homeschool situation. And sometimes, they don't even want to know. But I have found—and you will too—that most people just don't understand. They are curious and want to know more. And there are a few mean people that can just make us laugh.

> Let others have their own opinion. You have your own mission.

Homeschooling is a secret club. We are the only ones who know what it is like on the inside. You are the only one who knows what is inside your own home. Keep your mission.

14.2.4 What if I become arrogant toward others with different school choices?

Choose not to judge others' schooling choices. Homeschooling is right for our family. We made the decision carefully and thoughtfully. We are convinced that right now this is what God wants us to do. We are living out our homeschool *why*. But not every family joins us. Public school, private school, co-op school, online public school . . . there are a myriad of educational choices. Parents choose each for a variety of reasons.

The problem is our strongly held convictions, the convictions we know are oh so right. The convictions we hold but our neighbor across the church aisle does not share. The life choice that is imperative for our family but not for our friend.

We are all so tempted to judge other families by the standard God gave us. We expect that our lifestyle is the same God planned for everyone. We make ourselves judge over others.

But this ought not to be.

Christ did not come to save us from the public school. Christ came to show us himself. God did not command us to homeschool our children. His greatest command is to love God and love others.

You will either want to hug me because I wrote that or close this book and never read it again. You may identify with the judgmentalism, or you may believe there is no middle ground.

Regardless of our beliefs on childhood education, there is one thing we must all agree on. We must all agree to love and to support and to pray for one another in the body of Christ (see Colossians 3:13-15). It is sin to look down on our brother over such a fine point (see Ephesians 4:31-32). God commands us to not quarrel over petty issues (see 2 Timothy 2:23-24). Many may feel strongly that homeschooling is a vital aspect of their Christian walk. But we can cause no division over something never explicitly preached in Scripture.

We demonstrate our faith not by our homeschooling but by our love (see John 13:35).

14.2.5 What if I judge other people's parenting?

Remember that homeschooling does not save us, and homeschooling does not save our children. It does not ensure that your child or my child will turn to Christ and walk the straight and narrow way. Each child, every young adult has her own free will and can decide whether or not to take your homeschooling to heart.

There are homeschoolers who reject Christ. There are homeschoolers who become atheists. There are homeschool graduates who turn to a life of crime. There are homeschoolers who engage in sexual immorality or homosexuality. I have met them.

Does this mean my homeschool friends have homeschooled wrong? Not at all. In every case, I have known the parents to teach and pray fervently. They did everything they could to train up their child in the way he should go. Yet, a young adult's decision is just that—her decision. Her parents did not make that decision for her. Nothing her parents could do *could* make that decision for her.

We do the best we can. We teach, we pray, we live our lives as lovingly as we know how. Are we perfect? Not a one of us. Are we covered in grace? Every one of God's children. Are we omniscient to judge our fellow homeschool family? God forbid.

Will our children be perfect? Will our homeschool friend's child live for Christ? Only God knows. And only he can change a sinner's heart.

14.3 RELATIONSHIP DANGERS

14.3.1 What if I strain my marriage?

Homeschooling is stressful. And much of that stress goes directly on our relationship with our spouse. I'm not going to tell you how you two should be one team and nothing can pull you apart if you are living in perfect harmony. That sentence would be no help whatsoever to either me or you.

Usually, one parent (probably you) is responsible for the majority of the homeschooling. That is a tremendous burden. It takes time, it takes effort, it takes mental stamina . . . it takes all the issues in this book and fifty million more. And we cannot handle that strain alone.

Then there is the non-homeschooling parent (known to us, many days, as the *lucky one*). He has no idea what life is like all day. He has never heard the cries of a child trying to learn addition with carrying. He has never seen the destruction that *is* the floor under the kitchen table after lapbooking. He has never known the terror of a morning science lesson without coffee. He has never lived a day in the life of a homeschool warrior.

My own husband brags that he can handle housework. And, indeed, he is great at watching all the children while cleaning the house and doing all the errands. I love to leave him alone for a weekend, actually, because the bathrooms will sparkle when I return. *But* . . . I have told him many times that his bragging does not count *until he can do all of that while homeschooling.* Amateur.

He just doesn't get it. So when I have the worst day ever in the history of homeschooling (see section 14.1.2), he can't appreciate how truly catastrophic that is. And then he doesn't understand why I'm crying. And then he suggests that tomorrow will be better when, quite frankly, I don't want there to even *be* a tomorrow. And then he wonders aloud why he isn't getting a good-night kiss.

I'm all out of kisses at that point.

We spend all day long with the bad children and the hard math and the strewn laundry (if your children are never bad, your math is always easy, and your laundry is folded neatly, please stop reading this book). All day long of that and we lose a little of our minds. Usually, the part that can think.

So when the husband, bless his heart, asks what's for dinner, he may get a box of cereal thrown at his head. And if the box hits him in the head, he will protest that you are overreacting. If he says you are overreacting, you may decide to *show* him overreacting by hysterically bursting into snotty tears. When he sees your hysterical breakdown, he may ask why you are crying. And *then*, my friend, you will know *he doesn't get it.*

And that is when things get dicey.

Because deep, deep down, we all know that he will never get it. He can't understand because he doesn't live it. Just like I cannot understand how my husband's banking center runs because I have never lived it. I have never undergone a bank audit, and he has never taught long division while siblings yell like banshees or explode science volcanoes all over the dining room. He's never graded an essay, and I've never counted a bank vault. We don't understand each other's lives.

But you know what? I don't need to know what goes on at my husband's bank to know that he is working hard for our family. And my husband doesn't need to understand the depth of my stress to love me. We do love each other, and that's what matters.

I can too often allow myself to become so focused on homeschooling and my work with my children that I forget the bigger picture—my family life. But I am reminded often by the sad stories around me that homeschooling does not save a marriage. In fact, it takes extra commitment to keep that relationship strong through the strain of homeschooling.

I personally know several homeschool couples, including my own parents, who ended in divorce at the end of their homeschooling career. I could point to several factors that contribute to this tragedy: burnout, overscheduling, loneliness, depression, fighting. But the real reason my friends divorced, the reason many homeschool couples divorce, is simple: *they stop putting each other first.* They let their marriage come second after jobs, ministry, and children. They protect other things to the detriment of their own marriage.

We simply cannot let this happen. Homeschooling is wonderful. I believe in homeschooling. I have spent nearly two decades homeschooling. I have invested years of my life mentoring and encouraging others in their homeschooling (and don't even ask me how long this book took!). *But none of that compares to my marriage.*

Please, I beg of you, never let your homeschooling become more important than your spouse. Don't cry that he will never understand. Don't say there is no time. Don't make excuses that he is not doing things right. Stop what you are doing right now—put this book down—and schedule marriage time. Invest in the most important relationship you will ever have.

None of this matters—none of it—without your spouse.[2]

14.3.2 What if my student doesn't work well with others?

Life isn't tailored to our children. Only homeschooling is. Some homeschool children are not prepared for life this way. You see them in an art gallery, unable to follow the docent's directions in an orderly fashion. You see them in the science museum, unsure how to take turns at the display. You find them on field trips, interrupting each other and failing to follow directions. They can't walk in a line (yes, there are times to do that), they can't stand a long time for their turn, they can't wait patiently to ask a question. They cannot obey instructions given to them by a stranger. They think the entire environment revolves around them personally.

In other situations, like ministry or classes, they find themselves unable to work in a group. They don't respect leaders outside their own family. They have not learned to collaborate, to respect other opinions, to negotiate outcomes. They become unable to function outside their own small circle.

We celebrate an educational option that allows each child to do what she wants and learn the way she does best. But in life, she must learn to adapt to others' behaviors and wishes. This ability must be taught.

We can protect our child from self-centeredness with careful training. Model negotiation and waiting one's turn not only in board games but also in daily life. Put her in situations where she must work with others on a project more difficult than she can do on her own. Give her opportunities to learn and to interact with others in a variety of situations.

When my children were young, I sought out opportunities for them to work in groups outside their normal circles. I took them to zoo days, museum tours, and farm events where they would interact, along with a large group of children, with adult guides. They had to follow instructions and share resources (crafts and displays) with other children. They had to learn to wait to ask their own question and to listen carefully to those of others.

Last year, I took my three youngest children on an art museum tour. We went as part of a group of homeschool families that I did not know. The tour was led by a museum docent. We were so excited to see a collection we had not yet enjoyed.

As the tour began, the docent encouraged interaction and questions. She asked for feedback and ideas, for what impressions the pieces were making on the children. At first, no one was conversing with the docent, so my children jumped right in. Since they had frequently toured art museums and had participated in guided tours of many venues, they were raring to go. They asked insightful questions, they challenged assumptions, they pointed out details, they tried to make connections with other works. . . . They had a ball discussing the pieces with the docent and with one another. In just the first room. "Um, let's move on to the next room before our time runs out," another mom said.

As we filed into the next gallery, my face reddened with embarrassment. "Do NOT ask or answer any more questions! Let the other children talk from now on!" I hissed in their ears.

We stood before a large mural. The docent simply asked, "What do you see in this piece?" You could hear a pin drop. "Anyone? Do you see a person or an object that you recognize?" My twins squirmed beside me. My older son groaned under his breath, shifting his weight from one foot to the other.

Over a dozen children, and not one said a word. "Pleeeeease let me say something!" my eleven-year-old pleaded in my ear.

"Okay, just one question, and nothing more."

He asked about the connection between two individuals on opposite sides of the mural and what their placement represented. The group stood with stony faces as the docent waved her arms with great animation, describing the movement of thought from left to right across the piece.

We were enraptured. A huge wall of creative thought. And three young children simply *dying* to question and respond to it.

The tour came to an end, and the mother in charge walked straight up to me. I wanted to drop into the museum floor. "I'm so sorry. I truly didn't want my children to dominate the conversation. They just got so excited. I'm working on this with them."

"Please don't apologize." She reached out and touched my arm. "None of us know how to train our children what to do in a museum. How do we look at the art? What do we say? What questions should we ask? Your children were the only ones who knew how to talk with the docent. Maybe you can teach us all how to do this better. How did you teach your children that?"

"We go to a lot of museums. We take a lot of tours. And we don't usually take homeschool tours; we try to interact with students of a variety of backgrounds learning in the same space. This way, students not only learn the content, but they experience how to talk about their learning in a group."

On the drive home, the youngsters chattered on about their favorite pieces and what they had learned. "What did the others like?" my youngest asked. "I wish they had said what they thought."

Sunday school classes, youth groups, volunteer organizations, jobs, and more offer great opportunities for our young people. In large groups, they become part of a community, a social circle that teaches them to work and share and learn together. Just like the rest of their lives.

14.3.3 What if I delay my young person's adulthood?

We need to be careful not to raise a twenty-one-year-old child. Homeschooling allows us to carefully control our child's exposure to the world, to shelter her from dangerous situations and relationships. But at some point, our young adult must launch out into the future God has for her. Not a future that means long-term dependence on her family and little interaction with the outside world. A future of maturity.

The high school years are an excellent opportunity to gradually train our young people to take responsibility and to overcome mistakes. I like to tell my teens that they can have increasing privileges and responsibilities as long as they continue learning from the consequences. I would rather they make mistakes while they have the safety net of their parents. While they are still at home, we can help them through the natural consequences. We don't diminish these necessary teaching opportunities. But we can help point them toward a resolution of each difficult situation.

Adulthood requires that our teens know how to navigate the world around them. Too many homeschoolers do not have any experience with adult responsibilities in young adulthood and become dependent on their parents for food, clothing, shelter, and information. We need to prepare our teen to launch successfully.

One of the valid criticisms of homeschooling is that we tend to shelter our children too much. One homeschool speaker goes so far as to declare no family should participate in activities that do not include the entire family. But instead of permanently tethering our child to the family, we can take advantage of the homeschool years to gradually launch our young person into adulthood. We must be actively training our young people

IS MY CHILD PREPARED FOR ADULTHOOD?

- Does my teen know how to converse with an adult confidently?

- Does my teen know how to apply for a job and how to keep it?

- Does my teen know how to take responsibility for his own schedule, including making and keeping his own appointments?

- Does my teen coordinate schedules and transportation with kindness and wisdom?

- Does my teen keep deadlines reliably?

- Does my teen take control of his finances, ministry responsibilities, and health appointments?

- Does my teen understand the value of money and the expense of adult life?

- Does my teen have a deadline for leaving the house and supporting himself?

for life outside the home. Not every young person is ready to leave the house at eighteen or twenty-one or twenty-four, but we should be preparing them intentionally toward that future—a life they live confidently before God.

14.3.4 What if I feel unable to accept my adult child's decisions?

Understand that you can't control him anymore. While homeschooling, we have the freedom to control our child's environment to a certain extent. And within our own family, we can enforce our rules and expectations with varying degrees of success. But when our child becomes a teen and then an adult, we lose all control whatsoever.

That is so, so scary.

We can't control his marriage. We can't determine his career path. We can't make his friends. We can't force him to attend church, to adhere to our personal standards, or restrict his activities. That adult is out there on his own, and there is nothing we can do about it.

He knows that, so he starts saying and doing things we don't like.

They may be little things, but they seem big. Or they may be drastic decisions, but we can't control them. Growing an adult all day, every day leads to quite high expectations.

As homeschool parents, we can become critical, then afraid, then angry at the choices our young people make. I know—my young teens and young adults have scared me a few times, and I have lashed out in anger more times than I have apologized for. But I was wrong.

My teens did and still do learn more from their own bad choices and harmful consequences than they do from my yelling. And my young adults mature more by making their own decisions than they would from my control.

Last night, my adult son told my husband and me about a decision he was making. We gave our advice and warned against one part of his decision. As the conversation progressed, we kept going back to the error he was making. He burst out, "I know what you said. This is what I'm going to do! Stop nagging me now."

"We aren't trying to nag," I backpedaled quickly. "We honestly thought you were asking our advice, and we didn't feel like you heard us."

"I heard you the first time. Please just tell me and move on."

We continued the rest of the conversation amicably and parted happy for his choice overall. But the conversation was a success and probably even strengthened our relationship because we listened to him say one important thing: *tell me, but leave me to do what I decide.*

This goes beyond lifestyle choices. It's also about morality and biblical life. It is important for us to remember: young adults have a free will before God. Each of us—including our own children—must develop our own relationship with God. That includes our worship, our decisions, and our actions. *I cannot be the Holy Spirit for my adult child.* He stands before God on his own.

So while we may not like or even agree with every decision our young adult makes, we have only two options: accept his right to make his own choices, or reject his decisions. Only one of those contributes to a healthy relationship with our adult child, a relationship that deepens our love for each other. More importantly, accepting that we cannot control our child's every decision helps grow our faith in the God who loves our child more than we ever could. He leads each one along.

14.3.5 What if I am still afraid of the socialization question?

We are all sick and tired of the "How do you socialize your children?" question. But after hearing it dozens of times, we can start to wonder . . . are my children actually socialized?

> Peoples is peoples.
>
> **PETE TO KERMIT THE FROG IN** *THE MUPPETS TAKE MANHATTAN*

Google told me that to socialize means to participate in social activities with other people. I think there are people in our homes with whom we can practice this. And there are people at church. And in the library. And at the grocery store. And on our street. And at playgroup. And on the homeschool field trip. And at co-op. And in the online class. And on the sports team. And in the art class . . .

Our children know people.

Unless you keep your child hiding under the table with the blinds drawn, he knows people. He can talk to people, he can empathize with people, he can interact with people.

Your child is socialized. Bam. Done with that task. Check that one off the list.

14.3.6 What if I become odd?

You probably will. All of us are weird. We don't want to be *too* weird, though, do we? But on the other hand, do we really know what *normal* means? Most of all, we are homeschooling just so our children are *not* like the rest of the world. So, there's that.

Are we different? Absolutely. Our purpose, our methods, and our outcome are vastly different from those of people around us. Our friends and neighbors will know us by this difference.

But we don't need to raise oddballs.

Homeschoolers have a reputation for looking and behaving a certain way. We make fun of the stereotypes and even resent them. But these prejudices are there for a reason—homeschoolers sometimes act just plain weird. Some may dress inappropriately for the occasion or loudly protest against the behavior of those around them. Unfortunately, as a community, we sometimes draw the wrong attention.

My children and I were at the library along with another family who were obviously homeschoolers. You can always spot them—at the library during nonpeak hours checking out way too many books. The young man chose several nonfiction books off the shelf near us, and his mother walked over to check on his reading selection.

"WHAT IS THIS?! A biography of Barack Obama! Why did you choose such a thing? There is no way you should be reading that. WE ARE CHRISTIANS! WE DON'T READ THAT!" the woman shouted so the entire library could hear.

My children and I sat at the table beside them in shock. And we remained in shock as the family checked out their stacks of books and stomped out the door. Finally, my daughter remarked, "I should never tell her about my biographies of Stalin and Mao Tse-tung."

I was confused and embarrassed. I was also grateful that we had established a long-running, cheerful relationship with our librarians. Surely they knew we homeschoolers weren't *all* angry, biography-burning critics.

Of course, there are many aspects of our culture (and selections at our libraries) to which we strongly object. However, gentle and quiet teaching in private does so much more than ostentatious ranting.

Beyond learning to socialize appropriately, our children need to recognize the needs of others and reach out to meet those needs tangibly. We can help our children grow in this area by signing them up to serve in church. They need to not merely attend children's programs and sing in choirs. They need to also serve behind the scenes in nursery or VBS. They need to help with younger children and serve the elderly members. They need to understand that church is not just there to meet their needs but also for them to meet the needs of others.

They need to do the same for their community. We all depend on each other in the neighborhood around us. But even though we are home all day, it is easy to remain isolated from our neighbors. We can teach our children not just to get to know those around them but also to serve them. They can help out with yard work, pet walking, plant watering, and more. My son made a huge impact on one neighbor by regularly visiting her elderly mother who was at home on hospice care. By showing care and compassion to those around us, we teach our children to become contributing members of their community.

14.3.7 What if I begin isolating my family?

We want to protect our children—but that protection can too easily turn into isolationism. We homeschool because we want to keep the glory of God before and in our children. We want God to control our hearts and minds. But we forget that God wants us out there, involved in the world he created.

We live within a broader society. We are part of God's larger world. He calls us not to insulate ourselves from what he is doing, but instead to engage in the community around us. He commands us to go out to all nations, starting with the one we live in right now. To reach others in our own Jerusalem, to walk in our own city. We do not help the cause of Christ by hiding from the world. We do not help the ministry of our family by hiding our children. God wants to boldly use us where we are.

That's why, instead of isolating our family, we need to actively teach our children how God is working. They need to learn about sin and what temptations they will face in the world. They need to know how to make decisions for God without resorting to legalism. They need to practice going out into the community without overprotection, to have the opportunity to practice their own convictions.

We need to teach our children about the religions and philosophies of not only the past but also the present. They need to understand the basics of why others believe differently so they can know how their God is different.

We need to teach our children that others have different views on biblical issues. We need to model for them respect for differences in doctrine and practice. We need to fight sectarianism by demonstrating the unity of God's church.

We need to teach our children to have compassion for all people, not just those of the same background, social status, race, and church. They need to learn from us how Jesus befriended sinners and how to do the same. They need to learn how to live alongside their unsaved friends in a relationship that walks them toward God.

We need to teach our children what is right without vilifying other people. They need to know how to speak of others—even those in grave sin—with kindness and respect. They need to know how to differentiate between truth and bigotry.

We need to teach our children how to give. Isolating ourselves takes our abilities and our beliefs and keeps them all for ourselves. Instead, we must reach out to give hope and help in the community. We must show our children how to be good neighbors and good citizens in our own town.

We need to teach our children God's view of the world. Jesus, the perfect Son of God—totally separate from us sinners in every possible way—lived in this world and died to save it.

We need to stop isolating ourselves and instead joyfully send out our children to be God's love for the world.

•   •   •

Homeschooling is a beautiful life choice we can and should celebrate. At the same time, we need to be humble about the real difficulties and pitfalls inherent in the homeschool lifestyle. Be proud to homeschool! And be proactive to reach out, get help, and stay focused on your *why*—because homeschooling is important, but loving God and loving your family is oh so much more.

15

MAKING HOMESCHOOL
LIFE EASIER

HOMESCHOOLING IS A LIFESTYLE. But sometimes we think it's gonna kill us. Here's an example of today's killer routine:

- Work on the difference between *saw, seen, brought,* and *bring* with the twins. Discourage them from putting their heads in their hands and groaning when they realize that they can use them correctly in conversation but not on paper.
- Let the dogs out.
- Quiet down five people doing their schoolwork aloud in the same room.
- Look for pencils.
- Go back to working on verb usage.
- Someone has to use the bathroom.
- Start math. Remind children that they do know most of their multiplication facts, even the ones they breezed through yesterday but can't remember today.
- *Who let the dogs out?* Let them back in again.

- Review adding three-digit numbers.
- Look for rulers.
- Give up and use one-inch tiles to measure line segments.
- Look for pencils again.
- Ask the one practicing the piano to do so quietly.
- Take ibuprofen.
- Give apple slices to the ones dying of hunger.
- Spend five minutes looking for the map workbooks.
- Stop the dog from chewing on a workbook.
- Question the meaning of life.
- Pour another mug of coffee.
- Try one more time.
- Look at the clock and see it has only been forty minutes.

As homeschool parents, we experience unique challenges while we merge learning with our everyday lives. We can, though, overcome these bumps in the road with some creativity and planning. While not every mom will face these issues the same way, I'll share some strategies that help our family enjoy living with homeschooling. I have survived while home-schooling. At least I think I'm alive most days.

15.1 SELF-CARE

15.1.1 How do I take care of myself in the midst of this chaos?
Creatively. An important part of homeschooling is, indeed, **self-care**. This can mean anything from praying and meditating on a verse of Scripture, to eating properly, finding a few minutes to get outside and move a little (even if, like me, it's just strolling slowly around the block), or prioritizing seven to nine hours of sleep. Taking long enough showers to begin breathing again and to even use shampoo. All these things seem like luxuries, but if we homeschool moms do not take care of our bodies, our minds will suffer, and then our patience, and then our homeschool *why*. Self-care is the routine to start with before others.

Spend time alone planning. Get a general idea of what you want to accomplish that week or that year. Take a deep breath and create your small steps. Dream about the future, what you would like to feel and see and know next year and at the end of your homeschool journey. Get a positive outlook—a realistic idea—of where God is taking you and your family.

Contact with other homeschool moms is a tremendous encouragement. We all need a shoulder to cry on sometimes, someone to commiserate with, bounce ideas off of, or hug in encouragement. It is very important to find homeschool friend support.

> He who calls you is faithful; he will surely do it.
>
> **1 THESSALONIANS 5:24**

Get away from your family. Take an hour to hide in the closet or the coffee shop. Maybe put aside some money for a weekend alone at a local hotel. I set aside a fund each year to fly out of town to my friend's house for a few days. Get to the place where your mind is refreshed, your outlook is more positive, and you even miss your children . . . at least a little bit.

But most of all, remember that God called you, and he will enable you. He has planned this journey for your life just as he has planned it for your children.

God does not—he does NOT—intend you to lay down your life for homeschooling. Your lessons, your plans, your child's academics, even your child's happiness are NOT more important than your relationship with God AND your care for the temple of your body he gave you. Homeschool Mom, we too often martyr ourselves for our holy cause. But we cannot endure through the long journey unless we care first for what God has given us.

Self-care need not be selfishness. There is a balance, and let's err on the side of responsibility. I'm not telling you to run away from home very often. I'm begging you to enable yourself, with God's power, to continue doing his will in your life. If you shoot yourself in the foot, you won't be able to run the race.

God will, then, give you strength using your own individual talents and abilities. This is why your own homeschooling will look so different from that of your friends. You are homeschooling the way God intended you to.

15.1.2 How do I get into a routine?

First of all, decide if you even want one. Some moms do, and some moms just prefer to go with the flow. There is no law that says you need a routine.

You probably don't really want to follow a strict schedule. When you make yourself a schedule, you will surely get behind. When you get behind on your schedule, you will rush through something to catch up. When you rush through something to catch up, you will become frustrated and your child will become frustrated. When you and your child become frustrated, you will have a bad homeschool day. When you have a bad homeschool day, you will want more chocolate. When you want more chocolate, you will find you ate it all yesterday. When you do not find chocolate, you will lie on the kitchen floor and give yourself up for lost.

Don't lie down on the kitchen floor in a comatose state. Throw away your schedule.

If you are trying to set a new routine, be gentle with yourself. Try a simple morning routine. Maybe add an evening routine. Different sections of your day may fall into a nice rhythm. Most of all, do not try to copy someone else's routine exactly. Your family culture is unique, and so is your family. Check out some sample routines in appendix B to get some ideas.

It is most important to remain flexible. Daily life changes with interruptions, difficult assignments, exciting science experiments, historical discoveries, spring fever, and the flu. No matter what comes, God gives grace for each day's excitement.

15.1.3 How do I homeschool around a busy schedule?

Know what's essential—and what can be cut. I don't know a homeschool family that does not have a busy schedule. Simply adding teaching to your lifestyle immediately increases your workload, yet for some reason, no one compensates you by adding more hours to your day. Hours you might like to use catching up on your sleep. Even if we fight overscheduling (see section 14.1.4), we find there is not enough time to use the bathroom. Seriously. My husband did not understand why I used to greet him at the door with, "GREAT! Stand here and supervise so I can finally use the bathroom!"

> Commit your work to the
> LORD, and your plans
> will be established.
>
> PROVERBS 16:3

"Why don't you just go to the bathroom when you need to?"

"You have no idea what my life is like."

I said *used to* only because my children are older now, so I know they can find the front door when they set the house on fire.

When my schedule gets crazy, I make a chart on paper with the days of the week separated into hours from 8:00 a.m. to 8:00 p.m. Then I start filling it up to see what is left. There's usually nothing left. That's when I am forced to cut things out.

There are several nonnegotiable items in your family schedule. You have to sleep (whether you like it or not). You have to eat, which means taking time to cook or to pick up tacos. You have to clean the house just a little, you have to buy groceries, you have to make appointments. Those tasks need to go into your schedule first. Then you have your work and ministry. Those hours are usually dependent on other people, so they are set in stone on your calendar.

> All your children shall be taught by the LORD, and great shall be the peace of your children.
>
> ISAIAH 54:13

So now we have the time left over to homeschool. You may find a few hours in the morning, the afternoon, or both. You may be relieved to find your time set out. Or you may worry you don't have enough hours.

The longer you homeschool, however, the better you will become at simplifying your lessons. As you find how you teach best for the way your student learns best, you will also discover where you need to spend more time and how to best handle difficulties. You will find that in some subjects or assignments your student needs very little help from you. Your early learners will spend less school time and learn more through play. Your older students will become more independent. Soon, your teaching time will become more concentrated, more focused on what your child really needs.

If you are spending eight hours a day homeschooling, you may be doing it wrong. Even an institutional school with extra time for assemblies and busywork and walking between classes teaches a large group of children in less time. Don't push yourself.

"But my child needs more help," you say. Then he also needs a break. Let him learn over a longer period of time instead of cramming it into one or two sessions. If that means taking a year's curriculum and spreading it out over eighteen months, then so be it. You are teaching your own individual child, a child who doesn't need to feel burdened by learning. He will learn faster and better in the long run if you take your time.

This is the key to homeschooling a busy family: do not make your homeschooling busy. Let your child relax and enjoy learning. And then you will relax and enjoy teaching. Homeschool at the speed of your own family.

15.1.4 Do homeschool moms need to sleep?

We do need to sleep. This is the first principle of homeschooling while busy. The busier you are, the more important your sleep is. Yet we all are tempted to work a little later into the night or to get up super early in the morning to catch up on our housework or just to spend time without the children for a few precious minutes. And maybe shower. Hey, I get it.

But sleep is a nonnegotiable. For one thing, it is vital for our health. If we allow ourselves to become too tired and run down, we are susceptible to illness. Also, we then need to compensate for our lack of energy by eating more calories, and that causes other (ahem) problems in all of us.

Just as important as our physical health is our mental health. And we cannot function at our sharpest without some good sleep. Algebra problems and phonics rules are hard enough without trying to figure them out while impersonating a zombie. The pressures of life plus homeschooling can drag us down into darkness if we are not physically resilient.

Our emotional health is dependent on sleep. And this is perhaps the first and worst symptom of fatigue. We become frustrated and burned out. We find ourselves impatient with our children. We lose all the joy in homeschooling when we are just too tired.

How much do we need to sleep? Well, more than the five or six hours we are tempted to clock. Your body will likely tell you how much you need if you try several days in a row with no alarm clock. I have gotten to the point where I jealously guard my eight hours of sleep every night. I cannot function without it. Some of my homeschool mom friends make fun of me for saying, "I've got to go! Bedtime!" at nine o'clock. But I need to take care of myself (see section 15.1.1) if I'm going to remain stable while homeschooling.

15.2 HEALTH

15.2.1 How do I homeschool when my child or I am sick?

Don't. Homeschoolers get to take sick days, too. Some homeschool moms try sofa-homeschooling, having the sick child read or work quietly while lying down. That has never worked well for me. I can't find the balance between "you poor thing, get well soon" and "concentrate on this lesson."

Could the child drag out the sickness to get out of work? She may try. Most illnesses, though, have a general time frame for recovery. And we moms can often discern when the symptoms have pretty much subsided. Just go with your gut on when to ease back into studies.

What about a child with chronic illness? Now homeschooling is a blessing. Just as if the child were well, you can simply work at the child's own pace. Adjust how many years you spend on a textbook; you may take two years to finish a fifth-grade English book and then move into middle school work. Or you may just stay at the child's pace for the usual number of books and not worry at all about the move-up or graduation dates. You may enjoy reading aloud for a while. The most important principle is *don't worry about the pace of your homeschooling*. Do what you can—which may be nothing for a time—and then do what you can later. Your child's health is most important.

What about when *you* are sick? For Pete's sake, stop homeschooling and take care of yourself. Otherwise, you will be cranky at best and at worst, you will be even sicker. And that will likely draw out the sickness or pain even longer. Just put the books down, put a DVD on (educational, if you must), and lie on the sofa under a cozy blanket. The housekeeping may go to pot, and you may serve cereal for dinner, but you will get better eventually. Remember, there is no such thing as falling behind in homeschooling. Just do your best with what you have.

15.2.2 Can I homeschool if I'm on bed rest?

I did. It is not easy, but it is doable. I have been on bed rest with three of my pregnancies, nearly the entire time with my fourth. I know this is tricky. Just like other difficult times, this is not the season to press forward zealously. Rather, this is the time to love your middle child the most! (Sorry, my son got ahold of my manuscript. Don't worry, I just sent him back to do his math.)

As I was saying, this is the time to simplify and wait for the future. There are a few strategies that might help you gently homeschool during this time:

- **Do as little as possible if you are able to do anything.** Remember that early learning should be very minimal, anyway. Elementary subjects repeat the same content in more detail every year, so your student won't miss anything with a lighter treatment of the basics or even time away from it all. Your older students can be fairly independent, and you may be able to supervise them from your bed or ask your husband to look over the work. Let a little one crawl into bed and read with you. Explain nouns and verbs briefly each day until the elementary guy understands it. Drill multiplication facts. Make a goal of just one or two things to learn each week, and slowly make progress.

- **Focus on the basics if you must do something.** For most of your children, reading and math are enough for a while. If you are feeling really ambitious, maybe do some reading about science and history. I worked only on English and math while I was on bed rest and had my young learner practice phonics with me for fifteen minutes a day. We picked right up the following year.
- **Get a ride to co-op.** This is just what co-op is for—supporting your homeschooling. Ask another mom to shuttle your child back and forth for the time being.
- **Use a DVD or online schooling.** This is a great option if you feel guilty about older students. You can watch a DVD or online video together or let your student participate in an online class. Maybe you'll want to just enjoy snuggling in bed with documentaries and popcorn.
- **Find a babysitter.** Grandma or the teen across the street or a friend from church might come over for just an hour or two regularly. Let your helper check the math homework, go over the basics of fractions, supervise a science experiment, or grade a history test.
- **Consider doing nothing.** During one pregnancy, I ended up pushing all the books off my bed and concentrating on living and loving my family until after the baby was born. I felt guilty for about one day. Then I realized that (a) my health and my unborn baby's health were the most important, and (b) I could have *faith* that God would take care of everything later. And sure enough, we soon picked right up where we left off and caught up to where I felt comfortable in no time.
- **Rest and take care of yourself.** This may seem repetitious, but you need to believe it. There is a reason you are on bed rest. And that

reason is not to see how much you can do while lying on your side. The single most important thing you can do is to care for your own health and your baby's health. That is how you care for your family, too. Never, never, never let homeschooling get in the way of taking care of people.

15.2.3 How do I homeschool through mental and emotional pain?

I want to reach right through this page and hug you tight. I know that pain too. The pain of trauma, the pain of fear, the pain of depression, the unspeakable pain that can never be shared. I know the tears and the confusion. That's why I talked about this danger in section 14.1.16. And that's why I'm talking about it again now.

Mental anguish and mental illness are real. Dealing with parenting and homeschooling on top of it does not make things better.

In some respects, homeschooling can help. It gets me out of bed most days. It makes me look into my children's eyes and see my reason to keep going. It gives me hope that maybe the future will be clearer than the present darkness.

Homeschooling feels confusing when our brains are clouded by pain. I know that. Again, focusing on the simple basics sometimes helps. Make a list of what essentials you most want to cover. Ask your husband or your friend to check on you that you are still moving forward.

I set timers. I might try to spend fifteen minutes on reading. I may try to spend thirty minutes going over grammar. By concentrating on something else for a limited time I can increase my focus. This also helps me get out of my head and think about something else on those tough days.

I set a minimum subject requirement each day. One day, I make myself cover English and history. Another day, math and science. The children might do work in the other subjects, but those days I just make myself check work and teach those minimum areas.

I keep track of what we do. Recording the progress my children made, the difficulties we overcame, the concepts we conquered provides some light on my homeschool days. Over time, I can appreciate what I have done, even if it seemed little. I can see where God has carried us forward.

I get help. It took me entirely too long to learn to reach out, though. Once I got the counseling and care I needed, life slowly became clearer. And only then did homeschooling grow easier. I regained the joy of spending those hours with my children, resumed working toward my homeschool *why* with purpose and tenacity until I found the joy again. *Please, please, please if you struggle with panic, anxiety, depression, or other mental illness, you must reach out to your pastor, your nearby counselor, and your doctor until you find help.*

I fear there is still a stigma in the homeschool community attached to emotional scarring and mental illness. Yet statistics tell us that 20 percent of us are living with mental illness. That is one out of five of us, including your homeschool friends. That might be you. It is time we stopped judging, quit hiding, and helped one another through this, one of the most difficult trials homeschool moms face. God can and will work healing in the minds and spirits of suffering—and overcoming—homeschool moms. And God can give us all grace to uphold one another in love and prayer.

15.3 FAMILY

15.3.1 How can I handle this constant interaction with my child? I mean, I love him and all that stuff, but all day, every day feels like overkill.

Remember why you are doing this, and trust God for the outcome. Hey, I hear ya, sister. I have homeschooled up to five children at once (we adopted the twins after my oldest had graduated), and they seemed to never leave me nor forsake me. Remember that story from chapter 5 about the screaming in the front yard?

But here's the thing: I actually love those annoying people I call my children. Sometimes they are funny. Sometimes they are endearing. Sometimes they may even be helpful around the house. But more than that, they are my people, the people God gave me, and I just love them.

Did you know that your child is asking himself the very same question? That he is wondering how he can survive being around *you* all day, every day? And the older he gets, the more he asks himself, *Can I handle Mom much longer?* He loves you, but he does not want to be joined at the hip with you. So someday, he will pack up and leave for his own place, and you and I and every other homeschool mom will cry and wish we could live through this childhood stage all over again. (Do I sound like one of those old people?)

This present struggle to live together boils down to communication issues between you and your child. You both feel discouraged, annoyed, and stifled at times, and yet you will both have good days too. Trust God, stay hydrated, and focus on communicating positive emotions to your child. You don't need to love every day of homeschooling, but you can trust the next day will be better. "You are right, Son. I completely hate algebra. But we need to finish this, so finish it we will. Let's see if together we can't do just one more lesson and then get a cookie. I know this book will be finished at one point, and won't that feel really good?"

Everyone tells you that old cliché: "You'll miss these years someday!" But the fact of the matter is, yes, it feels like too much right now. In the following pages I'm going to tell you how to make it less painful. In the meantime, remember why you are doing this and stock up on chocolate and potato chips.

15.3.2 How do I homeschool a child who hates homeschooling?

Nearly all of us face this issue at some point in our homeschooling. A child is belligerent and refuses to do his homework and to listen to the lessons we try to teach. He just seems impossible to homeschool.

That child actually *is* impossible to homeschool. It is physically and mentally impossible to teach someone who does not want to learn. He obviously cannot learn if he refuses to, and we cannot force him to learn. We try, but it does not work.

So what are we to do with this stubborn child? Throw him out the window?

Actually, my children are usually too heavy for me to throw at this stage, so I ask my husband to throw them out the window. He always refuses, and I am disappointed.

There are several reasons a child may quit learning. But no matter what caused his learning strike, he may still need to learn one miserable life truth: we all have to work at things we don't like. In the housework, jobs, teaching children . . . there are myriads of things we need to do that we don't always enjoy. Sometimes we downright hate them. Teaching an unteachable child approaches that level.

Before you can improve the issue, consider what started it off. For example, your child may have reached a point in his studies that **seems**

too hard. He is discouraged from moving forward because the work seems impossible to him. No one wants to work long and hard at a job with no hope of a positive outcome. That's just ridiculous.

He may be completely **bored with the work**. The subject matter may make his brain freeze. The curriculum may make him want to gouge his eyes out. Homeschooling in general may have lost its fascination.

He may be **going through puberty**. This is a terrible time to home-school. Besides the unbelievable smell emanating from the kitchen table, the mood swings make consistent progress nearly impossible. The more stubborn his attitude, the less he wants to keep struggling through his work. His own emotions sabotage his efforts.

He may have a **learning disability**. Even a student who does great in his studies for several years may display learning issues later. In this case, you'll want to get him the support he needs (see chapter 16).

Finally, he may be **growing up**. As your teen approaches adulthood, he begins the very natural process of individuating. Teens need to establish their own personhood separate from their parents. So as the young person struggles with how to be different from and autonomous from his parents, that pushing away from us results in also pushing away from his school assignments. This sets him up for a power play over his studies. He probably did not come out of his room one day deciding, "I will define myself by never doing math again." But as he tries to be different, he begins asserting different priorities. And making homeschooling a low priority is very tempting.

All of these issues could set us as parents against our young people. We need them to learn, and they don't seem to want to learn. They may need help, or they may even need outward motivation. We went through some ideas for motivating preteens and teens in sections 12.3 and 13.3. Here are some consequences that stubborn students may face:

- **He might lose privileges.** In our house, if you don't have time to study, you don't have time to enjoy screens or to hang out with friends.
- **He might lose money.** Grades are worth money if the student goes to college. Getting mostly As will help him qualify for academic scholarships. Bs lower the scholarship level. Cs endanger receiving any money at all. Especially for a teen paying for all or part of his education, this could impact his choice of college.

- **He might lose valuables.** The keys to the car. His sports or clubs. His job. His free time.
- **He might grow up ignorant.** This does not seem to be much of a motivation for many teens at first. The entire reason they quit studying is that they simply don't care. But if your child hangs out with friends who *are* doing well in school, public or homeschool, he may begin to feel embarrassed when his own knowledge does not compare.

A stubborn student is very discouraging. I don't know a parent with an unteachable child who is not frustrated with the attitude. But somehow, we need to find a way to separate *ourselves* from our child and his decision. Because a stubborn attitude *is* his decision. Again, we simply cannot force him to learn. We can only set out the information, give him a way to learn it, and let him make a decision whether or not to apply himself.

Only God can change your child's heart. Until then, trust him and pray.

15.3.3 How do I homeschool a large family?

Homeschooling more than two children offers unique challenges. It often feels like running a three-ring circus in which the entertainers are consistently doing the wrong thing and falling down. But with a few simple strategies, I have found the chaos can be managed somewhat into a workable—and sometimes fun—homeschool environment.

Set a homeschool routine. A strict schedule is doomed to failure; someone is sure to mess things up. But a general routine helps everyone know what to do next and to mentally prepare for their next job. I put the more foundational subjects (for me, English and math) toward the beginning, so if we don't get to everything, I feel like I accomplished the biggies. Look at section 15.1.3 and appendix B for some ideas.

Teach your children, especially the older ones, to be flexible. Every day is a different adventure, and everyone just needs to roll with it. Remind them that it is okay if you skip an activity today. Stay positive when the day does not work out according to plan. Get used to saying, "maybe tomorrow" or "maybe next week."

Set time limits. With a large family, a long subject can easily wear everyone out and make all of you cranky. I have found that setting a time limit on each subject keeps all of us sane. Until the older children can tackle their subjects with near independence, the whole family will benefit from regular breathers. And even students studying on their own need breaks. I keep an eye on the clock or even set a timer. Whatever is left over can be tackled the next day. Homeschooling does not get better with cramming, anyway.

Learn subjects together. All or some of the children might learn from the same topics and the same curriculum at the same time. I purposefully bought a history curriculum that allows all of my children to study the same topics just to different depths. Now we can discuss the same events and themes all together, and everyone benefits from each other's perspective. I teach all of my elementary children the same science. All of my children, from elementary to high school, listen to the same read-alouds. Combining as much as possible helps save my time and my sanity.

Teach your children to work independently. This is a necessary skill as our children grow up, anyway. I start encouraging some independence in the mid-elementary years. With a little help and oversight, my children who are reading can do some of their work on their own until they need me to explain new concepts, help work through difficult questions, check their work, or give a test.

Work round-robin style. I love to teach my students all together around the kitchen table. It can become confusing sometimes, but when I can pull it off, this feels like the most *homeschoolish* thing we do. After our Bible reading and time with read-alouds or group lessons, I sit my children all around the table and get out their English assignments. The youngest work on their assignment one-on-one with me while I keep an eye on the others doing their work. I ask everyone to at least *try* to figure out the assignment during this short period (remember that early learners and elementary students shouldn't be working very long, anyway?). Then the youngest trace letters, color, or if they can, read quietly while I check the next youngest child's work. I can answer his questions or look over what he is doing to make sure he is going in the right direction. Then I move on to the next oldest child, who may just need a quick check-in. I ask my children not to move on to another subject until the little ones are done with their time (usually only twenty minutes or less, right?) or I'm satisfied the older ones have had enough help to finish on their own later. If someone needs a lot of help, we may put the assignment aside to work on later in the day. Keeping everyone on the same subject helps me not get too confused, but you may be smart enough to let the older children keep working at their own pace. If anyone finishes early, they might play quietly nearby, grab a snack, or read.

After I'm satisfied with my few minutes of English, we get out the math books and start the circle again. This time, I'm likely to have the little ones work with manipulatives, tangrams, or building toys when their time is done with me while I work with the older children. After the basic subjects are finished, everyone works on science or history. Since history is reading-intensive for the older ones, they usually save that for the afternoon and tackle science first. If anyone has an experiment, I stop the whole crew so they can join the excitement. I am finished hands-on teaching by lunchtime most days. This is how I taught when all of my children were in elementary school and middle school. The key is to keep the assignments simple and appropriate for their age and attention level.

This is just one strategy, though. It totally may not be for you. There were years when I worked with the littles all at once for an hour and then moved on to the older children. When I had a baby or toddler, I would do what I could in the morning while the little one sat on my lap or played alone. But much of my one-on-one work was during nap times. And most of all, I held elementary studies lightly during this season. Remember what we said in chapters 10 and 11: younger students should not be spending much pencil time, anyway.

Keep a sense of humor. Homeschooling can get a little crazy with several children at once. We may multiply the mistakes, but we definitely multiply the fun. If you can laugh your weird days off, the homeschool time will be a happy memory after these all-too-fleeting years pass. I'm not going to give you the cliché "cherish these years because you will want them back" speech. I'll just tell you . . . I want them back like you can never know.

15.3.4 I'm so busy taking care of the house and homeschooling multiple children and even working. How can I stay available to each child?

Focus on giving them small chunks. For the first weeks or months of homeschooling, your child *will* need more of your time to learn what homeschooling means, practice how to learn on his own, and adjust to the basic rhythm of learning. Be patient as everything else in your life seems to fall by the wayside.

Your home may look like a tornado hit it, or even worse—like mine.

You may be eating take-out tacos and frozen dinners for a few weeks. You may be arranging for others to pick up your children for soccer practice. You may even need to take some days off of work. But in a few days or a couple of weeks, you and your child will begin to find your own personal way of doing school at home.

Don't underestimate what your older children can do on their own. While you are teaching younger children how to read, write, and understand math, a teen can be reading a history assignment or even trying a science experiment alone. As they grow, your younger children will begin taking less of your time, and soon your older children will become more and more independent.

As all of this happens, you will find breathing room between teaching lessons. Use this time to answer a quick question, read some directions, and admire the mess of a science experiment gone horribly wrong. And then you may see, day by day, that you are spending more and more one-on-one time with each child. Regardless, do not criticize yourself for not spending an entire day with each child separately. Remember, in a classroom setting, each child receives very little or no one-on-one teaching. You are teaching your children just right.

15.3.5 How do I homeschool with babies and toddlers in the house?

With a lot of humor. And unbreakable objects nearby. And a growing tolerance for background noise. I have nursed and wrangled toddlers for many years of my own homeschooling, and once again, I would do it all over again in a heartbeat. Most of what we talked about in the previous section applies here too.

- **Hold your routine very loosely.** Most days, it just won't happen.
- **Don't spend much time homeschooling.** Seriously, my homeschool mornings were very short during those years. Fortunately, my children were very young, so they did not have long lessons anyway. Most moms wish their older children were more independent while they have babies, but teaching very young children brief lessons reminds us of what is important.
- **Hold your baby often.** This is not the time to worry about spoiling your child with too much attention. He's not getting much while

you absently let him sit on your lap, anyway. As long as he can sit or lie fairly still, he can just hang out there until your legs are numb.

- **Teach during nap time.** I know nap time may be very short, but, again, the younger children should only have short lessons, and the older children are more independent.
- **Use the normal baby-quieters more than usual.** Those swings, baby bouncers, and playpens are your best friends. The baby will not suffer from some alone time.
- **Let siblings play with the youngest.** You probably have some built-in babysitters, if only for a few brief minutes.
- **Hire a babysitter.** I never needed this option because my babies were unusually happy to homeschool and routinely napped, but many homeschool moms love and cherish their babysitter. Even an hour once or twice a week could make a big difference.
- **Teach during nursing/feeding or snack time.** These keep the baby or toddler busy for about twenty minutes, perfect for listening to a young reader or checking a math page.
- **Don't worry about homeschooling this year.** When my fourth baby was born, I declared it a light homeschool year. My other children were in early learning and elementary, so I knew that anything they would have been working on would just be repeated in more detail the next year. They did some work each day, but I did not push them to do every subject or every page. When I relaxed, I found that my children began to love learning even more, and they each grew at their own rate. And I was right; the next year was a great homeschooling year for everyone. Most importantly, I cherished that special time with my children.

15.3.6 Can I homeschool if I'm single?

I know several single homeschool moms. Many of them talked to me about their homeschool lives while I was writing this book. They all have the same reason for homeschooling: they are committed to giving their child the best possible education.

If you are a single mom, you are considering single-parent homeschooling for different reasons. You may be widowed. You may have lost your marriage while you were in the midst of homeschooling, so you've continued on. Perhaps you removed your children from school because of special needs or abilities. As a single mom, you will teach your own way too. Some single moms teach using classical, Charlotte Mason, text-book, unschooling, or online methods. All of them say they adapt their teaching—and their schedules—to how their child learns best.

Single homeschool moms are hardworking. Most work full-time at home, though some work out of the home. They have all different jobs at all different hours—day, afternoon, and night. As a single mom, you might feel lonely. Because homeschooling means you are working the equivalent of two full-time jobs, you might not have time for homeschool activities, support groups, or moms' nights out. Married homeschool moms, don't exclude these single friends from your fellowship—they desperately need our help and support.

One single friend says the key is to think outside the box. You may teach in the afternoons or on the weekends. You may get help with the children or help with the housework. You may need to work odd hours. But you can make it work because you are so committed.

Married homeschool moms, remember that this is the most important trait of these heroic moms. They are committed to homeschooling so much that many of them fight for custody and in other legal battles for the chance to teach their children at home. They continue on even though they have little support and little help. They are lonely, overworked, and exhausted.

But they are very committed.

One of the greatest opportunities right now for homeschool groups across the nation is to seek out, reach out, and support the single home-school moms in our communities. They could use help around the house, rides for their children, childcare, and friendship. This is a chance for us all to be the hands and feet of Jesus.

15.4 DADS

15.4.1 How can my husband be involved in homeschooling?

Your husband can and should be involved. Oh, my word, your husband should be involved in homeschooling. Husbands are there to be involved in everything, right? They got us into this whole child-rearing mess in the first place.

Your man can share the responsibility of teaching. Not all guys are excited about this, but it can really take a load off of you. And just tell him how much expertise he has and how much the children love spending time with him . . . it sometimes works. My homeschool dad taught me high school science and math. And now my husband helps my children with Spanish and South American history.

Dad can also be a great sounding board. Sometimes a mom just needs someone to listen while she thinks out loud about some new idea or curriculum or program or something. He can sit across the table at Olive Garden and listen with rapt attention while she spouts off dreams of new curricula and extracurricular activities and field trips and science projects and cheesecake. That is a big help.

Father of the Year can be a problem solver. There are days when we want to run from the house screaming in front of the judgmental neighbors. There are dark, stormy days when we can't send the little ones outside, so they destroy our knickknacks and our last nerve. There are (let's whisper it clandestinely) days when we want to quit.

That's when your knight in shining armor really . . . um . . . shines. Run those problems past him, cry over algebra in front of him, rant about the preteen attitude up in his face. Just go for it. Then throw your hands in the air and cry, "What can I do?"

Those are man-magic words. Men love to fix problems. And so he will mention how he would have done it better in the first place, but it is not too late to follow his wisdom. And after muttering under your breath, you may find he has some good ideas there.

I cannot tell you how many times I have ranted and raved to my husband. My children could give you an approximation, though, because apparently our bedroom door is kind of thin. But he never fails to give me a fresh perspective and a new idea or two. And, just like when homeschooling was all his idea, he always challenges me to try his suggestion "just a little while." Even though I am bound and determined to prove him wrong because he underestimates the gravity of the problem I have blown out of proportion . . . almost every time he is right.

So what can you do to get your husband involved?

Ask for help. This seems obvious, but it is easy to forget to even let him know you need him. All day long you manage a household and homeschooling by yourself, and even though you need help, you might forget there is someone right there for you. Sometimes, all you need to do is ask. Much of the time when I am overly frustrated in my homeschooling it is because I am trying to do it all on my own without God's or my husband's help. And that is not God's plan at *all*.

Ask for advice. Since you are doing the homeschooling all day, you might assume you know everything there is to know about homeschooling. But the fact of the matter is, when you become absorbed in what is right in front of you, it can be too easy to miss the big picture. Your spouse, on the other hand, may have a more objective view of the situation. From his vantage point, he may see a solution you have never considered. When you listen to his opinion, you may find other options to solve problems and to make your homeschool even better. As your partner in family life, anyway, he should be involved in the decision-making process. When you ignore his opinion, you could lose the strength of that teamwork.

Don't ambush him. When my husband would walk in the door, I used to descend on him crying, "You have no *idea* what I've been dealing with!" and then just blab on and on about my troubles. Right after I ran to the bathroom. The poor man didn't even have a chance to take his coat off. After a while, I learned that I get more help if I wait and feed the man and let him catch his breath. And maybe get the children down to bed.

Be honest about how you feel. Just let it all out. You can try to be strong, and you have struggled all day to be patient. But behind the bedroom door, you can honestly tell your husband what your day was like and why you are crying hysterically. He doesn't need to think you know it all. He needs to know what your emotions are so he can feel your pain . . . and enjoy the triumphs.

Tell him whether you want help or sympathy. Because sometimes you need one, and sometimes the other. I used to get frustrated when my husband would jump right to, "You should try . . ." and I would yell, "Just listen to me!" Sometimes after a day of no one listening to me, I just need someone to hear me rant. And sometimes I really do want advice. Lately, I've been wanting both: for him to listen to my feelings for a good thirty or sixty minutes, then when I take a breath, he can gently suggest how wrong I was.

Tell him something good about the day. We all go through difficult seasons in our homeschooling, times that seem like slogging through mud. But usually, I can find just *one* little bit of progress, or at least one ridiculous story. If I only complain, he gets a little tired of my whiny voice. But if I sprinkle in some lighter material, he gets a better picture of our homeschool life as a whole.

Share academic progress. Periodically during errands or dinner with just the two of us, I will bring up what the children are working on right now. I'll talk about what they are studying in history or what topic someone is tackling in science or how reading is going—just general updates on our studies. He has gotten so used to it that he now asks once in a while what we are doing in homeschooling. This helps him to stay connected and to understand me when I have a rough time. It also gives him some things he can bring up with the children during times with them.

Brag about a child. This is one of my favorite ways to keep Dad connected to our homeschooling. Periodically at dinner, I will burst out, "You won't believe what your son did today!" And of course, all the children and teens stop chewing for a moment and consider what crime they need to confess. I then share a child's accomplishment, whether it is a good grade on a hard test or learning a difficult process. The child beams and is encouraged to try even harder, and my husband hears about what we are working on and what difficulties we are tackling.

Let children present reports to him. I got this idea from a curriculum once, and I love it. When a student finishes a major aspect of a subject, I will often ask him to tell his dad all about what he learned, or if he writes a paper, I will ask him to read it to Dad. But one of my favorite homeschool memories was several years ago when we studied South American history. I asked my husband to take us to a Peruvian restaurant that was not too busy (this was easy because my husband *is* Peruvian). During dinner, my two oldest children read their reports on indigenous South American civilizations and the revolutions against Spanish occupation. My younger son presented a large map he had drawn with symbols of agricultural and historical significance. After each presentation, the children discussed their projects with their father, who congratulated them on their work and taught them aspects they didn't know. It was one of those rare moments when all of homeschooling came together beautifully. And it was mainly because I helped my husband and our children make a connection.

Suggest field trips. Some husbands, like mine, enjoy field trips more than at-home teaching. Mine will often plan museum or historical stops on our vacations. He finds it a personal challenge to take the children somewhere special.

One day, he took this to the extreme. I had signed up the children for a tour of the local mint. But I was tired beyond description. As in straddling the breaking point. He took a day off, dropped me and our infant at a bookstore/coffee shop, and happily chaperoned three children through what turned out to be a very boring tour. He even kept the children entertained by whispering stories about counterfeit money in the bank he works at. It is one of my favorite homeschool memories. Obviously.

Ask him what role he wants to take. As with many other aspects of marriage, it can be detrimental to expect something a husband doesn't want to do or isn't even capable of doing. Just like I homeschool best a certain way, he homeschools best his own way too. That's going to be different from how you homeschool and even different from how other dads homeschool. It may take him a few months or even years, but it helps to let your husband find his own style. It took my husband a little experimentation to find his own best way to help us, and now he confidently supports me and the children. He did not find his style and then announce, "This is what I'm going to do around here!" Instead, he just found his groove and lived out his own best way.

Respect him. He may be super involved; he may be hands off. He may have a lot of opinions; he may say he has no clue. He may not know what to say; he may say too much. But no matter what, he's probably doing his best at a really hard job: being married to a homeschool mom. Make sure he knows how much you value him, who he is, and what he does. Listen to his advice without immediately finding all the ways it is wrong. Give him opportunities to shape the homeschool toward his own vision. Respect how he parents as a homeschool dad. This is his homeschool too.

Thank him. No matter how much or how little your husband wants to be involved, he deserves gratitude: he makes it possible to homeschool; he helps provide financially for the homeschool; he lives with a tired, stressed-out homeschool mom; he keeps the homeschool family going. Those alone are big jobs. He is a hero.

15.4.2 What can I, as a father, do to help?

Dads, first of all, go back and read the previous section and take a look at the box in section 3.2.4. Then get out your highlighter and go through this list as well. (Moms, here is a section you can leave open on the coffee table and cough meaningfully every time you pass by.)

Help your wife think through your homeschool *why*. The purpose of your homeschool should reflect the mission of your entire family, especially your parenting vision. Think through these priorities with her so the two of you will be working toward the same goals. Check out chapter 1 for more about that.

Be a sounding board. Sometimes, your wife simply needs to talk through her issues. She may be wondering what curriculum to use next or how to handle a learning block. You have an excellent chance to just listen and maybe ask a few questions. Even if you don't know the answer, just letting her talk it out will help her clarify her thinking.

Discuss your child's learning. Ask your wife what your student is working on. Ask how he is doing in his subjects. Ask what conversations your wife would love to see you have with him. She may need you to give him a little nudge. She may like you to share some of your own knowledge. She may just want you to ask him if he is enjoying his subjects and why or why not.

Be a shoulder to cry on. Your wife may have a bad day. Or five dozen. She will think it is the most horrible day ever in the history of home-schooling. And that will make her rant and cry. When she rants and cries, she will need someone to vent to. And that is you. Listen kindly, even if you don't understand. She just needs someone to care.

Help out in one or five of her many roles. One of the reasons she may be crying is that she has too much to do in too little time. Besides over-looking the cluttered house and the hurried dinner (a definite must), you can also help her pick up the slack in small ways. Fold some towels. Wipe down a bathroom. Run an errand. Hold a crying baby. Drive a child to an activity. Put the young one to bed at night. A small act of help means so much to a tired, overworked woman. Bonus points if you completely take over a chore; my husband does much of the grocery shopping for me. He either drives each child to soccer practice or finds someone else who will. That alone makes me rise up and call him blessed.

Lower your expectations. She has high expectations, usually too high. And she can't reach them. Don't expect her to do all and be all (and remind her often that you don't expect it). The floor won't be picked up, the furni-ture dusted, the towels folded. She may still be wearing her jammies. You may step on a LEGO. You may have peanut butter sandwiches for dinner. Don't even care, and tell her you don't care. Tell her you want her to breathe and find rest, instead. Make sure she is taking care of herself.

Go to a convention. Many homeschool moms attend homeschool con-ventions to hear expert teaching and to look at curricula. You will likely find this boring. However, husbands who go to conventions are rock stars. Sit next to her and keep your eyes open during a session (bonus points if you tell her a fact you liked from the teaching). Look at some of the curricula and ask her what she likes about each one or how it compares with what she is using. Bite your tongue about your homeschool budget; instead, ask her if she can order her favorites later, and then you can talk about finances in private. Carry her books without complaining. Keep a smile plastered on your face the entire time. She will love you for this support and never forget it the entire year or until the next convention rolls around.

Teach a subject. Don't skip this paragraph. You can find ways to teach or at least to help out with one or more subjects. Even though your wife knows nearly everything about everything and flings curricula around like a ninja, there is probably a subject you know a little more about and may even enjoy a little more than she does. Consider teaching that subject just fifteen minutes every evening, twenty minutes three times a week, or an hour or so on the weekend. If you can't teach an entire subject, help out in some way. Discuss the topic of the week with your child at dinner or in the car. Listen to a podcast on the subject on the way to work so you will be prepared to share some fun facts over dinner. Find a way to either teach or help out with some of the academics. Consider taking your child on a field trip . . . without your wife. Your child will likely enjoy the change of homeschool styles, and your wife will enjoy the break.

Read aloud. This is a great alternative to teaching a subject. Find a book related to what your child is studying or even just a fun book you enjoy and read it regularly. Whether on the weekend or right before bed, this is an excellent way to bond with your child while once again relieving one of your wife's duties.

Check in daily. Just text to ask how her day is going. She will know you care, and you will have a heads-up on the attitude at home before you walk in the door. Rejoice with her over the day's progress. Promise to help out—or even better, to bring home tacos—when she is having a hard time. She will call you a hero and cry tears of joy.

Be the bad guy. There are days when your child bounces off the walls. There are days when she won't do her homework. There are days when she won't do anything but argue. There are days she drives your wife to the very frayed end of her rope. Come home at night ready to deal with the issues. Often a child just needs to hear correction from another parent. Other times, discipline from Dad just seems oh so much more meaningful. As much as possible, let Mom be good cop in the evening, and you be bad cop.

Guard her sleep and relaxation. One of the chief complaints of homeschool moms is that they never have a moment off duty. If they aren't homeschooling, they are juggling errands and housekeeping. They work longer than sunup to sundown. And they are constantly tired. The most important commodity your wife needs is rest; she does not have the strength to cope without it. Help out in the evening so she can go to bed at a decent time. Teach the children to fix their own cereal while you make coffee for her in the morning. Plan a day in which you will care for the children while she runs away. Be creative to find a way to give her regular rest and occasional breaks.

Praise her publicly. When your coworkers ask about homeschooling, tell them not only what it means but how great your wife is at it. When friends ask how homeschooling is going, tell them *great* because your wife is great. Every time someone says *homeschool* respond with *my wife rocks*. She needs to hear it, and she needs to hear about it from others. She needs to know you are proud of her. When I meet one of my husband's coworkers and they say, "Oh! You are homeschooling your children, too, right? He is always telling us about what you are doing and how great you are teaching! It makes me want to homeschool too!" There is nothing more encouraging than hearing that my husband is proud of what we are doing.

Thank her. If motherhood is thankless, homeschooling is even more so. She will likely never hear her children gush with gratitude, especially when they are in the thick of homework. Almost daily, she will struggle with the difficulties and trials, even while she remains committed to her cause. Thank her for staying the course, for enduring the frustrations, for making your home a safe place to learn. Thank her for being dedicated to your homeschool *why*.

15.4.3 What about dads who do the teaching?

Teaching fathers are a growing segment within the homeschool community. You may be one of them! Though some homeschooling fathers are stay-at-home dads while their wife is the primary breadwinner, many of these men work from home or out of the home. Homeschool dads, in fact, face the same challenges as homeschool moms. They are searching for the right way to teach each child (usually choosing an unschooling or eclectic style), overcoming insecurities about how their child is learning, and working hard to balance homeschooling, working, and home life.

Homeschool dad Chad Kent told me,

> In the end, you have to do what's best for your family. I've always managed to get things done. It might not look like it would if my wife did it, but our kids are happy and well-adjusted so who cares. Yes, I do get some sideways looks from people. But the way I see it, as a man it's my job to contribute to my family the best way I can. In our situation, it's for me to stay home and do school. If someone is going to look down on me for taking care of my wife and kids then that's their problem.[1]

Perhaps a father homeschooling flies against our cultural norm not only within society but also within the church. Homeschooling fathers challenge these assumptions by living counterculturally in more ways than one. Homeschool dads, in fact, take their responsibility to train their child personally. Many cite scriptural commands for fathers to train their child as the basis of their decision. They are dedicated to personally teaching their child not only academically but also spiritually.

> Leadership and learning are indispensable to each other.
>
> **JOHN F. KENNEDY**

Of the homeschool fathers I surveyed, nearly every one said isolation was the most difficult hurdle they face. Most homeschooling fathers do not know any teaching dads nearby. They turn for help and solidarity to online homeschool groups—the ones designed for and run by women. Unfortunately, some homeschool dads find the women in these groups to be unwelcoming or suspicious of male involvement. This contributes to their loneliness.

On the other hand, the homeschooling dads I talked to were very respectful of homeschooling women. They recognize the homeschooling advances made by female homeschool leaders, and they actively look for advice and fellowship from homeschool moms.

Homeschooling father Tim Tinkle encourages fellow teaching dads to learn from the broader homeschool community, especially homeschool moms. "Don't be afraid to just blaze your own trail but also don't be egotistical. Ask questions and listen to the ladies that have gone before you. Learn from them then take your own knowledge and add to it."[2]

Dad-taught homeschools are no different from any other homeschool. Families choose an alternative lifestyle—teaching at home—and the best-suited parent chooses to take part. Homeschool dads take the father's commitment to the next level, offering an excellent perspective on homeschooling. The dads I surveyed want every dad to know "you can do it."

15.5 WORKING

15.5.1 Can I work while homeschooling?

Yes! I have worked nearly my entire homeschool career. I have worked full-time and part-time, inside and outside the home. It always takes a little bit of creativity, but it can be done. The best candidates for working and homeschooling are women who can simplify their homeschooling, women who can patiently help their child work independently, and women who can be flexible with their expectations.

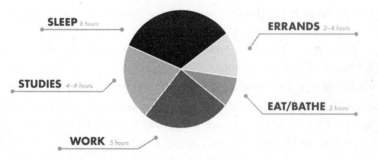

HOW MUCH TIME SHOULD WE SPEND?

SLEEP 8 hours

ERRANDS 2–4 hours

STUDIES 4–6 hours

EAT/BATHE 3 hours

WORK 5 hours

15.5.2 How can you homeschool while working outside of the home?

This is tricky, but doable. I have worked part-time outside of the home two separate times during our homeschooling. There are a few options. One, you can teach during hours you are home and have a spouse, family member, or friend stay with your child while you work and your child finishes his assignments (kind of like if he went to an institutional school, right?). Two, you can utilize a co-op for him to attend while you work, and you can help him with his remaining assignments afterward. Three, your child can use online homeschooling while someone watches him when you're working. I actually know a young lady who babysat for a family who utilized this method; she also helped with reading aloud and grading homework.

Four (and the method I used), you can find a way to take your child with you to your workplace. This takes some creativity on your part and understanding from your boss. During one job, I taught reading and math at home and let my early learner look at science and history books or use math manipulatives on my office floor. In another job, my toddler attended on-site preschool while my older children stayed with me doing their independent work. This obviously only works if your child is flexible and able to stay quiet for a period of time, so this may not be a good option for more rambunctious children. Also, not many employers appreciate this method.

The full-time, out-of-the-home homeschool moms I know work evenings while their husband works mornings, or vice versa. They usually share homeschool duties with their spouse.

15.5.3 How can you homeschool while working from home?

A flexible routine helps. A job requires time, and homeschooling requires time, so we need to set separate times to do each. Some of my friends wake up very early in the morning to work. Others stay up in the evening working. I cannot do either without falling asleep.

Since my children were infants, though, I have always had an afternoon nap time for my children. As they have grown older, I have still maintained a two-hour rest time every day. During that time, everyone must retire to their separate places to sleep, read, listen to audiobooks, play quietly, finish homework—whatever quiet activity they want. After that two-hour rest time, they usually run outside to play, enjoy a board game together, or find something else to do. That gives me about four hours or so to work in peace. I do all of my teaching in the morning (whatever doesn't get done can usually wait until the next day), and my older children can finish their assignments in the afternoon. This routine has worked well for me for years.

Many homeschool moms and dads use a home office and just close the door while their student and the other parent work separately; some even have a special knock for questions that just can't wait. Others have a tutor or babysitter for a few hours. Some allow their child to learn at a co-op or enrichment class while they work at home.

15.5.4 How do you juggle the demands of working, homeschooling, and the rest of life?

With a routine for everything. I homeschool in the morning and work in the afternoon. I spend time with my family and rest in the evenings (rest is the most important part of your routine!). I do homeschooling at the library on Tuesdays. I run errands and clean the house along with the children on Fridays, when we do less homeschooling. I attend soccer games and run the rest of the errands on Saturdays. I do as little as possible on Sundays so I can recuperate and begin every Monday somewhat refreshed. Everything has its own place in life, so I know when to do what. And if something does not get finished, I know exactly when in the future I will tackle it again.

Finally, I have to be flexible. If someone is sick or frustrated with something in homeschooling or struggling with something personally, I may need to chuck the routine and focus on what is important right then. If I am sick or completely worn out, I may need to push everything aside to take care of my health. If things fall apart, I just need to do the next thing God wants me to do in that moment, whether or not it was my plan.

The only way working while homeschooling works is with the support of your spouse. If he is not on board with it, then doing both at the same time is definitely not the right decision. If he has different expectations for how much you can work while homeschooling, he may need some patient explaining about how long homeschooling takes. If your child needs more help and attention, this may not be the right time to add something else to your plate. Working while homeschooling is not for everyone. There were a couple of years when working was not the right decision for my life and my family. As in every other area, we need to be sure this is what God wants us to do.

• • •

Sometimes homeschool life is just plain hard. There is illness, there are learning challenges, there are personal trials. You can survive—even thrive— through every homeschool season. **Give yourself a break and remember your *why*.** Remember your long-term goals. You are not homeschooling for today or tomorrow or the end of the week. You are homeschooling for a life you want your child to live, for a relationship you want inside your family, for your love of God.

On those hard days, put aside the lesson plans and make a list of good things from that day:

- I hugged my child.
- I provided food and clothing and shelter.
- I demonstrated love.
- I prayed with my child.
- I demonstrated faith in front of my child.
- I showed my child in word and deed what our family priorities really are.
- I let go of good studies in favor of the best relationship with God and others.
- I remembered why I am here with my family.

Write down or say aloud what you *did* well that day. Then rest assured that your labor is not in vain in the Lord.

16

SPECIAL CHILDREN, SPECIAL NEEDS

I AM NOT AN EXPERT on special needs, not by any means. I do not have experience teaching a special needs child. I do, however, want to give you encouragement and information. I know this chapter won't answer all of your questions. I do pray this chapter will give you encouragement that *you can do it* and provide the first steps toward getting support on your own unique homeschool journey.

What I can tell you is what I have learned from research and from interviewing therapists, doctors, and special needs homeschoolers. I wrote this chapter in close consultation with Kimberly Ferren, licensed professional counselor. From her training in psychology and Christian counseling, combined with work both in a psychiatric facility and private Christian therapy, she taught me so much about how a caring counselor identifies and treats the following issues from a Christian perspective.

Dr. Vincent Iannelli also reviewed and assisted with this chapter, besides advising me on the child growth and development standards in part three. Board certified, a Fellow of the American Academy of Pediatrics, author, and medical expert for publications and media, Dr. Iannelli has been my own trusted pediatrician for well over a dozen years. I would not have even attempted to include any child development or special needs information in this volume without his help.

It is important not to use this chapter as a diagnostic tool. For one thing, neurotypical children will exhibit many of the symptoms I describe here. For another thing, these indications are only a small list of things a professional might look for. Finally, we need to remember that only a trained professional can discern what, if any, special needs a child may be experiencing.

Twenty percent of parents choose to homeschool because of their child's special needs, fourteen percent due to their child's physical or mental health issues.[1] In addition, a growing number of homeschoolers, while working so closely with their child, discern issues early on. After having their child tested, they may see him diagnosed with special needs. Parents of special needs students often find public schools unable to meet the unique challenges their child faces. The school's promised educational plan—or an update to that plan—may take too long to sufficiently support the child's progress or may incompletely meet the child's unique needs. A school may not keep up with a child's development as quickly as parents at home. These parents want to meet their child's unique needs in a nurturing, specialized environment catering to his unique abilities.

Children of trauma, including foster and adoptive children, often experience special needs issues, as well. These children will need special counseling to deal with the pain they have experienced. In addition, these students often require diagnosis and treatment of special learning issues.

Regardless of whether the child's special needs are due to genetics, trauma, injury, or illness, the most important goal is *stability*. Homeschooling offers the unique opportunity to focus on what matters most to these students, and usually, this need is not academics. These children deserve our love and support most of all, regardless of their academic progress or achievements.

16.1 BASICS OF SPECIAL NEEDS

16.1.1 How do I know if my child has special needs?

Many parents worry at some point if their child experiences academic difficulties. In fact, homeschooling can help a parent notice these needs and seek early intervention. Your child may consistently reach milestones later than expected. It is sometimes difficult to know if your child's rate of growth is normal. And when you see your child struggling, it's natural to wonder if he would benefit from professional help. Here is a list of issues that may indicate your child is in need of special assistance:

- inability to reach development milestones within the expected range, especially verbal and social
- delayed or hampered speech
- difficulty remembering age-appropriate steps or following directions in schoolwork and in daily life, or easily becoming confused
- habitually learning something one day and then forgetting it the next
- difficulty retelling past events or a story
- difficulty staying in her seat or standing near a table to work
- difficulty organizing toys or materials
- difficulty putting thoughts on paper (for an older child)
- difficulty working puzzles
- difficulty differentiating right and left, top and bottom
- clumsiness, incoordination, difficulty controlling his body
- inability to make or keep friends
- difficulties adapting to other places besides home, like Sunday school or co-op

It is important, however, to remember that all children struggle from time to time. So just because a child exhibits some of these symptoms does not mean he needs intervention. But any time you feel concerned, you can seek out professional advice. See the following section for specific professionals you might contact.

16.1.2 Who do I talk to if I am concerned about my child's development?

Your pediatrician is an excellent place to start. She can compare your child's development to typical child development and let you know if your child is within expectations. Many times, your child's doctor can show you the wide range of child development and set your mind at ease. If additional evaluation is needed, she can give you solid advice as to a preliminary diagnosis and referrals for which specialists to see next. With my child, I called my pediatrician, and he gave me referrals for a specialist in my area of concern.

If your pediatrician seems unsure of your child's situation or brushes off your concerns, don't hesitate to move on to a therapist or specialist. You might even see a developmental pediatrician for evaluation or treatment. You can find referrals through your local children's hospital or insurance provider.

A trained educator or tutor can look at your child's learning skills and academic level. She may diagnose learning disorders, teach new study skills, or work to strengthen brain function. A trainer specifically certified in learning disabilities can customize a learning plan or tutor the child to overcome his obstacles. She may also teach you separately or along with your child to help you work better as a team.

A physical therapist can assess your child's gross or fine motor skills. She might test his coordination, balance, range of motion, and strength. I consulted a physical therapist when my son seemed behind his peers in many gross motor skills. The therapist gave me peace of mind that my son is still well within his expected range of growth and development, though he may seem younger than some of his peers.

A psychotherapist can help you and your child work out any emotional issues, behavioral habits, or traumas that may be hindering his emotional health and learning. She can teach you and your child coping skills and new habits to overcome difficulties in life and learning. She is also experienced in noticing behavior and mental issues that may need additional treatment.

A psychiatrist can diagnose serious behavior difficulties, brain-based disorders, and mental illness. She can determine what therapies may be necessary and even prescribe medication, if necessary.

You may also receive help from **a state or local early childhood intervention service for young children**. School-based evaluations are also available to homeschoolers in many states.

16.1.3 What is asynchronous learning in gifted students?

In homeschooling, asynchronous learning means learning at different levels at the same time. So if a ten-year-old were using a third-grade grammar workbook but is studying prealgebra, we would say she is an asynchronous learner.

Most children are somewhat asynchronous, especially between language skills and math skills. They seem to be great at one subject but not the other, or they may go back and forth with their best subjects. Sometimes, they do end up a few levels different in some of their courses, and this is not an issue. Homeschooling allows us to customize our child's program so he can take off in the things he knows and enjoys while spending more time in more difficult areas.

Asynchronous learning, however, is much more common with gifted students. Gifted students are estimated to make up approximately 20 percent of the homeschool population[2], and many gifted students are at least partially homeschooled[3]—precisely because of the opportunity it provides for asynchronous learning. Different from talented students, gifted children possess a profound ability in linguistics, logic, math, kinesthetic (athletics and dancing), music, interpersonal skills, or natural science. Many gifted students have an IQ of 130, test in the top one or two percent on intelligence tests, or show extreme ability in one area, an ability more than talent and hard work would explain. Giftedness is not taught but rather is believed to be a combination of genes developed in the right environment.

In fact, giftedness is defined as asynchronous learning itself. A definition of giftedness developed by the Columbus Group is

asynchronous development in which advanced cognitive abilities
and heightened intensity combine to create inner experiences
and awareness that are qualitatively different from the norm.
This asynchrony increases with higher intellectual capacity. The
uniqueness of the gifted renders them particularly vulnerable
and requires modifications in parenting, teaching, and counseling
in order for them to develop optimally.[4]

A student exhibiting learning difficulties that interfere with the use of her gift is often called *twice-exceptional*. For example, she may be extremely gifted in math but struggle with dyslexia. In spite of her profound ability, she will need particular help with her weakness. These learning difficulties may hinder the use of her gift and frustrate her learning. Her parent may become confused about how to meet this child's unique needs.

The twice-exceptional student does need help with his learning disabilities. As with typical students, he will benefit from an evaluation and a specific program to help him overcome his learning and/or sensory challenges.

Standard curriculum is often not sufficient for a gifted or twice-exceptional student. Materials usually are not challenging enough, proceed at too slow a pace, and contain too much repetition. Because she often memorizes quickly, a gifted student needs help to concentrate on thinking skills and practical application of her gift and interests. She also needs plenty of free time to develop her gift. If this student does not continue to develop her gift, some experts believe she could even lose it.[5]

The asynchronous or gifted student can become very sensitive to his grades. He might expect near perfection from himself and become frustrated with his weaker subjects. He needs less emphasis on grades (maybe no grades at all) and encouragement on progress rather than achievement.

In her gifted area, however, the asynchronous student should be allowed to take off. She will likely prefer working independently on this subject in which she excels. She may even benefit from unschooling in that subject. In her area of strength, she can take part in internships or take AP or honors classes. Regardless, she will need a customized curriculum program that will both challenge her and enable her to develop her ability.

A common mistake is to treat a gifted student as if he is older than he is. He and his parents may become frustrated with poor achievement in his areas of weakness or with his immature behavior. If he also has a learning or sensory issue, it can become magnified because of these imbalances. Encouraging him to enjoy the stage of life he is in can help alleviate the pressure to grow up too quickly.

With creativity, parents can balance the unique challenges of an asynchronous student. Homeschooling offers the perfect environment that both meets learning needs and allows gifts to flourish.

16.2 LEARNING DISABILITIES

16.2.1 What is a learning disability?

It's not just trouble with schoolwork. According to the U.S. Department of Education,

> a learning disability means a disorder in one or more of the
> basic psychological processes involved in understanding or in
> using language spoken or written, that may manifest itself in
> an imperfect ability to listen, think, speak, read, write, spell, or

to do mathematical calculations, including such conditions as perceptual disabilities, brain injury, minimal brain dysfunction, dyslexia, and developmental aphasia [losing the ability to speak or understand speech]. The term does not include learning problems that are primarily the result of visual, hearing, or motor disabilities, mental retardation, emotional disturbance, or environmental, culture, or economic disadvantages.[6]

In other words, a learning disability is a problem with the child's mental process that affects his ability in reading, writing, and math. It's a disability not caused by a physical disability or trauma. Up to 50 percent of students diagnosed with a learning disability have a family member with a learning disability that may or may not be correctly diagnosed.[7]

Trauma may lead to difficulties that appear similar to learning disabilities. These difficulties could resolve with trauma therapy in conjunction with academic help. However, a traumatized child also could possess a learning disability due to prenatal substance exposure, injury at birth or in early childhood, or a genetic predisposition. (This is also why children from foster care and adoption commonly experience issues manifesting as learning difficulties.)

Up to one-half of all special needs children have a learning disability. There is a wide range of learning disabilities. The most well-known are dyslexia (difficulty with reading, writing, and spelling) and dyscalculia (difficulty with numbers, time, and math). Sometimes learning disabilities occur in conjunction with neurological disorders (see section 16.3).

It is important to remember that *learning disabilities are not about intelligence*. A highly intelligent—even gifted—child may struggle with a learning issue. Dr. Laura McGuinn, professor of pediatrics at the University of Alabama at Birmingham and coauthor of a published report on learning disorders for the American Academy of Pediatrics agrees. "Children not proceeding academically are usually not lazy. . . . There's usually a problem underneath it, and it's usually a complex problem—all children pretty much want to succeed."[8]

Lastly, be assured that if your child is diagnosed with a learning disability, *it is not related to your teaching ability*. Don't even worry about that. Researchers have found a variety of contributing factors to learning disabilities, including genes, injury, and environmental factors.

16.2.2 What are the signs of a learning disability?

A trained learning specialist will look for several signs of a learning disability. It is normal to have a few learning issues; the specialist will be evaluating your child for multiple signs that together may indicate a specific disability. A few of those symptoms include the following:

- unexplained underachieving in most subjects
- normal intelligence not reflected in academics
- difficulties specifically in reading, writing, and/or math
- struggling to find the right words to say
- guessing instead of sounding out words or working through a math problem
- difficulty reading while enjoying being read to
- poor handwriting
- reverses letters and/or numbers
- struggles with phonics and reading comprehension (dyslexia)
- struggles with shapes, number values, measurements, and fractions (dyscalculia)
- appears frustrated or cannot pay attention
- has a family history of a learning disability or undiagnosed difficulties
- exhibits behavior symptoms similar to attention deficit/hyperactivity disorder (ADHD)

That last symptom is very interesting. Many children with learning disabilities are mistakenly diagnosed with ADHD, though students with ADHD may also have a learning disability. Students with learning disabilities may exhibit inattention, distractibility, inability to sit still, lack of focus, frustration, and even anger at their schoolwork.

For many children, however, these characteristics could be symptoms of frustration or a struggle with life changes like moving, a family death, or divorce. These children cannot understand or perform what is expected, so they take their frustrations out with inappropriate behavior or difficulties learning. For these children, a combination of therapy to help deal with their emotions along with intervention for their academic difficulties may relieve the frustration and enable them to learn peacefully.

Also, most children who do not have a learning disability will exhibit many if not all of the above symptoms at some time. Learning frustration is common and may even come and go. You may see improvement by slowing down your child's rate of work, by working for shorter periods of time, and by cultivating a relaxing learning environment. If your child's difficulties persist, then you may want to consult your pediatrician or learning expert for evaluation.

16.2.3 How is a learning disability diagnosed?

By a trained professional. If you suspect a learning disability, talk to your pediatrician. He will likely screen for vision, hearing, and other physical issues that may affect learning. He can then point you to a trained learning specialist who will evaluate your child for a learning issue. Your child will likely be tested for intelligence and academics; a large discrepancy may indicate a learning issue. You can also find testers certified in identifying learning disabilities in reading or testing centers.

16.2.4 How do I homeschool a child with a learning disability?

A child with a learning disability will benefit from patient, one-on-one instruction in his particular areas of weakness. She may, however, find herself increasingly independent in her areas of strength. A learning disability continues for life, but with help, your student's abilities will most likely improve.[9]

You may try breaking up his assignments into smaller sections. Giving him time during the day to rest may help his concentration. Allowing him to break up lessons over several days may also increase his confidence.

Your child's ability to learn may also improve with environmental changes such as a different type of lighting, soft background noise or music, silence, sitting/standing, or a more comfortable work location. Giving her the space and time she needs can help her to concentrate, and

> STEPS TO MAKE LEARNING EASIER FOR YOUR STUDENT
>
> - Set a consistent routine.
> - Repeat expectations often.
> - Help him organize information and materials.
> - Assist him with reading comprehension.
> - Use books with pictures and illustrations to help him understand his reading.
> - Reward him for effort and encourage his hard work.

before long she may exert a little more effort in those areas where she most struggles.

There are many materials that those with learning disabilities enjoy. You may use audiobooks and videos to supplement some of his reading assignments. He may prefer using a word processor and spellchecker to help him write without distraction. With help organizing his papers and other materials, he may find studying easier. The professional who diagnoses your child will likely have suggestions as well for methods and materials that will meet his needs.

Some homeschool curricula are specifically designed for students with learning disabilities. The special needs homeschool community also shares products that have helped their children. Of course, nearly any materials can be customized to help your child best.

Remember, your child with a learning disability is working so much harder than other children to do the same work. She will need extra support and encouragement. Giving her periodic breaks will help her relax and focus. And of course, encouragement and tangible rewards will help her keep working hard.

16.3 NEUROLOGICAL DISORDERS

16.3.1 Attention Deficit Hyperactivity Disorder (ADHD)

16.3.1.1 WHAT IS ATTENTION DEFICIT/HYPERACTIVITY DISORDER (ADHD)?

Despite sometimes erroneously being considered a behavior issue, attention deficit/hyperactivity disorder (ADHD) is in fact a neurological issue. The student's behavior is often a response to outside stimuli. When the child is overwhelmed by the sights, sounds, or activity around him, he becomes unable to concentrate on what he is doing. Becoming frustrated by overstimulation, he may become hyperactive or undisciplined. His over-activity is, in reality, a coping mechanism to help him ignore the difficult task in front of him or to deal with other things around him. There are two subtypes of ADHD, inattentive and hyperactive.

ADHD affects nearly 9 percent of students and twice as many boys as girls. American Academy of Pediatrics guidelines stipulate a doctor rule out anxiety, depression, and other disorders as causes of the symptoms before medically treating a child for ADHD, but these children often struggle with another disorder, in conjunction with ADHD.

Some children may develop ADHD-like behaviors during stressful events in their lives. My own adopted child exhibited some symptoms of ADHD, but trauma therapy and consistent home life has noticeably helped. Some children may need both therapy and medical treatment before a cause is diagnosed and symptoms recede.

16.3.1.2 WHAT ARE THE SIGNS OF ADHD?

Children diagnosed with ADHD will often exhibit some of the following characteristics:

- impulsive actions
- inattention to directions and details
- difficulty focusing even on play
- hyperfocused on one sensory stimulation or action
- difficulty switching activities when engrossed in his task
- hyperactive energy
- difficulty playing quietly
- blurts out words or talks incessantly
- cannot wait his turn
- disorganization with materials and work
- behavior issues that interfere with academics and classroom situations
- temper tantrums inconsistent with the problem (for example, flying into a rage because someone bumped into him)
- symptoms persist in all areas of life, not only academic work
- behaviors interfere with daily life

16.3.1.3 HOW IS ADHD DIAGNOSED?

The American Academy of Pediatrics revised their own diagnostic standards in 2019. These guidelines emphasize the need to first train parents before medical treatment is needed. Parent training in behavioral management (PTBM) and educational interventions should be your doctor's first line of treatment.[10] According to Dr. Joseph F. Hagan, Jr., coauthor of the AAP guidelines and vice chairperson for the AAP Subcommittee on Children and Adolescents with Attention Deficit/Hyperactivity Disorder, "A child diagnosed with ADHD will benefit most when there is a partnership between families, their doctors, and their teachers, who may need to create special instructional plans and support."[11] A good doctor should suggest appropriate interventions and therapies before beginning medical treatments.

Though medication often results in quick improvement, it is not without side effects. As a result, many children resist taking medication. Some are also sensitive to the changes in their feelings, which should be considered another negative side effect. A good pediatrician should carefully monitor these issues to find the right treatment for each child.

Like all learning disabilities, many of these symptoms are completely normal for a growing child. For this reason, some would rather call these symptoms *ADHD-type behavior*, since the disorder itself may not be diagnosed. Others believe that many children diagnosed with and medically treated for ADHD are simply active children who have not yet developed the capacity to deal with multiple stimuli and concentrate on one sense for a length of time. Thus too much rigidity in routine, rules, and academic work can result in ADHD-like behaviors.

A child with ADHD or similar behaviors craves physical activity and perhaps physical contact. Flexibility and outlets for energy like outdoor play and sports can often diminish or completely remove these symptoms. As in all areas of growth, the mental and physical capacity to be still and concentrate for a length of time develops at different rates for each child.

It is important to remember that, as in other neurological disorders, ADHD is not a discipline issue. With increased activity, sensory management, and coping skills, these children may achieve higher levels of concentration and then academic performance.

ADHD itself may persist into adulthood. With training and environmental changes, both students and adults may in time learn to manage their symptoms without medical treatment.

16.3.2 Sensory Processing Disorder

16.3.2.1 WHAT IS SENSORY PROCESSING DISORDER?

Sensory Processing Disorder (SPD) is characterized by an overload of sensory functions in the brain, resulting in difficulties with behavior and thought processes. According to the STAR Institute for Sensory Processing Disorder, "SPD is a neurophysiologic condition in which sensory input either from the environment or from one's body is poorly detected, modulated, or interpreted and/or to which atypical responses are observed."[12] A student who is hypersensitive may become overwhelmed by the coarseness of clothing, the brightness of light, or the volume of sound. These distractions cause concentration difficulties and may result in behavior issues. He may burst out in anger over interruptions, yell when the room becomes noisy, refuse to wear clothing he considers uncomfortable, or gag on certain textures of food. He may appear to be often angry, stubborn, and disruptive. What would cause a small adjustment for others creates a crisis for the child with sensory disorders.

SPD commonly occurs in conjunction with other neurological disorders, including those on the autism spectrum. At times, SPD may be mistaken for mental disorders like depression or anxiety. Mild SPD may be exacerbated by family issues, life changes, the environment, or diet. Therapy and coping skills often improve the discomfort and dysregulation of these children.

Though SPD is commonly diagnosed because of behavior issues, it is important to remember it is actually a brain-based disorder characterized by an overreaction to what most people would consider normal sensory levels. Though most of these students will struggle with their disorder through adulthood, they can achieve academic and behavioral improvement by limiting stimulation, learning coping skills, and perhaps taking medication.

Students with sensory disorders may also exhibit symptoms of autism spectrum disorder or learning disabilities. None of these issues, however, are a sign of lower intelligence. These students are often very creative and highly intelligent. Their outbursts or disruptive behaviors result not only from sensory stimulation but also from their own inability to reach their potential while coping.

16.3.3 Autism Spectrum Disorder

16.3.3.1 WHAT ARE THE SIGNS OF AUTISM SPECTRUM DISORDER?

Autism spectrum disorder (ASD) causes difficulties with communication and behavior. Students with ASD may exhibit some of the following symptoms:

- being nonverbal
- regression in speech
- inappropriate verbal outbursts

- difficulty giving and receiving nonverbal communication
- difficulty understanding nonliteral speech, like jokes or figures of speech
- difficulty participating in a conversation
- avoidance of eye contact
- not recognizing and empathizing with others' emotions
- repetitive body movements or motions with objects (spinning or shaking or hitting things repeatedly)
- staring at lights or moving objects
- insistence on rigid routines
- symptoms persisting consistently since early childhood

It is important to remember this is not an exhaustive nor a prescriptive list. Neurotypical children will often demonstrate many of these behaviors as they grow and develop. ASD, however, is persistent and interferes with daily life, although it exists on a spectrum, meaning a child may have a mild, moderate, or severe form of the disorder. Only a doctor can diagnose ASD. If you suspect your child may experience these issues, you should consult your doctor soon. Early intervention is important.

16.3.4 How are neurological disorders diagnosed?

Neurological disorders should be diagnosed and treated by a doctor or therapist. If you suspect any neurological disorder, early intervention is key. Speak with your pediatrician, who can compare your child's emotional and mental development with expected standards, and who should screen for ADHD, SPD, and ASD during regular well-baby visits in any case. Seek out a pediatrician who is knowledgeable in identifying special needs, and if your pediatrician seems dismissive, don't hesitate to look for a second opinion. A licensed counseling therapist can also give a preliminary diagnosis. Neurological disorders are also identified and treated in your local children's hospital. A good professional will present several treatment options and guide both parent and child toward symptom management.

16.3.5 How do I homeschool a child with a neurological disorder?

In a homeschool setting, the parent can help the child study with a few modifications. First of all, the parent should consider **deschooling** for a time, putting all academics on hold while adjusting to the new diagnosis and treatment. Whether the child is coming home from a school setting or even homeschooling with a new diagnosis, both you and your child need some time to rest and reevaluate. Over time, you can observe what helps and hinders your child's responses and how you can help him. Now that you both are adjusting to his diagnosis, your care and attention will help him look to you as a member and teammate, rather than an authoritarian adversary. Strengthening your relationship is most important to home-schooling him effectively.

As you observe your child, you may get ideas about what **curriculum and methods** she will best respond to. Through trial and error, you may find just the right program to meet her needs. And of course, no matter what program you use, you can customize it to help her best. The special needs community is especially helpful as they share what materials have worked for them.

Remember to **teach him one-on-one**. If you have other children in the home or are participating in a co-op, you might want to spend some time teaching him alone. With your undivided attention, you can adjust his learning and stimulation while remaining sensitive to his strengths and weaknesses. Your child may learn, after a while, how to work more inde-pendently on the program you customize for him. Children with more serious forms of neurological disorders may require help throughout their schooling. One-on-one teaching allows you to customize his learning to his needs, and this is a vital strength of homeschooling special needs students. You can literally teach your child "when you are sitting in your house, and when you are walking by the way, and when you lie down, and when you rise" (Deuteronomy 11:19).

You will want to **start slowly**. You may feel like your child is "behind" (whatever that is), but she needs to work from where she is mentally and emotionally. Don't hesitate to work through curricula designed for lower grades than you would initially expect. Remember, you are not teaching to her chronological age but to her own unique ability. Her abilities may be asynchronous, meaning she will be more advanced in some subjects than in others. Don't be afraid to experiment. Many curriculum companies also offer samples and/or placement tests to help you find the product that meets your needs.

You might **break assignments down** or even cut out some repetition.

Students with sensory issues may be overwhelmed by numerous equations or questions on a page. Working on just a few seems more manageable.

Spend **less time** each day on academics. His overstimulated senses make studying more difficult for him than for you. Be sensitive and allow him to move at his own pace in the time period right for him.

Your child will likely benefit from **environmental changes**. Reducing the stimulation around her while she studies will likely help her concentrate. She may prefer a certain lighting or workplace. She may need special soft clothing. She may prefer soft music or noise-canceling headphones. Finding her preferences can really help reduce frustration. This is another reason why a time of deschooling can help you learn your child's needs better.

Experiment with his **diet**. Many parents of children with autism spectrum disorder report improvement with dietary changes. Your doctor may have information to help you find which foods your child is sensitive to. Since overly restrictive diets can become harmful to child development, any changes to your child's diet should be in consultation with your child's doctor or dietician.

Teach your child **coping skills**. Your therapist and psychologist will likely give you ideas for both you and your child. As you learn how to respond to her behaviors and needs, you can patiently help her learn to manage and cope with the frustrations around her. When life changes or difficult situations arise, perhaps allow your child time to process and react before continuing academics.

Remember to **communicate**. Let your child know what you are doing for him and how he can respond. With time, he may learn how to better communicate his needs, at least to a certain extent. Because these are neurological disorders and not behavioral issues, it is important to work on communication rather than discipline.

Give her an **outlet**. A child on the autism spectrum in particular may be hyperinterested in one subject or activity. Allowing your child time to meet these needs may reduce some of the frustration when she needs to concentrate.

The child with a neurological disorder often thrives in homeschooling. Since you have more control over his environment, his curriculum, and his time management, you can uniquely meet his needs and help him reach his own potential.

16.4 OPPOSITIONAL DEFIANT DISORDER

16.4.1 What is oppositional defiant disorder?

The most common behavioral disorder is oppositional defiant disorder (ODD). ODD includes intense opposition to all authority and directions, opposition to any "no" from authority, and rebellion against all rules, even the law. Those with ODD will often react with violent rage against authority or restrictions. Children with ODD have limited sensitivity to the feelings of others, including animals; they can be dangerous around pets. Symptoms are constant and disrupt the student's life. Those diagnosed with ODD are often dealing with other learning or mental health issues, as well. Between 1 and 16 percent of children are affected.[13]

Oppositional defiant disorder is quite different from ADHD. For one, ODD is a behavioral disorder, and ADHD is a neurological disorder. ODD is a rebellion against authority, and ADHD is a frustration with overstimulation. ODD is manifested by violent rage, and ADHD causes hyperactivity, impulsiveness, and frustration.

ODD can be the result of trauma, so it is sometimes seen in foster and adoptive children. ODD can also be caused by severe head injury or severe illness. Sometimes, ODD is a result of family issues or other current trauma. In this case, the resolution of these issues may lessen or relieve these symptoms.

A child with ODD requires family therapy. Everyone involved in the child's immediate life needs to learn how to respond to him while he is learning to respect authority and boundaries. Any organic or behavioral issues can then be addressed with the family as a whole. This child must work on behavioral and cognitive skills before he can begin working on his academics.

In addition, treatment for ODD often includes problem solving therapy for the child. Though there is no medical treatment for ODD, if other disorders are also present, medical treatment for these issues may lessen the symptoms of ODD. In severe cases, the child may be placed in a special facility.

With treatment, children typically improve within a few months. Up to 67 percent of children with ODD appear symptom-free within three years.[14]

16.4.2 How do I homeschool a child with Oppositional Defiant Disorder?

Homeschooling is not vitally important to this child. The single most important issue for her is behavioral skills. Without respect for authority and obedience to directions, she simply cannot learn. Intense therapy, forgiveness, and love are the only things she needs at this point.

A child with ODD may be able to participate in limited academics. He may excel in one subject while refusing to study the hated ones. Thus you often see asynchronous academic performance in such cases. A child's learning may improve if he is given choices along with patient consistency.

16.4.3 Is there a cure for ODD?

A child with ODD can improve over time. Both therapy and medication may help him manage his behavior while dealing with the underlying cause. He may remain easily triggered into his adult life, however. He may feel as though his life is often in crisis. You can help your child with ODD by remaining consistent. Learning calm reactions to his violent behavior may relieve a little bit of stress on your part.

As a parent, please seek support from therapists and doctors not only for your child but also for yourself. Many parents find reading on ODD and other behavioral issues gives perspective and valuable information. Some find assurance and comfort from support groups. Parenting a child with ODD can be extremely difficult and discouraging. It is of the utmost importance that you gather help and support.

16.5 MENTAL AND PHYSICAL DISABILITIES

16.5.1 What about children with mental or physical disabilities?

Different children have differing homeschool needs. Depending on the level of disability, your child's academic goals may be similar to those of typical homeschoolers. Whatever his ability, adapt the child's program of study to help him succeed to the best of his ability. Your child's doctor, physical therapist, and occupational therapist can help determine how to best teach your child for his strengths. They can also suggest helpful tools like larger pencils, more space, or other accommodations.

Many parents teaching a child with a disability find help from a tutor or specialized class. A child with a greater disability may spend less time on academics and more on life skills. Some children spend their days learning basic reading (or sight words) and number skills. Others may focus on personal care and housekeeping. Many respond best to recreational learning.

Regardless, homeschooling allows you to cater to your child's unique strengths while meeting his needs for now and for the future.

16.6 MENTAL ILLNESS

16.6.1 What is mental illness?

Children can develop mental illnesses, including depression, anxiety, obsessive-compulsive disorder, bipolar disorder, and eating disorders. As in adults, these can be the result of biological issues, or they may be a reaction to trauma. Or, traumatic events can trigger a latent chemical issue.

Licensed professional counselor Kimberly Ferren estimates that in up to 75 percent of childhood mental illness, the condition is tied to parental emotional health, a parent's reaction to the child, family crisis, or a sick sibling. This is not to blame the parents but, rather, to indicate ways a parent can help alleviate the child's symptoms.[15]

16.6.2 What are the signs of childhood mental illness?

Each mental illness has specific indicators an expert will look for. Depression, in particular, has several indicators, including the following:
- sudden decrease in academic performance in all subjects
- sleeping too much or not enough
- eating too much or not enough
- disproportionate anger and irritability
- preoccupation with death, not just of personal death, but the death of others or pets
- excessive, unreasonable fears, like birds, bug bites, the outdoors, or eating certain foods

16.6.3 How is childhood mental illness diagnosed?

Only a licensed professional should diagnose mental illness. A pediatrician should make a referral to a specialist, like a psychologist or a therapist.

Often a therapist can treat the child for a time before determining what diagnosis or medical treatment is appropriate.

Some children with mental illness do not require medication; they learn coping strategies and better thought processes through therapy. Parents themselves should also seek therapy for strategies and perspectives. It is important for parents to remember they do not cause the mental illness; it is a true illness with which the child—and thus the parents—must struggle.

Mental illness is dangerous to your child. You must get her help for her mental and emotional pain. If your doctor brushes off your concerns, seek a second opinion from a specialist. And if you suspect your child is struggling with a mental illness, do not wait to obtain help.

16.6.4 How do I homeschool a child with mental illness?

Address the illness first and foremost. The single most important goal is stabilization. Seek psychological help if necessary and obtain regular therapy from a licensed professional. *Do not hesitate to take your child to the hospital if you have any suspicions she is in physical danger.* A children's hospital can not only treat her immediate problems but can also offer diagnosis and referrals for ongoing care.

Christian parents might hesitate to seek mental health care, fearing wrong advice and treatment from non-Christian practitioners who may not share their values. This hesitation, though, will prolong her misery at the very least and could even put her life in danger. We would rush our child to the hospital if she were in severe stomach pain, just in case she had appendicitis. In the same way, we must rush to get help from the nearest professional when our child is in mental and emotional pain.

After the child is safe and stabilized, parents can look around for doctors and treatments they are comfortable with. In the heat of the moment, however, we must trust the doctors around us to make the life-and-death call for our child.

Aftercare is just as important as that immediate treatment. A child with mental illness will likely need long-term care from a therapist and doctor and will perhaps need such support for life. There may be a temptation to stop treatment when symptoms subside. But parents must recognize that this does not indicate they should stop treatment, but rather be grateful that the treatment is working. "Start low and go slow," says Dr. Joseph Hagan, former chair of the American Academy of Pediatrics' (AAP) Committee on the Psychosocial Aspects of Child and Family Health, "but [keep adjusting] until desired effect of recovery. Remember if you are 100% anxious and miserable, you'll look and feel great when you're only 50% anxious, but you're still only halfway better! It's also important to discuss with your patient when you start meds how long you are going to continue them, lest they feel good and stop prematurely."[16]

When the child is strong and mentally healthy, then she is ready to return to academics. During a mental crisis and early in treatment, she may be able to participate in little of her studies. But the single most important priority is to stabilize her mental, emotional, and spiritual health.

• • •

By faith, you can successfully homeschool and parent your special needs child. We can all trust that the professionals God puts into our lives—the therapists, doctors, and hospitals—will give us the care our children desperately need. Instead of fearing the resources available to us, we should trust these to help treat very real needs in our families. Try not to overthink it; once you are doing all that you can humanly do, simply leave the future with the Lord. He will give you hope and the assurance that you are on the right path, that he will guide and protect your child through treatment.

Have faith to care for yourself. Intense teaching of a special needs child depletes your physical, mental, emotional, and spiritual reserves. "Good self-care can't be overemphasized. It helps us as parents to see options we might not otherwise be able to see due to our own exhaustion and frustration. More importantly, it affords us a better perspective, giving us a heart to celebrate our child, sometimes even amidst the challenges," says Kimberly Ferren, LPC.[17] You must sleep and eat and take care of your physical body. Find times to step away to maintain perspective and rest. Hire certified caregivers to help your child and yourself step away. Find an outside interest or activity to release the mental tension. Find Christian support from friends and church family that is loving, not judgmental. And maintain your own identity—a parent God created not only to care for this child but also to serve him, to enjoy him, to bring glory to him.

Have faith that this child is a gift from God. He gave you this child for a reason—not because you are strong enough to handle the challenge, but to show you that only he can. He gave you this child to demonstrate his love, care, forgiveness, and strength. We all must have faith that our family is for our own good, for the glory God will show by his grace.

CONCLUSION

MY HOMESCHOOLING is different every year. And this book is a little different now than it was last year. From the time of writing to editing, I made a lot of changes, because my homeschooling has gone through a lot of changes.

If I were to write this book again now, I would change stuff again. Because my children are not the same age. I'm not using the same curricula. I'm teaching a little differently. My children are learning a little differently.

I'm in a slightly different life stage. I've made new friends. I've (Lord willing) strengthened my walk with the Lord. I've faced new challenges. I've tweaked my routine. I've changed the day I go to the library. I've swept the kitchen floor once.

So the changes I would make are small. I have changed what I'm doing and maybe who I am, but God hasn't changed. He still uses homeschooling to change me and to mold my family.

And God is working through your homeschooling too.

I earnestly pray that this book has helped you see some of that. Helped you see how uniquely God has made you, your family, and your home-schooling. Given you ideas to try in your teaching. Given you insight into your child's mysterious and unique learning. Given you strength to continue changing your homeschool for good. Given you peace that you can homeschool purposefully your own way. Given you a vision of how the Lord is, indeed, working within you.

Because he is. God loves you. God loves your family. God loves your work for your children. And God only wants good for you and for your family. God wants, in your homeschool, love, joy, peace, patience, kindness, goodness, faithfulness, gentleness, and self-control.

God wants you to teach how you teach best for the way your child learns best and to see how he works his best in your lives.

APPENDIX A:

FINDING YOUR TEACHING STYLE

NOT SURE EXACTLY what homeschool style you should choose? We looked at several in chapter 6. A couple of them probably resonated with you. The following list of questions will help you think through which style may fit you best. This is just to get you started; your teaching style will likely evolve over time. Your style may even be a mishmash of several strategies. It's possible you'll get to the end of this list and completely disagree with the answer the questionnaire provides. That means you already know your style! Great job!

1. How confident do you feel about the idea of homeschooling?
   a. Parents have been doing this for centuries, and I can too.
   b. Give me some good books, and I'm all set to go.
   c. I'll do this if someone tells me how to teach each day.
   d. I really wish I could homeschool AND leave this to the experts.
   e. My child will learn if I just give her the freedom.

2. What kind of support do you want?
   a. I wish I had infinite knowledge of times past, or else a plethora of reference books.
   b. Please build me a new bookshelf yesterday.
   c. I want a daily script or list of assignments.
   d. I need to know every day that my child has learned exactly what he needs to.
   e. I don't need much—my child and I have got this.

3. How involved do you want to be?
   a. I yearn to spend hours reading and discussing what we learn; helping my child think is really important to me.
   b. I want to spend hours reading to my child and enjoying the outdoors; helping her love literature and nature is really important to me.
   c. I want to teach my child directly some of the time and see measurable work the rest of the time; seeing that she is learning every day is really important to me.
   d. I don't need to personally teach; ensuring a quality education with expert teaching is really important to me.
   e. I want to let my child teach herself; creating an atmosphere of exploration is really important to me.

4. What does your ideal curriculum look like?
   a. I like a time line of events and information on how multiple subjects fit together in a given period of history.
   b. I would love a long booklist, sketch pads, and notebooks.
   c. Workbooks make everything easier.
   d. I really want to leave the curriculum to the experts.
   e. I don't need any silly curriculum. It's stifling.

5. How much technology do you want to use?
   a. I prefer mostly books, with limited technology for research.
   b. I prefer mostly books and nature specimens.
   c. I prefer mostly books, with some technology for research.
   d. Technology is an excellent learning tool we should make full use of.
   e. Learning through technology is a very good thing when the child's interests lead him in that direction.

6. How do you prefer to present your subjects?
   a. All of the humanities are interrelated; you can't separate them.
   b. Literature and nature naturally cover most subjects, but I prefer to study each subject individually in-depth. The outdoors has so much to teach us.

    c. It is just easier to study subjects separately by dividing them into separate textbooks.

    d. It is just easier to study subjects separately through individual online course modules.

    e. I prefer to present all subjects as they naturally occur in life, whether together or separate.

7. What do you think is your child's primary VARK learning style?
    a. Probably visual or reading/writing with a little auditory
    b. Probably auditory and kinesthetic
    c. Probably reading/writing
    d. Probably auditory, visual, and/or reading/writing
    e. Probably kinesthetic or all of them combined

8. How do you feel about hands-on projects?
    a. If you open a glitter bottle, I will pass out.
    b. My child loves hands-on projects related to what he is learning.
    c. I can take hands-on projects or leave them.
    d. I would rather not deal with crafts or projects.
    e. You can't learn if you are not hands-on.

9. How many children are you teaching, and do you want to teach them together or separately?
    a. I have several children who are close in age, and I want to teach them together for some subjects, but not all.
    b. I have several children of widely varying ages, and I want to teach them together for most subjects.
    c. I have three or more children, and I would prefer for them each to learn at their own levels.
    d. I have one or two children, and I would prefer for them each to learn at their own levels.
    e. Does it even matter?

10. If you have a baby or toddler, how easy is it to work around her?
    a. She stays on a routine.
    b. She's not always following her schedule, but I can easily work around her.

    c. It is really hard to work around her right now.

    d. She takes all my attention all day.

    e. Does it even matter?

11. How much time do you want to spend on homeschooling?

    a. I like to spend three to four good hours a day.

    b. I like to spend a couple of hours broken up throughout the day.

    c. I like to spend a couple of hours in one clearly delineated time.

    d. My time is very limited, so less than an hour of teaching time.

    e. I can't quantify it; learning occurs all day long.

12. How much structure do you like in your day?

    a. I follow a very strict schedule or routine.

    b. I'm fairly flexible but want moderate structure.

    c. I try to follow a schedule, but sometimes it is hard to keep to it.

    d. I have a lot to do besides homeschooling, so I want a schedule for myself and one for my kids.

    e. I thrive on flexibility and want very little structure.

13. What is your ideal field trip?

    a. I love to take museum tours and visit historical sites on vacation.

    b. I love a good nature walk.

    c. Anything is great as long as a support group will plan for me.

    d. I don't have a lot of time for field trips except on the weekends or breaks.

    e. We would go everywhere, every day if we could.

14. What are your hopes for your child's college plans?

    a. I want to prepare my child for the rigor at a top college.

    b. I want to prepare my child for college in case he wants to go, but there are many other wonderful options open to him if not.

    c. I want to prepare my child to attend college, so I am focusing on developing his reading comprehension to the college level.

    d. I want to prepare my child to attend college, so I am focused on helping him navigate a digital environment.

    e. My child can do whatever he wants; it's his decision.

15. What do you want your child to get out of homeschooling?
    a. I want to teach my child to reason through life's issues.
    b. I want my child to love learning forever.
    c. I want my child to be able to learn new concepts through studying books and articles.
    d. I want my child to be able to learn new concepts in a digital environment.
    e. I want my child to be confident.

16. What teaching style most attracts you?
    a. classical
    b. Charlotte Mason
    c. textbook
    d. online
    e. unschooling

How did you answer?
Mostly a's: you might prefer classical.
Mostly b's: you might prefer Charlotte Mason.
Mostly c's: you might prefer textbooks.
Mostly d's: you might prefer online classes.
Mostly e's: you might prefer unschooling.
A mixture of several letters: you are probably eclectic, using multiple styles the way you love best.

APPENDIX B:

SAMPLE ROUTINES

I TOLD YOU I HATE SCHEDULES. I forced myself and my children into a schedule for several years, and it just caused misery and heartache. Every time my husband called asking for an errand, or the baby determined to nurse five minutes longer, or I tripped on the floor, or a child coughed, my entire day was thrown off. Then I was cranky and tried to drag my children through the day faster, then they were cranky and unable to concentrate. And no one—no one—was smiling.

Finally, I listened to my fellow homeschool friends and mommies everywhere and threw out my time schedule. And then I started breathing again.

I have changed my routine dozens of times since then. Life changes, needs change, children grow and change. Holding my routine loosely has enabled me to both organize my thoughts *and* accomplish at least the bare minimum. With maybe time left to finish my lukewarm coffee.

I don't always get "mommy time." But right now, I'm thankful to be in a season of my life when I sometimes can. I usually enjoy my devotions, take a shower, make coffee, and maybe check social media before my children need me in the morning. That is really nice when it happens.

Here are some of the routines that have worked for me. For some points, I've given approximate time periods I aim for, but they are not set in stone. Go, my friend, and find the routine that works for *you*. Then go change it again every time it doesn't work!

EARLY LEARNING

- Mommy time
- Morning routine: breakfast, teeth, dress, chores
- Playtime
- Bible story
- Phonics time—10 minutes
- Numbers time—10 minutes
- Snack time
- Other activities (craft, coloring, memorizing a poem)
- Play outside
- Lunch
- Read aloud
- Rest time
- Play until dinner

ELEMENTARY

- Mommy time
- Morning routine
- Bible and memory time—20 minutes
- Reading—20 minutes
- Grammar—20 minutes
- Snack time
- Math—30 minutes
- History or science—30 minutes
- Electives—20 minutes
- Playtime
- Lunch
- Read aloud
- Rest time (reading, playing quietly, listening to audiobooks)
- Play until dinner

MIDDLE SCHOOL

- Mommy time
- Morning routine

- Bible—20 minutes
- Literature and/or grammar—30 minutes
- Snack time
- Math—30 minutes
- History or science—30 minutes
- Independent work
- Lunch
- Read aloud
- Electives—30 minutes
- Rest time (reading, independent work, audiobooks)
- Play until dinner

HIGH SCHOOL

- Mommy time
- Morning routine
- Bible—30 minutes
- Go over previous day's work—30 minutes
- Independent work on most difficult subject / answer questions / review lesson together
- Snack time
- Independent work / answer questions / review lesson together
- Relax—30 minutes
- Lunch
- Read aloud
- Quiet time (finish work, read, work on a project)
- Answer questions on homework
- Play until dinner

MULTIPLE CHILDREN

- Mommy time
- Morning routine
- Bible—20 minutes
- Discuss the day's assignments—20 minutes
- Reading time with youngest child / others work independently—20 minutes

- Youngest child writes or colors / answer next child's questions or give brief lesson
- Continue working through the age levels of children, giving the youngest a brief project to work on or letting him play
- Snack time
- Math time with youngest
- Work through the ages again (youngest plays)
- Group lesson (history, science, elective)
- Lunch
- Read aloud
- Youngest rest time, help older students finish
- Rest time for everyone
- Play until dinner

MULTIPLE CHILDREN ALONG WITH TEENS

Same as the one above, except answering teen questions after the younger ones are finished with their schoolwork. Teens can work independently at their own rate, following their own routine.

WORK-AT-HOME MOM

- Mandatory mommy time
- Morning routine
- Bible—20 minutes
- Routine for appropriate age level above
- Mandatory stop at lunchtime (resume subjects the next day)
- Lunch
- Read aloud
- Rest time for everyone—2 hours for children, 20 minutes for Mom
- Mom works while children continue to rest
- Children play, Mom may work some more
- Dinner
- Evening routine
- Mom perhaps works an hour or two
- Mom's mandatory decent bedtime (allowing for 7 to 9 hours of sleep)

APPENDIX C:

STUDENT ESSAY EDITING CHECKLISTS

THE FOLLOWING PAGES INCLUDE sample editing checklists for both a one-paragraph essay and a multiple-paragraph essay. Copy the appropriate list and give it to your student to help her edit her writing. Adapt the list by crossing off items she has not learned yet and adding areas you want to emphasize. Make it your own!

As a teacher, you might also use these checklists to help you grade your students' essays in lieu of the editing rubric in appendix D.

ONE-PARAGRAPH ESSAY CHECKLIST

Topic sentence
- ☐ clearly states what the essay is about
- ☐ fulfills the purpose of the assignment
- ☐ contains a clear, decisive verb
- ☐ begins the essay in a descriptive, interesting way
- ☐ states or alludes to the supporting facts to follow

Paragraph
- ☐ presents the supporting facts in an interesting manner
- ☐ supports the topic sentence with clear details, such as
  - examples
  - reasons
  - events
- ☐ organizes these facts in one of the following ways:
  - from first to last
  - by strong reason, weaker reason, strong reason
  - by location, near to far or far to near
  - chronologically
- ☐ conclusion sentence restates topic sentence with different words or tells why we should care about the essay

Word choice
- ☐ uses strong, descriptive words
- ☐ uses active verbs
- ☐ avoids weak words like *very*, *good*, *like*, or *a lot*
- ☐ avoids repeated words

Grammar

- ☐ contains only complete sentences (i.e., contains no fragments)
- ☐ compound sentences are separated by a comma and a coordinating conjunction like *and* or *but* (i.e., contains no run-on sentences)
- ☐ varies sentence structure
- ☐ maintains consistent verb tense (present, past, future) throughout
- ☐ maintains consistent person throughout (he/she *or* you *or* I)
- ☐ uses correct subject-verb agreement
- ☐ uses correct pronoun-antecedent agreement
- ☐ keeps adjectives and adverbs in the correct place, not creating a humorous misplacement
- ☐ uses correct spelling
- ☐ uses correct punctuation
- ☐ uses correct capitalization

Presentation

- ☐ contains correctly formatted heading including name, date, and assignment topic
- ☐ contains title
- ☐ uses correct font
- ☐ uses correct spacing
- ☐ properly indents paragraph

Other

- ☐ _____
- ☐ _____
- ☐ _____
- ☐ _____
- ☐ _____

MULTIPLE-PARAGRAPH ESSAY CHECKLIST

Topic paragraph

- ☐ includes a thesis statement that
  - clearly states what the essay is about
  - appears at the beginning or end of the paragraph
  - fulfills the purpose of the assignment
  - contains a clear, decisive verb
- ☐ begins the essay in a descriptive, interesting way
- ☐ states or alludes to the supporting facts to follow
- ☐ demonstrates why we care to read the essay, what is the purpose of the essay, or why the facts matter
- ☐ develops the *why* of the essay
- ☐ may contain a concluding sentence introducing the paragraphs to follow

Body paragraphs

- ☐ each contain a clear topic statement supporting the thesis statement
- ☐ each introduce the supporting facts in an interesting manner
- ☐ each support the topic and thesis statement with clear details, such as
  - examples
  - reasons
  - events
- ☐ are each organized in one of the following ways:
  - from first to last
  - by strong reason, weaker reason, strong reason
  - by location, near to far or far to near
  - chronologically
- ☐ as a whole are organized in one of the following ways:
  - from first to last
  - by strong reason, weaker reason, strong reason
  - by location, near to far or far to near
  - chronologically

Concluding paragraph

- ☐ includes a conclusion statement that
  - restates the thesis statement in a different way
  - is placed at the beginning or end of the paragraph
- ☐ persuades the reader to change his mind or take action
- ☐ emphasizes the *why* of the essay
- ☐ supports the conclusion statement with examples or creative retelling of previously mentioned facts
- ☐ includes a final sentence that restates the thesis

Word choice

- ☐ uses strong, descriptive words
- ☐ uses active verbs
- ☐ avoids weak words like *very, good, like,* or *a lot*
- ☐ avoids repeated words

Grammar

- ☐ contains only complete sentences (i.e., contains no fragments)
- ☐ compound sentences are separated by a comma and a coordinating conjunction like *and* or *but* (i.e., contains no run-on sentences)
- ☐ varies sentence structure
- ☐ maintains consistent verb tense (present, past, future) throughout
- ☐ maintains consistent person throughout (he/she *or* you *or* I)
- ☐ uses correct subject-verb agreement
- ☐ uses correct pronoun-antecedent agreement
- ☐ keeps adjectives and adverbs in the correct place, not creating a humorous misplacement
- ☐ uses correct spelling
- ☐ uses correct punctuation
- ☐ uses correct capitalization

Presentation

- ☐ contains correctly formatted heading including name, date, and assignment topic
- ☐ contains title
- ☐ uses correct font
- ☐ uses correct spacing
- ☐ properly indents paragraphs
- ☐ uses correct form of citations, if applicable

Other

- ☐ _____
- ☐ _____
- ☐ _____
- ☐ _____
- ☐ _____

APPENDIX D:
SAMPLE ESSAY GRADING RUBRIC

ON THE NEXT PAGE IS AN EXAMPLE GRADING RUBRIC to demonstrate how a rubric works. For each category, evaluate which description most closely matches your student's paper, then assign the corresponding points for that section. Add the points for each section and write the total in the bottom right corner of the chart. You will likely want to develop your own chart that fits your teaching style and priorities. If you prefer not to use a rubric, the editing checklists in appendix C can also serve as grading tools.

	SUPERB (10 PTS)	EXCELLENT (8 PTS)	GOOD (6 PTS)	POOR (4 PTS)	TOTAL POINTS
THESIS AND INTRODUCTION	▫ Thesis is clearly stated and well phrased. ▫ Thesis fulfills assignment purpose in an original or unexpected manner. ▫ Introduction clearly states supporting facts. ▫ Introduction demonstrates the essay's *why* in a particularly compelling way.	▫ Thesis is clearly stated. ▫ Thesis fulfills assignment purpose. ▫ Introduction states supporting facts. ▫ Introduction demonstrates the essay's *why*.	▫ Thesis is stated but unclearly. ▫ Thesis imperfectly fulfills assignment purpose. ▫ Introduction alludes to some supporting facts. ▫ Introduction imperfectly demonstrates the essay's *why*.	▫ There is no thesis statement. ▫ Introduction fails to mention supporting facts. ▫ Introduction does not demonstrate the essay's *why*.	
BODY OR PARAGRAPHS (GRADE EACH BODY PARAGRAPH INDIVIDUALLY)	▫ Body paragraph has a clear topic sentence supporting the thesis statement. ▫ Several clear and relevant facts support the topic sentence in an interesting and polished way. ▫ Sentences are organized clearly and persuasively.	▫ Body paragraph has a topic sentence supporting the thesis statement. ▫ Several clear and relevant facts support the topic. ▫ Sentences are organized clearly.	▫ Body paragraph has a topic sentence that imperfectly or unclearly supports the thesis statement. ▫ Some facts support the topic sentence, but the connection is not always clear. ▫ Sentences are partially organized.	▫ Body paragraph lacks a topic sentence supporting the thesis statement. ▫ Very few facts support the topic sentence, and/or the connection is not clear. ▫ Sentence organization feels haphazard.	
CONCLUSION PARAGRAPH	▫ Includes a strongly persuasive conclusion statement. ▫ Includes strong support for the conclusion.	▫ Includes a persuasive conclusion statement. ▫ Includes strong support for the conclusion.	▫ Includes a basic conclusion statement. ▫ Includes little support for the conclusion.	▫ Includes a weak conclusion statement. ▫ Includes no support for the conclusion.	

WORD CHOICE AND GRAMMAR	□ Uses many strong, descriptive words and few repeated words. □ Uses complete and correct sentences (no fragments or run-ons) with varying sentence structure. □ Maintains consistent verb tense and pronoun use throughout. □ Demonstrates correct subject-verb and pronoun-antecedent agreement with no errors. □ Demonstrates correct spelling, punctuation, and capitalization with no errors.	□ Uses strong, descriptive words and few repeated words. □ Uses complete and correct sentences (no fragments or run-ons). □ Maintains consistent verb tense and pronoun use throughout with few errors. □ Demonstrates correct subject-verb and pronoun-antecedent agreement with few errors. □ Demonstrates correct spelling, punctuation, and capitalization with few errors.	□ Uses a mix of strong and weak words and occasional repeated words. □ Sentences are usually complete and correct (few fragments or run-ons). □ Verb tense and pronoun use are relatively consistent. □ Demonstrates some awareness of subject-verb and pronoun-antecedent agreement with several errors. □ Demonstrates awareness of correct spelling, punctuation, and capitalization with several errors.	□ Uses mostly weak words and many repeated words. □ Uses a number of fragments or run-ons. □ Verb tense and pronoun use are inconsistent. □ Demonstrates little awareness of subject-verb and pronoun-antecedent agreement with many errors. □ Demonstrates little awareness of correct spelling, punctuation, and capitalization with many errors.
PRESENTATION	□ Has correct number of paragraphs. □ Paper is formatted correctly. □ Citations are formatted correctly.	□ Has correct number of paragraphs. □ Paper is formatted correctly, with a few exceptions. □ Most citations are formatted correctly, but a few incorrectly.	□ Paper is missing one paragraph. □ Paper is not formatted correctly. □ Many citations are formatted incorrectly.	□ Paper is missing two or more paragraphs. □ No attempt at formatting has been made. □ Needed citations are not present.
				/40

APPENDIX E:

HIGH SCHOOL TRANSCRIPTS AND COURSE DESCRIPTIONS

CREATING A HIGH SCHOOL TRANSCRIPT is not a complicated process. Colleges do not expect—nor want—a dissertation on the validity and thoroughness of your homeschool education. They simply need to verify that the requisite courses have been completed. Most colleges just want a straightforward list the admissions office can glance at and keep on file for scholarships.

Many universities help homeschoolers out by posting online what they want a transcript to look like. Viewing these example transcripts taught me that my transcript was way, way too detailed. I had to edit it down from several pages to only one when I submitted my firstborn's paperwork. I kept the same format, then, for subsequent graduates. You might want to research examples from a few possible colleges to see what I mean. If all else fails, keep a detailed transcript, then simplify it after you contact the college admissions office and ask them what they would like to see.

Throughout my children's high school years, I keep a running transcript in a Google Doc. I share that as view-only with my student so she can see her grades. At the end of each semester, I fill out the classes finished and grades earned. This way I don't need to remember anything (which I wouldn't, anyway). Sending this transcript off to schools for early admissions and final paperwork is a breeze, since it is always ready.

For early admission, then, I have a completed transcript up through the first or second semester of junior year. This is easy to send in to the admissions office. Both colleges my children have applied to offered them academic scholarships based solely on that early transcript.

In addition, just in case it was needed, I kept track of subject content on separate pages of the same document for my firstborn. I listed the subject, a brief description of what that subject covers, and the main resources used (I discuss this further in section 13.3.5). I tried not to go into detail about every single little thing included in that class, nor did I list every resource. Many curriculum websites give specific examples for how to include their published course on a transcript. Making your own description, though, is as simple as explaining what the student was learning over the semester and what the outcome was. For subjects like English that are studied over multiple years, I just numbered them 1, 2, 3, and 4 for each year of high school. This list was a "just in case" feature I didn't end up needing. I skipped it with my subsequent transcripts, knowing I could complete such a list in a couple of hours if I needed it.

My other "just in case" effort is example work. If you keep portfolios for the state or for your personal records, you already have plenty of proof of work. (I discuss portfolios in section 13.3.6). For the rest of us, it can be a security blanket to save lab notebooks, sample writing, and records of projects completed. I have heard urban legends that some universities ask for these examples, though I have never met a real person who needed them. I do save a few things just in case, but obviously, I'm not stressing out over it.

Below, I share with you an example transcript similar to the ones my students used to gain entrance to their first-choice colleges.

SAMPLE HOMESCHOOL TRANSCRIPT

Student: Mark Doe
Birth Date: April 22, 2001
Gender: Male
Parents: John and Jane Doe

Address: 305 Appletree Lane, Wheaton, IL
Phone: (722) 403-2041
School: Homeschooled
Graduation Date: May 30, 2019

Grade	Year	Course Title	Fall	Spring	Final	Credits	GPA
9	2015–2016	Bible I	100A	100A	100A	1	3.63
		English I	89B	94A	92A	1	
		Algebra I	88B	85B	87B	1	
		Honors World History I	82B	92A	87B	1	
		Honors Biology	82B	88B	85B	1	
		Spanish I	94A	93A	94A	1	
		Honors Music I	100A	100A	100A	1	
		PE I	100A	100A	100A	1	
10	2016–2017	Bible II	100A	100A	100A	1	3.88
		Honors English II	95A	96A	96A	1	
		Geometry	86B	90A	88B	1	
		Honors World History II	91A	93A	92A	1	
		Chemistry	85B	95A	90A	1	
		Spanish II	95A	100A	98A	1	
		Honors Music II	100A	100A	100A	1	
		PE II	100A	100A	100A	1	
11	2017–2018	English III	91A	95A	93A	1	3.83
		Algebra II	86B	84B	85B	1	
		Honors World History III	95A	96A	96A	1	
		Anatomy	90A	93A	92A	1	
		Spanish III	91A	91A	91A	1	
		Honors Music III	100A	100A	100A	1	
12	2018–2019	Honors English	90A	89B	90A	1	4.0
		Bible Survey	90A	88B	90A	1	
		Honors World History IV	92A	87B	90A	1	
		Cultural Philosophy	95A	90A	93A	1	
		Honors Music IV	100A	100A	100A	1	

Total Credits: 27
Final High School GPA: 3.84
GPA is unweighted
Credits and Grading Scale: A 90–100; B 80–89; C 70–79; D 60–69; F below 60
Weight for one-credit courses (120 hours): A = 4; B = 3; C = 2; D = 1; F = 0
Activities: principal violinist, New Life Symphony Orchestra | piano teacher | church youth choir president | church orchestra | Awana Cubbies leader (3-year-olds teacher) | soccer referee | volunteer, Life Message Food Pantry
This 2019 transcript is valid and complete: Jane Doe, parent/teacher

SAMPLE COURSE DESCRIPTIONS

Sample course descriptions are easy to prepare. In the following examples, notice the simple way they are phrased, including general subject matter covered and textbooks used. The Bible course below I pulled together from different resources. Algebra was a textbook course. Grammar was a combination of two full courses, giving it an Honors standing. History was a classical course with extra time and effort given to geography, government, philosophy, and church history, making it also an honors course. Music was a listing of activities that together required nearly twice the usual 120 to 180 hours of study, making it too an honors course.

Bible I—Weekly Scripture memorization on topics of doctrine and Christian Living. Old Testament (first semester) and New Testament (second semester) overview course. Texts: Awana's *Trek*, Meade's *The Most Important Thing You'll Ever Study*, vols. 1–4.

Honors English I—English grammar and composition in detail for two semesters. Combined with World Literature III, which includes *Pride and Prejudice*, *Les Misérables*, *Great Expectations*, *The Scarlet Letter*, and *Crime and Punishment*. Shorter works from authors such as Goethe, Twain, Dickens, Stowe, Crane, Melville, Ibsen, Conrad, Tolstoy, and Wilde, as well as other short works of poetry, are read and analyzed. Texts: Abeka's *Grammar and Composition III*, Ryken's *Words of Delight*, Strand and Boland's *The Making of a Poem*, and classic literature listed above.

Algebra I—A first-year algebra course, covering proofs, statistics, and probability as well as algebra-based real-world problems. Text: Saxon's *Algebra I*, Khan Academy (online).

Honors World History III—World history course beginning with US President John Adams and continuing through William McKinley, covering major events of the 1800s. Follows developments in the United States, South America, Europe, Australia, China, and Japan. Of particular focus are the Congress of Vienna, Victorian England, Manifest Destiny, Marx and Communism, the American Civil War, and European Imperialism. Course includes a half-credit's worth of American history, geography, government, philosophy, and church history. Texts: Breunig and Levinger's *The*

Revolutionary Era, Dudley's *Antebellum America*, Ojeda's *The Civil War*, Smith's *Imperialism*, Wood's *The Gilded Age*, Rich's *The Age of Nationalism and Reform*, Foster's *Abraham Lincoln's World* and *George Washington's World*, Withrows' *Courage and Conviction*, as well as supplementary reading and independent research.

Physical Science—Includes such topics as the atmosphere, the hydrosphere, weather, the structure of the Earth, environmentalism, the physics of motion, Newton's laws, gravity, and astrophysics. Concentrating on the controversies around the modern environmentalist movement. Includes lab work. Text: Wile's *Exploring Creation with Physical Science*.

Spanish I—Basic Spanish conversational skills, including greetings and introductions, simple questions and answers, shopping, and much more. Text: Rosetta Stone's *Spanish I* along with conversations and evaluation with a native speaker.

Honors Music I—Intensive private study in classical technique and repertoire for piano and viola with mandatory once-per-semester performances. Study of music theory and music history. Evaluation of classical form and composition. Regular choral training and performance. Regular handbells training and performance.

PE I—Recreational soccer referee, grade 9. Training and experience in officiating recreational soccer for noncompetitive teams under age 14. Twenty-five games.

HOMESCHOOL RESOURCES

THIS SECTION INCLUDES a listing of many resources and curriculum suppliers specifically catering to homeschooling. This list is not exhaustive, but it does contain many products and resources to get you started. Now, I am intentionally not sharing with you specifically which resources and teaching materials I use. I encourage you to look around, experiment, and find the right products for your teaching style and your student's learning style.

GENERAL HOMESCHOOLING

Answers in Genesis Creation science resources and Christian curriculum from Ken Ham and others. Answersingenesis.org

Cathy Duffy Homeschool Curriculum Reviews The homeschool standard of curriculum and homeschool resources with more than 1,500 reviews. Duffy's book *102 Top Picks for Homeschool Curriculum* is available digitally. *How to Choose Homeschool Curriculum* guides parents through questionnaires and information to help sort through curriculum choices. Free newsletter and website listings. Cathyduffyreviews.com

Charlotte Mason Research Company Books and articles on the Charlotte Mason teaching style by Charlotte Mason expert Karen Andreola. Charlottemason.com

Christianbook (formerly Christian Book Distributors) Online retail of homeschool curriculum from a variety of publishers, plus biblical resources. All subjects including Bible and electives. Preschool through adult. Catalog and online store. Christianbook.com

Classical Conversations Education groups meeting locally to enhance classical learning through group lessons and parent support. Online bookstore with curriculum and products. Classicalconversations.com

Grace and Truth Books Online retail of homeschool resources, Christian books, character training materials, and more. Available online, through select retailers, and at the Sand Springs, Oklahoma, store. Preschool through adult. Graceandtruthbooks.com

Home School Legal Defense Association Legal advocates and experts on homeschooling since 1983. Offers support, legal representation, consultation, and information for members. Hslda.org

Jim Hodges Audio Books Unabridged recordings of G. A. Henty novels, classic children's literature, and old-time radio programs. Recorded professionally by homeschool father Jim Hodges. Discounted Download-a-Month Club available. CD or digital. Elementary through high school. Jimhodgesaudiobooks.com

Moore Expressions New and used homeschool textbooks. Offers consulting to choose materials for your child's learning style. Mooreexpressions.com

Rainbow Resource Center Online retail of homeschool resources, curriculum, and Christian materials. Preschool through adult. Rainbowresource.com

Raising Real Men Books on education and test preparation as well as parenting and family. Online parenting seminars targeted for homeschoolers also available. Raisingrealmen.com

Shekinah Homeschool Books Online retail of homeschool books and resources from a variety of publishers, with lowest-price guarantee. Preschool through high school. Shopshekinahglory.com

The Back Pack Used curricula including out-of-print titles, selling both individual books and curriculum packages. Elementary through high school. Thebackpack.com

Timberdoodle Online retail of homeschool books also offering curriculum packages in secular or Christian sets at different levels of study within each grade. All subjects including Bible, STEM, and other electives. Preschool through high school. Timberdoodle.com

PUBLISHERS OF COMPLETE CURRICULA OR MULTIPLE SUBJECTS

A Reason For Workbook curriculum and leveled readers from a Christian perspective. Science curriculum appropriate for teaching multiple ages together. Spelling, handwriting, reading, and science. Kindergarten through middle school. Areasonfor.com

Accelerated Christian Education (A.C.E.) Online courses or self-paced mini-textbook Packet of Accelerated Christian Education (PACE). Student studies at his own rate, allowing different grade levels for subjects. All subjects. Online course or print. Kindergarten through high school. Aceministries.com

Abeka Traditional textbooks from a Christian viewpoint. Stand-alone textbooks and teachers' manuals. Courses also offered in digital form and online classes. All subjects, including Bible and electives. Preschool through high school. Abeka.com/homeschool

Alpha Omega Student-led LIFEPAC courses in three- to four-week intervals. Available also in teacher-led materials or online classes. Online and phone support. All subjects. Workbooks or online. Third grade through high school. Aop.com

AIM Academy Online classes in most subjects and test prep. Fifth grade through high school. Debrabell.com

BJU Press Traditional textbooks from a Christian perspective. Print textbooks, e-textbooks, and online classes available. Online videos explaining concepts also available through their AfterSchoolHelp. Available online and through select retailers. All subjects including Bible and electives. Preschool through high school. Bjupress.com

BookShark Complete curriculum kits combining literature-based and textbook materials written by them and a variety of publishers. Curriculum designed for a four-day school week. Individual subjects also available. Preschool through middle school, with some high school subjects. Bookshark.com

Bright Ideas Press Courses from a Christian perspective for individual homeschools or co-ops. Many courses adaptable for multiple ages. History, geography, science, English, and electives. Digital and print options. Elementary through high school. Brightideaspress.com

Calvert Education Online self-paced program utilizing games and videos. Available in individual courses or complete curriculum. Third grade through high school. Calverteducation.com

Christian Liberty Press Accredited coursework in textbook form and online classes. Includes modified courses and advanced studies in all grades including kindergarten. Individual classes also available. All subjects including Bible and electives. Preschool through high school. Shopchristianliberty.com

Cornerstone Curriculum Biblical worldview-based approach utilizing textbooks, literature, and videos. Most subjects including Bible and electives for elementary; worldview, science, and math for high school. Kindergarten through high school. Cornerstonecurriculum.com

Easy Peasy All-in-One Homeschool Free Christian curriculum for all grades, using daily assignments combined with free resources on the internet. Developed by a homeschool mom and expanded regularly. Preschool through high school. Allinonehomeschool.com

Geography Matters History and geography courses from a Christian perspective. Curriculum sets for all subjects (except math) available. Print or download. Kindergarten through high school. Geomatters.com

God's Little Explorers Preschool curriculum covering multiple subjects based on Bible lessons. Includes letters, numbers, science, and life skills. Download. Motherhoodonadime.com/gods-little-explorers-preschool-curriculum

Heart of Dakota Integrated curriculum program with prepared lesson plans designed around skill levels rather than grades. Covers reading/literature, English, history, geography, Bible. Appropriate for teaching multiple ages. Early learning through high school. Heartofdakota.com

Homeschool Complete All-in-one Christian curriculum based on unit studies, manipulatives, and worksheets. Includes lesson plans, flash cards, and manipulatives needed. Calendar and student lesson planner included. All subjects including Bible and physical education. Kindergarten through fourth grade. Homeschoolcomplete.com

Annenberg Learner Free online video lessons in foreign language, English, literature, science, math, and more. Kindergarten through college. Learner.org

Logos Press Classical Christian curricula and Christian living titles. Curricula and boxed sets available for first grade through eighth grade. Online high school classes. Logospressonline.com

Master Books Complete curricula or individual subjects from a Christian viewpoint. Also providing parenting resources. Print and digital. Preschool through high school. Masterbooks.com

Mott Media Reprints and updates of classic curriculum and resources, including McGuffey's Readers and Ray's for Today Arithmetic. Kindergarten through middle school. Mottmedia.com

My Father's World Literature-based integrated curriculum based on classical and Charlotte Mason teaching styles in a five-year history cycle. Intended for teaching multiple ages together. Includes humanities subjects and Bible. Primarily real books. Preschool through high school. Mfwbooks.com

Savvas Learning Textbook programs in language arts, math, science, and social studies. Courses include games, online videos, and more. Print and online. Kindergarten through high school. Homeschool.savvas.com

Queen Homeschool Supplies Charlotte Mason–style curriculum by Keith and Sandi Queen. Includes curriculum-in-a-box for preschool through high school or single subject curriculum, including Bible. Queenshomeschool.com

Rod and Staff Curriculum and resources from an Anabaptist viewpoint. Select subjects, including Bible. Preschool through tenth grade. Only available on Amazon.

Sonlight Curriculum Complete curriculum and individual subject packages featuring integrated humanities based on literature. Appropriate for teaching multiple ages at once. All subjects including Bible. Primarily real books. Preschool through high school. Sonlight.com

Tapestry of Grace Integrated classical Christian curriculum centered on a four-year history cycle utilizing classical and modern literature. Subjects and topics coordinated across age groups for group teaching. Curriculum includes history, literature, writing, Bible, philosophy, and more. Teacher's guide digital or print. Preschool through high school. Tapestryofgrace.com

The Good and the Beautiful Literature-based curriculum emphasizing family, God, character development, and nature. The open-and-go courses require no daily prep time and combine multiple subjects. Available online and in the Lehi, Utah, store. Print or digital products available. Preschool through high school. Goodandthebeautiful.com

The Noah Plan Curricula and teaching guides centered around American Christian history. All subjects. Offers CD, digital, and print options. Kindergarten through high school. Face.net/curriculum/

Veritas Press Classical curriculum from a Christian perspective. Complete curriculum kits available for parent-taught, web-based self-paced, or online classes. All subjects including Bible. Physical or online. Preschool through high school. Veritaspress.com

Well-Trained Mind Classical curriculum from a Christian perspective. Specializing in history, yet offering many resources for English, writing, languages, and literature. Print preschool through high school. Online academy for middle school and high school. Welltrainedmind.com

WinterPromise Charlotte-Mason style curriculum including humanities and other subjects. Designed around themes accessible to multiple ages. Print or digital. Preschool through high school. Winterpromise.com

BIBLE

Bible Road Trip Three-year Bible survey curriculum. Takes students through a Bible survey course five times throughout the homeschool years. Offers corresponding notebooking journals and Bible memory verse card sets. Preschool through high school. Thinkingkidspress.com

Cat and Dog Theology Bible course emphasizing selfless Christianity. Eight years available. Print. Kindergarten through high school. Amazon and catanddogtheology.com

Deeper Roots Curriculum emphasizing Christian character and worldview. Print and download. Middle school and high school. Amazon and deeperroots.com

Discover 4 Yourself for Kids Six-week Bible study series by Kay Arthur. Stories guide the child through the topic of each study. Includes puzzles and activities. Print. Ages eight through twelve. Amazon and shop.precept.org/collections/discover-for-yourself-kids

Grapevine Studies Bible course for homeschool and small classes (co-ops). Utilizes stick figure drawings to help children understand and retain their learning. Print or digital. Preschool through high school. Amazon and grapevinestudies.com

The Picture-Smart Bible Teaches Bible facts by helping the child draw one detailed picture over time. Print. Kindergarten through high school. Amazon and shop.celebratekids.com/picture-smart-bible/

Positive Action for Christ Curriculum developed for schools, utilizing teacher's manual and workbooks. Includes Scripture memory and quizzes. Print. Preschool through high school. Positiveaction.org/school

Sound Words for Kids Bible studies on theology, including devotions, memory work, notebooking, and activities. Digital. Elementary. Proverbialhomemakerstore.com

Summit Ministries Bible curriculum focused on biblical worldview. Print. Kindergarten through high school. Digital high school. Amazon and summit.org/curriculum

PHONICS, READING, VOCABULARY

Alpha-Phonics Reading primers and tutorials used by homeschoolers since 1984 Print, CD, e-book, and video workshops. Alpha-phonics.com

Explode the Code Phonics course focusing on reading comprehension. Skill assessment available. Online or workbook. Kindergarten through fourth grade. Explodethecode.com

Saxon Phonics and Spelling Introduces letters and sounds before learning words and more complex blends, prefixes/suffixes, and compound words. Homeschool kit includes teacher's manual and student materials. Kindergarten through third grade. Available on Amazon.

Spelling Power Single course teaches spelling rules and words in fifteen-minute lessons including a review test, word practice, and new principles. Print. Kindergarten through high school. Spellingpower.com

Spelling You See Multilevel spelling program emphasizing visual memory. Lessons include reading and copy work. Courses are designed for developmental stage rather than grade levels. Print. Elementary. Spellingyousee.com

Teach Your Child to Read in 100 Easy Lessons One book that contains step-by-step twenty-minute lessons to teach a child to read from beginning phonics to a second-grade reading level. Print. Available on Amazon.

ENGLISH WRITING

Brave Writer Language arts curriculum focusing on writing. Courses adaptable to teaching multiple ages together. Online classes offered in three- to six-month increments. Kindergarten through high school. Digital download. Bravewriter.com

Institute for Excellence in Writing (IEW) Writing curriculum used by both neurotypical students and those with sensory or learning needs. Recommended teacher training available online. Online classes, digital downloads, and print curriculum. Kindergarten through high school. Iew.com

Readers in Residence/Writers in Residence Courses in reading and writing. Textbooks or online classes. Fifth grade through high school. Debrabell.com

WriteShop Writing curriculum that helps parents to not only teach writing but also to edit and grade. Grammar books also available. Curriculum also available for co-ops. Workbook and video. Kindergarten through high school. Writeshop.com

WriteAtHome Courses in nonfiction (including research, essay, and persuasion) and creative writing. Available in thirty-two, sixteen-, and eight-week courses. Includes grading. Online. Middle school through high school. Writeathome.com

Write Source English language arts and writing workbooks. Social-emotional courses also available. Online resources included. Kindergarten through high school. Thoughtfullearning.com

ENGLISH LITERATURE

Circle C Adventures Yearlong reading and literature bundles. Each package includes books, study and activity books, and hands-on creative packets (lapbooks). Also contains a daily schedule for independent learning. Second grade through eighth grade. CircleCAdventures.com/literature-bundles

Common Sense Press Christian homeschool publisher known for the series Learning Language Arts through Literature. Resources for math, science, and Bible also available. Print and e-book. Elementary through middle school. Commonsensepress.com

Five in a Row Easy-to-use teacher lesson plans using classic library books. Reading the same book five days in a row, students learn a new concept each day, including geography, art, character qualities, science, and more. Print and digital. Preschool through elementary. Fiveinarow.com

Progeny Press Study guides from a Christian perspective for classic literature. Print, CD, or digital. Elementary through high school. Progenypress.com

Total Language Plus Language arts taught through literature. Study guides focus on spelling, vocabulary, writing, and more. Print. Third grade through high school. Totallanguageplus.com

MATH

Art of Problem solving Challenging math curriculum for grades five through twelve, beginning with prealgebra. Separate volumes for math contest preparation also available. Younger students study from a comic-book-style text with accompanying workbook. Online curriculum also available. Second grade through high school. Artofproblemsolving.com

Chalk Dust Company Christian company offering math instructional sets including textbooks, DVDs, and student manuals for upper elementary through high school. Math drill set available for first grade through fourth grade. Print and DVD. Elementary through high school. Chalkdust.com

Life of Fred Mathematics presented in a humorous, ongoing story of how Fred uses math. Print. Elementary through early college. Lifeoffred.uniquemath.com/lof-elementary.php

Math-U-See Hands-on math instruction adaptable to all teaching styles. Elementary math levels are numbered by Greek letters rather than grade numbers, encouraging students to work at their own pace. Upper-level math available in print or online courses. Elementary through high school. Mathusee.com

Miquon Math Hands-on math using Cuisenaire rods to illustrate number concepts. Workbook and materials. First grade through third grade. Miquonmath.com

RightStart Mathematics Math instruction utilizing an abacus for visualization. Workbooks divided by alphabet letters to avoid grade levels and encourage students to progress at their own pace. Placement tests available. Print, video, and online. Elementary through middle school. Rightstartmath.com

Saxon Math Used by homeschoolers for over thirty years, Saxon has become the curriculum against which homeschool math programs are compared. The textbook-style courses in lower ages utilize manipulatives and household items to teach math concepts. Older children learn each step of a problem in consecutive lessons while daily reviewing past concepts. Print and CD. Kindergarten through high school. Available on Amazon.

Singapore Math Curriculum teaching math in a concrete, then pictorial, then abstract, and finally mental sequence. Print. Preschool through middle school. Singaporemath.com

Teaching Textbooks Online program with e-book text designed for completely independent learning. Grading included. Third grade through high school. Teachingtextbooks.com

VideoText Interactive Combines prealgebra, algebra 1, and algebra 2 into one course with a full credit for each level. Course includes video lessons and workbooks. The geometry course combines geometry, trigonometry, and calculus. Based on parent-student dialogue during lessons. High school. Videotext.com

SCIENCE

Apologia Publishers of science and worldview courses from a creationist viewpoint. Also offering curriculum in select language arts subjects and general homeschool resources. Kindergarten through high school. Online classes for grades seven through twelve. Apologia.com

Home Science Tools Science laboratory supplies, including curriculum-specific kits. Homesciencetools.com

Homeschool Science Press Science curriculum and science notebooks from a creationist viewpoint. Labs require materials from grocery or hardware stores. Biology, chemistry, and physics. Print and digital. Preschool, elementary, high school. Homeschoolsciencepress.com

Lyrical Learning Science courses taught by one weekly song. Texts include line drawings. Life science and earth science. Book with CD. Elementary through middle school. Lyricallearning.com

Media Angels Science resources and homeschool podcast. Print. Kindergarten through high school. Mediaangels.com

TOPS Learning Systems Science labs and hands-on activities including teaching and student notes. Physics, chemistry, Earth, and life science. Print and digital. Kindergarten through high school. Topscience.org

HISTORY

Beautiful Feet Books History curriculum and historical literature. Print and download. Kindergarten through high school. Bfbooks.com

Diana Waring Presents world history in a three-year cycle from a Christian perspective. Written for a Charlotte Mason, unit study approach. Other subject matter, including art and science, included in each course. Can be used for multiple ages at once. Lessons written for multiple learning styles. Print and audio CDs. Fifth grade through high school, with optional activity books for younger children. Dianawaring.com

Figures in Motion Paper dolls of historical men and women for hands-on history activities. Each book of a different time period contains jointed puppets that can be constructed and used to tell the story of their lives. Use as a supplemental history project or for other educational projects. Figuresinmotion.com

Greenleaf Press Bible, literature, and history books and study guides, including reprints of many classic titles. Print and e-book. Elementary through high school. Greenleafpress.com

Homeschool in the Woods History project packs, maps, lapbooks, and time lines. Downloads and CDs. Kindergarten through eighth grade. Homeschoolinthewoods.com

Jim Weiss Audio recordings of classic literature, including works by G. A. Henty. History and science titles also available. CD and MP3. Ages three and up. Available from Amazon. Jimweiss.com

Notgrass History History courses from a Christian worldview using narrative lessons, primary sources, quality literature, and hands-on projects. Elementary through high school. Notgrasshistory.com

Tapestry of Grace Integrated classical curriculum from a Christian worldview. Based on a four-year history cycle. Subjects and topics coordinated across age groups for group teaching. Also includes literature, writing, Bible, philosophy, and more. Teacher's guide digital or print. Preschool through high school. Tapestryofgrace.com

TruthQuest History History combined with humanities from a biblical perspective. American history for elementary, world history for middle school and high school. Based on literature and real books. Print teacher's edition with optional digital downloads. Elementary through high school. Truthquesthistory.com

GEOGRAPHY

Knowledge Quest Geography courses, map resources, time lines, and history resources. Print, e-book, and interactive website. Preschool through high school. Masterbooks.com/knowledge-quest

FOREIGN LANGUAGE

Rosetta Stone Language-learning software. Homeschool edition includes grading reports. Software and app. Elementary through high school. Rosettastone.com/homeschool

ELECTIVES

Art of Eloquence Studies on general communication skills from a Christian perspective. Includes speech, debate, overcoming shyness, leadership, conflict resolution, and more. Preschool through adult. Artofeloquence.com

ARTistic Pursuits Drawing and sculpture lessons focused on real-world observation. Students draw what they see rather than practice exercises. Preschool through high school. Artisticpursuits.com

How Great Thou ART Drawing and painting lessons focused on the fundamentals of art. Courses in classical art history. DVD, digital, and workbooks. Preschool through adult. Howgreatthouart.com

UNIT STUDIES

Design-A-Study Course frameworks allowing the parent to design lessons to the child's learning style and interests. Contains learning objectives. Appropriate for teaching multiple ages. English, math, science, and social studies. Print and e-book. Kindergarten through high school. Designastudy.com

Konos Month-long unit studies based on an individual character trait. Lessons encompass all subjects including safety and Bible. Appropriate for teaching multiple ages. Print and download. Elementary through high school. Konos.com

UnitStudy.com One- to four-week unit studies and lapbooks on a variety of topics. Lessons are cross-curricular (spanning multiple subjects). Digital. Kindergarten through high school. Unitstudy.com

SPECIAL NEEDS

Dianne Craft "Right Brain" Learning System Educational support from Dianne Craft (MEd special education) on dyslexia and other learning disorders as well as sensory issues. Articles, curriculum, development courses, and personal consultations available. diannecraft.org

Different by Design Learning Articles on homeschooling special needs students with learning disabilities, sensory issues, and mental illness by special education teacher Shawna Wingert. Print and e-books also available. Differentbydesignlearning.com

Hoagies' Gifted Education Page Information on educating gifted children. Includes lists of products tailored to developing gifted children. Hoagiesgifted.org

Homeschooling When Learning Isn't Easy by Heather Laurie. Discusses how to make the decision to homeschool a special needs child, choosing curriculum, and how to teach. Paperback and e-book. Available on Amazon.

Homeschooling the Child with Autism: Answers to the Top Questions Parents and Professionals Ask by Patricia Schetter and Kandis Lighthall. Deals with homeschooling a child with autism, including how to make the decision and how to set up a personalized program. Paperback. Available on Amazon.

Homeschooling with Dyslexia Articles and books by Marianne Sunderland with courses and mentoring groups to support parents of students with dyslexia. Homeschoolingwithdyslexia.com

Learning Abled Kids Articles with information and encouragement to homeschool students with both learning and sensory issues.

Includes subject-specific information. Print and digital books by author Sandra K. Cook and others available on Amazon through links. Learningabledkids.com

Our Crazy Adventures in Autismland Articles on homeschooling the child with sensory needs, as well as articles on faith and nontraditional medicine by Penny Rogers. E-books and printable resources also available on site. Ourcrazyadventuresinautismland.com

Pro-Ed Publishers of *Edmark Reading Program* and other curricula for special education students. Resources categorized by subject and special need. Print and digital. Proedinc.com

Raising Lifelong Learners Articles on homeschooling the gifted child, homeschooling individual subjects, and parenting by Colleen Kessler, EdM gifted education. MP3s and e-books available on site. Raisinglifelonglearners.com. Also provides "The Ultimate Guide to Homeschooling Gifted Children" which includes definitions, blog suggestions, and multiple articles on identifying and homeschooling gifted students at raisinglifelonglearners. com/the-ultimate-guide-to-homeschooling-gifted-children.

Special Needs Homeschooling Facebook Group Over 16,000 parents sharing homeschool strategies, parenting tips, and more. facebook.com/groups/specialneedshomeschooling/

HOMESCHOOL PLANNERS

A Simple Plan Print planner including monthly calendar, weekly lesson planner, attendance, grading, budget, reading lists, activity lists, and more. Tabbed dividers. Twelve months. Up to six students. Student planner available. Mardel.com/asimpleplan

Check Your Planner Online planner including assignment tracking. Moves late assignments forward while giving the student a reminder. Assignments marked complete by student then approved by parent. Computer, tablet, phone. Checkyourplanner.com

Ferg N' Us Print *Home Schooler's Journal* and *Homeschooler's High School Journal* for record keeping. Fergnusservices.com

Flexible Homeschool Online planner for flexible lesson planning and progress tracking. Designed to adapt to each child's individual pace rather than to a calendar or schedule. Computer, tablet, phone. Aflexiblehomeschool.com

Homeschool Day Book Computer software planner for simple record keeping. Homeschooldaybook.com

Homeschool Lesson Planner Print planner by Jan Teacher for goal setting and lesson planning. Monthly and weekly schedules. Dated. One student. Available on Amazon.

Homeschool Manager Online planner for lesson planning, grading, weekly schedule, and booklists. Student login to make notes on activities and mark tasks complete. Computer and tablet. Homeschoolmanager.com

Homeschool Minder Online planner for lesson planning, grading, and reporting. Student login to mark assignments complete. Student login to view calendar and mark tasks complete. Computer and tablet. Homeschoolminder.com

Homeschool Panda Online planner for lesson plans, budgeting, and to-do list. Panda Kids program encourages the student's input on lessons, meals, and more. Computer and mobile. Homeschoolpanda.com

Homeschool Planet Online planner integrating lesson plans, grading, transcripts, family calendar, chores, and shopping lists. Over 1200 lesson plans contributed by many different publishers. Student login. Computer, tablet, and mobile. Homeschoolplanet.com

Homeschool Portfolio Print book by Ashley Fox to record state or local portfolio requirements. Space to track attendance, curriculum, projects, booklists, and more. Lined and unlined pages for saving student projects. Available on Amazon.

Homeschool Tracker Online planner integrating lesson plans, grading, transcripts, and family calendar. Students can have limited access. Computer and tablet. Homeschooltracker.com

The A+ Homeschool Planner Print planner by Amy Sharony based on goal planning and tracking. Includes attendance and grading records. Undated. Up to six students. Available on Amazon.

The Complete Homeschool Planner and Journal Print planner by Larry Zafran for teacher or student to enter assignments and brief notes on twenty pre-printed subjects. Undated. One student. Available on Amazon.

The Eclectic Homeschooler's Plan Book Print planner by Sarah Janisse Brown for parent or student to record daily activities and lessons. Undated. One student. Available on Amazon.

The Ultimate Homeschool Planner Print planner by Debra Bell including goal setting, priorities, spiritual reflections, reading list, and field trips. Undated. Up to six children. Student planners available. debrabell.com/homeschool-planners/

Uncomplicated Homeschool Planner Print planner by Rebecca Spooner including grades, field trips, read-alouds, unit studies, and meals. Includes inspirational quotes. Undated. Large daily box for all subjects and children. Print or download. Available on Amazon.

CONVENTIONS

Each year, states and regions host conventions featuring speakers, publishers, and resellers. You can learn more about homeschool topics and see some of the curricula and resources available for your homeschool. Check with your local support group for information about your area's convention. **You can also find a listing of many of these events at homeschoolconventions.com.**

National conventions feature even more speakers and vendors. They are an excellent way to compare methods and products. My own parents decided to homeschool after visiting a national convention in Ohio. Check out the following convention organizations to find the next event near you:

Great Homeschool Conventions greathomeschoolconventions.com
Teach Them Diligently teachthemdiligently.net

PERIODICALS

Homeschooling Today Quarterly magazine on homeschool issues. Includes lesson plans and activities. Print subscription. Homeschoolingtoday.com

Practical Homeschooling Magazine Quarterly magazine from Mary Pride, homeschool expert for over 25 years. Print or digital subscription. Practicalhomeschooling.com

The Home School Digest Quarterly magazine on homeschooling and discipleship. The oldest homeschool magazine. Print subscription. Homeschooldigest.com

The Old Schoolhouse Magazine Quarterly 120-page homeschooling magazine since 2001. Print magazine available by subscription and in stores. Also available in online magazine and on app. Theoldschoolhouse.com

BIBLIOGRAPHY

THE FOLLOWING BIBLIOGRAPHY lists the works I consulted in writing this book. While you may be tempted to read everything on the list, I don't recommend it. Many of these titles, even homeschooling books, I referenced for opposing viewpoints. As I have said many times, you need to homeschool the way God called you and the way you do best, so read with discernment—and please don't consider this list as my personal endorsement of any particular resource.

Abboud, Soo Kim, and Jane Kim. *Top of the Class: How Asian Parents Raise High Achievers—and How You Can Too*. New York: Berkley Books, 2005.

Ackerman, Shira, and Kelsey Kloss. "The Guide to 5th Grade." Parents. Scholastic, July 3, 2019. https://www.scholastic.com/parents/school-success/school-success-guides /guide-to-5th-grade.html.

American Academy of Pediatrics. "What Are Learning Disabilities?" from *Caring for Your School-Age Child: Ages 5 to 12*. HealthyChildren.org. Accessed June 3, 2020. https:// www.healthychildren.org/English/health-issues/conditions/learning-disabilities /Pages/What-are-Learning-Disabilities.aspx.

———. "AAP Updates Guidelines on Attention Deficit Hyperactivity Disorder with Latest Research." HealthyChildren.org. September 30, 2019. https://www.healthychildren .org/English/news/Pages/Practice-Guideline-for-the-Diagnosis-Evaluation-and -Treatment-of-ADHD.aspx.

American Montessori Society. Accessed October 31, 2018. https://amshq.org/.

Andreola, Karen. *A Charlotte Mason Companion: Personal Reflections on the Gentle Art of Learning*. Elkton, MD: Charlotte Mason Research and Supply, 1998.

Babauta, Leo. "The Beginner's Guide to Unschooling." *Zen Habits* (blog). Accessed November 22, 2018. https://zenhabits.net/unschool/.

Bauer, Susan Wise, and Jessie Wise. *The Well-Trained Mind: A Guide to Classical Education at Home.* New York: W. W. Norton, 1999.

Bell, Debra. *The Ultimate Guide to Homeschooling Teens.* Anderson, IN: Apologia Press, 2010.

Bluedorn, Harvey, and Laurie Bluedorn. *Teaching the Trivium: Christian Homeschooling in a Classical Style.* Muscatine, IA: Trivium Pursuit, 2001.

Borba, Michele. *Building Moral Intelligence: The Seven Essential Virtues That Teach Kids to Do the Right Thing.* San Francisco: Jossey-Bass, 2001.

Duffy, Cathy. *102 Top Picks for Homeschool Curriculum: Choosing the Right Curriculum and Approach for Each Child's Learning Style.* Westminster, California: Grove Publishing. 2015.

Centers for Disease Control and Prevention. "Positive Parenting Tips." Child Development. Reviewed March 6, 2020. https://www.cdc.gov/ncbddd/childdevelopment/positiveparenting/.

Chitwood, Deb. Living Montessori Now. Accessed November 15, 2018. https://livingmontessorinow.com/.

Christian Unschooling: Living in Freedom in Christ. Accessed July 22, 2019. http://www.christianunschooling.com.

Clarkson, Clay, and Sally Clarkson. *The WholeHearted Child: Home Education Handbook.* Walnut Springs, TX: Whole Heart Ministries, 1994.

Deurlein, Rebecca. *Teenagers 101: What a Top Teacher Wishes You Knew about Helping Your Kid Succeed.* New York: AMACOM, 2014.

Dunn, Rita, Andrea Honigsfeld, Laura Shea Doolan, Lena Bostrom, Karen Russo, Marjorie S. Schiering, Bernadyn Suh, and Henry Tenedero. "Impact of Learning-Style Instructional Strategies on Students' Achievement and Attitudes: Perceptions of Educators in Diverse Institutions." *Clearing House* 82, no. 3 (January/February 2009): 135–39. https://www.tandfonline.com/doi/abs/10.3200/TCHS.82.3.135-140.

Dunn, Rita. "Rita Dunn Answers Questions on Learning Styles." *Educational Leadership.* ASCD.org. October 1990, 15–19. http://www.ascd.org/ASCD/pdf/journals/ed_lead/el_199010_dunn.pdf.

Farenga, Patrick. "John Holt Biographical Information." John Holt GWS. Accessed November 13, 2018. https://www.johnholtgws.com/who-was-john-holt.

Garfias, Lea Ann. *Homeschool High School Made Easy.* Amazon Digital Services, LLC, 2017. Kindle.

Goff, Sissy, David Thomas, and Melissa Trevathan. *Are My Kids on Track? The 12 Emotional, Social, and Spiritual Milestones Your Child Needs to Reach.* Bloomington, MN: Bethany House, 2017.

The Good Housekeeping Book of Child Care, rev. ed. . New York: Hearst Books, 2004.

Gregorc, Anthony F. Accessed June 3, 2019. https://www.anthonyfgregorc.com/.

Griffith, Mary. *The Unschooling Handbook: How to Use the Whole World as Your Child's Classroom.* Rocklin, CA: Prima, 1998.

Growing without Schooling: A Record of a Grassroots Movement, vol 1. Cambridge, MA: Holt Associates, 1997.

Hagan, Joseph. "Pediatricians as Mental Health Doctors: An Interview with AAP Presidential Candidate, Dr. Joseph Hagan." By David Rettew. Psychology Today,

September 19, 2014. https://www.psychologytoday.com/us/blog
/abcs-child-psychiatry/201409/pediatricians-mental-health-doctors.

Healy, Jane M. *Your Child's Growing Mind: Brain Development and Learning from Birth to Adolescence*. New York: Broadway Books, 2004.

Hertzog, Nancy B. *Ready for Preschool: Prepare Your Child for Happiness and Success at School*. Waco, TX: Prufrock, 2008.

Holt, John. *How Children Learn*, 50th anniversary ed. New York: Da Capo, 2017.

Holt, John, and Patrick Farenga. *Teach Your Own: The John Holt Book of Homeschooling*. Cambridge, MA: Da Capo, 2003.

Home School Legal Defense Association. "High School and Beyond." Accessed March 25, 2019. https://hslda.org/teaching-my-kids/high-school-beyond.

The International Montessori Index. Accessed November 7, 2018. http://montessori.edu/.

Ishizuka, Kathy. *The Unofficial Guide to Homeschooling*. Foster City, CA: IDG Books Worldwide, 2000.

Khazan, Olga. "The Myth of 'Learning Styles.'" *Atlantic*, April 11, 2018, https://www.theatlantic.com/amp/article/557687/.

Klicka, Chris. "The Myth of Teacher Qualifications." Federal Relations. Homeschool Legal Defense Association Current Issue Analysis, September, 2007. https://nche.hslda.org/docs/nche/000002/00000214.asp.

Kottmeyer, Carolyn. "Home Schooling the Gifted Child." Hoagies' Gifted Education Page. Updated November 6, 2019. https://www.hoagiesgifted.org/home_sc.htm.

Kuzma, Kay. *Teaching Your Own Pre-School Children*. Garden City, NY; Doubleday, 1980.

Liesveld, Rosanne, and Jo Ann Miller with Jennifer Robison. *Teach with Your Strengths: How Great Teachers Inspire Their Students*. New York: Gallup, 2005.

Linsenbach, Sherri. *The Everything Guide to Homeschooling*. Avon, MA: Adams Media, 2015.

Loeber, Rolf, Jeffrey D. Burke, Benjamin B. Lahey, Alaina Winters, and Marcie Zera. "Oppositional Defiant and Conduct Disorder: A Review of the Past 10 Years, Part I." *Journal of the American Academy of Child and Adolescent Psychiatry* 39, no. 12 (December 2000): 1468–84. Quoted in *ODD: A Guide for Families by the American Academy of Child and Adolescent Psychiatry* (2009). https://www.aacap.org/App_Themes/AACAP/docs/resource_centers/odd/odd_resource_center_odd_guide.pdf.

Mason, Charlotte. *Home Education*. Carol Stream, IL: Tyndale, 1989.

———. *A Philosophy of Home Education*. Carol Stream, IL: Tyndale, 1989.

Mayer, R., J. M. Anastasi, and E. M. Clark. *What to Expect & When to Seek Help: A Bright Futures Tool to Promote Social and Emotional Development in Infancy*. Washington, DC: National Technical Assistance Center for Children's Mental Health, Georgetown University Center for Child and Human Development, in collaboration with the National Center for Education in Maternal and Child Health, 2006. Accessed January 3, 2019. https://www.brightfutures.org/tools/index.html.

———. *What to Expect & When to Seek Help: A Bright Futures Tool to Promote Social and Emotional Development in Early Childhood*. Washington, DC: National Technical Assistance Center for Children's Mental Health, Georgetown University Center for Child and Human Development, in collaboration with the National Center for Education in Maternal and Child Health, 2006. Accessed January 3, 2019. https://www.brightfutures.org/tools/index.html.

———. *What to Expect & When to Seek Help: A Bright Futures Tool to Promote Social*

and Emotional Development in Middle School. Washington, DC: National Technical
Assistance Center for Children's Mental Health, Georgetown University Center for
Child and Human Development, in collaboration with the National Center for
Education in Maternal and Child Health, 2006. Accessed January 3, 2019.
https://www.brightfutures.org/tools/index.html.

———. *What to Expect & When to Seek Help: A Bright Futures Tool to Promote Social
and Emotional Development in Adolescence.* Washington, DC: National Technical
Assistance Center for Children's Mental Health, Georgetown University Center for
Child and Human Development, in collaboration with the National Center for
Education in Maternal and Child Health, 2006. Accessed January 3, 2019.
https://www.brightfutures.org/tools/index.html.

McQuiggan, Meghan, Mahi Megra, and Sarah Grady. *Parent and Family Involvement in
Education: Results from the National Household Education Surveys Program of 2016:
First Look.* U.S. Department of Education: National Center for Education Statistics,
September 2017. https://nces.ed.gov/pubs2017/2017102.pdf.

McGuinn, Laura. Quoted at Perri Klass. "Is Your Child Struggling in School? Talk to
Your Pediatrician." New York Times, October 7, 2019. https://www.nytimes
.com/2019/10/07/well/family/is-your-child-struggling-in-school-talk-to-your
-pediatrician.html.

Moore, Raymond. "School Can Wait." Interview by James Dobson. Focus on the Family,
1982. Video, 25:55. Posted by Joshua Kan, March 31, 2015. https://www.youtube
.com/watch?v==XLI5joMjOyQ.

National Home Education Research Institute (NHERI). Accessed March 29, 2019.
https://www.nheri.org/.

The Peak Performance Center. "Gregorc Mind Styles Model." Accessed June 3, 2019.
http://thepeakperformancecenter.com/educational-learning/learning/preferences
/learning-styles/gregorc-mind-styles-model/.

Rogers, Penny. Our Crazy Adventures in Autismland. Accessed May 21, 2019.
https://ourcrazyadventuresinautismland.com/.

Salkind, Neil, ed. *Child Development.* Macmillan Psychology Reference series. New York:
Macmillan Reference USA, 2002.

Self-Portrait Power Traits Assessment. http://redp.com/ (accessed December 17, 2018).

Smith, Deborah Deutsch. *Introduction to Special Education: Teaching in an Age of
Opportunity,* 5th ed. Boston, MA: Pearson Education, 2004.

Standing, E. M. *Maria Montessori: Her Life and Work.* New York: Plume, 1998.

STAR Institute for Sensory Processing Disorder. "Understanding Sensory Processing
Disorder." Accessed November 7, 2019. https://www.spdstar.org/basic/understanding
-sensory-processing-disorder.

Sterling, A. M. *Montessori at Home Guide: A Short Guide to a Practical Montessori
Homeschool for Children Ages 2 to 6.* Lexington, KY: Sterling Production, 2016.

Stoppard, Miriam. *Complete Baby and Childcare: Everything You Need to Know for the
First Five Years.* New York: Dorling Kindersley, 2006.

Suarez, Paul, and Gena Suarez, eds. *Homeschooling Methods: Seasoned Advice on Learning
Styles.* Nashville, TN: Broadman and Holman, 2006.

Texas Education Agency. "Texas Essential Knowledge and Skills." Accessed June 4, 2020.
https://tea.texas.gov/academics/curriculum-standards/teks/texas-essential-knowledge
-and-skills.

VARK: A Guide to Learning Preferences. Accessed December 14, 2018. https://www.vark
-learn.com.

Wayne, Israel. *Education: Does God Have an Opinion? A Biblical Apologetic for Christian
Education and Homeschooling*. Green Forest, AR: Master Books, 2017.

———. Homeschool Pioneers. Accessed December 15, 2018. http://homeschool
pioneers.com/.

———. "The History of Homeschooling." MP3. Lecture presented at Teach Them
Diligently conference, 2014.

Willis, Mariaemma, and Victoria Kindle Hodson. *Discover Your Child's Learning Style:
Children Learn in Unique Ways—Here's the Key to Every Child's Learning Success*.
Roseville, CA: Prima Publishing, 1999.

NOTES FOR CALLOUT QUOTES

CHAPTER 1: FINDING YOUR HOMESCHOOL *WHY*
Chad Kent, email to author, June 12, 2019.

CHAPTER 4: WE AREN'T IN SCHOOL ANYMORE
Soo Kim Abboud and Jane Kim, *Top of the Class: How Asian Parents Raise High Achievers—and How You Can Too* (New York: Berkley Books, 2005), 14.

CHAPTER 5: HOW TO BE A GREAT TEACHER
Mariaemma Willis and Victoria Kindle Hodson, *Discover Your Child's Learning Style: Children Learn in Unique Ways—Here's the Key to Every Child's Learning Success* (Roseville, CA: Prima Publishing, 1999), 192.

CHAPTER 6: THE WAY YOU TEACH BEST
Albert Einstein, English translation of German inscription on plaque of dedication, Pasadena City College building, speech and dedication February 26, 1931.
Charlotte Mason, *A Philosophy of Education* (Carol Stream, IL: Tyndale, 1989), 159.
John Holt, *How Children Learn*, 50th anniversary ed. (New York: Da Capo, 2017), 279.

CHAPTER 7: HOW CHILDREN LEARN
Daniel Willingham, quoted at Olga Khazan, "The Myth of 'Learning Styles,'" *Atlantic*, April 11, 2018, https://www.theatlantic.com/amp/article/557687/.
Neil D. Fleming, "I'm Different; Not Dumb: Modes of Presentation (V.A.R.K.) in the Tertiary Classroom," in ed. A. Zelmer, *Research and Development in Higher Education, Proceedings of the 1995 Annual Conference of the Higher Education and Research Development Society of Australasia (HERDSA)*, HERDSA, vol. 18, 308–13, https://www.vark-learn.com/wp-content/uploads/2014/08/different_not_dumb.pdf.
Anthony Gregorc, email message to author, June 14, 2019.
Mariaemma Willis and Victoria Kindle Hodson, *Discover Your Child's Learning Style: Children Learn in Unique Ways—Here's the Key to Every Child's Learning Success* (Roseville, CA: Prima Publishing, 1999), 113.

CHAPTER 9: WHAT GRADE ARE WE IN?
Jane M. Healy, *Your Child's Growing Mind: Brain Development and Learning from Birth to Adolescence*, rev. ed. (New York: Harmony, 2011), chap. 1, Kindle.
Healy, *Your Child's Growing Mind.*

CHAPTER 10: EARLY LEARNING: THE PRESCHOOL AND KINDERGARTEN YEARS
Harvey Bluedorn and Laurie Bluedorn, *Teaching the Trivium: Christian Homeschooling in a Classical Style* (Muscatine, IA: Trivium Pursuit, 2001), 371.

CHAPTER 11: ELEMENTARY SCHOOL: THE FIRST- THROUGH FIFTH-GRADE YEARS
John Adams, quoted in Harvey Bluedorn and Laurie Bluedorn, *Teaching the Trivium: Christian Homeschooling in a Classical Style* (Muscatine, IA: Trivium Pursuit, 2001), 377.
Albert Einstein, "Science and Religion," (address, The Conference on Science, Philosophy, and Religion, New York, 1940), Religious Naturalism, https://religiousnaturalism.org/science-and-religion-2/.

CHAPTER 13: HIGH SCHOOL: THE NINTH- THROUGH TWELFTH-GRADE YEARS
Soo Kim Abboud and Jane Kim, *Top of the Class: How Asian Parents Raise High Achievers—and How You Can Too* (New York: Berkley Books, 2005), 12.
Einstein to Barbara, Washington, DC, January 7, 1943, in *Dear Professor Einstein: Albert Einstein's Letters to and from Children*, ed. Alice Calaprice (Amherst, NY: Prometheus Books, 2002), 140.
Theodore Roosevelt, "A Square Deal" (speech, Syracuse, New York, September 7, 1903).

CHAPTER 15: MAKING HOMESCHOOL LIFE EASIER
John F. Kennedy, undelivered remarks prepared for speech (Dallas, Texas, November 22, 1963), Archives, John F. Kennedy Presidential Library and Museum, https://www.jfklibrary.org/asset-viewer/archives/JFKPOF/048/JFKPOF-048-022.

NOTES

INTRODUCTION

1. In a landmark court case, Mark and Christine De Jonge faced removal of their children for homeschooling. Their ensuing trial set a precedent for later homeschool freedom in Michigan. See "Mark and Christine De Jonge—History of Homeschooling in Michigan," interview by Israel Wayne, MICHN: Michigan Christian Homeschool Network, September 12, 2015, https://michn.org/mark-christine-de-jonge-history -of-homeschooling-in-michigan/. Read the court ruling People v. DeJonge, 442 Mich. 266 (1993), at Michigan.gov, accessed March 11, 2020, https://www.michigan.gov /documents/MDE-P2_attachc_13528_7.pdf.
2. Okay, that's a gross oversimplification of the story. There's a lot of heartache and healing that I'm glossing over, but you can read more about it in my book *Rocking Ordinary: Holding It Together with Extraordinary Grace.*
3. Obviously, not always. But sometimes, for sure.
4. Our adopted twins spent one semester in public first grade before they could come home to us. That is the extent of our institutional school experience.

CHAPTER 1: FINDING YOUR HOMESCHOOL *WHY*

1. Meghan McQuiggan, Mahi Megra, and Sarah Grady, *Parent and Family Involvement in Education: Results from the National Household Education Surveys Program of 2016: First Look,* U.S. Department of Education: National Center for Education Statistics, September 2017, table 8, https://nces.ed.gov/pubs2017/2017102.pdf.
2. McQuiggan, Megra, and Grady, *Parent and Family Involvement,* table 8.
3. McQuiggan, Megra, and Grady, *Parent and Family Involvement,* table 8.
4. Pier Penic (founder of black homeschoolers support group Culture at Home), in discussion with the author, June 10, 2019.
5. McQuiggan, Megra, and Grady, *Parent and Family Involvement,* table 8.
6. Monica Olivera, email message to author, June 15, 2019.
7. Centers for Disease Control and Prevention, "Study Shows Benefits of Biculturalism," CDC Newsroom, August 7, 2009, https://www.cdc.gov/media/pressrel/2009 /a090807.htm.

8. Pier Penic, quoted at Melinda D. Anderson, "The Radical Self-Reliance of Black Homeschooling," *Atlantic*, May 17, 2018, https://www.theatlantic.com/education /archive/2018/05/black-homeschooling/560636/.

CHAPTER 2: GET READY FOR THE QUESTIONS
1. Brian D. Ray, "Research Facts on Homeschooling," National Home Education Research Institute, November 27, 2019, https://www.nheri.org/research-facts -on-homeschooling/.
2. Ray, "Research Facts on Homeschooling."
3. Pierce v. Society of Sisters, 268 U.S. 510 (1925), Cornell Law School, Legal Information Institute, accessed March 21, 2020, https://www.law.cornell.edu /supremecourt/text/268/510.
4. Wisconsin v. Yoder, 406 U.S. 205 (1972), Cornell Law School, Legal Information Institute, accessed March 21, 2020, https://www.law.cornell.edu/supremecourt /text/406/205.
5. Raymond Moore, "School Can Wait," interview by James Dobson, *Focus on the Family*, 1982, video, 25:55, posted by Joshua Kan, March 31, 2015, https:// www.youtube.com/watch?v=XLl5joMjOyQ.
6. Ray, "Research Facts on Homeschooling"; Megan Brenan, "K-12 Parents' Satisfaction with Child's Education Slips," Gallup, August 25, 2020, https://news.gallup.com/ poll/317852/parents-satisfaction-child-education-slips.aspx.
7. "Education Spending per Student by State," Governing: The Future of States and Localities, accessed March 21, 2020, http://www.governing.com/gov-data/education -data/state-education-spending-per-pupil-data.html.
8. Vicki Bentley, "What Does It Cost to Homeschool?" *Everyday Homemaking* (blog), August 26, 2020, http://everydayhomemaking.com/what-does-it-cost-to-homeschool-2/.

CHAPTER 5: HOW TO BE A GREAT TEACHER
1. Rosanne Liesveld and Jo Ann Miller, with Jennifer Robison, *Teach with Your Strengths: How Great Teachers Inspire Their Students* (New York: Gallup Press, 2005), 21.
2. Brian D. Ray, Ph. D., "Research Facts on Homeschooling," National Home Education Research Institute, November 27, 2019, https://www.nheri.org/research -facts-on-homeschooling/.

CHAPTER 6: THE WAY YOU TEACH BEST
1. Dorothy Sayers, "The Lost Tools of Learning" (speech), 1947, Oxford University.
2. See Daniel 1:1-5. The Babylonians sought out Hebrews already versed in the trivium (knowledge, understanding, and wisdom) so they could catch them up on the language and history of the Chaldeans and move forward with the quadrivium.
3. Space doesn't permit me to expound on this most interesting biblical study. Examples of this trivium of knowledge, understanding, and wisdom can be found in numerous passages like Job 15:8-9; Proverbs 2:6; 3:19-20; 24:3-4; and Daniel 1. In the New Testament, the principles continue in passages like Romans 11:33-34; Ephesians 1:8-9; and Colossians 1:9-10. A study on any of these words—knowledge, understanding, and wisdom—finds that they are often connected with one another.
4. Harvey Bluedorn and Laurie Bluedorn, in their book *Teaching the Trivium: Christian Homeschooling in a Classical Style* (Muscatine, IA: Trivium Pursuit, 2001), propose

that the three levels of grammar, dialectic, and rhetoric are actually the biblical stages of knowledge, understanding, and wisdom.

5. Charlotte Mason, *Home Education* (Carol Stream, IL: Tyndale, 1989), preface.
6. Charlotte Mason, *A Philosophy of Education* (Carol Stream IL: Tyndale, 1989), 159.
7. E. M. Standing, *Maria Montessori: Her Life and Work* (New York: Plume, 1998), 118.

CHAPTER 7: HOW CHILDREN LEARN

1. Michael Gurian et al., *Boys and Girls Learn Differently!: A Guide for Teachers and Parents*, rev. 10th anniv ed. (San Francisco: Jossey-Bass, 2010).
2. Anthony Gregorc, email message to author, June 14, 2019.
3. Rita Dunn, *How to Implement and Supervise a Learning Style Program* (Alexandria, VA: Association for Supervision and Curriculum Development, 1996) chap. 1, http://www.ascd.org/publications/books/196010/chapters/All-About-Learning-Styles.aspx.

CHAPTER 9: WHAT GRADE ARE WE IN?

1. Eve Wixtrom, "What Are Multiple Intelligences and How Do They Affect Learning?" Cornerstone University, February 6, 2018, https://www.cornerstone.edu/blogs/lifelong-learning-matters/post/what-are-multiple-intelligences-and-how-do-they-affect-learning.
2. Jane M. Healy, *Your Child's Growing Mind: Brain Development and Learning from Birth to Adolescence* (New York: Broadway Books, 2004), 82.

CHAPTER 10: EARLY LEARNING: THE PRESCHOOL AND KINDERGARTEN YEARS

1. Peter Gray, "Early Academic Training Produces Long-Term Harm," *Psychology Today*, May 5, 2015, https://www.psychologytoday.com/us/blog/freedom-learn/201505/early-academic-training-produces-long-term-harm?eml.
2. "Research Finds No Advantage in Learning to Read from Age Five," University of Otago, December 21, 2009, https://www.otago.ac.nz/news/news/otago006408.html.

CHAPTER 11: ELEMENTARY SCHOOL: THE FIRST- THROUGH FIFTH-GRADE YEARS

1. Mariam Arain et al., "Maturation of the Adolescent Brain," *Neuropsychiatric Disease and Treatment*, 2013, no. 9 (April 3, 2013): 449–61, https://www.ncbi.nlm.nih.gov/pmc/articles/PMC3621648/.
2. Rob Coppock, "For Educators Pushing Eighth-Grade Algebra, an 'F' in Brain Science," *Washington Post*, July 15, 2011, https://www.washingtonpost.com/opinions/for-educators-pushing-eighth-grade-algebra-an-f-in-brain-science/2011/05/25/gIQAFuVyGI_story.html.

CHAPTER 12: MIDDLE SCHOOL: THE SIXTH- THROUGH EIGHTH-GRADE YEARS

1. Iroise Dumontheil, "Development of Abstract Thinking during Childhood and Adolescence: The Role of Rostrolateral Prefrontal Cortex," *Developmental Cognitive Neuroscience*, 10 (October 2014): 57–76, https://www.sciencedirect.com/science/article/pii/S1878929314000516?via%3Dihub.

CHAPTER 13: HIGH SCHOOL: THE NINTH- THROUGH TWELFTH-GRADE YEARS

1. Meghan McQuiggan, Mahi Megra, and Sarah Grady, *Parent and Family Involvement in Education: Results from the National Household Education Surveys Program of 2016: First Look*, U.S. Department of Education: National Center for Education Statistics, September 2017, 18, https://nces.ed.gov/pubs2017/2017102.pdf.
2. Guillermo Montes, "The Social and Emotional Health of Homeschooled Students in the United States: A Population-Based Comparison with Publicly Schooled Students Based on the National Survey of Children's Health, 2007," *Home School Researcher* 31, no. 1 (January 10, 2015), National Home Education Research Institute, https://www.nheri.org/home-school-researcher-the-social-and-emotional-health-of-homeschooled-students-in-the-united-states-a-population-based-comparison-with-publicly-schooled-students-based-on-the-national-survey-of-child/.
3. Brian D. Ray, *Home Education Reason and Research: Common Questions and Research-Based Answers about Homeschooling* (Salem, OR: National Home Education Research Institute, 2009), 6, https://www.nheri.org/HERR.pdf.
4. The following information is from my own article, "Why My Teens Don't Dual Credit," Lea Ann Garfias website, January 19, 2016, https://lagarfias.com/why-my-teens-dont-dual-credit/.
5. Brian D. Ray, "Homeschool SAT Scores for 2014 Higher Than National Average," National Home Education Research Institute, June 7, 2016, https://www.nheri.org/homeschool-sat-scores-for-2014-higher-than-national-average/.
6. Kevin Quealy and Claire Cain Miller, "Young Adulthood in America: Children Are Grown, but Parenting Doesn't Stop," *New York Times*, March 13, 2019, https://www.nytimes.com/2019/03/13/upshot/parenting-new-norms-grown-children-extremes.html.

CHAPTER 14: THE DANGERS OF HOMESCHOOLING

1. Brian D. Ray, *Home Education Reason and Research: Common Questions and Research-Based Answers about Homeschooling* (Salem, OR: National Home Education Research Institute, 2009), 2, https://www.nheri.org/HERR.pdf.
2. My friends who are single . . . I salute you. God has given you superhuman strength to homeschool solo that I will never understand. I don't know how you do it. God is giving you grace and an intimate relationship with him that I will never know. I love and respect each one of you. Keep on. (Also, I speak a bit into solo homeschooling in section 15.3.6.)

CHAPTER 15: MAKING HOMESCHOOL LIFE EASIER

1. Chad Kent, email message to author, June 12, 2019.
2. Tim Tinkle, email message to author, June 11, 2019.

CHAPTER 16: SPECIAL CHILDREN, SPECIAL NEEDS

1. Meghan McQuiggan, Mahi Megra, and Sarah Grady, *Parent and Family Involvement in Education: Results from the National Household Education Surveys Program of 2016: First Look* , U.S. Department of Education: National Center for Education Statistics, September 2017, 19, https://nces.ed.gov/pubs2017/2017102.pdf.
2. Laura J. Lee, "Cutting Class: Experiences of Gifted Adolescents Who Switched to

Homeschooling," *Home School Researcher* 32, no.3 (July 10, 2016), National Home Education Research Institute, https://www.nheri.org/home-school-researcher-cutting -class-experiences-of-gifted-adolescents-who-switched-to-homeschooling/.

3. "Home Schooling the Gifted Child," Hoagies' Gifted Education Page, updated November 6, 2019, https://www.hoagiesgifted.org/home_sc.htm.

4. "The Columbus Group," Institute for the Study of Advanced Development, Gifted Development Center, accessed May 31, 2020, https://www.gifteddevelopment.com /isad/columbus-group.

5. "No Child Is Just Born Gifted: Creating and Developing Unlimited Potential," National Association for Gifted Children, April 20, 2016, https://www.nagc.org /blog/no-child-just-born-gifted-creating-and-developing-unlimited-potential.

6. U.S. Department of Education, 1999, quoted by Deborah Deutsch Smith in *Introduction to Special Education: Teaching in an Age of Opportunity,* 5th ed. (Boston, MA: Pearson Education, 2004), 110.

7. "What Are Learning Disabilities?" HealthyChildren.org, American Academy of Pediatrics, updated November 21, 2015, https://www.healthychildren.org /English/health-issues/conditions/learning-disabilities/Pages/What-are-Learning -Disabilities.aspx.

8. Laura McGuinn, quoted at Perri Klass, "Is Your Child Struggling in School? Talk to Your Pediatrician," *New York Times,* October 7, 2019, https://www.nytimes.com/2019 /10/07/well/family/is-your-child-struggling-in-school-talk-to-your-pediatrician.html.

9. "What Are Learning Disabilities?" HealthyChildren.org.

10. "AAP Updates Guidelines on Attention Deficit Hyperactivity Disorder with Latest Research," HealthyChildren.org, American Academy of Pediatrics, September 30, 2019, https://www.healthychildren.org/English/news/Pages/Practice-Guideline-for -the-Diagnosis-Evaluation-and-Treatment-of-ADHD.aspx.

11. Joseph F. Hagan, Jr., quoted at "AAP Updates Guidelines," HealthyChildren.org.

12. "Understanding Sensory Processing Disorder," STAR Institute for Sensory Processing Disorder, accessed November 7, 2019, https://www.spdstar.org/basic/understanding -sensory-processing-disorder.

13. Rolf Loeber, et al., "Oppositional Defiant and Conduct Disorder: A Review of the Past 10 Years, Part I," *Journal of the American Academy of Child and Adolescent Psychiatry* 39, no. 12 (December 2000): 1468–84. Quoted in *ODD: A Guide for Families by the American Academy of Child and Adolescent Psychiatry* (2009), 2, https://www.aacap.org/App_Themes/AACAP/docs/resource_centers/odd/odd _resource_center_odd_guide.pdf.

14. *ODD: A Guide for Families*, 12.

15. Kimberly Ferren, email to author, October 5, 2019.

16. Joseph Hagan, "Pediatricians as Mental Health Doctors: An Interview with AAP Presidential Candidate, Dr. Joseph Hagan," by David Rettew, *Psychology Today*, September 19, 2014, https://www.psychologytoday.com/us/blog/abcs-child-psychiatry /201409/pediatricians-mental-health-doctors?amp.

17. Kimberly Ferren, email to author, October 5, 2019.

INDEX

A

Abboud, Dr. Soo Kim *52, 343*
academic development stages *172–177*
   early learning *173–174, 179–232*
   elementary *174–175, 233–289*
   high school *176–177, 341–394*
   middle school *175–176, 291–340*
academic goals *62–65*
ACT exam *376–379*
Adams, John *250*
adult children *441–444*
adulthood, delayed *441–444*
adulthood, preparation for *107, 176–177, 345–350, 441–444*
AP exams *370, 372*
arrogance about school choices *436*
art *284, 323–324, 365–366*
assessment. *See grading*
asynchronous learning *482–484*
attention deficit/hyperactivity disorder (ADHD). *See neurological disorders; special needs*
auditory learners. *See VARK model*
autism disorder (ASD). *See neurological disorders; special needs*

B

babies, homeschooling with. *See young children, homeschooling with*

bad days *58–59, 407, 458–459*
bed rest *455–457*
beginning. *See getting started*
behavior issues
   argumentativeness *326–327, 391–392*
   not listening *35, 230–231*
   struggling to work with others *439–441*
   upset at wrong answers *48–49*
   won't do work *46, 47, 72–73, 286–287, 313–314, 390–391, 459–461*
Bible *191–193, 243–245, 301–302, 353–354*
Bluedorn, Harvey and Laurie *215*
Bombeck, Erma *383*
Bonwell, Charles C. *124*
books *201. See curricula*
brain development, support for *170*
budget *33, 154*
burnout *398–406*
   causes *398–400*
   surviving *400–406*
busyness *452–454, 463–464, 477–478*

C

capitalization *253*
carschooling *74*
challenges of homeschooling *395–447, 457–465*

character development, typical *181–186,*
237–239, 293–295, 345–347
Charlotte Mason homeschooling *90–96*
  history of *91*
  how to grade *94*
  how to simplify *96*
  how to teach *91–94*
  materials for *94*
  pros and cons *94–96*
  resources for *93*
  stages of *91*
child development. *See academic*
  development stages; character
  development; emotional development;
  mental development; physical
  development; social development
child-directed homeschooling.
  See unschooling
choice *16*
chores *225, 287*
classical homeschooling *84–90*
  biblical criticism of *88–89*
  classical conversations *87*
  history of *84–85*
  how to grade *88*
  how to simplify *90*
  how to teach *86–87*
  materials for *87*
  pros and cons *89*
  sources *86*
  stages of *85–86*
classroom *28, 54, 156*
CLEP exams *370*
college
  applications *377*
  choosing *373*
  dual-credit courses *372–375*
  portfolio *370, 371*
  preparing for *351–352*
  testing *370, 371, 375–379*
  trade school *380*
  transcripts *367–370, 523–527*
comparison *46, 71, 95, 430–437*
complicating the process *411–412*
co-ops *109–113*
  how to choose *111*
  how to find *111*
  how to start *111–113*
  pros and cons *110–111, 417–418*
  resources for starting *113*
copying other people's
  homeschooling *432–433*
cost of homeschooling. *See budget*
course descriptions *369, 526–527*
credits *352–353, 368–369*
curricula *147–157*
  choosing *55–56, 149–150, 152–153*
  finding *148–149*
  saving money on *154*
  storing *156–157*
  types *150–152*
  using *63–64*

D
dads
  supporting moms *47, 466–472*
  teaching *55, 473–475*
dangers of homeschooling *397–447*
debate *364*
deciding to homeschool *11–14*
defending the decision to
  homeschool *23–32*
depression
  child *497–500*
  friend *429, 430*
  parent *425–430, 457–458*
deschooling *42, 102–108*
devotions *301–302*
diagnosing special needs *480–482*
diagramming sentences *253–254,*
  306–307
different from public school. *See versus*
  public school
difficult subjects. *See teaching*
diploma *381–382*
drama *322, 363*
driver's education *383*
dual-credit courses *372–375*
  help *372*
Dunn and Dunn model *139–144*
  emotional aspects of learning *141*
  environmental aspects of
    learning *140–141*
  five aspects of learning *140–143*

implementing *143–144*
physiological aspects of learning *142*
psychological aspects of learning *142*
sociological aspects of learning *141*
dyslexia. *See special needs*

E
early learning *179–232*
  activities *190*
  chores *225*
  concerns *190*
  curriculum *222*
  development, character *181–186*
  development, mental *187–189*
  development, physical *186–187*
  development, social-emotional *189–190*
  goals for early years *180*
  memorization *216–217*
  patterns learned *182*
  play *226–228*
  readiness for preschool or
      kindergarten *220–221*
  screen time *222–223*
  self-care *224–225*
  sex education *225–226*
  sitting still *228*
  social skills *229*
  speech and pronunciation *223–224*
  starting early *221–222*
early learning subjects
  art *217, 220*
  Bible *191–193*
  electives *217*
  health and safety *217, 219–220*
  history *217, 218–219*
  math *213–216*
  music *217, 220*
  phonics *203, 204*
  reading *193–203*
  science *217, 218*
  social studies *217, 218–219*
  spelling *207, 212–213*
  technology *217, 218*
  writing *207–212, 217*
eclectic teaching style *116–117*
eighth grade. *See middle school*
Einstein, Albert *78, 278, 357*

electives *29, 217, 282–284, 321–322,*
  365–366
elementary school *233–289*
  concerns *242*
  development, character *237–239*
  development, mental *240–241*
  development, physical *239–240*
  development,
      social-emotional *241–243*
  grading *285–286*
  memorization *276–277*
  starting late *284*
elementary school subjects
  art *282–284*
  Bible *243–244*
  electives *282–284*
  foreign language *282–284*
  grammar *248–249*
  handwriting *250*
  health and safety *283–284*
  history *279–282*
  math *257–276*
  music *282–284*
  physical education *285*
  reading *245–248*
  science *277–279*
  social studies *279–282*
  spelling *250–252*
  writing *248–250, 254–257*
eleventh grade. *See high school*
emotional aspects of learning. *See Dunn*
  and Dunn model
emotional development, typical *189–190,*
  241–243, 298, 349–351
English *355–357*
encouragement for homeschooling *408*
environmental aspects of learning.
      See Dunn and Dunn model
environment and learning *99, 140–141,*
  167–168, 403
  positive *167*
essays *254–257, 307–314*
  editing checklist *513–518*
  grading rubric *519–521*
evangelism *25–26, 244–245*
expectations *389–390, 410–411*

F

family life *34, 54–56, 59–60, 461–463*
    See also marriage
famous homeschoolers *31*
field trips *67*
fifth grade. *See elementary school*
finances *33*
finding your homeschool why *11–22,*
    58–59
fine arts *217, 220, 282–284, 321–322,*
    365–366
fine motor skills. *See motor skills*
first day *40–41, 43–50*
first grade. *See elementary school*
Fleming, Neil *124*
foreign language *282–284, 321–322,*
    365
fourth grade. *See elementary school*
Franklin, Benjamin *33*
friendships *25, 229, 327–328*
frustration *71*
future planning *380–381*

G

Gardner, Howard *169*
GED test *29–30, 382*
General Educational Development test.
    See GED
genetics and learning *164–166*
getting help *422*
getting started *37–38*
    supplies *153*
gifted students *29, 482–484*
goals *65. See academic goals*
gospel *25–26, 244–245*
grade level *41–42, 55–56, 161–166*
grading *54–55, 164, 285–286, 366–367*
    sample rubric *519–521*
graduation *351–352, 380–382*
    delayed *382–383*
grammar *248–249*
    rules *252*
Gregorc, Anthony *130, 133*
Gregorc Mind Styles model *130–133*
    applying to student learning *132–133*
    four quadrants *131–132*
    student learning *132–133*

    two continuums *131*
gross motor skills. *See motor skills*

H

handwriting *250*
Head Start *221–222*
health and safety *217, 219, 283–284, 322*
Healy, Jane *166, 168*
high school *341–394*
    ACT exam *376–379*
    AP exams *370, 372*
    argumentativeness *391–392*
    CLEP exams *370*
    college admittance *351–352*
    concerns *350*
    credits *352–353, 368–369*
    development, character *345–347*
    development, mental *349*
    development, physical *348–349*
    development, social-emotional *349–350*
    diploma *381–382*
    driver's education *383*
    dual-credit courses *372–375*
    GED test *29–30, 382*
    grading *366–367*
    graduation *351–352, 380–382*
    graduation, delayed *382–383*
    independence in schoolwork *386–388*
    motivation *389*
    portfolio *370, 371*
    readiness for high school *337–340*
    SAT exam *376–378*
    trade school *380*
    working while in *383–386*
high school subjects
    art *363–364*
    Bible *353–354*
    drama *363–364*
    electives *365–366*
    English *355–357*
    foreign language *362–363*
    history *360–361*
    math *357–358*
    music *363–364*
    physical education *361–362*
    science *358–359*
    social studies *360–361*

speech and debate *364–365*
high school transcripts *367–370, 374, 523–527*
  course descriptions on *369–370, 526–527*
  middle school credits on *368–369*
  sample *525–527*
history *217–218, 279–282, 319–321, 360–361*
history of homeschooling *30–32*
Holt, John *102–103*
homeschool readiness *14*
honors courses *369, 526–527*
hslda *26*

I
identity as a homeschool mom *418*
independence *388*
independent learning *53, 297, 299–300*
infants, homeschooling with. *See young children, homeschooling with*
intelligence, types of *169*
inventing disposition. *See Willis and Hodson's model*
isolation *446–447*

J
judging other people's parenting *436–437*

K
Kennedy, John F. *474*
Kim, Jane *52*
kindergarten. *See early learning*
kinesthetic learners. *See VARK model*

L
lapbook *108*
  kits *109*
large family, homeschooling with *229–230, 461–464*
Latin *88*
laziness *389–391, 415–416*
learning
  effect of areas of intelligence on *169–170*
  effect of environment on *167–168, 403*
  effect of genetics on *164–166*
  effect of mental age on *170–171*
  effect of past learning on ongoing learning *168–169*
  love of *73*
learning disabilities *484–488*
  diagnosis *487*
  homeschooling a child with *487–488*
  signs of *486–487*
learning modalities. *See learning styles*
learning styles *119–146*
  Dunn and Dunn model *139–144*
  Gregorc Mind Styles model *130–133*
  number of *124*
  talents and *144–146*
  VARK model *124–130*
  why to care about *121–122*
  Willis and Hodson's model *133–139*
legal issues *32*
lesson planning *66–67, 70, 154–156*
limiting opportunities *29, 416–417*
Lincoln, Abraham *151*
literature *303–305, 355–357*
loneliness *26, 423–425*

M
making homeschooling your god *418–419*
marriage *34, 437–439*
Mason, Charlotte *58, 90–96*
math *213–216, 257–276*
  algebra *357–358*
  decimals *268–269*
  difficulties with *276*
  division *263–265, 271–273*
  fact families *265*
  fractions *269–273*
  geometry *273–275, 357–358*
  literal *260–263*
  multiplication *263–265, 271–273*
  prealgebra *275, 314–317*
  real-life application *213*
  supplies *214*
  teaching *258–276*
  trigonometry *357–358*
  worksheets *265–266*
mature subject matter *293, 298*

memorization *216–217, 276–277*
mental development, typical *187–189,*
    240–241, 296–297, 349
mental disabilities *496–497*
mental health, parent *425–430,*
    457–458
mental illness *497–500*
middle school *291–340*
    argumentativeness *326–327*
    concerns *297*
    development, character *293–295*
    development, mental *296–297*
    development, physical *295–296*
    development, social-emotional *298*
    friendships *327–328*
    independent work *334–335, 338*
    note-taking *335–336*
    phones *329–330*
    problem solving *330–331*
    puberty *324–326*
    readiness for high school *331–334,*
        338–340
    screen time and media *328–329*
    sex education *325–326*
    test-taking *336–337*
    why not to skip *292, 299–300*
middle school subjects
    art *321–322, 323*
    Bible *301–302*
    drama *321–322, 323*
    electives *321–322*
    foreign language *323*
    health and safety *322*
    history *319–321*
    language arts *303–304*
    literature *304–305*
    math *314–317*
    music *322, 323–324*
    physical education *322–323*
    science *317–319*
    social studies *319–321*
    speech *322*
milestones *163–164*
Montessori homeschooling *96–102*
    environment for *99*
    history of *96–97*
    how to grade *100*
    how to simplify *101–102*
    how to teach *98–99*
    materials for *99–100*
    pros and cons *100–101*
    resources for *101*
    stages of *97*
Montessori, Maria *96–97*
motivation *72–73, 205–206, 389*
motor skills
    fine *206–207, 210, 226*
    gross *187, 226, 227*
music *217, 321–322, 363–364*

N
nature vs. nurture *164–172*
neurological disorders
    attention deficit/hyperactivity disorder
        (ADHD) *172, 488–490, 492*
    autism spectrum disorder
        (ASD) *491–492*
    sensory processing disorder
        (SPD) *490–492*
ninth grade. *See high school*

O
online learning *113–114*
oppositional defiant disorder
    (ODD) *495–496*
organization *35*
overscheduling *409–410, 452–454*

P
perfectionism *48–50, 205–206,*
    389–390, 410–411
performing disposition. *See Willis and*
    Hodson's model
Pete *444*
phonics *203, 204*
physical development, typical *186–187,*
    239–240, 295–296, 348–349
physical disabilities *496–497*
physical education *286, 322–323,*
    361–362
physiological aspects of learning. *See Dunn*
    and Dunn model
portfolio *370–371*
preschool. *See early learning*

Principle Approach *114–115*
problem solving *330–331*
producing disposition. *See Willis and Hodson's model*
psychological aspects of learning. *See Dunn and Dunn model*
punctuation *254*
pushing your student too hard *410–411*

Q
qualifications for teaching. *See teaching*
questions about homeschooling *23–36*

R
reading *193–206, 247–248*
  comprehension *247–248*
  head start on *194–195*
  helps *202*
  independently *204*
  perfectionism *205–206*
  readiness *194–195, 204–205*
  steps to learning *198*
  struggling with *247*
  teaching *196–203*
reading/writing learners. *See VARK model*
real-life learning *180, 181, 221, 225, 229*
real-world readiness *24–25*
reasons to homeschool *11–22*
  academic preparation *15–16*
  cultural heritage *17–18*
  faith *15*
  positive social connections *16–17*
  saving money *17*
recipes for fun *227*
records *156*
relating/inspiring disposition. *See Willis and Hodson's model*
resources *529–546*
  Bible *535*
  conventions *545*
  electives *541*
  foreign language *541*
  general *529–531*
  geography *541*
  history *540–541*
  literature *537*
  math *538–539*

multiple subjects *531–534*
periodicals *545–546*
phonics *536*
planners *543–545*
publishers of complete curricula *531–534*
reading *536*
science *539*
special needs *542–543*
unit studies *541–542*
vocabulary *536*
writing *536–537*
rites of passage *25*
Roosevelt, Theodore *385*
routine. *See schedule*

S
SAT exam *376–379*
schedule *43, 53–54, 452–454, 509–512*
schoolroom *156*
science *217–218, 277–279, 317–319, 358–359*
screen time *222–223, 328–330*
second grade. *See elementary school*
self-care *450–454*
sensory processing disorder (SPD). *See neurological disorders; special needs*
seventh grade. *See middle school*
sex education *225–226, 325–326*
shared classes *109*
sickness *454–458*
single moms *465–466*
sixth grade. *See middle school*
sleep *454*
social development, typical *189–190, 241–243, 298, 349–351*
socialization *24–26, 446–447*
social studies *217–219, 279–282, 319–321, 360–361*
sociological aspects of learning. *See Dunn and Dunn model*
Socratic discussion *87*
special needs *29, 479–500*
  asynchronous learning *482–484*
  attention deficit/hyperactivity disorder (ADHD) *488–490, 492–494*

autism spectrum disorder
(ASD) *491–492*
diagnosing *480–481*
dyslexia *483–486*
gifted students *482–484*
learning disabilities *171–172, 284–285,
484–488*
mental disabilities *496–497*
mental illness *497–500*
neurological disorders *488–494*
oppositional defiant disorder
(ODD) *495–496*
physical disabilities *496–497*
sensory processing disorder
(SPD) *490–491*
speech *321–322, 365–366*
spelling *212–213, 250–252*
spiritual pride *419–421*
sports *29, 286, 322–323, 361–362*
stereotypes about homeschoolers *25,
445–446*
success, signs of *415*
support group *26, 87*

T
teaching
challenges of *26–27, 45–50, 407–418,
459–466*
confidence at *58–61*
difficult subjects *28–29, 70–72*
effectiveness *68*
gift of *27–28*
how to teach *54–56, 57–75*
qualifications for *27, 60*
responsibility for *28*
subjects you don't know *70*
success *45–46, 60–61, 68–69,
407–408*
teaching styles *77–117*
Bible *302, 353*
Charlotte Mason *90–96*
classical *84–90*
electives *365*
English language arts *303–304, 355*
finding your *79–80, 503–507*
fine arts *363*
foreign language *362*

history and social studies *281, 321, 360*
grammar *256*
math *215, 275, 315, 358*
Montessori *96–102*
other subjects *219*
philosophy of *78–79*
physical education *362*
reading *197, 247*
science *279, 318, 359*
speech *364*
spelling *212*
survey to determine *503–507*
textbook *80–83*
unschooling *102–108*
writing *211, 256*
technology *217–218. See also screen time*
tenth grade. *See high school*
tests *54–55, 336–337. See also grading*
textbook homeschooling *80–83*
how to grade *81*
how to simplify *83*
how to teach *80*
materials for *81*
pros and cons *81–83*
resources *81*
stages of *80*
thinking/creating disposition. *See Willis
and Hodson's model*
third grade. *See elementary school*
toddlers, homeschooling with. *See young
children, homeschooling with*
trade school *380*
transcripts *367–370, 523–527*
course descriptions on *369–370*
middle school credits on *368–369*
sample *525*
twelfth grade. *See high school*
twice-exceptional. *See Asynchronous
learning*

U
unit studies *108–109*
unschooling *102–108*
biblical criticism of *105–106*
history of *102–103*
how to grade *105*
how to simplify *108*

how to teach *103–104*
materials for *104*
pros and cons *106–108*
stages of *103*

V

VARK model *124–130*
  auditory learners *125–126*
  having multiple styles *130*
  kinesthetic learners *128–129*
  reading/writing learners *126–127*
  time frame in which style develops *129*
  using other styles *130*
  visual learners *125*
versus public school *52–54*
visual learners. *See VARK model*

W

WholeHearted Learning *115–116*
  resources for *166*
why. *See finding your homeschool why*
Willingham, Daniel *122*
Willis and Hodson's model *60, 133–139, 144*
  five aspects of *134*
  inventing disposition *136–137*

performing disposition *134–135*
producing disposition *135–136*
relating/inspiring disposition *137–138*
thinking/creating disposition *138–139*
witnessing *25–26, 244–245*
working while homeschooling
  from home *476–477*
  outside the home *475–476*
  parents *33, 475–478*
  teenagers *383–386*
worldviews *25–26*
worrying about other people's
  judgment *434–435*
writing *207–212, 250–257, 307–314, 355–357*
  essays *254–257, 307–314, 355–357*
  grammar *252–254, 305–307*
  handwriting *250*
  process *255*
  steps to a great paragraph *309*
  struggling with *211–212, 312–314*
  teaching *209–211*

Y

young children, homeschooling
  with *229–231, 464–465*

ACKNOWLEDGMENTS

NO ONE CAN KNOW EVERYTHING there is to know about home-schooling. It took one large community of people to get this information in one place, and I'm so grateful to each one.

Thank you, Mary DeMuth, for mentoring me through my writing career. Thank you for pushing me forward the dozens of times I was too tired or too scared to keep going.

Thank you to the many experts who enthusiastically answered questions and reviewed portions of this book: Dr. Greg Ammons, ancient education; Laurie Bluedorn, classical education; Stacy Schaffer and Deb Chitwood, Montessori homeschooling; Israel Wayne, homeschool history; Jenny Herman, special needs learning; Shawna Wingert and Penny Rogers, sensory issues homeschooling; Sarah Andrews, co-op teaching and organization; Pier Penic and Monica Olivera, homeschooling in minority groups.

Thank you to the many medical and research professionals who wholeheartedly helped me research, discussed their work, and reviewed major portions of this book: pediatrician and author Dr. Vincent Iannelli; therapist Kim Ferren; therapist Suzanne Fullerton; researcher Anthony Gregorc; and educator Neil Fleming.

Thank you to my Facebook friends who enthusiastically contributed not just encouragement but ideas, tips, explanations, and connections. You are truly friends IRL.

Thank you to the professionals who championed the book and brought it to completion: Jessie Kirkland, my agent, for taking a chance on me; Sarah Atkinson, for believing in the project; and the entire Tyndale family for making this a joy. Debbie King, my editor: you made this what it is, and I can't express my gratitude.

Thank you to my family. You put up with so much drama from me through this entire thing and acted interested in every detail. My children, Gian, Adana, Leandro, Xzavian, Juliana, Roman: you put up with my homeschooling, you forgive my many failings, and you succeed in spite of my inadequacies. I couldn't be prouder. My husband, David: I can't find words to say thank you for being the reason there is this book. Thank you for your love.

Thank you, dear reader. This book is for you.

Sincerely,
Lea Ann

ABOUT THE AUTHOR

LEA ANN GARFIAS is a homeschool graduate, a homeschooling mother of six, and the author of four books, including three on homeschooling. She and her husband, David, live in Dallas, Texas. Besides "author," she holds the titles of "professional violinist," "French-press owner," and "friend."